Cohassett Beach Chronicles

World War II in the Pacific Northwest

Dedication

TO THE MEMORY OF OUR PARENTS

Kearny & Dorothy Clark

Lance & Clare Hart

Cohassett Beach
Chronicles

World War II in the Pacific Northwest

by Kathy Hogan

edited by

Klancy Clark de Nevers

Lucy Hart

ILLUSTRATIONS BY LUCY HART

OREGON STATE UNIVERSITY PRESS
CORVALLIS, OREGON

The paper in this book meets the guidelines for permanence and durability of the Committee on Production Guidelines for Book Longevity of the Council on Library Resources and the minimum requirements of the American National Standard for Permanence of Paper for Printed Library Materials Z39.48-1984.

Library of Congress Cataloging-in-Publication Data

Hogan, Kathy, 1890-1973.
Cohassett Beach chronicles : World War II in the Pacific Northwest / by Kathy Hogan ; edited by Klancy Clark de Nevers & Lucy Hart
   p. cm.
   Includes bibliographical references.
   ISBN 0-87071-384-1.
1. World War, 1939-1945—Washington (State)—Cohassett Beach Region. 2. Cohassett Beach Region (Wash.)—Social life and customs. I. de Nevers, Klancy Clark. II. Hart, Lucy. III. Title.
D769.85.W22C644 1995
979.7'95—dc20   94-47571
                                             CIP

Preface

KATHY HOGAN was a charming eccentric who lived in a small cottage on the coast of Washington State. Though she lived a quiet life, she wrote a weekly column called "The Kitchen Critic" full of stories about her friends and neighbors coping with the frustrations and inconveniences of wartime. These stories reflect the pride and industry of her home front community. "The Kitchen Critic" columns in this book were written during World War II from December 7, 1941, to August 14, 1945.

Comments from Editor Klancy Clark de Nevers

"THE KITCHEN CRITIC" appeared in Aberdeen's *Grays Harbor Post* at the invitation of my father, publisher Kearny Clark. He took over the paper when his older brother Jack's Marine Reserve unit was activated in 1940. The brothers corresponded about the Kathy Hogan deal and Jack approved: ". . . it is a hell of a good job of writing. Kathie (sic) has plenty between the ears—in fact is brilliant—but doesn't have enough common sense to come in out of the rain (or scotch mist) most of the time. The [first] two articles have been top notch—in fact rate along with some of the recognized 'down-to-earth' writers of present times, especially in the expression of homey philosophy." Kathy Hogan stayed down to earth for ten years, telling tales about life on the West Coast during the 1940s.

After the *Post* ceased publication in 1961, the files containing Hogan's columns were stored in our basement in the hope that someone would collect them into a book. I found the yellowed and mildewed volumes a few years ago. After reading some of Hogan's articles, I knew the task was mine. In Seattle a few months later, I showed some proposed chapters to Lucy Hart, whom I've known since we met in the late 1940s at Cohassett Beach.

Lucy's great-aunt operated a hotel at Cohassett Beach, and in the 1940s her family still owned several cottages in the compound where our families spent summers. Many of the houses still bore the scars of the Army's wartime occupation. Lucy and I played in the sand dunes near Kathy Hogan's cottage, but kept our distance on column writing days because Kathy hated to be disturbed.

Klara Nancy Clark, 1949, at Cohassett

Kathy Hogan loved good listeners but was uneasy around children. We never got to go with the grownups for morning coffee at Kathy's, nor for drinks when the sun had gone "over the yardarm." Happily we each got to know her later. My mother, Dorothy, remembered going out with Kathy to Westport taverns where she would entertain the locals with amusing stories of life as a newspaper reporter years earlier—stories that got better with each telling.

After reading some proposed Hogan chapters, Lucy wrote, "Gad [as Kathy was known to say frequently], wouldn't this make a wonderful book?" Kathy Hogan's writing deserves new readers. She has created admirable characters and memorable scenes that recreate life in the 1940s. We can imagine her acting out some of the stories. Lucy wrote, "I can still see her sitting in a cloud of gray smoke, with an unfiltered Chesterfield in one hand, the other hand wrapped around one of the endless cups of coffee she nursed during the day." Tilting her head, her eyes squinting behind thick lenses, she would chuckle after a good line. "We all adored Kathy," my mother remembered. After reading Kathy's stories, we hope you will too.

Salt Lake City, September 1, 1994

Recollections by Editor Lucy Hart

IN 1943, after the U.S. troops left our cottages, my family returned to Cohassett Beach for the summer. My sister burst into tears when she discovered that the wooden rocking horse, "January," had been burned in the fireplace by inexperienced boys from the New Jersey National Guard unschooled in surviving in the woods.

There were gashes on our hearth where the soldiers had cut firewood, furniture was rearranged and scattered among the cottages, axes and hatchets were as dull as andirons, wicker porch furniture was rotting from exposure in the pasture, family pieces thought missing turned up in the neighbors' sheds. The high sand dunes were lined with barbed wire fences and we were told to keep away from the no-man's-land between the dunes and the ocean's edge after dark, lest we be shot.

Over the years the barbed wire rusted, the fence posts collapsed—sand covering

Lucy Hart (center) at Cohassett Beach with sister Astrid (Lisa) on left and Janet MacIlyar

the remnants of the "occupation." Our memories of those summers are faint. But now we have Kathy Hogan's "The Kitchen Critic" to bring the early 1940s to life once again.

Seattle, September 1, 1994

Acknowledgments

Vicki Jones, Michael and Amanda Jones of Salt Lake City scanned and proofed the Hogan columns, making the manuscript possible. Kelley West provided genealogical work, unearthing 80 years of Hogan information. Noel de Nevers, who is a World War II buff, supported the project with patience, historical commentary, and many good phrases. Tom Lubbesmyer, Historical Archives of the Boeing Company, Seattle, supplied valuable World War II photographs. Martha Ferguson, Miller Horticultural Library, Urban Horticulture Center, University of Washington, assisted with botanical research. William S. Hanable, Director of the Westport Maritime Museum, facilitated access to the museum's collection. Barbara Hart allowed us to raid her 1940s photo albums. Michal Patterson assisted with research and Bob Hereford provided photographic support. Kind friends and acquaintances helped in accessing information, including Furford's Cranberry Museum and Kaye Walsh, both of Grayland. Donald Wesley Smith provided constant encouragement and support. The editors would also like to thank Jo Alexander, Managing Editor, OSU Press, for making this book a reality.

About the Sketches

Kathy Hogan often writes about Cohassett Beach's flora and fauna. Although it is approximately on the same latitude as Bangor, Maine, and Duluth, Minnesota, the Washington coast enjoys a mild ocean-moderated climate similar to that of Southern England. The sand dunes, boggy fields, and evergreen forests create an environment favored by many plants including blackberries, cranberries, and huckleberries. The cottage dwellers plant flowers including nasturtiums, honeysuckle, and rambling roses. The animals and plants sketched for this book by Lucy Hart are common to Cohassett Beach and its seashore.

Chronologies

The information shown in sidebars throughout this book is taken from chronologies prepared by the Western Newspaper Union and published in the *Grays Harbor Post* at the end of each year of the war. Because this information summarized current news, events now considered significant may seem buried in detail. In addition, some words now deemed offensive, such as "Jap," will be found in the chronologies, as in Hogan's text.

Table of Contents

Preface   v

Map: Location of Cohassett Beach   xiv

Introduction   xv

Map: Cohassett Beach During World War II   xxviii

1941

December 13   **Blackout**   2
December 27   **A Wreath in the Window**   4

1942

January 3   **Soldiers at Dinner**   6
January 10   **Civilian Defense Meetings**   8
January 17   **Hysterics—Beans**   10
January 31   **Dogs—Wildcats—Wolves**   12
February 7   **Bread**   13
February 14   **Men—Mothers—Menus**   14
February 21   **Travel—Trousseau—Team Work**   16
February 28   **American Tragedy**   19
March 7   **Fun—Fear—Food**   22
March 14   **Civilian Sorrows**   24
March 21   **Cats as Cats Can**   26
March 28   **National Emergencies**   27
April 4   **Boys—Billets—Baths**   29
April 11   **This Mechanized Army**   32
April 18   **Health—Hollers**   34
April 25   **Creation**   35
May 2   **Figures—Farmers—Flyers**   36
May 9   **Sugar**   38
May 16   **Shapes—Shifts**   39
May 23   **Business—Art—War**   40

May 30	**Labor—Education**	42
June 6	**Literature—Agriculture—Sports**	44
June 13	**Labor—Industry—Science**	46
June 20	**Sinks—Sonnets**	47
June 27	**Sugar Shenanigans—Shadows**	49
July 4	**Cranberries—Clams**	50
July 18	**Catching—Cleaning—Cooking**	52
July 25	**Dishes—Drains—Diplomacy**	54
August 1	**The Vanishing Victuals**	56
August 15	**Ducks—Donations—Dogs**	58
August 22	**Houses—Hawks—Harvest**	60
August 29	**Penalties—Parlors—Products**	62
September 5	**The Kalaloch Cow**	63
September 12	**Comings and Goings**	65
September 19	**Traveling—Tinned Foods—Itinerants**	67
September 26	**War Stories**	69
October 3	**Animal Story**	70
October 10	**War—Art—Agriculture**	72
October 17	**Education—Sanitation—Astronomy**	73
October 24	**October Days and Nights**	75
October 31	**Sailor's Return**	77
November 14	**Pete's Progress**	79
November 28	**Country Life**	81
December 5	**Economics**	82
December 12	**Ways and Means**	84
December 26	**Every Man for Himself**	86

1943

January 9	**Turn of the Year**	90
January 16	**Frosty Weather**	92
January 23	**Mutiny in the Pantry**	94
January 30	**What's News?**	95

February 7	**Wives and Mothers**	97
April 10	**Ration Pains**	99
April 17	**City Life**	101
May 1	**Women at Work**	102
May 8	**Mop Psychology**	104
May 15	**Coming Up the Hard Way**	106
May 22	**Local Geography**	108
May 29	**Making the Most of Things**	110
June 5	**How We're Doing**	112
June 12	**Happy Combinations**	114
June 19	**Fighting Words**	115
June 26	**Peace Talk**	117
July 3	**Tooling with Food**	117
July 10	**Joe Takes Time Out**	119
July 17	**Changing Times**	121
July 24	**Other Ways Than Ours**	123
August 7	**Defending Democracy**	123
August 21	**Where to, Utopia?**	125
August 28	**Chopping Wood**	127
September 4	**Sea Changes**	129
September 11	**Infiltration of Culture**	130
September 18	**Harvest Moon**	133
September 25	**Luncheon Party**	134
October 2	**Men Must Work**	137
October 16	**An Open and Shut Case**	139
October 23	**Annabelle**	140
October 30	**Big Game**	142
November 6	**Rioteer**	144
November 13	**What Every Woman Knows**	146
November 27	**Polish the Kettle**	148
December 4	**Classified Funnies**	150
December 11	**The Next Best Thing**	151
December 18	**Blundering Through**	154

1944

January 1	**Changing Times**	158
January 8	**Clams**	159
January 22	**All Quiet**	160
January 29	**Various Dinners**	162
February 5	**House and Garden**	163
February 12	**—and Pursuit of Happiness**	165
February 19	**Local Gossip**	166
February 26	**We, the People**	168
March 4	**Things to Think About**	170
March 11	**Bonfires—Dogs**	171
March 18	**Home on the Range**	173
March 25	**The Mayor's Parlor**	174
April 1	**To Bee or Not to Bee**	175
April 8	**Crime in the Country**	178
April 15	**Alone—by the Telephone**	179
May 6	**Wild Life**	181
May 20	**Man vs. Nature**	182
May 27	**What Every Sheriff Knows**	184
June 3	**Live and Let Live**	186
June 10	**Business as Usual**	187
June 17	**Down on the Farm**	189
June 24	**June . . . on the Dunes**	190
July 1	**Under Dog**	192
July 8	**Natural History**	193
July 15	**Archaeology**	194
July 29	**Crop Failure**	196
August 12	**Time & Tide**	197
August 19	**Rewards of Toil**	199
August 26	**Things to Come**	200
September 2	**How to Write a Column**	202
September 9	**The Ghost Ship**	204
September 16	**More Mysteries**	206

September 30	**Weatherman**	207
October 7	**Getting Ahead in the World**	209
October 21	**Good Hunting**	210
October 28	**Taken for a Ride**	211
November 4	**Buck Fever**	213
November 11	**Turn of the Year**	214
November 18	**Beach Business**	216
November 25	**Club Night**	218
December 2	**Business as Usual**	220
December 9	**Local Improvement**	220
December 16	**Night Life**	221
December 23	**December**	224
December 30	**The "Schoolhouse"**	225

1945

January 6	**Music in the Making**	228
January 13	**Written in Sand**	229
January 20	**The Pipe Dream**	232
January 27	**Private Lives**	233
February 3	**Making the Best of Things**	235
February 17	**For Better or For Worse**	236
February 24	**The Care and Feeding of Insects**	238
March 3	**Our Lost Battalion**	240
March 10	**Lights to Literature**	243
March 17	**Down to the Sea**	244
March 24	**Riding out a Gale**	246
March 31	**Man vs. Nature**	249
April 21	**Journey's End**	250
April 28	**Work for a Living**	252
May 5	**How to Build a Good Hot Coal Fire**	254
May 12	**May Days**	257
May 19	**One Man's Business**	258

May 26	**News about Neighbors**	260
June 2	**The Late Mr. Holmes**	260
June 16	**June on the Dunes**	263
June 23	**Getting Ahead of the World**	264
June 30	**Natural History**	265
July 7	**Time Marches On . . .**	266
July 14	**Professional People**	267
July 21	**Keeping in Touch with the World**	269
July 28	**Sea Gardens**	271
August 11	**Applied Science**	272
August 18	**Modern Museum**	275
	Glossary	277
	Washington Geographical Names	280
	Map: Grays Harbor Area ca. 1941	281
	Annotated Select Bibliography	282
	Photo Acknowledgments	284
	Index	285

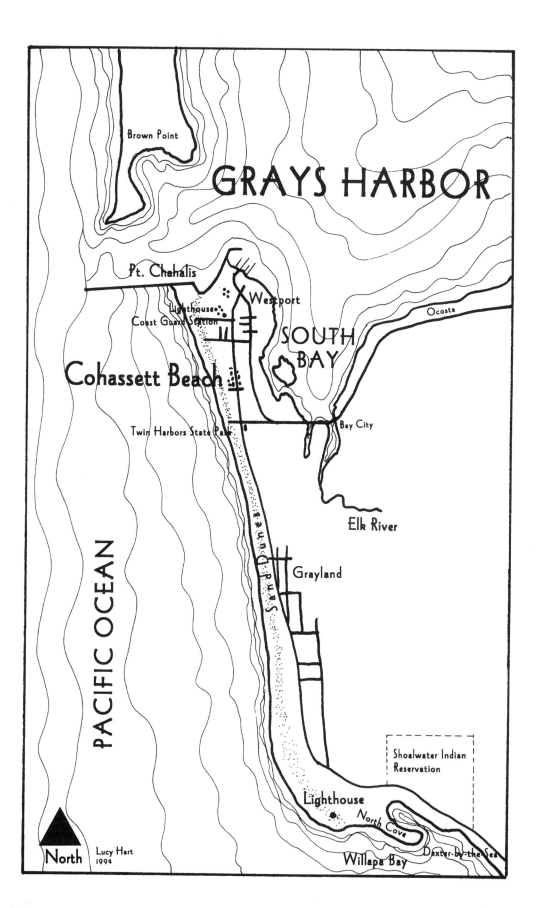

Brown Point

GRAYS HARBOR

Pt. Chehalis

Westport

Lighthouse

Coast Guard Station

SOUTH BAY

Ocosta

Cohassett Beach

Twin Harbors State Park

Bay City

Elk River

Sand Dunes Rd.

Grayland

PACIFIC OCEAN

Shoalwater Indian Reservation

Lighthouse

North Cove

Dexter-by-the-Sea

North

Willapa Bay

Lucy Hart
1994

Introduction

AFTER THREE FAILED MARRIAGES, fifty-year-old Kathy Hogan was banished by her father to live at Cohassett Beach on the Washington coast. She lived frugally in a small cottage, cultivating her garden and writing for a weekly newspaper. With World War II as a backdrop, Hogan turned everyday incidents into entertaining articles for a column called "The Kitchen Critic," published weekly in Aberdeen's *Grays Harbor Post.*

In this collection of newspaper columns from December 1941 to August 1945, Hogan writes about the home front—sugar shortages, rationing, civil defense meetings, President and Eleanor Roosevelt, victory gardens, her neighbors' fear of being invaded, the Japanese, the soldiers stationed on the beach, and fishermen and cranberry growers.

This introduction provides a context for the columns, including a description of Grays Harbor and its economy, a brief history of World War II and home front activities, especially in the Pacific Northwest, and a brief biographical sketch of Kathy Hogan.

Grays Harbor

WASHINGTON'S COAST consists of sandy beaches, rocky headlands, and three harbors which can accommodate large ships. Grays Harbor was discovered in 1792 by sea captain Robert Gray, the first American to circumnavigate the world. The harbor, which borders the south slopes of the Olympic Peninsula, was at that time surrounded by dense forests of enormous evergreens. Early explorers complained about storms, steady rains, and overcast skies—a perfect place for growing trees and for cool salmon-spawning streams.

The land surrounding Grays Harbor was the scene of one of the last and most efficient harvests of virgin forest in the country. In the sixty-four years prior to World War II, aided by steam engines, the county's forests yielded more than 31 billion board feet of lumber, an amount equal to lumber production in the entire U.S. in 1940. The towns of Aberdeen, Hoquiam, and Cosmopolis boasted sawmills, plywood factories, and docks filled to capacity with logs and lumber of Douglas fir, Western redcedar, and spruce.

Lumber production in the Grays Harbor area peaked in 1926. The timberline had moved up the rivers into steeper terrain, but trees were still being cut down as if the supply was unlimited. Old growth dwindled. By 1940 the boom was over and there began an era of careful timber management and tree farming (an idea originated on Grays Harbor). The lumbering operations were transformed into the "forest products industry," which produced chemicals, plywood, pulp, paper, furniture, and veneer products in addition to logs and lumber. At the war's end Grays Harbor was one of the largest producers in the U.S. of wooden doors, shingles, and lath.

The Grays Harbor Post

John C. Hogan

THE GRAYS HARBOR POST was founded in 1904 as a weekly newspaper by a "curmudgeon . . . with a querulous pen, all set to cuddle up to the trade unions and needle the timber barons," J.W. Clark.[1] A carpenter and unionist, Clark had come to the rough new mill town of Aberdeen from South Dakota. He wrote unflattering stories about mill operators he disliked and featured news and editorials sympathetic to the unions. His son, John W. Clark II, took over the publication in 1935 and continued until he was called back into the marine reserve in 1940. The next son, Q. Kearny Clark, father of co-editor Klancy Clark de Nevers, carried on the publishing tradition until the paper closed in 1961.

One day in 1940, lawyer John C. Hogan suggested to friend Kearny Clark that his daughter, Kathy Hogan, could write entertaining stories for the newspaper. Kearny agreed, and Kathy Hogan began writing a weekly feature column, "The Kitchen Critic," from her quiet cottage as talk of war swirled the globe.

The Kitchen Critic

BY *K. H.*

★ The "Schoolhouse"

Set a building down in cow clipped pasture land, give it a background of stretching marsh and misty bay, place a couple of tall, sky swishing spruce trees in the middle distance and a sprinkling of munching cows in the lee of the white sand dunes which tumble in from the north. And, if your building is one basement and two stories high, with a tower, and made of wind grayed clapboards with a faded red roof, a double staircase and a general air of having been dreamed up in the Nineties and forgotten these many years, why—well, then you have our schoolhouse. All out of scale with the little white houses and the bleached slab sided cottages of the village across the way, it looms in perpetual elegance above the plain, and recalls, if you want to let yourself go in for that sort of thing, the day when the town was a resort and not a fishing village; when a great curlicued veranda-ed hotel kept it company; when the stern wheeled steamers dumped their passengers into waiting horse-drawn stages at the end of the long dock, from whence they were whisked away to Lowery's Hotel or Mrs. King's boarding house where good clam chowder was the order of the day and where picture post cards could be purchased showing various scenes—the town's fine new schoolhouse, among others—all with the identical caption:—"At the Seashore."

A new, modern, one storied schoolhouse stands at the other end of the town, and the old building hasn't seen a boy or girl for years. Nevertheless, it remains the important building of the town. It took me a little time to get on to the state of things. I was sitting in the kitchen of the wife of my fisherman friend along about suppertime one evening when she shoved the potatoes back on the stove and said, with what I couldn't help but feel was a touch of envy, "He's going to be late again, I guess. Probably sitting over there at the schoolhouse with his long Norwegian legs curled around a stool."

When I wanted to know what He would be doing at the school house at that hour she said, why drinking beer, of course. What did anyone do at the schoolhouse? And she went on to tell me that once let a Norwegian get his long legs curled around a bar stool at the schoolhouse and nothing could pry him loose. Not even salt herring and boiled potatoes for supper.

So that's how I learned about the schoolhouse. There's a beer hall in the basement. It is the town club. If, in the afternoon, you want to get a new crochet pattern from a neighbor and she isn't home you'll find her at the schoolhouse. Clicking her needles, probably, and sipping a modest glass. At night the place

blazes with light, and along the bar the white capped fishermen sit through the hours, while in the cavernous rear basement grotto the polka blares from the music box and young and old fling their heels with gusto. Father and son are there; mother and daughter. About the walls a crew, fresh off a big shark boat from the Behring sea, stand watchfully, taking things in. They wear knitted watch caps, and their eyes are dark in their unshaven faces. One wears a gold ear ring. They bring with them a feeling of foreigners. There is Portuguese blood here. And Indian. And a dark conglomorate brew distilled from heaven knows what chance landings in a hundred years of Pacific landings. Now they stand watching the pretty Scandinavian girls dance the polka. They do not drink beer.

Above the din and brightness of the basement beer hall the old schoolhouse stands with its sightless, empty windows. Every two minutes the beam of the light house swings about and brushes warmly across the faded red roof and the tower. Then the stars prick through the empty windows again, and the sound of the sea echoes from the old hollow structure. Down in the basement my fisherman friend unwinds his long Norwegian legs from the stool, adjusts his white peaked cotton cap in the back bar mirror, looks himself steadily in the eye and runs over in his mind his homecoming speech which is something about why in hell isn't dinner on the table when a man gets home from the sea.

Setting the Stage: World War II before Pearl Harbor

WORLD WAR II BEGAN in Europe in September 1939, but seemed far away for most Americans until German military victories in the spring and summer of 1940 removed much of the complacency in the U.S.

Hitler and the Nazis rose to power in Germany in the 1930s; Germany and Italy— also ruled by a fascist government—rearmed in spite of earlier peace treaties, and developed modern war machines that threatened their neighbors. Hitler annexed the Rhineland, Austria, and Czechoslovakia, and then began war in earnest. In September 1939 the German "blitzkrieg" (lightning warfare) defeated Poland in three weeks, invaded Finland, and, in early 1940, captured Denmark and Norway. The Germans' innovative use of armor, air support, speed and mobility then defeated the combined French-Belgian-English army in six weeks. France surrendered in June. England survived the Battle of Britain (the German Luftwaffe's air attack in the fall of 1940), but remained in serious danger of defeat as well. The Americans, though still bystanders, shipped tons of Lend-Lease aid to Britain through the submarine-infested waters of the North Atlantic in 1941. Hitler's June 1941 invasion of Germany's former ally, Russia, had stalled as winter descended; his troops were forced to pull back from Moscow and along the southern Russian front. Nevertheless, by the end of 1941, German armies occupied most of Europe and parts of North Africa.

Isolationist sentiment was strong in the U.S. prior to Pearl Harbor and was a theme in Roosevelt's 1940 presidential race against Wendell Willkie, although both Willkie and Roosevelt believed that America's participation in the European war was inevitable. Roosevelt persuaded Congress to approve the Lend-Lease program, but only after they added restrictions on the president's powers.

Hostilities in the Far East had begun in 1937 when the Japanese invaded China. In 1941, the Japanese were fighting in both China and northern Indochina. Journalists, missionaries, and the government helped to orchestrate sympathy for China and antagonism toward Japan. Diplomatic relations between the Japanese and the U.S. were strained because of the American embargo in August 1941 on war materiel, scrap metal, and petroleum products. When the Japanese moved forces into southern Indochina, the U.S. warned them not to engage in further military movements and froze their assets in the U.S.

Getting Ready for War in the Pacific Northwest

IN 1940 AND 1941 the U.S. began to prepare for the war it wanted to stay out of but feared it would be drawn into. The preparations focused on the European war; only on the West Coast was Japan considered a likely enemy. This preparation meant a major increase in weapons production, which put more people to work everywhere, including the Pacific Northwest, and finally ended the Great Depression of 1929-40. Congress approved the first peacetime draft in the fall of 1940; reserve units were called up for active duty and troops were sent to remote outposts in the Pacific, Alaska, and Iceland. This effort was small compared to the full mobilization that came later.

Washington National Guardsmen activated their units to refurbish and staff the run-down artillery installations overlooking the Straits of Juan de Fuca. The Western Washington Marine Reserve unit was called to San Diego in November 1940 to join the Sixth Marines on active duty. After an emotional leave taking at the Aberdeen station, the marine troop train passed under the new Tacoma Narrows bridge just hours before it collapsed in high winds. This was seen as an omen—most of the Sixth Marines were sent to defend the Philippines, and their survivors were taken prisoner at Bataan or Corregidor in the spring of 1942.

Coastal artillery mobile units came to the Grays Harbor beaches in the summer of 1941 for anti-aircraft practice and camped in Twin Harbors State Park. The Army's 194th Tank Battalion regularly convoyed units back and forth to the coast, clogging traffic on the narrow, winding road from Fort Lewis, near Tacoma.

The Army staged a major war game in southwest Washington in August 1941. More than 100,000 troops from Washington and California engaged along a 40-mile front in open farmland near Brady. Since this was a peacetime operation, a mid-game liberty was declared, allowing troops to enjoy a serviceman's dance in Aberdeen.

When the maneuvers resumed in heavy rains, the defenders from Fort Lewis, who knew how to survive in a downpour, executed a brilliant flanking movement that gave the home forces the victory.

In Aberdeen in October 1941, mock air raids signaled by mill whistles and fire sirens tested civilian air raid wardens during a six-day alert.

At War

THE JAPANESE ATTACK on Pearl Harbor on December 7, 1941, shocked Americans. The U.S. could no longer stay out of the war and, in spite of official denials, it was clear that it had suffered a major defeat at the hands of the Japanese—a people most Americans had regarded as inferiors.

In the next four months the Japanese conquered the Philippines, the Malay Peninsula, Indochina, Burma, and the Dutch East Indies. American and British troops were defeated quickly and easily by Japanese forces even when they outnumbered the Japanese, as at Singapore and Bataan. The Japanese seemed invincible. People on the West Coast wondered if the Japanese were about to land on their shores without warning. The military considered the threat serious enough to station troops on the beaches, establish beach patrols, and set up gun emplacements.

Pacific Northwest Industries in World War II

INDUSTRIAL PRODUCTION had increased in the Northwest even before Pearl Harbor; once the war began, President Roosevelt urged America to become "The Arsenal of Democracy," and war production moved into full swing. The two largest war industries in the Northwest were the Boeing aircraft plants in Seattle and Renton and the Kaiser shipyards on the Columbia and Willamette rivers in the Portland-Vancouver area. A top-secret facility to produce plutonium for the world's first atom bombs began under guarded development at Hanford, in eastern Washington, by 1943.

American's overwhelming productive power was decisive in defeating the Germans and Japanese. By the last year of the war, U.S. factories produced seemingly endless quantities of artillery shells, bombs, replacement aircraft, and tanks. Boeing and Kaiser compiled impressive productivity records. During the war Boeing's Seattle plant built seven thousand B-17 "Flying Fortresses." The advanced bomber, the B-29 "Superfortress," came out of Boeing's Northwest plants at the rate of one every five days in 1943, and at six a day by 1945. The Kaiser plants constructed oil tankers, "baby flattop" aircraft carriers, and merchant "Liberty" ships. A Kaiser ship built in 72 days in 1942 could be built in five days at war's end. Kaiser's Swan Island Yards near Portland christened their 143rd Liberty ship the *S.S. Grays Harbor*, and it transported supplies and men to the South Pacific.

To help achieve their production goals, Boeing organized ten branch assembly plants in western Washington, including plants in Aberdeen and Hoquiam that employed 1,150 people and produced riveted parts for the B-17 and the B-29. In addition to the Boeing plants, Grays Harbor contributed to the war production with expanded production of lumber, pulp, canned fish, cranberries, and a special marine plywood favored for high speed launches and PT (patrol-torpedo) boats. Local shipyards produced barges, and more than 72 tugs and mini-yawls that were used in the Allied invasion of France in 1944; another plant built rudders for Liberty ships. The war plants brought a welcome increase in jobs after the lean years of the 1930s.

Roosevelt and the U.S. Political Scene

THE GREAT DEPRESSION changed the political climate of the United States. The Democrats came to power when President Franklin D. Roosevelt took office in March 1933 and stayed in power until 1953. Roosevelt's New Deal legislation of 1933-1939 helped bring America out of its economic doldrums and transformed the social and economic fabric of the country through programs such as Social Security, farm price supports, the National Labor Relations Board, FDIC bank insurance, rural electrification, stock market regulations, housing agencies, and minimum wage laws.

Roosevelt was serving an unprecedented third term in the White House when the Japanese bombed Pearl Harbor. The next day, Congress heard Roosevelt's dramatic speech with the words, "Yesterday, December 7, 1941—a date which will live in infamy," and declared war against Japan. Roosevelt was effective in uniting the country behind the war effort.

Eleanor Roosevelt enlarged the role of First Lady. Both Eleanor and her husband believed in using their wealth and position to improve society. She worked to relieve poverty in the Appalachians, and for rights for women and for blacks. In 1939 when black contralto Marian Anderson was denied an appearance in Washington's Constitution Hall by the Daughters of the American Revolution (DAR), Mrs. Roosevelt resigned her DAR membership and helped arrange for the singer to perform on the steps of the Lincoln Monument to a crowd of seventy thousand.

Eleanor Roosevelt's books and her syndicated newspaper column "My Day" were widely read. At the beginning of the war she was given an unpaid post as head of volunteers for the Office of Civilian Defense (OCD), but she soon became the lightning rod for criticism of the OCD and was forced to resign.

In 1944, as the Allied invasion pushed across France toward the Rhine and MacArthur's forces were recapturing the Philippines, Roosevelt was reelected for another term. He died of a cerebral hemorrhage on April 12, 1945, a death widely mourned. "President Harry S. Truman takes over his new office and command at a dickens of a time," wrote Kearny Clark in a *Grays Harbor Post* editorial. He noted that Truman's test was coming, and ". . . no newspaper that carries 'The Pledge of Allegiance' in its masthead will deny him support nor render judgment in any way until that test. This way . . . might be called the American way." Truman authorized the use of the atomic bomb and the Japanese surrendered on August 14, 1945.

A Vulnerable West Coast

GRAYS HARBORITES felt vulnerable after Pearl Harbor, well aware that their undefended harbor was known to the Pacific enemy. For generations Japanese schooners had been plying the north Pacific trade routes with loads of Northwest lumber. The shipments to Japan stopped, but beach residents feared their wide and unprotected beach would be a perfect place for a nighttime invasion. Their fears were aggravated by the shelling by Japanese submarines off the coast of Southern California in the days immediately following Pearl Harbor. At Christmas of 1941 a remarkable fleet of military and private planes and boats of all kinds was commandeered by the Army and Coast Guard to patrol the western shoreline. This improvised defense force is said to have caused the Japanese to abandon a planned Christmas submarine bombardment of West Coast cities that would have confirmed coastal residents' worst fears.

In the first days of the war, several West Coast commercial vessels were attacked and four were sunk. During the next nine months several Japanese submarines roamed the Pacific coastline, looking for targets. They sank two ships off Canadian and northwestern U.S. waters, damaged four others, and shelled Fort Stevens, a coastal artillery post at the mouth of the Columbia River. On September 9, 1942, a small Japanese seaplane was catapulted off a submarine. It penetrated the Oregon coastline twice near Cape Blanco, and dropped incendiary bombs expected to start devastating forest fires. But in the cool, wet forests of Southern Oregon the small fires were easily extinguished by forest rangers.

Japanese submarines amplified their presence by setting afloat dummy periscopes made of weighted bamboo sections. These decoys could fool human observers but not radar, which soon became a secret part of the Army's coastal defense.

In April 1942, sixteen B-25s bombed Tokyo in the Doolittle raid. The Japanese wished to retaliate on the U.S. homeland. They searched for ways to threaten the American continent—and their answer was to release thousands of cleverly engineered high-altitude paper balloons into the jet stream, each carrying four incendiary bombs. Although there were 345 verified discoveries of balloons or bombs on the North American continent, no devastating fires were started, and only one of these bombs caused fatalities. A woman and five children on a picnic near Bly, Oregon, were killed when one of them accidentally set off the bomb. After that incident in May 1945 the War Department issued the first public statement warning Americans of the balloons and their bombs.

Rumors of Japanese invasions were rampant, especially in early 1942, and defensive actions taken by the military seemed to confirm the threats. Anti-submarine nets were placed at the mouth of the Columbia River and in the Straits of Juan de Fuca; planes and blimps were sent out on regular submarine search patrols; and barbed wire barriers, pillboxes, and gun emplacements were constructed on the beaches. The U.S. Coast Guard patrolled the coastlines 24 hours a day, deploying beach patrols of sailors and guardsmen assisted by dogs and horses. Patrolling the wilderness beaches of the Olympic Peninsula near Lake Ozette was considered a hardship duty because of the area's high rainfall, wind, cold summers, fogs, impenetrable forests, rocky shores, and narrow beaches.

Home Front Conditions

BECAUSE INVASION SEEMED POSSIBLE, the civilian defense measures imposed on the country seemed relevant in the Grays Harbor area. Civilians willingly participated in the home front effort, volunteering to assist with the OCD, rolling bandages, learning first aid, becoming air-raid wardens, or spotting airplanes in the night skies. Grays Harborites contributed to a "Clothes for Britain" drive—"clothes of every kind are needed, but only woolen clothes can be accepted"—and many suitable clothes were sent from one damp climate to another.

Lana Turner on a War Bond Drive

Americans were forced to accept government regulations affecting every aspect of life—price controls, rationing, war taxes, and war bond campaigns. Mail to and from the troops was censored. The Office of Price Administration (OPA), the Office of War Information (OWI) and many other "alphabet soup" agencies created rules, regulations, and paperwork that were irritating but were designed to spread the irritation fairly.

The War Production Board sent out directives to control scarce materials. To save fabric they called for the elimination of extra cloth in men's suits (ending the two-pants suit), ordered shorter, narrower skirts for women and encouraged two-piece bathing suits. The OPA froze prices and controlled wages to prevent profiteering and price hiking.

Twenty essential items were rationed, among them gasoline, tinned foods, sugar, coffee, meat, and shoes. American shoppers had to master a complex set of ration books containing color-coded and dated coupons that had to accompany the purchase of rationed items. Rationed items were given point values that changed as supplies changed; red ration stamps allowed purchase of meat, fish, and dairy products, blue were for canned goods. Gasoline allotments were based on priority. Driving for pleasure was the lowest. Farmers and fishermen and others who needed gasoline to do their jobs got the highest priority, E for emergency, but had to fill out countless forms in triplicate every time they bought gas.

Stores were plagued with irregular supplies of goods and customers with money in their pockets either couldn't find the things they wanted or didn't have enough ration stamps or points to purchase them. Household items made of metal, such as an alarm clock, were particularly scarce. When a line formed outside a store people would join it without knowing what they would find inside—perhaps only some hard candy or a pack of cigarettes.

Morale was boosted by widespread participation in the drives to collect scarce materials—rubber, tin cans, scrap steel, bacon grease, coffee jars, aluminum, newspaper. Throughout the war years, collected scrap supplied significant amounts of the steel and tin needed for American weapons production.

Americans were willing to support the war effort, enduring inconveniences, the mandated 48-hour work week, housing shortages, and endless waits at the rationing board office. The average citizen worked hard, bought savings bonds, frowned at people who bought black market goods, and tried to obey the laws. Signs posted everywhere urged, "Use it up, wear it out, make it do, or do without." For many, the wartime hardships just continued the frugality and thrift their families had practiced since pioneer days and through the Depression years of the 1930s.

Industries Close to Home

WHEN THE FIRST WHITE SETTLERS arrived on the Washington coast, cranberries grew wild behind the dunes and the Northwest Indians lived off the bounty of the sea. Kathy Hogan's beach communities still depended largely on the traditional occupations of fishing, farming, and dairying.

Before World War I a group of Finnish immigrants working in Grays Harbor timber heard about the natural peat bogs on the south shore of the harbor. They bought and cleared bog land in Glen Grayland (now just Grayland) and planted cranberry starts from Cape Cod. They and their descendants still dominated the thriving cranberry industry in the 1940s. The 1942 harvest of cranberries broke previous records, and more than half of the new crop was allocated to Army kitchens. Each fall during the war, off-duty soldiers at the beach helped bring in the cranberry harvest.

Women Contribute to the War

THE MANUFACTURING WORK FORCE nationwide was depleted when millions of men went to war. Many jobs previously held by men out of necessity became available to women. More married women sought work outside the home, and factories began to train women as welders, riveters, and heavy equipment assemblers. Women learned to pump gas and drive taxi cabs, trucks, and city buses. Other women rolled bandages, served food at the USOs (United Service Organizations), drove ambulances, knitted scarves, and saved rubber, tin cans, and fat for the war effort. And two hundred thousand women served in the armed services.

Victory Gardens

THE U.S. DEPARTMENT OF AGRICULTURE encouraged people to plant vegetables in home gardens called "Victory Gardens," and northwesterners had good reasons to cooperate. Farm workers had gone to war or to better-paying factory jobs. The Japanese truck farmers of Seattle's Duwamish Valley had been evacuated to relocation camps. Foodstuffs were being shipped overseas to feed the troops, making fresh produce even more scarce in the stores.

The Victory Garden Program was designed to solve the food supply problems, to improve people's physical health, and to stimulate cooperation with the entire war effort. Americans everywhere responded to the government's urgings, digging up and planting plots in backyards, vacant lots, parks, and community gardens. In 1944 half of all American households claimed to have grown a Victory Garden.

A View of the Enemy

ACCORDING TO THE 1940 CENSUS, two-thirds of the 127,000 Japanese Americans were native-born American citizens and most lived in Hawaii and on the Pacific coast, with the largest clusters on the mainland in Los Angeles and Seattle. After the attack on Pearl Harbor, known sympathizers with Japan and Germany were arrested, but hysteria grew, enabling advocates of removal of the Japanese from the western parts of the Pacific states to prevail. In February 1942, President Roosevelt signed Executive Order 9066 which allowed the Army to evacuate more than a hundred thousand Japanese and Japanese Americans from the Pacific coast states to "relocation camps" inland, where most of them remained throughout the war. Former Aberdeen attorney Colonel Karl R. Bendetsen, chief of the Aliens Division in the War Department, was one of the most vocal in pushing for the order, and received a distinguished service medal for supervising the evacuation and relocation.

Throughout the war, the public's view of the Japanese and Germans was shaped by government propaganda programs. Posters and political cartoons pictured the Japanese as small, sinister, slant-eyed people. Movies explained the Axis threat in Europe using animated black spiders repeatedly exploding (like the sorcerer's brooms in *Fantasia*) into tens of spiders in close ranks, goose-stepping out of the map of Germany to cover the world with a web of swastikas. Newsreels bombarded Americans with images of ferocious Japanese troops attacking American positions in the Pacific islands.

This was no time for a quiet study of the ancient and highly developed culture of Japan. This was no time to recall the individual hard-working farmers or shopkeepers who had been neighbors prior to the war. The U.S. was at war and the enemy was clear.

War Stories

THROUGHOUT THE WAR, courageous war correspondents wrote vividly about battles in the Pacific, North Africa, and Europe. Edward R. Murrow broadcast eye-witness accounts of the bombing of London. Bill Mauldin's *GI Joe* cartoons said more than all the censored letters from the front. Ernie Pyle told the human side of the fighting in Italy and lost his life during the final Pacific campaign. Kathy Hogan's front lines were quieter, but she shared Pyle's interest in the lives of the men "in the trenches."

Hogan's trenches were the sand dunes above her house, the neighboring cottages and the improvised barracks in the communities near Cohassett Beach where battalions of army troops were stationed during the early years of the war.

Kathy Hogan

BORN IN DECEMBER 1890, Katharyn Lyle Hogan was the first of three daughters of John Carol and Lillian Miles Hogan, who had come to Aberdeen from Wisconsin. John C. Hogan's career as an attorney began slowly; he worked nights in a mill to support the family until his law practice took hold. In the late 1890s he practiced law in Seattle as well as in Aberdeen. He was soon successful, winning a large damage suit against the Northern Pacific railroad; he incorporated the first logging companies, won a seat in the legislature and affected laws that govern the logging industry; he served briefly as Aberdeen's City Attorney.

Kathy Hogan was brought up with an upper-class Victorian view of a woman's role. Her mother died when she was eight and she and her sisters, Margaret and Mary, were raised by housekeepers and later by a stepmother, Lizzie. She attended a finishing school near Washington D.C. for "girls. . .who wish to be broadly cultured and prepared to live their lives worthily."[2] She returned home, married lawyer George Acret, had two children, engaged in amateur theatricals, and enjoyed an active social life.

But married life wasn't easy for Kathy—she tried it with three husbands. "I loved them all dearly, but couldn't live with 'em," she said. She assisted her second husband, a florist, and her third, a journalist, in the working world at a time when few married women were employed outside the home.

In the late 1930s she and her third husband lived in Kalaloch, an isolated beach community north of the Quinault Indian Reservation, trying to operate a small newspaper. When the newspaper and the marriage failed, her father, who by this time had raised her children, sent her to live in one of his cottages at Cohassett Beach to avoid the embarrassment and scandal that went with divorce in those days. Kathy Hogan did not know that it was her father who urged Kearny Clark to give her writing a chance.

Kathy Hogan had learned the art of storytelling from her Irish grandmother, Bridget. Her father, a "gentle scholar with a thorough knowledge of Shakespeare,"[3] had named her Katharyn after Shakespeare's unruly "Shrew" and taught her to share the Bard's love of the English language. She had a keen ear for colorful phrases and observed wartime expressions creeping into the language. With this background, she started writing "The Kitchen Critic" columns in January 1941.

In a column with kitchen in the title, one might expect a recipe and Hogan obliged with a few, once forgetting to list an important ingredient, the

Kathy Hogan's grandmother, Bridget

milk in the clam chowder. However visitors were more central to her stories—people like "my Fisherman friend," and the "canneryman with the curly-tailed dog."

During the war she kept a National Geographic map of the Pacific Ocean on her living-room wall to follow the war and her son's travels as a merchant seaman. Living away from cities, alone among unpretentious people, "living close to nature" as she described it, agreed with Hogan. After the war she bought the property at Cohassett called "the Barn" (because of its origin), tried to grow Croft (Easter) lily bulbs in its pasture, and continued writing "The Kitchen Critic" until 1950. She later built a modern house on the dunes nearby that had the feeling of that barn and a view of the ocean, where she lived until her death in 1973.

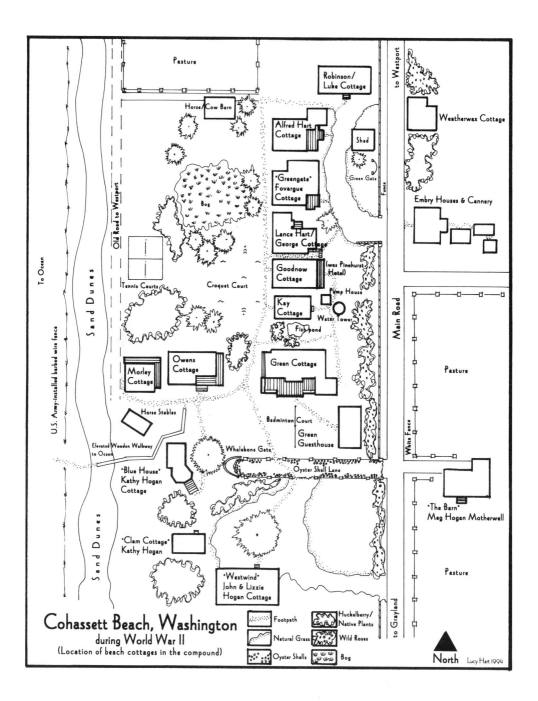

Cohassett Beach, Washington during World War II (Location of beach cottages in the compound)

Pasture

Robinson/ Luke Cottage

Weatherwax Cottage

Horse/Cow Barn

Alfred Hart Cottage

Shed

Green Gate

to Westport

Fence

Embry Houses & Cannery

"Greengate" Fovargue Cottage

Bog

Lance Hart/ George Cottage

Goodnow Cottage

(was Pinehurst Hotel)

Pump House

Tennis Courts

Croquet Court

Kay Cottage

Water Tower

Fish Pond

To Ocean

Sand Dunes

Old Road to Westport

Main Road

Pasture

Morley Cottage

Owens Cottage

Green Cottage

White Fence

U.S. Army-installed barbed wire fence

Horse Stables

Badminton Court

Green Guesthouse

Elevated Wooden Walkway to Ocean

Whalebone Gate

"Blue House" Kathy Hogan Cottage

Oyster Shell Lane

"The Barn" Meg Hogan Motherwell

Sand Dunes

"Clam Cottage" Kathy Hogan

Pasture

to Grayland

"Westwind" John & Lizzie Hogan Cottage

Footpath

Huckelberry/ Native Plants

Natural Grass

Wild Roses

Oyster Shells

Bog

North

Lucy Hart 1994

Cohassett Beach

KATHY HOGAN'S COMPOUND of weathered Victorian cottages was the remnant of an earlier elegance. In the 1890s city folks from many parts of western Washington journeyed to Cohassett Beach to enjoy the distractions of ocean breezes, to bathe in the surf, and to be seen by other visitors. Historian Ed Van Syckle describes the development:

> *Behind the high sand dunes south of Westport . . . grew what was in its day the most fashionable resort on the Washington coast . . . it was . . . called Cohassett, named after a similarly situated town on Massachusetts Bay.[4]*

Cohassett's "day" began in the 1890s and ended with the fiery destruction of the old hotel in 1917. The resort boasted of private cottages, Mrs. A. D. Wood's Pinehurst Hotel, and the two-story Essex Hotel. On top of the dunes was the "Tie House," built of railroad ties which had come ashore from a shipwreck years before. Early visitors arrived in stages, taking a train to Aberdeen, then a stern-wheeler to the boat landing at Westport, and a horse-drawn carriage to Cohassett. Accommodations were not luxurious; a water system was not installed until 1907.

During much of the war Kathy Hogan lived in the "Blue House," an octagonal building that had been a gazebo for the old hotel. Her family owned "Westwind" and "Clam Cottage," which were built in the 1920s on the grounds of the former Essex Hotel.

The compound of cottages at Cohassett Beach which billeted the troops during the war.

What charms remained to Cohassett Beach by the time of Pearl Harbor? A lane paved with crushed oyster shells passed under a huge whale-bone arch and led into the former hotel's front yard; many silvered fences outlined grass-filled meadows and the dozen or so surviving houses. Paths that threaded among the shingled houses led to a planked walkway that wound up a hill through scotch broom and pines to the first dune, then straggled across the inter-dune wasteland, vanishing at the high water line. The compound was surrounded by tall pines and cypress, and was sheltered from the ocean by high sand dunes crowned here and there with clumps of a tall beachgrass imported, according to some legends, from Massachusetts' Cohasset [sic].

The cottages (most of which were two storied) were full of evidence of earlier sophisticated visitors. Bookshelves contained forgotten volumes of G.B. Shaw plays, "The Voice of the Turtle,"[5] old *New Yorker* magazines, and hand-blown periwinkle glass bottles.

In the rush to defend the coast early in World War II, the Army sent troops to Hogan's area before any barracks were available. Sheds, barns, and summer homes were taken over to billet the soldiers. Cohassett Beach was no exception. The permanent residents immediately found themselves overwhelmed and outnumbered by the troops, an experience they called an "occupation."

December 1941 found Santa Claus on posters offering unusual Christmas presents: "This year give a share in America's Defense, buy bonds and stamps." The Navy recruiting office in Seattle stayed open seven days a week, 24 hours a day, and averaged fifty applicants a day. When available, radios sold for $17, or $35 for a deluxe model. The airways were competing for wartime listeners—CBS offered Amos 'n' Andy, the Glenn Miller Orchestra, NBC's Quiz Kids, Army Camp News, while MBS [Mutual Broadcasting System] presented the Lone Ranger and Serenade in Tangotime. Housewives listened to Ma Perkins, Guiding Light, Young Widder [sic] Brown, and John's Other Wife. Bob Hope and Paulette Goddard in "Nothing But the Truth" could be seen for 20 cents at Aberdeen's D&R theater. Joe DiMaggio of the New York Yankees was voted outstanding male athlete with a .357 batting average. And Kathy Hogan sat at her typewriter each week to write another episode about life on her Cohassett Beach home front.

Klancy Clark de Nevers
Lucy Hart

Notes

1. Van Syckle, Edwin, *The River Pioneers: Early Days on Grays Harbor,* Pacific Search Press and Friends of the Aberdeen Public Library, 1982, page 277.
2. Catalogue for National Park Seminary, Inc. for Young Women, Forest Glenn, Md.,1907. Hogan attended a not-so-fancy school next door.
3. Obituary, *Grays Harbor Post*, November 29, 1947.
4. Van Syckle, ibid. page 213.
5. Popular play by John Van Druten (1939).

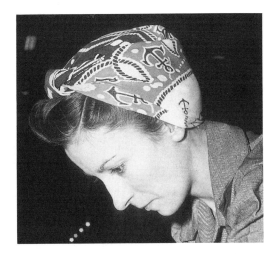

1941

Blackout

December 13, 1941
(In Aberdeen)

SOME DAY, GOD WILLING, we can tell our great grand-children of the night of December 8th, 1941, when we turned from the radio (you know that funny instrument they used then—no, not the melodeon, but something like it) and with lips compressed with determination, and the hard light of resolution in our eyes, and with the admiring gaze of a trusting family upon us, we went immediately to the—well, we went in search of something to cover the windows for a blackout.

Everyone was looking at us, weren't they? And expecting us to produce the miracle of darkness which the radio, the army, the navy, the air force, and our own self-esteem, commanded that we produce. Women had been called upon in the national emergency. We couldn't fail, could we? But for a moment—for several moments perhaps, we were stumped. Halfway upstairs we lost our first enthusiasm for cutting up the spare-room blankets into window-sized panels, and tried desperately to think of some compromise. That old flannel bathrobe of grandpa's? No! We'd given it to British relief. The bathroom rug wasn't wide enough. Would two sheets do? No, they couldn't. Not even three sheets—not even four sheets, with corresponding pillow cases.

Where were we? Oh, yes! We were after something to black out the windows. The rag bag! First line of defense in our grandmother's day for every emergency from gallstones to gun wadding. Heavens! where was it? Already we felt the comfort of its bulky weight in our hands. Dumped out in the upper hall, it would surely produce something upon which we could lay our hands, fly downstairs, and hold our face before the family. And then we remembered. Horrors! We didn't have a rag bag!

The full realization of this catastrophe tied up in our subconscious mind somehow with the naval disaster at Pearl Harbor, and for an instant we felt that the world was lost. The rag bag had disappeared insidiously, depleted first by the rag rug craze, thence looted by the rummage sales, and finally completely demoralized by Bundles for Britain.

Rag bags were out. And time was fleeting. It was fleeting nearer and nearer to that moment when the army, the navy, the international news service, the BBC, Johnson's floor wax, the president of the United States and Carter's Little Liver Pills commanded, on threat of disaster, darkness, total and stygian. What if we failed? What if we were the one to leave a chink of light, whose beam would guide raiding enemy war planes to the North American continent? Things just as small had caused almost as great disasters. Take Mrs. O'Leary's cow.

But this was no time to go into abstractions about cows. Heavens! Why does the mind balk and go off at inconsequential tangents when it should be running forward with lightning precision on well-oiled tracks? Something must be had to cover the windows, and that at once. Wasn't there an old tarpaulin in the attic? Or was it in the basement? Or didn't we leave it at the lake that time we camped in the pasture?

Downstairs there was the sound of furniture being moved. Thumpings and poundings recalled us to sanity, and to the fact that an impatient family had taken command below decks. With a final sigh of resignation, and commending ourselves for a praiseworthy sacrifice, we grabbed from the spare bedroom the extra blankets, and descended the stairs to nail them to the mast of the emergency.

We were met by the proud smiles of a smug, complacent, and triumphant family. The windows had already been covered. While we had been having a brain storm upstairs with Pearl Harbor and Mrs. O'Leary's cow, the family had jumped into the breech, and the situation was well in hand. One glance was enough to assure us that the process by which the blackout had been accomplished was earmarked with the simplicity of genius. We dropped into a chair to get our breath— and to better grasp the significance of what had been done.

Yes, we should have known in the first place that the big rug was the only logical covering for the big window. And whose deft touch was responsible for ripping the felt cover from the playroom billiard table and lashing it over the south bay? Two kneading boards over the transom of the front door—what could be neater, or more efficient? And the card table nailed over the breakfast-room window! And the best napkins, and the kitchen towels, and the sweater we were knitting, stuffed simply everywhere. That coat, the one that just came from the cleaners, is nailed over the dining-room casement, and the other coat, the old worn one that we didn't send to the cleaners, is still hanging in the hall!

Well, it's a good thing we had all those nails on hand. Spikes, I guess they're called—the ones we got for laying the new planking in the garage.

Chronology of 1941

December

2 Attempt to kill Mussolini fails.

6 Britain declares war on Finland, Hungary, and Rumania.

7 Japan unleashes devastating surprise attack on Hawaii (Pearl Harbor, where 2,897 U.S. armed forces are killed) and Philippines and follows this with declaration of war on U.S.

8 U.S. declares war on Japan, as does Great Britain.

11 Germany and Italy declare war on U.S. and congress votes declaration against them within 4 hours after news is received.

17 Admiral Kimmel, commander of Pacific fleet, and two top-ranking army officers in Hawaii removed as aftermath of Pearl Harbor losses.

A Wreath in the Window

December 27, 1941

IT IS CHRISTMAS AGAIN. Outside my window a company of young soldiers has been digging "fox holes" in the sand dunes. They are wearing helmets, and carrying their wartime gear. Etched against the stormy surf of the Pacific Ocean they make a beautiful living frieze, as they bend in labor at their shovels. Occasionally a little group gathers at the top of a particular fort-like dune, and surveys the surrounding terrain.

"I'd like to be right here," says one boy, "when they come over." And he looks hopefully out into the Pacific.

Inside my house, red ribbons, sprigs of holly, and a confusion of wrapping papers and tinsel ornaments clutter a card table. What am I doing with little bits of paper and tinsel, I ask myself, when out here—outside my very window—life and death are fighting for position of vantage on a tight rope?

My ribbon and tinsel seem so silly and futile. And yet if Christopher Columbus, or William Shakespeare, or some long-dead peasant from the steppes could come back here tonight, the only familiar thing in this strange new world would be the holly, the red ribbons, and the tinsel of Christmas.

Boys like those outside my window are the ones who have kept Christmas going for us. We want to tell them that we know this. But we are inarticulate. All we can do is shove aside the blackout curtains and hang a wreath in the window—right there behind them, beyond the little fox holes.

1942

Soldiers at Dinner

January 3, 1942

HAVE YOU HAD A SOLDIER at dinner? If you haven't, you'd better go out and get one right away. You will never feel that this is your war unless you do. After you have gotten your soldier, and fed him, and talked to him, this will have become your war—and the soldier, the one you had to dinner, will be fighting it for you.

We didn't get our soldier until the evening of Christmas day. Due to government business, my host was unable to be at home until eight o'clock. Most of the boys on this beach had been nobly fed by that time as guests of honor in our hundred homes. But my hostess was determined. "There must be some boy who hasn't had Christmas dinner," she insisted, and so her husband put on his things again, got out his car, and went off. "Bring all you can find," she called after him.

But he only brought one. He brought him in proudly, as one brings home a rare hunting trophy. "I tried dozens of 'em," said my host, "and they'd all been fed. So I drove down to the water's edge and found this fellow just coming off a watch. He's cold, and hungry, and everything else that you'd want in a soldier," and my host looked approvingly at the soldier as if he'd invented him.

He was a big young fellow. His nice brown eyes accepted with a glance of appreciation the crackling fire, the decorations of pine branches and cones, the yellow fringed tablecloth on the pine table. He took off his muffler and folded it up, put his coat on a hanger—you'd have thought it was London made, the way he handled it—washed his hands, and sat down.

Two red candles lighted our feast. We talked of trivial, comfortable things. Outside, the North Pacific roared and rattled as it does on a fine night. Sometimes we stopped talking to listen to it. We looked into each other's eyes and thought of landing parties, submarines, and other enemy deviltry under the stars. But no one mentioned these things.

Our soldier talked of soldiering and the new army. He hailed from the Middle West, and his eyes were big with the wonders of this new country. Up on Hood Canal, he said, a watchman for oyster beds had told the boys they could have all the oysters they wanted for stews. So they got all they needed, and milked a nearby cow for milk. And it was such a grand oyster stew that they tried it again the next day—and the next, always falling back on the same cow. At the end of the fourth day, the company received a bill from a farmer for $24 worth of milk, so the stews came to an end.

When they found themselves bedded down in one of our forests during a wind storm, many of the boys from the plains country suffered acute discomfort and confessed that they felt like bolting. It would be easier to face enemy fire than to stay in the forest during a wind storm, they said.

Most of the boys in his company were in their early twenties, our soldier said. But they had one old fellow of thirty-five. He came from Arkansas. He didn't like the army much. His wife had had a fine job back in Arkansas and he'd lived on the fat of the land. And he would have been living on the fat of the land until this day, if his wife hadn't arisen to the national emergency and gone herself to the draft board and said, "Come and get him." So they came and got him, and since that day he didn't mind telling the world he'd been cheated. "Such a big healthy girl . . . and then to lay down on the job like that," was the way he put it to his comrades.

At eleven o'clock, we let our soldier out the door. His natural good manners would permit him to dine at Windsor Palace without untoward incident. Our hearts were large with pride. When we heard the garden gate click, we closed the door. Somehow the candle light seemed dimmer. And yet, we have something that we didn't have before— we have a soldier at the front. Our own personal soldier.

━━

Today army regulars are to be seen about. They wear wintry ear-muffed caps to the post office, and carry their gear on their backs with professional jauntiness. They are older than our Christmas friend. They do not stop to watch the schoolchildren at their games, and they do not pet the neighbor's dog, but instead they order it not to follow them. It is plain to see that a certain esprit de corps is to be maintained. They are above eating cookies on the road. They do not rush with boyish shouts to sift the softness of the sand dunes through their fingers. They do not race to the top of the dunes to let the first vision of the Pacific write tell-tale ecstasies on their faces. No indeed! They are old experienced troops—twenty-five years, or older, to the man.

Civilian Defense Meetings

January 10, 1942

THE OTHER NIGHT we muffled ourselves into our coats, put on our mittens and galoshes, and went to the rural schoolhouse for a civilian defense meeting.

I feel sorry for those Americans who can't go to the rural schoolhouse for elections, socials, and rural defense meetings.

The square stove in the corner was there. And above the blackboards which skirted the room, the handiwork of the juvenile population showed that the youth of this age were still wrestling with the intricacies of colored crayon technique. The same squirrels holding nuts to their jaws looked down upon us, interspersed with drawings of red apples which were no worse nor better than we did in our day. Initials, hearts, and triangles, not to mention grooves and gouges, were carved plentifully atop the wooden desks. The younger generation, it was plain to be seen, was growing up in the tradition of its ancestors.

Heartened by these sights, we wedged ourselves into the seats of these moderns—who weren't so modern after all—and prepared ourselves to face the facts. That there were facts to be faced no one doubted. But we were somewhat vague and doubtful as to what they were. To speak of bombs and blastings, of bloodshed and bandages in this atmosphere of our youth seemed blasphemous, somehow. For a moment we hoped that such things wouldn't be spoken of—that someone would stand up and make a motion that the ladies be delegated to furnish boxes and the gentlemen decorations for some forthcoming basket social. We closed our eyes and willed Mr. B., our coordinator, to say something cheerful.

Well, he didn't. But he presented his incendiary bombs, poison gases, evacuation plans, and pleas for an emergency dressing station as well as he could. Those women who had come wearing hats and gloves and looking efficient were put at the heads of committees. The rest of us, weak but willing, in mittens and mufflers, made up the working crews. The men went in for splints and stretchers, fire-wardening, and blackout patrol.

We are organized. We know each other better and like each other more than we did before the meeting in the schoolhouse. My neighbor—the one whose infant ducklings my cat ate up last spring—seconded my motion about collecting the steam cookers for sterilizing bandages. I have forgiven him for the subsequent event in which the father and mother of the ducklings ate the water plants out of my pool. Mrs. E., who has never even had any of us in for so much as a cup of coffee, has given her home to the supplies committee, along with a five-dollar bill.

Chronology of 1942

January

1 Hitler himself takes command of retreating Nazi army on Moscow front.
Sales of new cars banned pending rationing.
Football results: Rose Bowl, Durham, N.C.—Oregon State 20, Duke 16.

2 Manila and Cavite naval bases fall to Japs.

6 War draft of 20-44 announced.

11 OPM orders halt in private home building.

12 Dutch East Indies invaded by Japanese; MacArthur's men again hurl enemies back to Luzon.

14 Joe DiMaggio, Yankee outfielder, named "player of the year" for 1941 baseball season.

16 Carole Lombard, screen actress, her mother and 19 others killed in plane crash near Las Vegas, Nev.

22 South American anti-Axis compact completed.

23 Australia calls on U.S. for help.

25 Dutch and Yanks take toll of 33 Jap ships in Macassar strait.

26 U.S. American Expeditionary Force (AEF) lands in North Ireland.

28 Nation told 80 Nazi U-boats off East coast.
Colorado's worst coal mine disaster in 25 years snuffs out 34 miners' lives.

30 Price control bill passes.
President's 60th birthday.

31 Malaya falls—Japs drive on for Singapore.

And we need it. A week ago the Red Cross carried away the community bankroll of $11. If they don't forward us the promised first aid kit pretty soon, it will amount to absconding. That is the general feeling.

In the meantime, we are getting together our old sheets and our worn out shirts and sugar sacks for bandages. We are making stretchers and splints, and equipping a dressing station, and passing from one to the other such old wives' lore as we know. If a submarine rises out of the Pacific in some future dusk and sends a shell into our midst, or if raiding enemy bombers, having found no better objective, unload their cargoes on us before they leave this shore, we will do the things we are expected to do.

We've got to make this schoolhouse safe for colored-crayon squirrels, and red apples, and American children, for ever and ever. That's not a very comprehensive plan, you will say. But if you multiply it by thousands of schoolhouses and hundreds of thousands of American hearts, it becomes comprehensive.

Hysterics—Beans

January 17, 1942

I WONDER IF A LITTLE hysteria wouldn't be a good thing after all. A news dispatch says Washington had plenty of advance notice that Tokyo was geared for attack. The information was pressed by anti-Japanese, Koreans, the British secret service, and several members of Congress with Far Eastern connections. "But," says the dispatch, "these tips were disregarded as hysterical and unfounded."

Now we are preparing our own coastline to resist attack, but we are repeatedly warned not to get hysterical. Civilian defense activities are instructed to prepare the people for poison gas eventualities, but to keep a firm hand on the control gear of public hysteria. Some communities have been told to have ready a 30-pound pack containing bedding and a can (preferably) of beans.

It would be easy to get hysterical about the bedding but the beans somehow seem to lead things back to the commonplace. Who could get hysterical with a can of beans in his bedroll?

No one in the communities which have received these instructions but visualizes himself setting out as a leading actor in one of those terrible forced migrations of a populace. And then, just when he is getting up steam and preparing his spirit to plod heroic miles to safety, along comes that dampening thought of the can of beans. If it could be bully beef, or a dried herring, or any thing with a historic background or heroic import! If it could be foie gras or truffles or any other fine food, cast with a fine reckless gesture among the blankets! But to arrive weary and wet at the end of a day's trudge with nothing but beans in your bedding is an implied insult to the American spirit of adventure.

No, you could never get hysterical with that can of beans on your back. The very thought of it takes all zip out of the prospect. Its weight would stay the eager foot, dull the shining eye, and regiment into numbness a fine-fettled American hysteria which would carry thousands through marsh and forest, over hill and prairie to a sort of victorious covered wagon objective.

On second thought, perhaps we won't evacuate at all. Perhaps we will stay here on our shores and emulate the one thousand civilians at Wake Island,* who had every reason to get hysterics, and who, no doubt, did get hysterics—and made a sizable dent in the fenders of the Japanese navy before they got calmed down.

A number of our citizens have stood on their dunes during the past weeks and seen Japanese submarines attempt to throw monkey wrenches into west coast shipping. They have seen our ships attacked, and they have seen the attacks repulsed—and they have gone home and milked their cows, scolded their wives, and turned on their radios. Is that hysteria?

There are reasons, of course, why the army and the navy and the newspapers and the ready tongue should be stilled when it comes to releasing information of value to the enemy. But to withhold other information from the people because they might have hysterics is an insult to American intelligence. If we have to have beans in our bedding or bombs in our bays, we want to know about it. It is our war, isn't it?

A well-developed case of grade A hysterics such as the Russian people are having today can accomplish a miracle.

---

* Wake Island is an atoll with three islets in the central Pacific Ocean between Hawaii and Guam. It was defended only by a few companies of marines and some civilian workmen who repulsed the first Japanese invasion attempt on December 11 and inflicted some casualties before the island was captured on December 23, 1941.

Dogs—Wildcats—Wolves

January 31, 1942

I **ONCE OWNED** a sheep dog who grew up and celebrated her first birthday without ever having laid eyes on another four-legged creature larger than a rabbit. The community in which we lived consisted of fourteen souls and one dog—and the dog was ours.

A sign in front of a settler's home advised the passerby that the place boasted a "Wildcat in cage," and an arrow directed the curious to the rear of the property. I had never stopped to view the wildcat in cage myself, but I decided one day that the time had come to let my dog know that she wasn't the only animal on the face of the earth, as she was developing quite a superiority complex.

So one day I stopped the car in the vicinity of the advertised attraction, and took the path to the rear of the cabin. My dog pranced boldly ahead. As we turned the corner, we came abruptly upon a cage full of yellow, snarling, evil-toothed, red-fanged venom, spitting and clawing threateningly.

Completely stunned by the sight, my dog stopped dead still. With her forepaws almost against the cage, she turned her head away from the fearful vision and froze into immobility. She never budged and never took another look at the wildcat. She resisted all urging to take a "look at the pretty kitty" and kept her eyes turned instead on the familiar sights of the forest.

When I turned to go she withdrew her paws gingerly from the edge of the cage, as if from the edge of a bottomless crevasse. As soon as we turned the corner of the house, she occupied herself furiously by digging for an imaginary mole and snapped viciously at various nonexistent mosquitoes.

As far as I could determine, her reaction to the little horror in the cage was to simply pretend it hadn't existed. She refused to accept this thing—outside the range of her experience—into her consciousness. It was ugly, and terrible, and fearful. To her, therefore, it became on the instant the little wildcat who wasn't there.

For a long time now, we Americans have refused to contemplate the nature of the little monster in the Pacific. We haven't told ourselves it wasn't there, exactly, but we have refused to take a good look at it. Because it hasn't produced a literature we would understand, we have written our own fantastic books about it. We didn't care for Japanese music, so we sang Madame Butterfly. We told ourselves that these people thought and felt as we did, and finally we were anesthetized by our own inventiveness.

So we were surprised and chagrined when the cat came out of the cage at Pearl Harbor the other day, and showed its fangs. It came out armed with American scrap iron and an imitation of a German plane for conquest. Besides these purely occidental attributes, it came with other native gifts of treachery, age-old instincts of deceit, a feeling of national inferiority, and a capacity for reproducing cannon fodder at a rate comparable to the army ant—and the same willingness to bridge the gap of conquest over the bodies of its own dead.

America recoils from this specter of spiritual puniness. We'd like not to have to look at this wildcat. But we are not so fortunate as my dog. We not only have to look at it, but we have to set our teeth in its unwholesome hide. We have to drive it back to its island, and keep it there until it learns the meaning of civilization.

——

To ape the accoutrements of civilization does not make civilization. When the wolf put on grandma's cap and glasses and crawled into her bed, it was only to fool someone. It wasn't because he really liked to sleep in beds.

To his brutish eyes, the cap and the glasses and the bed, were devices to use for deceit—just as the diplomatic structure at Washington was used while Pearl Harbor was attacked.

What to do with some thousands of Japanese citizens of the United States is a moot question on the Pacific coast. They are wearing their caps and glasses very nicely. But their presence here constitutes a dangerous hotbed from which the FBI has dragged many a wolf.

Perhaps in due time we can present them with one of the lusher islands of the Japanese Archipelago.

Bread

February 7, 1942

A GOOD THING TO DO when you are assailed by war worries—and who is not?—is to get out your large yellow bowl, some milk, shortening, sugar, and salt, and add a yeast cake. The instant you add the yeast cake you will have something to cope with. You can't put off coping until tomorrow, or until the afternoon radio reports that General MacArthur is still fighting without reinforcements. You won't have time to worry about where our fleet is, or why we haven't got a landing field at Corregidor, or why we don't hurry and bomb Tokyo. To keep the situation you have created well in hand will require your concentrated attention for a number of hours.

The successful loaf of bread requires energy, a sense of timing, an understanding of temperature, imagination, resourcefulness, and other gifts, which, when enumerated, look like the list of qualifications for a good airplane pilot. However, the object of bread making, as I recommend it, is not merely to land a good loaf of bread at the end of the day's flight, but to turn your repressed warlike feelings to some good account.

The important part is the kneading. When you have the dough on the board you can pummel it to your heart's content. You can put everything you've got into the job, including your feelings about congressional pensions. Bright ideas will pour into your brain—for instance, congressmen accepting pensions could be decorated on the back of the collar with a number, such as "Pensioner No. 62." Then everybody would know what team he was on—yours or his.

Also I prescribe bread making for women who don't knit. When those superior people who knit settle themselves into the best chairs and commence reeling their skeins, you can say with a tone of super superiority and a slight tinge of pity, "Excuse me, please, I've got to make some bread."

It's a good form of counterattack.

Men—Mothers—Menus

February 14, 1942

AFTER EVERYBODY in the village store had been served, the little group which had been waiting near the door approached the meat counter. There was an air of authority about the quiet-voiced young man who had evidently been elected spokesman of the group. He looked the chops over carefully, and the butcher, sensing the momentousness of the occasion, went into the cooler and came out with the best loin he had and cut off ten chops.

When they had been wrapped, under the careful scrutiny of five pairs of eyes, the group moved over into potatoes and vegetables. They watched silently while the spokesman selected several pounds of medium-sized potatoes, examining each one as if in search of a flawless stone. The vegetable question was simple. There were only carrots and spinach, so it was spinach of course—lots of it. Apples were gone into next. The group crowded about the box, and everyone took a turn at going over the apples thoroughly. They were weighed while five pairs of eyes watched the flicker of the scale dial. The transaction having been completed in a businesslike fashion, the group went into a whispering huddle. Then one of their number detached himself and walked with resolution to the bunch of bananas and selected five, and a bottle of cream.

The spokesman then put the exact amount of change and tokens on the counter. A perfect arithmetical problem had been worked out.

At this juncture, I could contain myself no longer. "Is the army cooking for itself these days?" I asked the quiet voiced one—the one with two chevrons on his sleeve.

"Oh no!" he assured me solemnly, "it's just that we get homesick for things cooked the way the folks do it—at home," he added.

I watched them going down the road in close formation. In the flurry of moving trucks, and the activity of the road on which you can count a jeep a minute, they were a thing apart. They were a group consecrated for a few hours to playing, in a feverish world of war, that they were at home.

They turned into the path which led to one of the summer cottages where many of our troops are bedded down. The last man through shut the picket gate and latched it carefully. If I ever saw a pantomime of "Do Not Disturb," it was in the closing of that gate.

As I write this, five young soldiers down the road are playing house—no, not house, they're playing Home. They're doing things the way the folks do them.

━━━

Well, the least we can do is to play home, too. After all we're the folks, aren't we? We can't change things in the Pacific or comprehend congress, or Mrs. Roosevelt, or grasp the magnitude of the billions of war dollars the press tells us about every twenty-four hours. Perhaps we hadn't better try. Perhaps all we can do, out of all there is to do, is to keep on playing house. Someday,

Chronology of 1942

February

3 Nazis rush air and tank reinforcements to southern Russia battlefront.

4 AEF speeds aid to Far East Allies.

5 Giant Jap spy ring disclosed on West coast.

6 Key oil town in Borneo captured by Japs.

13 Hitler's fleet escapes from Brest to Kiel.

15 Singapore falls to Japs.

16 Dutch destroy 100-million-dollar oil fields in Sumatra.
    U.S. registers nine million more for draft, 20-44.

19 First Jap bombing of Darwin, Australia.

20 New cabinet for Churchill; Japanese land on Timor Island.

21 U.S.-Dutch air fleet sink or damage 19 Jap ships.

25 Two waves of planes over Los Angeles, immediate blackout.

28 British 'chutists and Commandos raid France.
    Bill to end 40-hour week defeated.

when they come back, it will be home again. Being the folks is something that this swiftly changing world cannot change. To get home to the folks is the ultimate objective of hundreds of thousands of American boys today. Being "the folks" is a pretty important job.

———

The army mess is located in the basement of the community hall. A counter divides the room. Two big gasoline cookers, looking like square metal boxes, contain compartments for kettles, and emit steam. On the floor around the room are boxes of lettuce and celery. Otherwise not a crumb is in evidence in the cleanly scrubbed room. A mess sergeant and his aides preside. Hanging near the door is a sheaf of typewriter paper containing thirty-one printed pages—the menus for the month. They are identical with the menus of Fort ——, and every other place where Northwest soldiers are stationed. And the same meals are eaten simultaneously by thousands of troops.

It was New Year's Day when I visited the mess hall. Ham omelette had been served for breakfast, a turkey dinner at noon, and supper called for cold meat cuts.

"I suppose it will be cold turkey?" I said to the sergeant.

"Not a chance," he replied. "In the first place, there won't be any turkey left, and in the second place it isn't on the menu. It's gotta be cold meat cuts."

In reply to my query about foraging on the country and serving local salmon or clams once in a while, he said, "No Siree, ma'am! They're not on the menu."

The reason is that every bite of food is subjected to a rigid test before it is served to our troops. It is a good thing too. But that cast-iron menu is also the reason why the boys in the cottages play house once in a while.

Travel—Trousseau—Team Work

February 21, 1942

ONE OF THE THINGS we'll have to get used to is travelling by bus. Buses are of three types—overcrowded, late, and special. And it isn't a bit difficult to find one combining all three of these attributes, now that the American public has become tire minded, and is leaving its cars home in the garage. The special bus that I took from Olympia the other afternoon was an hour late. We got into it on time, but it stood there

without budging for the best part of an hour, while some mysteries of transportation were being solved in the station office.

When we finally got underway, everyone was bristling with annoyance. The important-looking man up in front put away the watch he had been holding, and said in a loud voice that he was going to miss an important business engagement. The large bristling woman across the aisle snapped her bag shut with a loud click, and said that she would be an hour late for the dentist "and you know what that means." We did. Everyone shrugged and wriggled at the thought of being late for the dentist. We pondered on the unchangeableness of dentists in a changing world. Buses are late, tankers are sunk, tires are scarce, important men miss important engagements, but dentists still expect people to be on time. They should be forced to change their ways, we agreed.

"It's maddening," said the large bristling woman, and she snapped her bag shut two or three times in quick succession.

"I hope we're not too late," said the young girl beside me. "I'm getting married at four o'clock."

———

She was very young, and pretty in a brown-eyed, sleek-haired way. She wore a brown skirt, and a green jacket, and she carried a small cardboard overnight bag in her lap, and a paper bag.

"I'm marrying a soldier," she said and laughed, and looked out of the window happily. Everyone smiled, except the large bristling woman, who clicked her bag disapprovingly.

"He's stationed at E——," said the bride. "He's rented a cabin for two days. I hope it has a good stove," she added, and for a moment she looked worried. Everyone else looked worried for a moment too. We couldn't help hoping that the cabin would have a good stove. We wanted her to make a success of her two days of matrimony.

"I've got to go back to work on Monday," she told us. "I'm shelling walnuts in Oregon. It's nice work, but you can't get the stain off your fingers," and she held up her hands and showed us her brown-stained fingers. Then she reached into the paper bag and took out a little white cake. "His mother made it," she said with pride.

"Does he like the army?" demanded the important-looking man. And even though he was trying to be friendly, his voice sounded gruff, and he looked more important than ever.

"Yes, he does," said the bride. "At least he did until he met me six months ago. He says I annoy him," and she laughed again. "I make twenty-five dollars more a month than he does."

At the town of E——, we were met by the wedding party—five soldiers carrying between them a bunch of pussy willows, a red heart-shaped box of candy, and a punchboard table lamp. Even in the excitement of being clasped in the arms of one of them, the bride managed to keep the paper bag containing the cake from being crushed.

——

"I think it's disgraceful," the large bristling woman announced as the bus went on its way.

"What is, ma'am?" asked the little wiry man, who had been chewing a toothpick since we left Olympia.

"Getting married like that, without a thought in the world," said the large bristling woman. "After the war we'll have to support them. They haven't got a thing in the world."

"Oh, yes, they have," said the little wiry man. "They've got the only thing in the world that you don't have to pay for, and that you can't buy no matter how much you have. They've got youth."

The large bristling woman shook her head doubtfully. "Well, I don't believe in it anyway," she said, and she closed her bag. But there was no snap in it this time.

"Oh, come now, ma'am, you do too," said our wiry passenger. "Why, you're young yourself. I'll bet you haven't had a bite since breakfast. That's the trouble with these buses. They don't seem to realize that folks have to eat once in a while. Why, I met a man the other day all the way from Montana, and what with one thing and another, and poor connections, and mixed up time tables, he didn't have a mouthful of food until he got to Seattle. Now if you'll show me where there's a good restaurant I'll be happy to buy your supper . . . "

The large bristling woman started to say something, but no words came. She looked down at her bag. It was open, but she did not snap it shut. Instead, she took out a compact. She looked at herself in a little mirror. "I don't know . . ." she said. The bus lurched over the Wishkah Street bridge. Everyone reached for their belongings, and coughed and scraped their feet, and got into the aisle. It had been unanimously agreed in that telepathy that exists between bus passengers that she should go out for supper with the little wiry man. He had nice blue eyes, crinkled with humor and kindness. We made a lot of noise and confusion and gave her a chance NOT to snap that bag shut if she didn't want to.

I don't think she did.

American Tragedy

February 28, 1942

THE BIG NEWS in women's affairs is that Mrs. Roosevelt has finally agreed to agree to the wishes of the American people, and has resigned her post with the Office of Civilian Defense. As Mrs. Roosevelt expresses it, she "left" the job, but as columnist Westbrook Pegler puts it, "she didn't leave her job, but was stormed out of it by public opinion."

Mrs. Roosevelt in "My Day" says that two New York newspapers, the *Herald Tribune* and the *Times*, published the first valid criticism of her connection with civilian defense. These newspapers pointed out to her, she says, "that the wife of any president cannot be looked upon as an individual by other people in the government. She must always carry the reflection of the usual governmental public servant."

"I had hoped this was not true, but I found out that it was . . . even when the position is unpaid," she writes.

She sums up on a note of hope, "people can gradually be brought to understand that an individual, even if she is a president's wife, may have independent views and must be allowed expression of an opinion; but actual participation in the work of the government we are not yet able to accept."

Just what Mrs. Roosevelt means by expression of opinion is not quite clear. Does she mean that she isn't permitted to express opinions as freely as other Americans, or does she mean that she should be entitled to express more and freer opinions than any other Americans? But if we take it that she means a president's wife should be allowed to express herself in the same way the average American expresses himself, I think she

should be allowed that latitude. And if we take it that that is all the latitude she has made use of, we can also take it that the same things have happened to her that happen to every one of us who express opinions—people either like our opinions or they don't. In Mrs. Roosevelt's case, they don't like them.

———

That the wife of a president cannot be an individual is, I think, untrue. If Mrs. Roosevelt had won a place for herself in public affairs before the election of her husband to office, I very much doubt if the fact that she inadvertently found herself a president's wife would mitigate against her career in public service. Unfortunately, we have only learned about Mrs. Roosevelt's opinions because we elected her husband to the presidency. To our uninstructed eyes, her talents are not rooted in the solid ground of personal endeavor, but are raised to imminence on the parent stem of the presidency.

To use another figure of speech, Mrs. Roosevelt is like one of those "added attractions" that accompany the movie feature—you have to sit through it in order to see the feature picture, or you don't. It depends on how attractive the added attraction really is.

———

In action, Mrs. Roosevelt has expressed herself with determination in favor of a certain group or groups of American peoples, including certain labor union factions, mountain barn-dancing communities, and artistic personalities whose talents were predestined to blush unseen. There have been many fine men and women devoted to the same groups—just as there have been other fine men and women devoted to the preservation of American wild birds, foreign missions, reforestation, baseball, ballet, the eight-hour day, horse breeding, husband holding, agate hunting and similar interests. Every one of those men and women who have attained eminence in these fields and who have done anything for themselves and their professions have taken a firm grip on the bottom rung of the ladder, set their teeth with determination, and started the long slow climb to the top. They have been allowed to express themselves just as much, and no more, than nature and things-as-they-are allow people to express themselves. To lift any one of these groups, or the ideas of any of these groups, into quick success by means of the presidential lever is to employ an artificial stimulus which even the common man recognizes as unsound. America is not a proving ground for a group of social service workers to cut their milk teeth on, no matter how sincere they may be. When it comes to being tamed, and civilized, and hand fed by self-appointed arbiters, America is not amused.

———

As to Mrs. Roosevelt's sad reflection "that we are not yet ready to accept the idea of a president's wife actually participating in the government," she is right. We aren't. Even in England, where the wife of the ruler is considered very much of an individual, she is not allowed to participate in what Mrs. Roosevelt means when she says "the government." Any opinions that the queen expresses are carefully prepared by the prime minister. If she has any of the independent views which Mrs. Roosevelt feels a woman ought to be allowed, she keeps them for her intimates.

If such procedure has been found feasible in a monarchy where a woman actually shares a crown, it ought to work pretty well in a democracy. And, so far, it has.

Fun—Fear—Food

March 7, 1942

I'S NOT FUNNY to be funny anymore. All the high-priced boys who write the columns are going in for the deadly serious. As a matter of fact, there isn't much that is funny in the world today.

Take the little affair of the Women's Ambulance Corps which occurred in an eastern city last month. An unscrupulous columnist wrote a whole column about the incident which, if he hadn't been nosing about the newspapers and discovered it, would have gone down to oblivion in its proper place on the obituary page under an eczema ad.

There is a proper place for every story in a newspaper, and one of the major jobs of the editor is to give a story its just deserts, and if it hasn't any, to hide it, preferably under an eczema ad.

———

Well, the story I speak of had been nicely buried, according to Hoyle, for the good of the public morale, when along came this columnist and dug it up and made a lot of

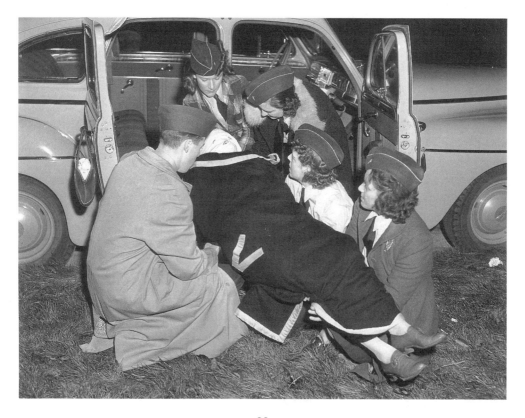

loaves and fishes out of one little paragraph. Whether he should have done so or not, you will have to decide for yourselves when you read the story. The story which has to do with the misadventure of the Women's Ambulance Corps, I will state in as few words possible, to-wit:

The ladies had completed their prescribed number of hours of first aid, and were giving an exhibition before the assembled townsmen. A public spirited citizen of about 50 years had volunteered to model the ordeal of bandaging, splinting, and an ambulance trip to a theoretical dressing station. After he was bound and gagged, so to speak, the ladies, in carrying him to the ambulance, dropped one end of the stretcher and he broke his leg.

Undismayed (and of course keeping cool), they picked him up, splinted his broken leg, and shoved him into the ambulance, whether or no. The ambulance started with a jerk, the door flew open, and he flew out and cracked his skull. At this junction, the public spirited citizen resigned his job. If he had kept on modeling for another round he could have made "Believe It or Not."

———

The saddest story of the week is that of the small boy who advertised that he'd do odd jobs for nothing—it would be impossible for him to buy anything with any small change he might make anyway, he said. Immediately following upon this wisdom from the mouth of a babe, Secretary of the Treasury Morgenthau doubled the taxes on soda pop, candy, and chewing gum, which makes the boy a prophet as well as a philosopher.

"The sooner we come to complete food rationing, the better," says Secretary Morgenthau. Americans eat more sugar than any other people, and have more diabetes, according to the medicos. They smoke more cigarettes, and have more heart trouble, say the statisticians. To make food restrictions easier to swallow, why couldn't these boys be organized to find something wrong with all restricted commodities as they come to hand? The process could be simplified and made readily understandable by alliteration, such as coughs in coffee, boils in butter, flu in flour, etc.

Chronology of 1942

March

2 Auto rationing begins.
4 Burlington, Iowa, ordnance plant explosion kills 16, injures 51.
7 Japs invade New Guinea at two sectors.
11 U.S. fixes used tire prices.
14 Yanks land in Australia.
17 MacArthur and aides escape from Phillipines, land in Australia.
19 Jap invasion fleet heading for Australia is smashed by Allies.
24 U.S. takes over strike-bound Toledo, Peoria, and Western railroad.
25 U.S. navy rips Makin island 1,000 miles off Jap capital.
27 Chinese smash Burma trap, relieve retreating British.
29 British Commandos wreck Nazi-held St. Nazaire port.

What with the evacuation of Japanese residents, green vegetables on the Pacific coast are liable to be scarce and expensive. Many people will want to raise their own lettuce, radishes, onions, parsley, carrots, peas and beans, and all those things which do so well in our own climate. Even California admits that we are superior in one thing—green vegetables.

Civilian Sorrows

March 14, 1942

LIFE, WHATEVER ELSE it is doing, is decidedly not going on as usual these days. If our troops on the far-flung fronts glean from our censored newspapers and our letters telling of the daily routine that the home folks are apathetic, and that life, in any sense of the word, is going on as usual, it is too bad. Life is going on, but in a most unusual way. There is not a man or a woman, or a child, or a business, or a schoolhouse, or an office whose daily pattern of life has not been changed by the war.

Expressions on peoples faces are intent and abstract. Loss of some sort is imminent. The American people are philosophical about congress' conjured-up billions. They can always replace money again. It isn't the changed and uncertain economic situation that causes our hurried, abstract, nervous manner, but it is the fact that every American family can now name a son in deadly danger of his young life. Somewhere on a transport in the Pacific, somewhere in an American village in the theater of war, are young men who will take with them, if they do not return, something which can never be replaced.

All of us civilians know this fact. We know it intensely. And strange to say, so do our sons, and our nephews, and the neighbors' boys, wise beyond their years. To believe in war and the slaughter of American manhood is to set our chart by an abstraction. We are fighting because we have to fight. There is no glory in it, except the strange, mysterious, unfamiliar glory that rides with death.

What is there about the uniform of our troops that brings the pulse into our throats? It is simply that it is a symbol of men dedicated to death. Our anger, our frustration, and the helplessness we suffer despite success slogans and the fanfare of mobilization is caused by the fundamental knowledge we have that war skims the cream of youth from life's milk pan. And whether we like it or not, the diet of many of us who are left behind will consist of skim milk from now on in.

———

Another timely tragedy that we witness every day is that of the slightly middle-aged patriot who would give his eye teeth to be "out there" somewhere in the Pacific. Who doesn't know one of these staunch, slightly girthy-about-the middle citizens who will tell you with real feeling that, while he can't hike twenty miles a day, he is a good shot, and what with this being a mechanized army, he could do just as good a job as a young sprout who feels the tug of life in his veins?

And who living in Grays Harbor County doesn't know a bar pilot or a fisherman, or just a local boy grown older, who chafes because time and the United States navy regulations prevent some practical use of his stored-up knowledge of this coast and the vagaries of the Grays Harbor channel? To know how to do something well, and not be allowed to do it—that is hard.

———

As I write this, in this little beach community on our Western front on this 10th day of March, 1942, army traffic is thick on the narrow road. Olive drab trucks, tractor-type vehicles with big guns, jeeps and ambulances are racing up and down the road. Groups of soldiers are coming from the village post office where some of them have got the mail, which has at last caught up with them in a new world where troops move faster than the U.S. mail.

The camellias are shedding their first petals. The first daffodils are blooming in rutted rows in the dooryards. From some of the cottages, bedrolls are being flung into waiting trucks, trucks waiting with their engines running. There is movement and departure. There are no goodbyes. There is no time for goodbyes. And there are no words in which to say goodbye. It is a lingering, letting go, of all the dear, loved familiar things which will become doubly dear, and are seen sometimes for the first time at the moment of leaving. The pale March sunlight glints with false brightness on the yellow gorse. Who is going to be wooed by this promise of a summer that may never come.

Gorse
Ulex

———

Tomorrow there will be new faces at the canteen. Hungry faces that ask questions without words—and which you cannot answer. Well, you can at least shove the chocolate layer cake into a position of vantage, can't you, madam?

C'est la guerre!

Cats as Cats Can

March 21, 1942

MOVING ALL YOUR household goods from one beach cottage to another is nothing compared to moving one cat from one beach cottage to another. This week I did both. You can take down a stove and move it a quarter of a mile and set it up again, and it stays there. But you take down a cat and set him up again, and again, and again, and he won't stay put.

Claude Furbottom was the final item on the moving schedule. Yesterday I lured him into an old blanket and started down the road. On two previous occasions, he had escaped my clutches and fought his way to freedom, only to return to the deserted house. But this was to be my last trip in favor of one cat, I told myself, as I took a double hitch in the blanket and admonished the squirming animal within to be still.

"Nothing is going to happen to you," I assured him. And he was still. And nothing did happen until a honking jeep aroused him into the equivalent of a tempest in a teapot—or a blizzard in a blanket, or a tornado in a tarpaulin. Any way you put it, he was aroused, and he braced himself into a steel spring and backed through the maze of the double hitch, and jumped to the ground.

Once on the road, his green eyes made a lightning-like reconnaissance of his position, and with uncanny acumen he fled to cover beneath the underpinning of a nearby camouflaged gun battery.

"Here, kitty, kitty!" I called rather helplessly, looking under the mass of piled-up muzzles, tractor wheels, and the what-have-you of a gun battery. And if I had said "open sesame," or knocked on the door of a beehive, nothing more could have happened than did happen. Uniformed men appeared from nowhere, everyone sprang to position, guns were manned, and one big muzzle swung about with ominous precision among the cedar boughs, while a hard-eyed sergeant wanted to know the meaning of "all this."

"It's only my cat," I said, adding, "Kitty, kitty!" in a tone calculated to soothe the sergeant more than the cat.

Everyone looked under the guns, where kitty's green eyes shone with bright inquisitiveness. He was squatted on his paws, alert and interested in what was going on, but not a bit frightened, I could see. I know that cat. He loves drama. And this was drama, wasn't it, being looked at by an entire gun crew?

Everyone got down on their haunches and said, "Here, kitty, kitty!" School let out just then, and the primary grades, seeing the strange maneuvers around the guns, stopped and blocked the traffic on the road. A jeep with a general was obliged to come to a full stop. "What's going on here?" asked the general, with a great deal of authority.

"It's the lady's cat, sir," said the sergeant, coming to attention.

"It's my little cat," I said. "He got away from me." And I looked at the general and smiled hopefully. But the general didn't smile. Instead, the lines tightened about his mouth.

I tried again. "It's a good cat," I said, watching the general's unchanging face. But from his expression, I gathered that he suspected the animal of being an enemy alien. He muttered something and got back into the jeep. The schoolchildren fell back, and everyone stood stock still while the general's jeep drove off. It wasn't permitted to be interested in the cat any longer, it was plain to be seen. So I thanked the sergeant and the men and went off down the road, giving kitty a dirty look over my shoulder. He returned my glance with one of joyful malice.

Later in the evening, there was a knock on my door, and the sergeant came in and proudly unwrapped a large bath towel and produced a cat. It was a nice cat, but it was not my cat. I thanked him. And after he had gone, I dismissed the animal—a lethargic old Persian who belonged to the woman across the road.

But the day was not done yet. Another knock came on the door. This time it was the nice young wife of the nice young lieutenant. She carried a picnic basket from which the vacuum bottles had been removed and which contained, believe it or not, the same nice lethargic old Persian which belongs to the woman across the road.

After that, there was nothing for me to do but to go to bed, before someone brought him back again.

This morning when I opened my front door, there was a cat on the door step. It was my cat. He had his back toward me and he was washing his face. He did not turn around when he heard me open the door, but continued to lather his paw and swab his face. Every now and then he would stop and look complacent, epicurean approval at the goldfish pool which is one of the attractions of my new garden. In a little while, the sun will strike the pool, the fish will rise, and kitty will manage to live through another, not too boresome, day.

National Emergencies

March 28, 1942

THIS WEEK I HAD the most important man in the district at luncheon. Envious glances were cast over neighboring fences as we went into the cottage and shut the door. And no doubt some hard words were said too. After all, who was I, a comparative newcomer, to snatch and snare the most important man, when so many other women were willing and eager to lay hands on him? To tell the truth, I felt quite elated at the conquest, and I determined, while I had the opportunity, to make hay while the sun shone.

We lunched in a sunny corner by the kitchen window, on fresh side pork, country gravy, and cornbread, with a big pot of coffee on tap, as I gathered from the look of him that he would like that sort of food. And while he attacked the meal with a sort of relentlessness, I sat and drank coffee, and conspired in my mind ways and means of holding him. Men are scarce as hen's teeth these days. But a gifted man, one with the talents of my guest (who at the moment in question was swabbing an outsized corn muffin in milk gravy), was a man without price—well, almost without price anyway.

He wasn't particularly handsome, I realized, really looking at him for the first time. Nor did I know his age. He may have been thirty-eight, or it may have been fifty-eight. You couldn't tell by looking at him. But that was not important. The important thing was that here was a man of genius sitting at my table; and unless I could think up something in a hurry, I wouldn't have the slightest excuse for detaining him.

I could think of plenty of things, all right, but it must be something imperative, something that would hold him! Hadn't I heard him promise Mrs. G. that he would spend the afternoon with her? It must not be! Already he was down to the last muffin, and nothing had come into my mind. Why hadn't I made an apple pie? A hot apple pie with cinnamon in it would have swung time into the breech. Besides, he was the kind of man who liked hot apple pie with cinnamon in it for lunch. Some instinct told me so.

Now he shoved his chair back and stood up.

"Don't go," I begged, coming out of my abstraction and putting more feeling than I had intended into my voice.

He stood looking down at me with a hint of compassion in his eyes. "You know I can't get along without you," I said, throwing caution to the winds.

A slow smile appeared at the corners of his mouth, and was replaced by a determined setting of the muscles. "I promised Mrs. G. I told her last week I'd come today . . ."

It came over me then in a flash that I'd lost the skirmish. But only the first round, perhaps! I fell back to the second line of defense. "What are you doing tomorrow?" I asked. At the sound of my own voice, asking that question which is admittedly one which should never cross a canny woman's lips, I felt a premonition of defeat in my veins.

"I'm going to Miss M.'s," he answered. His hand was on the door knob. Now he was opening the door. He said something about seeing me next week.

Horrors! Was this the way it was going to end—on this indefinite note, and after all those corn muffins and apple pie? But no, there hadn't been any apple pie. But pie or no pie, he was getting away from me.

"Wait!" I called, and followed him into the shed. "You know I've got to have that oil barrel hitched up yet. And the tin flashing you put up around the chimney! How do I know it will work? If it rains tomorrow, you'd better stop and look at it. And the porch light! You didn't fix that yet."

"I know! I know!" he said, and there were tired lines beneath his eyes, in spite of all the corn muffins and coffee. "But there are so many ladies who need things done, now that there are no men about. I can't keep up with you all. But I'll do my best."

"You're the only handy man on the beach," I told him. "Everybody's so tied up with war jobs. I don't know what we'd do without you."

"Well, I'll be seeing you," he said.

"Yes, come tomorrow," I called after him. "I'll have an apple pie."

"You set an awful nice table, ma'am," he assured me earnestly. And he went across the road to put flashing around Mrs. G.'s chimney, and mend the kitchen stove, and fix the garage doors, and put the hook for the canary's cage in a place out of the draught. What would we do without him?

━━━

This community crossed another Rubicon at first-aid class the other evening—we mastered the traction splint. The young lieutenant who modeled the part of a broken-legged man was so thoroughly trussed up that we had to cut him loose with drawn knives. He came out of the ordeal with nothing worse than a wrenched shoulder. The trouble was that when we got him all tied up in the splint, we pulled the wrong string and levered his arm out of joint, instead of his leg into place. These are perilous times.

Boys—Billets—Baths

April 4, 1942

IT IS A NICE LITTLE schoolhouse painted brown, with yellow trimmings, and a cupola. Right now the gorse is blooming, and over the gorse can be seen the sand dunes and the Pacific Ocean. It is a sixth-and-seventh-grade-sized school, with everything built to a corresponding scale. Therefore, it is funny, these days at recess, to see soldiers pile into the schoolyard and take possession of the basketball. At first they toss it to one of the older boys, but pretty soon they are tossing it only to other soldiers. The game becomes fierce and lively. The children take to the fence. The principal comes out and scratches his head. Here is a national emergency, all right.

━━━

Down the road, Paul gets out of the jeep. Civilians don't often ride in jeeps. But he has ridden in a jeep, and with an officer too. He isn't one of those slim young officers that you can't tell from a private. He is not as neat as a private, he is older, and he wears a pair of dusty boots of an early vintage. Together they cross the road and look down at the only vacant house left in the village. It has a tarpaper roof that leaks, and three small rooms. It will house nine men. But there are many more men to be housed.

The officer ponders, and looks hopefully at the village handyman as if he expects Paul to conjure up something better; something larger, anyway.

And wonder of wonders, Paul does. Hidden from view in an overgrowth of alder and brambles is the old bog house, the original cranberry sorting house of the first bog, built nearly thirty years ago, and long since abandoned, when the Finnish settlers found deeper peat to the south.

The two of them cross the drainage ditch on a footbridge. The water is dark and sluggish, and salmonberry and thimbleberry brush is thick on the bank. Stooping under the alders, they follow a rut in the rotted planks of an old road, and come to the doorway before they have even seen the house.

It is large. The officer is pleased. There are no windows, but the men will soon see to that, he says. It will hold fifty men.

Salmonberry
Rubus spectabilis

Over on the new bogs where every Finnish house has an accompanying warehouse for the sorting and storing of cranberries, soldiers are living in the lofts of the warehouses. Everything is neat and scrubbed. There are starched curtains at the windows. Baling wire and reels of twine hang on hooks. In the corner are piles of knocked-down wooden boxes. There are heating stoves to keep the sorters warm. It is a pleasant place to live. When the housewives bake their fine white sweet bread, they ask the soldiers into their kitchens for warm bread and coffee.

———

Max is a pet at the house where he lives. On St. Valentine's Day, he brought his hostess a box of candy tied with red ribbons, and gave her a big smack. He calls her "Mommer." Mommer is as old as the hills. She has the girth and expansiveness of Schumann-Heink. Max is very handsome. He is small with fine shoulders, dark hair, and blue, blue eyes. His father was a Jew, and his mother is a Lithuanian. Once he came from the post office with a package containing a loaf of pumpernickel bread and some homemade salami. He cut two slices of the bread and put the sausage between. Then he held the sandwich away from him at arm's length, firmly with both hands. "My mother made that," he said. And he bit into it, and two tears fell on the bread. "Mommer" got two more tears in her eyes when she told about it.

———

On Saturday night, fires are cooked up in the Finnish bath houses. Puffs of smoke can be seen coming from the squat little bath houses. Pretty soon the women run to the warehouses to tell the soldiers that the bath is ready.

"But I had a bath last night!" someone protests.

"It makes no difference; you can bathe again. It is good for you," is the answer.

If there are more baths than boys, someone goes over to the canteen to muster in a few more recruits from the pool table. The good hot water shall not be wasted!

———

The first lieutenant looked about the waxed and shining kitchen where the Finnish women sat at their crochet work. None of them spoke. Their expressions were calm, but unreadable. He would learn nothing by looking at them, he realized that. And yet . . . he felt a silence.

"Perhaps you have misunderstood me," he said. "I expect to pay rent, if you can find a house for my wife to live in. I'll pay well. I'm not asking something for nothing."

Everyone hooked thread for a minute. Then an older woman spoke. "Your wife said she wants to board. She doesn't want to cook. And we haven't time . . . we eat differently."

"She wants a bathroom," said another woman, and she looked at the lieutenant as if that settled everything.

A slow grin appeared on the lieutenant's face, and a look as if he were enjoying a secret joke.

"Nonsense!" he said. "She's a fine cook. Why, she's cooked for years. And as for a bathroom, why a little outside plumbing won't hurt her. It'll do her good to learn a little pioneering," and he smiled broadly. Everyone smiled, then.

So it was arranged that the lieutenant's wife should have one of the little two-room cabins, with the bright linoleum rug, and the well-polished stove, and the sink enclosed in wooden boards painted blue, and of course, a bed in the other room. A big double bed piled high with wool patchwork comforters, smelling faintly of soap.

This Mechanized Army

April 11, 1942

THERE WAS A KNOCK on the door. Three soldiers stood there. They said they were "sorry, ma'am," but. They looked sorry for me in a way that boded no good. "It has come," I said to myself. "The army wants my house. Last week they took the house two doors away, yesterday they took the house next door, today they want my house."

I could hear this bad news better sitting down, so I asked them to come in. They came in. But they would not sit down. "Perhaps you'd better hear the bad news first," said the small Irish one with the gold identification bracelet.

I braced myself. "Well, give it to me," I said, as my mind plowed through the patriotic furrow I have been cultivating of late, and stalled on the word "sacrifice." Who was I to escape it, after all? "Go ahead," I said and managed to sound not too hopeless.

"You tell her, O'Houlihan," said the big one in the sweat shirt looking at the small Irish one.

O'Houlihan stepped forward, looked me straight in the eyes and said, "Could we use your washing machine?"

"You could do that, and welcome!" I answered. And wished that I had three washing machines to give to my country, so relieved was I. The ice was broken and introductions followed, O'Houlihan doing the honors. The big one in the sweat shirt was Bill of Baltimore, and the pretty quiet boy was Pete from the Bronx. "I'm a small town boy myself," said O'Houlihan, "from the sticks of New Joisey."

"We're engineers," explained Bill of Baltimore, and in spite of the dirty sweat shirt, I knew instantly that he came from the right side of the tracks. My instinct also told me that O'Houlihan of New Jersey and Pete of the Bronx hadn't yet penetrated his incognito—and never would, if Bill of Baltimore could manage it.

So I didn't ask if he was Princeton, which was on the tip of my tongue. "I've got hot water all day," I said instead.

"But we woik all day," said Pete of the Bronx.

"And wash all night," added O'Houlihan, with a grin.

How true that was, I was about to find out.

At seven o'clock the setting sun was blotted out by three coolies passing the kitchen windows bearing burdens. It was my soldiers in blue fatigue uniforms, each with a galvanized tub on his head, burgeoning over with unwashed clothes.

"Is this the washing of a whole company?" I asked a moment later in the laundry.

"Oh, no! ma'am," O'Houlihan said. "It's every man for himself in this army." There must have been weeks of dirty clothes, and I said as much.

"Oh, no, ma'am," O'Houlihan assured me. "It's just two weeks to a T." And he proceeded to stuff six shorts, six undershirts, eight pairs of socks, six khaki shirts, two pairs of dungarees, two towels, two wash cloths, and a couple of blue denim hats into the machine with beautiful impartiality. "Regulations are that we have to make a complete change three times a week."

Pete of the Bronx cut up a villainous cake of soap on the chopping block and added it to the brew. "This army soap will take the paint off a battleship," he announced.

The lever was pulled, the machine started chugging, and the first load was on its way.

———

There remained Pete's of the Bronx and Bill's of Baltimore yet to go through the washer. I flew to the kitchen. I hadn't bargained on that much hot water. I seized an armful of wood and stoked manfully at the range.

"I figure in about an hour she ought to be clean," O'Houlihan told me optimistically from the doorway. I calculated hastily—an hour for New Jersey, an hour for the Bronx, and an hour for Baltimore made three hours! I grabbed more wood.

"Lady, come here!" begged O'Houlihan's voice.

"Jeepers—Creepers!" whispered Pete of the Bronx as I appeared.

The washing machine, it was plain to be seen, had bit off more than it could chew and was slowly strangling to death on a wringerful of dungarees—but no, it wasn't dungarees! Bill of Baltimore in a desperate struggle with the dying monster managed to drag a length of khaki wool from its jaws.

"Holy cats!" sobbed O'Houlihan. "It's the lieutenant's pants! How did they get in here?"

But it was only half the lieutenant's pants, the other half being firmly wound around the wringer.

Chronology for 1942

April

1 Hand-to-hand fighting with Japs on Bataan.
   Senate defeats ban on 40-hour week, closed shop upheld.
2 All bicycle sales halted.
4 Navy admits three U.S. warships sunk by Jap planes.
8 Axis desert forces move against British in Libya.
9 Bataan falls . . . 36,000 U.S. soldiers taken prisoners.
16 RAF blitz on German industrial centers roars into 5th day.
18 Tokyo bombed by U.S. air force (Doolittle's raid)
22 Commandos raid France at Boulogne, rout Nazis.
23 Sugar for restaurants and other food services cut 50 per cent.
24 U.S. opens sedition quiz of suspects.
30 RAF again bombs Paris industries.

"Well, how did they get in here?" I asked with more than a little asperity in my voice. I could see unpleasant official investigations looming ahead. This thing had gone far enough.

"They were to go to the cleaners," said Bill of Baltimore. "We must have grabbed them up with the rest of the stuff."

———

There followed a few tense moments of reversed levers, and delicate manipulations worthy of an operating room, before the lieutenant's pants were freed, intact.

"They can still go to the cleaners," I told them, after a huddled inspection.

"And they won't be back until next week!" said Pete of the Bronx.

"In the meantime, India may revolt!" said Bill of Baltimore.

"A thousand things can happen in a week, to lessen the news value of the lieutenant's shrunken pants," I said. And I reached for the coffee pot and another armful of wood.

Health—Hollers

April 18, 1942

I DON'T KNOW WHAT magazines soldiers buy, but I do know the ones they don't buy. Down at the village store and post office, where everything considered readable is snapped up from the comprehensive magazine counter almost before it is laid down, there remain unhonored, unsung, and unread *True Confessions*, *Life Romances*, and *Women*. They are dog-eared from repeated spurnings. To me that is another indication that we have the healthiest army ever mobilized.

———

My neighbor who has one of the pleasantest homes on the bogs gets more mail each day than anyone else who calls at the post office. For several months she has been mothering various and diverse flocks of soldiers. "Are those all from your boys?" I asked her today, when she came out with a large packet in her hand. "No," she told me, "most of the letters are from the boys' mothers. They come from all over the United States. I write back and tell them all about their lovely sons, and the good times we've had, and the little coffee feasts. But I can't tell them what they want to know most," she added. "I can't tell them where their boys are now."

Pacific Dogwood
Cornus nuttallii

In times of stress, you find out what people are really made of. In these war times we are finding out what a nation is made of. Various peculiarities of our people, which pass unobserved in peace times, arise like lumps of tough earth under the harrow of the emergency, and are exposed to national view. Take the bunch of Tennessee soldiers who stood it as long as they could, and then voiced amazed indignation because black-eyed peas weren't served for breakfast. We had a similar incident in a Northwest CCC camp where boys went on a hunger strike because hominy grits were not part and parcel of their diet.

Personally, I think the army ought to make a practice of occasional black-eyed peas for breakfast, and give the rest of the boys something to holler about. Sergeant York came from black-eyed pea stock. Those boys never owned a pair of store shoes, but they cut their milk teeth on the butt end of a squirrel gun, and help to raise the marksmanship standards of the American army. They ought to be humored.

Every good American got a sinking feeling in the pit of his stomach this week when he heard about the short rations of our troops in the final heroic struggle on Bataan. To us on the Pacific coast, what is happening in Europe and Asia is not as important. Our hearts belong to Corregidor. The war, as far as we are concerned is being fought in the Pacific. That is where our prayers go, anyway.

Creation

April 25, 1942

WOMEN BEATEN BACK upon themselves are wont to produce such subversive activities as knitted bedspreads. If all the knitted bedspreads in the world were placed end to end and left there, it would be all right with me. Well, anyhow, women have got to do something with their odd moments, it seems. Having the kind of eyes predestined never to see the eye of a needle (I have taken someone's word for it that needles have eyes), I have, nevertheless, mastered an outsized darning needle, sort of a little brother to a crowbar. When I feel the primordial urge toward smugness of accomplishment, I darn socks.

"Have you got any darning to do?" I ask my hostess when the ladies have settled down to their stitching. This question, if it isn't politely ignored, is greeted with a nervous laugh, and an attempt to continue the conversation where it left off. But if I persist, and go so far as to thread a spike, showing I mean business, my hostess disappears and eventually emerges with her husband's fishing socks, or the ones he wore that time he got lost three days on an Olympic Peninsula elk hunt, and I am given the uppers to play around with.

Sock darning as an outlet for the creative spirit has its limitations. If they would let you choose your own colors . . . but they won't!

Figures—Farmers—Flyers

May 2, 1942

AT THE VILLAGE STORE some of us were buying the last five pounds of sugar we will be allowed until May 7th.

"And how about you, Roger?" the proprietor asked a small boy hovering over the ice cream counter. "Hadn't you better take home some sugar to your mother?"

"Nope," said Roger, with proud satisfaction, "we've got a whole sackful in the attic."

After Roger had gone down the road lapping at an ice cream cone, we fell to talking prices with the grocer. To my surprise he didn't agree with the government's contention that the wholesaler charges more because the manufacturer has to pay more to produce the goods.

"It's still the wholesaler that's peeling off the profits," he said, "I don't care what they say. You see that can of salmon? I'm selling it for 44 cents. I've got the number of the pack from the case, and it's the same pack that sold last year for 34 cents. The wholesaler has just added a profit of $6 a case by wishful thinking. It didn't cost the manufacturer one cent more. How could it, when it was packed at the prices that prevailed a year ago? And by the way, you'd pay 50 cents for the same can in Aberdeen today.

"A woman came down here yesterday and bought up all the tuna fish I had on hand," he continued, "because it was 6 cents a can cheaper than in town. A Seattle woman who comes down here for weekends always takes home seven or eight dollars worth of meat from our store, and says she saves more than the cost of her gasoline bill. Somebody's making money that you can't blame on the manufacturer.

"The reason we haven't got any liver is because veal is being sold to Alaska contractors. The wholesaler is selling it to Alaska because Alaska offered a better price for it. The price control business can't come a minute too soon for me. It'll be a good thing."

Many women who stocked up on paper napkins, paper towels, and other items have been awaiting the arrival of that dark day when they will be informed that there are no more to be had.

Our President's speech on Tuesday night, with its seven points designed to use every American to help win the war (and to keep some buying power in the American dollar after the war is over), was accepted wholeheartedly by most of the people. To hear that a minority group, the farm bloc in congress, is asking 10 per cent more for farmers than for other workers, doesn't set well with the rest of the country.

Somebody wrote a comprehensive article in the *Saturday Evening Post* a year or so ago, debunking the poor American farmer. The author did his debunking in a three-point treatise: (a) you can't get rich farming; (b) you don't have to farm; (c) you farm in spite of drawbacks, crop failures, and hardships, because farming offers more freedom, more pleasure, and more rock-bottom security than any other calling. Men farm because they want to farm, not because they have to.

President Roosevelt ought to form a "You Can't Eat Your Cake and Have It" commission to explain this adage to our cousins in the hog belt. Whole hog or none seems to be their motto.

Last night I watched the Sunset patrol come in from the Pacific. A flock of pursuit planes flying in from the southwest converged on shore, and bespoke each other with joyous swoopings and wing tilting. Then, only a hairsbreadth above the dunes, they sped off northeast-ward full tilt, kicking up their heels like spring calves in the pastures of the sky. They put everything they had into their homeward flight, and it was beautiful!

Even while they were coming in, the night flight, high above their heads, was putting out to sea.

Sugar

May 9, 1942

THE COLUMNISTS on the women's pages are going to come out in a few days and tell us how to get along without sugar. We will be reading enough sugarless cake recipes (just half a cup, my dear, and a little honey thrown in) to create an unprecedented shortage. If all the recipes are taken seriously, there will be a national emergency.

Right now there is an ominous silence on the pages devoted to food and recipes. The recipe-writing ladies are lying in their lairs, figuring out ways whereby we can go without sugar and still eat cake. If they can figure that out, they will have something.

The editors of the food pages are recovering from an unexpected blow below the belt, due to the unforeseen disappearance of honey from the market. For the past two weeks, they have been telling us with blithe assurance that honey is a fine substitute for sugar. And now lo and behold, there is no honey.

If we are going to get by with what sugar we are allowed, it is going to be on a basis of every woman for herself. If you find that a raisin pie for instance takes very little sugar, for heaven's sake keep it to yourself. Don't publish it in the paper. If you do, the price of raisins will rise, and eventually they will disappear from the markets. That's the way it works.

Shapes—Shifts

May 16, 1942

HOW WILL YOU LIKE wearing clothes designed by the Department of Agriculture? We have been warned for some time that things were going to happen to clothes, and—well, we were philosophical about it. We could see why pleats and pockets have to go and skirts remain static, but we thought little else about it. We had the best designers in the world, didn't we? We could leave the problem safely to them.

But now it appears that the problem isn't going to be left to them. And even that could be overlooked—but to turn it over to the Department of Agriculture seems rather an indignity.

I suppose it had to be turned over to some department. I have mentally run through all the departments—the Department of the Interior, the Postmaster General, the Labor Department, the Attorney General! None of them seem particularly promising. Things just seem to shift back naturally to the Department of Agriculture, but why, I cannot say. The only thing the Department of Agriculture has designed in the way of clothes, so far as I know, are cotton coats for sheep—to keep their wool clean.

Well, anyhow, they are now going to take over. A new system for setting sizes for retail women's wear has been worked out. A scientific study of women's weights and measurements has resulted in "figures showing actual proportions and is expected to result in better fitting ready-made clothes," says agriculture.

It may be for the good—women can be just themselves. For the first time in ready-made history, clothes will be made to adapt themselves to the woman, instead of the other way about, with women struggling to reshape themselves to fit the clothes. Cognizance is about to be taken of the fact that the preponderance of women take on an expansiveness of girth shortly after

Chronology for 1942

May

1 Hitler, Mussolini meet at Salzburg, leave Japan out.
   Plans to draft women for war service temporarily abandoned.
4 National sugar registration for ration books begins, first of four days.
5 British, backed by U.S., occupy Madagascar.
6 Corregidor falls to the Japs; 7,000 U.S. troops surrender.
18 All New York City night baseball banned for duration by New York police commissioner. Sky glow endangers shipping.
19 East coast gas rationing to be put on national scale, Roosevelt hints.
25 Allied plane sinks Axis sub off Brazil.
28 On the grounds he is a Communist party member, Harry Bridges, Australian-born West coast CIO leader, ordered deported.
29 Death of radio, stage, and screen star John Blythe Barrymore, 69.

they pass the girl scout age, and from this fact the designing profession has turned away with shudders and denied in practice as nonexistent.

———

In order to be clothed at all, a good life-sized woman had first to lash herself in an extra-curricular rubber hide, and then pay the alteration department time and a half for reefing out more sail. Now all that is to be changed, says Agriculture, by new standards of weights and measurements. Rubber as a lasher-upper has vanished from the scheme of things, and the American designer, having nothing to stick pins into, has thrown up his hands in horror and run screaming from the scene. The Department has jumped into the breech, and now proposes to create dresses that women can jump into without even a look in a mirror and wear away from the scene of the crime without even a backward glance. They will fit because they will be made for women as nature made them—and not for women as the designers wish they were made.

Whether these gowns are to be purchased in the grocery department along with a sack of potatoes and two pounds of asparagus, or in garden tools and accessories, or in hay, grain, and feed, the Department has not announced.

Other fashion news is that the shoe business ought to be looking up.

By and large, this is a pretty cheerful world.

Business—Art—War

May 23, 1942

ON MONDAY I gathered a couple of pairs of needy shoes in my arms and went to the shoemaker's house. You don't wrap your shoes when you take them to be resoled in this community—you just tuck them under your arm and stroll down the road. Then everyone who sees you knows, without undue effort, where you are going, and can say upon returning home, "I met so-and-so going to the shoemaker's."

Along the picket fences, baby broom trees were sprouting a bonanza of bloom. The fences sagged under burdens of rambler roses, as yet in bud, and blue myrtle blossoms shot out from the driveways. As I passed the barber's house, I saw a little plot beside the road devoted to sixteen (I counted them) potato vines, neat and prim as a pansy bed.

At the shoemaker's house, I opened the door in the ell and went into the shop. A little man with a ruddy face and wearing a large flat hat was busily humming among his wares.

"Ah, business!" he said. "Well, that is what I want. I will put leather soles on these. Real leather." I also knew that many good stitches, made with the aid of an awl, and put there to stay, would go into the job. Our shoemaker has an exacting clientele. The Finnish people have never accepted shoes casually. Shoes are one of the important things of life. They must be good. That stands to reason, doesn't it?

Hearing our voices, Mrs. Shoemaker opened her door and crossed the porch to the shop. "I have just made a dish of clams," she said. "Come and taste it. And I want you to see my grandson's picture."

We crossed the porch and went in the front room. Finnish front rooms are all alike—a good radio, two of the grandest upholstered chairs that money can buy, and the rest just shining space. A leaf-patterned linoleum glistened on Mrs. Shoemaker's floor, from the front door to the kitchen sink—also the best that money can buy.

On a table was a photograph of a young boy. He was wearing a sailor suit, and looking reminiscent of foreign ports.

"That is his picture of last year," Mrs. Shoemaker said. "Before Pearl Harbor." She picked up a larger, shinier picture from another table. Sonny was shown in white shorts, a pith helmet and cartridge belt, and holding a small rifle with a bayonet. There was an expression of fierce determination on his face. "Since Bataan!" his grandmother told me proudly.

———

In the kitchen she drew from the oven of one of the best stoves that money can buy an aluminum baking dish that shone like a mirror, and spooned out two helpings of the dish I was to "try." Whole clams baked with beaten eggs, a dash of young onions, and topped with buttered crumbs. A handful of red radishes and cups and cups of coffee went with the taste.

Lupine
Lupinus littoralis

The window looked out over new grass waving under a mist of lupine. Farther away the cranberry bogs spread a rust-colored blanket at the feet of the forest. While we ate, an airplane chased its tail in mad circles so close to the ground that you thought of it subconsciously as a bull instead of a bird, and went on with your coffee. There was a stout fence to keep the animal from snorting into the back dooryard.

"Every day it is the same," said Mrs. Shoemaker. And we shook our heads. If you have to have airplanes in your back yard every day, why you just have to have them, don't you?

———

Walking home, I was overtaken by a column of soldiers marching at route step. They were not happy. Halfway down the column, "the general" marched beside them. "The general" is a sergeant of Italian parentage; handsome, aloof, and with a bitter quiet voice. In fact, he is everything that a sergeant shouldn't be, according to the movies, which is one of the reasons he is called "the general."

The other reason is that he wants to be a general.

Whispered mutterings were heard. What a march! Eight miles. No one but a sergeant who wanted to be a general could think of such an indignity. Not in this mechanized day! Can you beat it! Jeepers!

The column faded into the road through the dunes.

Labor—Education

May 30, 1942

A NEW MEANING for an old word has been evolved here. The same thing no doubt occurred in other communities. The word "army." Whereas it once meant an armed force, it may now mean merely a couple of soldiers coming from the post office. You hear the neighbors say, "I met the army coming from the post office—the army has taken the house next door—the army bought all the cream puffs before the baker got them into the store—the army wants to borrow the waffle iron!"

Today the "army" in the guise of one platoon is drilling in the road. Everyone going to the post office stops to see the show. Sixteen men in blue dungarees—the uniform of the inductee—are being put through their paces. The drill sergeant has the deadpan face of Ned Sparks of movie fame, and the agile body of an ace chorus master. He cruises up and down the column, plowing through the undergrowth at the side of the road in a sort of hippity-hop step, barking the word "Hut!"

"Hut! hut!" he says, dancing along the line, and his eyes take in every movement of every recruit. He puts out an occasional hand to change by the thousandth of a millimeter the angle at which a gun is held. He cocks his head to one side to study the set of a pair of shoulders. All adjustments are made while the column is in full swing, and the sergeant never misses a hut—unless it is to give the command to count. "Count!" he roars, and the men yell "One! Two! Three! Four!" in a gruff composite staccato, and pound their feet on the road.

At a command for gas alert, they come to an abrupt halt, put down their guns, and remove from their chests flexible contraptions which turn out to be gas masks. The sergeant views this operation with a critical eye from a distance and then comes hut-hutting along the line like an angry locomotive overtaking a stalled freight on a siding. Putting down your gun, taking off your hat, and adjusting a gas mask without getting its wires crossed with the straps of your pack is a difficult operation. And it doesn't help much to have old hut-hut snorting alongside!

Eventually the thing is accomplished, and the gas-masked crew looking like something out of Jules Verne's *Twenty Thousand Leagues Under The Sea*, pass the schoolhouse just as recess is declared for the primary classes. The children take one look and shrink back into the vestibule. But some of the little boys take brave breaths and soon come out again. The small girls follow. Only a few gasps and shrinkings, and gas masks are an accepted part of life.

Standing there, and seeing my first gas masks along with the children, I suddenly feel very primary-grade myself.

I also recall that day before yesterday Mayor La Guardia of New York City pounded his chest and asked, "Where is all my equipment for civil defense?"

And Civil Defense Authority James Landis answered, "It's out on the West Coast, at Seattle, Washington!"

Literature—Agriculture—Sports

June 6, 1942

IN A SMALL COMMUNITY, all you have to do to understand how the war program is working out is to take up your stand in the village store and post office—in a short time you will know all.

"What, no bread today!" exclaimed an indignant woman.

"No ma'am!" said the proprietor. "The bakery wagon has had to cut down—doesn't even know whether he will be able to come at all anymore."

"You women will have to bake your own bread," announced a local prophet from behind the stove.

The driver of the laundry truck came in. "Tell the 00th company that we can't press their uniforms anymore," he told the postmistress. "We have orders to cut out all army laundry. We're allowed just enough cleaning fluid to care for our old customers."

Tony, the faithful driver of the vegetable truck, folded his tent and disappeared a month ago, along with the last inner tubes and the first strawberries.

Today the bookmobile made its final round, picking up books, but giving none out. Mr. Walter Cummings, who drives the truck, and Mrs. Helen Gilbert, librarian, are saying a last goodbye to 22 rural communities which they serve. That means 2,000 less books will be read in Grays Harbor country during the course of each month. For the past two years the bookmobile, sponsored by the state library association, Hoquiam public library, and the county commissioners, has traveled a route of 750 miles serving rural communities from McCleary to Tokeland, and from Melbourne to Quinault inclusive.

At the next general election, the people of the county will be asked to pay two more mills to reestablish the service as a county project.

My victory garden isn't doing so well. So far nothing has appeared above ground—not even a weed! Not even an onion!

"The onion," says the encyclopedia, "may be grown from the tropics to the coldest verge of the temperate zone."

Well, maybe so, maybe so!

Other irrelevant information about common vegetables, gleaned from the same authoritative source, says that the French discovered how to make sugar from beets during a sugar shortage in the Napoleonic wars. A good beer may be brewed from beets. Invading Romans introduced the apple into Britain. You can get opium out of lettuce in a pinch. Asparagus grows wild and luscious on the Russian steppes.

What really made me lay down the hoe though, were the cabbages of the Channel Islands. They grow 6 feet tall there, and the stalks are used for fence rails. And walking sticks. And for rafters for the thatched houses. Five of these Channel Island cabbages will feed 10 oxen or 100 sheep.

━━

He is a small cat belonging to my neighbor. He has deep black fur which makes him appear fairly sizable, but when you pick him up, you realize that his body is not much larger than that of a squirrel. He is such a runt that nobody has ever dignified him with a name, and until this morning, he was just another one of those anonymous cats known as "Kitty."

Nobody made friends with him. The pampered pets of the neighborhood disappeared under davenports when he came in, or went out of the back door when he came in the front door. He was a lonely soul, apparently. The aura of loneliness seemed to cling about him like a cloak.

When he came to the door this morning and mewed his plaintive mew, I felt sorry for him. I shoved my big gray cat out the door. "Go out and make friends with him," I urged.

Claude Furbottom took one look and sprang to the roof with the speed of an exploded shell. Kitty, mewing in a heartbreaking treble, climbed painfully up the shingles and vanished over the eave trough. Immediately ear-splitting shrieks rent the air, the house echoed with a thumping sound as if a giant were pounding the roof with a broom, and wads of fur parachuted earthward.

I flew outside to take a look. Claude had taken refuge behind the chimney, and Kitty was advancing toward him with the deliberate intention of giving him another trouncing—for those wisps of fur in the air were from the hide of my pet. Claude looked the advancing menace in the eye as long as he could. Then he turned tail and jumped off the roof and rattled off at full speed in the salal brush.

Kitty paced the ridge pole, victorious.

He still mewed. But it wasn't company he wanted, I realized belatedly, it was another fight. And he hadn't been snubbed, only avoided—avoided with terror.

"Come on down, Timoshenko," I called, "and have some breakfast."

Labor—Industry—Science

June 13, 1942

"DO YOU SELL BB SHOT?" I asked the proprietor of the village store.

"Yes," he answered.

"Ah!" I said, "I'll take the lot of it."

He dumped the contents of a cardboard box into a paper sack.

"Are you sure that's all you have?"

"That's all," he told me. "There won't be any more. War priorities, you know."

"Well, thank heaven!" I said, and I departed with the purchase clutched to my bosom. I hadn't an earthly use for BB shot. And yet, this cornering of the local market would mean split wood, mowed lawns, and the lives of innumerable birds and chipmunks in the neighborhood, to say nothing of an occasional winged cat.

It has been three weeks now since Roger has laid a hand to the plow of odd jobs. Thirteen years old, and a very sparse and gangling thirteen at that, Roger represents the remaining manpower for hire in this community. Never avid for jobs, he is nevertheless available now and then for occasional dreamy preoccupations with the hatchet. Having chopped as much kindling as you could put in your eye, it is his wont to collect his wages and spend them on riotous ice cream cones. At 25 cents an hour, he manages to prolong the day into an orgy by working five cents worth and eating five cents worth, *ad infinitum.*

Then one day, between a chocolate jumbo and a strawberry strangle, he disappeared. That was three weeks ago. The kindling pile melted and the grass grew, but still no Roger. Today I met him on the road.

"When are you coming back to your job?" I demanded somewhat brusquely.

Before he answered me, he raised a rusty BB gun and let fly at a single splinter of glass which was all that remained of the window of the clam buyer's shack. There was a gratifying tinkle. Roger smiled with slow satisfaction. Then he granted me the favor of a sort of vague somnambulistic attention.

"Ooooh, I'll be along . . . one of these days. When this BB shot gets used up. There's a priority on it," he added with some pride.

So that is why I cornered the ammunition market, and nipped squirrel-potting season in the bud!

———

There were five soap broadcasts every day last week. I haven't counted them this week. Soap manufacturers are buying more and more radio time. In the first place, there must be money in soap. And in the second place, it doesn't appear that we are threatened with a shortage of that commodity.

The basis of soap is fat—animal or vegetable in combination with potash and soda. One quart of perfume will flavor 200 pounds of soap. Two ounces of coloring matter will tint the same poundage. It all sounds very simple. But it isn't. Everybody uses soap, but everybody doesn't use the same brand. Crooners, swing bands, blues singers, dramatic skits, and news broadcasts are locked in a life-and-death struggle to capture the trade.

If soap were standardized for the duration, what a lot of freight cars, crooners, and colored-paper wrappers would be released for the war effort. And without the loss of a single sud.

———

Before the war, the greatest percentage of billboard advertising in England went to digestive panaceas. And no wonder; cabbage and brussels sprouts are apparently the only known vegetables there, according to returned travelers. Our lovable ally has managed to preserve the tradition of being one of the worst cooks in the world.

———

They handed out those new helmets to our army down here this week. A truck drew up to the warehouse, and a soldier stuck his head out of the cab. "Hand me a load of those banana boats, will you brother?" he called out. And a new name was born!

Sinks—Sonnets

June 20, 1942

HAVE YOU TRIED to buy a sink lately? Because if you haven't, don't try—unless you want to spend a day making out affidavits, getting depositions, and swearing on the Bible that your old one is incompetent, irrelevant, and unsanitary. At least that is what my neighbor advises. She went to town the other day to do some shopping, and, among other things, buy a sink. Getting the sink took the whole day—and she still doesn't know whether the deal is going through.

She had to tell her age, how long she'd had her permanent wave, and promise not to use the sink for illegal purposes. After the sheriff, a notary public, and the FBI have okayed her application she will get the sink—if there is a sink!

Chronology for 1942

June

2   Nazi city of Essen smashed by 1,000 RAF planes.

4   Dutch Harbor, Alaska, bombed twice by Japs.

5   Japs attack Midway Island.

6   U.S. navy smashes Jap fleet at Midway Island. Later considered turning point of Pacific war.

7   Virtually entire Japanese population of West coast (99,770) moved inland.

10 British announce 183,550 casualties during first two years of war ending September 2, 1941, including 48,973 killed, 46,363 wounded.

12 Japanese land at Kiska Harbor in Aleutians.

21 Tobruk, British stronghold [in North Africa], held since January 22, 1941, surrenders to Nazi desert fighters.

27 Eight highly trained Nazi saboteurs caught by FBI. Four landed on beach in Florida, other four landed on Long Island. Nazi sub used in operations.

They gave me no ammunition,
They said I could learn to shoot;
By squeezing on the trigger
And shining all my boots.
Now that I'm back at the station,
They say that I can shoot;
But all I do is clean my rifle
And put polish on my boots.
When I joined the army
I had but one ambition;
I wanted to be a good soldier,
But they gave me no ammunition.

Sergeant Albert Hopper is the author of the lines above which are part of a poem published in a little newspaper gotten out by the signal detachment here. It expresses a very real sorrow—Uncle Sam isn't handing out any extra shells, it seems. And if the army can tell it so can I. Everyone wonders why, but the fact remains that there isn't much target practice on this natural range.

Last week, while we were on the alert, every gun around was borrowed by soldiers who wanted to try their hand at really shooting one of the things. Most Western boys have been raised with guns, but to many of our Eastern recruits, the gun still remains a thing of mystery.

Yesterday a soldier walked up to a civilian who came on the dunes with a gun and told him he couldn't shoot it there.

"But I came clear from Everett to shoot this gun," the man protested.

"Well, I came clear from New York to keep you from shooting," the soldier told him. "But I didn't tell him I never shot one of the darn things myself," the soldier told us later.

One buck private doled out the price of a .22-calibre rifle and gave it to a shopper going to town with instructions to buy him a gun and ammunition. "I've polished one of 'em so long, I'd like to see how they work," said he.

Well, there'll probably be some changes made—now that the boys have started writing poetry about the situation.

Sugar Shenanigans—Shadows

June 27, 1942

I WENT BLITHELY to the schoolhouse to register for canning sugar. A businesslike registrar picked up a typewritten form and indicated an empty desk. We sat down. "What do you can?" she asked, her pencil poised for action.

"I always make some jam," I answered with proud innocence.

"You can't have sugar for jam." She ran her pencil through a line, and waited for my next move. I looked around the room. It was filled with women—and men too. There were more people registering for canning sugar than ever attended a defense meeting. And all of them didn't make jam, I realized with slowly dawning amazement. Very well, then, I thought, if jam isn't good enough for them and the United States government, it isn't good enough for me either.

"I won't make any jam," I said.

"How many quarts of fruit did you put up last year?" was the next question.

"I didn't put up any quarts of fruit last year," I answered truthfully enough. "I just made jam—pints of jam."

"But you can't make jam," insisted my inquisitor in a voice edged with a scallop of exasperation.

I made haste to assure her that all thoughts of making jam had left me. I didn't intend to have any truck with jam, I told her, and I regretted that I had ever even considered jam. From now on, I said would consecrate myself to "putting-up" things—peaches, pears, plums. If I got careless and mentioned jam again, it was plain to be seen that I wouldn't get any sugar for canning. And not to have any sugar for canning, when everyone else was getting ready for the season of steaming fruit jars, piles of damp peach skins on the drain board, and peach pits on the floor, was to admit that I couldn't cope with the emergency. "There's rhubarb too," I announced brightly.

"The rhubarb season's over," snapped my interlocutor.

"So it is!" I exclaimed with false affability. "Well, the orange season isn't over. I always make some orange marmalade."

"Marmalade is jam," she pronounced with finality, and made as if to rise. Things looked very black for me for an instant, but there had been something in her last words that caught at my hopes. Marmalade was jam, she had said. But that was not true—not of my marmalade anyway. For twenty years I have tried to make it jam, but it never has.

"The marmalade I make is a kind of sauce," I said. "You take some water, and an orange or two, and some more water . . ." I waved a vague hand in an attempt to describe the vacuousness of my product. "It's an old Southern recipe," I explained, prompted by a stroke of inventiveness. "They used it during the Civil War when sugar was impossible to get. That is, it was very scarce," I corrected hastily, "but you could get a little. Just like now. Our forefathers who fought, bled, and died at Gettysburg used this very recipe, and if it was good enough for them, it ought to be good enough for us hadn't it?" Whereupon, I got up, turned my back on my one-man jury, and went and looked out of the window in the manner of the best legal tradition. And after the manner of the worst legal tradition, I had dissembled to the very best of my ability, and slain logic in its cradle—but I had to have that sugar. I couldn't go around being the only sugarless citizen in the community, could I, being forever set apart from my betters?

There was a rustling of papers and my judge cleared her throat and pronounced sentence. "You are entitled to fifteen pounds of sugar," she said.

I walked out of the schoolhouse a free woman.

—————

We are on the alert. Just before dusk an old sedan equipped with a proud new siren drives up and down the road emitting soul-chilling wails. Immediately in the little houses around, you can hear the tap-tap-tap of the tack hammer as householders rush to arrange their blackout equipment. You begin by picking up the nearest rug, and progress toward a thorough confusion and upsetting of the household goods, which ends very neatly with a bath mat over the transom.

In a little while, not a chink of light is to be seen—except the blaze from an unshaded bulb which hangs over the head of old Ivor as he dozes in blissful unawareness in the front room of his cottage. The sedan stops in front of his door and the warden goes in and taps the old man on the shoulder. He is almost stone deaf.

"Put your light out, Ivor," the warden says kindly.

The old man gets up and obligingly puts out the light. On that instant we are a hundred per cent blacked out.

Cranberries—Clams

July 4, 1942

WAS AWAKENED AT DAYBREAK, which comes at about 4:30 o'clock, by rapid gunfire coming from the bogs—but it turned out to be only the cranberry spraying machine being operated by a thrifty Finn. After you have lived here a while, you get to understand that these sparkling homes on the bogs with their shining modern plumbing, and their well-tired cars in the little garages, didn't get there by accident or a stroke of luck. The Finns are early birds—and late birds too.

There is a prosperity about these marshland homes that is stimulating. The pennies are no doubt counted—but when and where it is impossible for the eye of the stranger to perceive. There is always homemade rye bread cooling on the kitchen counter, or fine white sweet bread, almost like cake, to which you are welcome. There are fresh eggs to be given away, or a digging of new potatoes, and an occasional quart of cream.

The cream is the more surprising as the Finns do not run strongly to cows. They have the art of considering their economic scheme as a whole, and keep only enough cows to go around. If a neighbor keeps a cow, you buy your milk from him. You do not rush extravagantly into a cow of your own.

I have noticed at the post office-grocery store that the Finnish residents take their change in defense stamps as a matter of course. There is unrestrained pride, however, in their manner as they make the purchases. What they think of our national characteristic of taking no thought for the morrow I do not know. I believe they get a certain delight out of our childlike improvidence, without, however, any desire to emulate.

As for myself, I experience at times a strong desire to emulate a Finn. For instance, I envy that fellow operating the spraying machine. Out there at 4:30 o'clock in the morning, he is keeping a date with success. Furthermore, he is having a lot of fun—what with the waking birds twittering about his head, and a splendid sun due to come up and gild him with warm encouragement.

By a sort of unspoken agreement I do not discuss the position of Finland in the war with my neighbors.* The subject is, I feel, a puzzling, sore one with them. But this I do know—the Finns are very good Americans. In the search for enemy aliens, when rumor and suspicion had their day here, there was not one instance where doubt cast even the breath of a shadow on the integrity of a Finn. Fortunately for us, their children and their children's children will continue to interject the early bird virus into our national veins.

—

Yesterday six soldiers carrying trench shovels rushed onto the beach and, facing each other, began to dig furiously. In a matter of seconds, they had made a hole big enough to bury an ox in. They bent over and examined the hole for an instant and then jumped to a new position. Again they dug furiously. The results were apparently unsatisfactory. They sprang to a third position, clenched their teeth with determination, and dug another ox's grave.

I kept on with my walk. In the heat, the waves came shoreward in long rollers of liquid glass frothed with white ruffles. The jetty hung, suspended in a mirage, so near that I felt that I could touch it. Clumps of beach grass in the shimmering distance had become black islands floating in the air. I used to stop and show our new soldiers how to dig razor clams. But this is getting to be an awfully big army.

---

* In June of 1941 Finland joined Germany in attacking the USSR in hopes of recovering territory taken from them by the Soviet Union in the unprovoked war of 1939-40.

Catching—Cleaning—Cooking

July 18, 1942

THE BEST TIME to visit the Westport dock is late afternoon, or even just before dusk. You have to have something to go for, so you go for a fish. The rigging of the first troller can be seen coming around the sand spit, and a few minutes later the top riggings of other boats are to be seen throbbing in the racy turmoil that is the aftermath of the bar. Smart puffs of wind buffet the long dock. Now the first white troller breaks cover and comes into full sight, her trolling poles folded like up-turned wings, the tiny cross bar at the mast head reminiscent, somewhat, of the Crusades.

There is something gallant about these little boats which put to sea each day in the proximity of coast defense, shore patrol, and hovering aircraft—like defenseless birds caught in a flight of eagles. The arrival of a loaded fishing boat makes everybody go to the edge of the dock and take a prideful look. The success of the fisherman is success for everyone, as is the symbol of one more conquest of man's archenemy, the sea. Once again we have walloped her, is the feeling.

The cargo is dumped on the floor of the fish-buying scows. A great heap of salmon slithers into the gloom of the lower deck; water drips from the slowly heaving scow, and ripples of reflected light shimmer on the fish buyer's face, and on the huge coal scuttle scales suspended on a chain. Set apart from the heap of salmon is a neat little row of oddments of the deep—a couple of shark, a red snapper, and two or three ling cod, the usual dregs of the salmon catch.

You keep your eye opened for an infant black-mouthed salmon, as you can't undertake the purchase of a really full-grown monster, and the selling rule is whole fish or none. This evening you are in luck. There are two small fish, allowing you the added pleasure of deciding between the two. For a dollar, you finally come up the gang plank with a six-pound nugget of firm red meat under your arm.

Before you can eat this prize, there are two very special processes to be undergone, and the first of these is cleaning your catch. It is possible to bruise and mutilate a good salmon beyond recognition in the cleaning. In my case, it is not only possible, or even probable, but inevitable. Turn me loose with a salmon to clean, and I will bring you, sooner or later, a fish with every bone in its body broken, and not one firm red flake clinging to another. So I don't clean them anymore. When I come off the dock with a fish, I turn my steps to the cottage of a Norwegian friend, Chris. Chris takes the fish, a batch of newspapers, and a spotless carving board and departs for a hydrant in the back yard, stopping to grab from a drawer a gleaming machete-sized piece of steel, commonly called in the family a knife.

From the kitchen window, I watch the expert swish of the machete as the fish is scaled, scrubbed within an inch of its life, and then cut into thick slices—an inch and three quarters, to be exact.

Then, "You might as well let me cook it," says the wife of Chris. She claps one of those old-fashioned oval hot-cake griddles on the stove, and ties on a starched apron. The heated griddle is brushed (and only brushed) with olive oil, and when it has reached the proper crackle, the salted and peppered fish is put on the griddle. When it is a ruddy brown on one side, and when a delicate test with a fork reveals that it is cooked exactly halfway through, the fish is turned. An epicurean aroma smites your nostrils.

In the meantime, the potatoes have been boiled, the tomatoes sliced, a lemon quartered, and the white luncheon cloth with the embroidered blue butterflies is put on the table. A fat aluminum percolator protesting on all four cylinders is removed from the fire and placed beside the cups and saucers, where it settles down with a final admonitory cluck, like a hen among chicks.

We sit down. There is a special plate for the bones. "Six bones to a piece," says Chris, and removes them deftly. I do likewise. After that there is no sound but the clink of cutlery, except from the open window where you can hear the north Pacific turning over on its side. After a while, Chris sits back with his last cup of coffee. "I remember one night off Destruction Island," he began. "We were ten—Johnnie and Gus were there, and Arne, I remember, and we had anchored together for the night when . . ."

And so it goes. There isn't anything about fishing that I don't like.

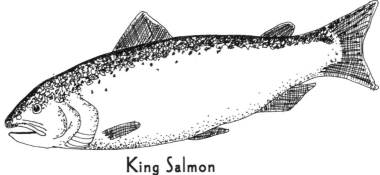

King Salmon
Oncorhynchus tshawytscha

Chronology of 1942

July

1 Navy's giant 70-ton patrol bomber, Mars, makes official tests over Chesapeake Bay, Md.

6 U.S.-made General Grant tanks battle Nazis in African war.

8 Nazi 35,000-ton ship *Tirpitz* torpedoed twice by Soviet sub. Seven-man military commission, appointed by President, begins secret trial of eight Nazi saboteurs in Washington.

16 Soviets place German losses for period May 15-July 15 at 900,000 men. Admit 399,000 of their own killed in action.

23 One of the largest U.S. convoys (the fifth) to cross Atlantic reaches North Ireland.

26 U.S. pilots in action over France, flying British Spitfires. One American-piloted Spitfire shot down by Nazis.

31 According to U.S. naval official, 10,000 Jap soldiers stationed in the Aleutians.

Dishes—Drains—Diplomacy

July 25, 1942

"COME AND SEE my present," said Eddie, after he had finished putting up my order. So I followed him through the door beside the counter that leads into the big white modern kitchen, and from the kitchen into the living room. There was white woodwork in the living room, and walls papered in blue and white striped paper, and a corner cupboard lined with a darker shade of blue. A row of windows gave on the back garden where 100 trees and shrubs, purchased through the wiles of a radio broadcast, were planted in neat rows in which the tallest tree was not yet one foot high. There were comfortable chairs in the room, pictures, books, and magazines. Over against the wall a large walnut table was covered with piles of recently unpacked fine American china. Wisps of excelsior still clung to the cups and plates. Eddie took a large card from a gravy boat and gave it to me. I read: "To Eddie with the love of the 00th Battalion."

"That was the finest bunch of boys I've ever known," said Eddie, and he shook his head and looked solemn and sad. "They've reached their station on the other side now. They bought the dishes before they sailed, but you aren't allowed to send any mail even, before you go, so this was held up for a couple of months . . . until they got there. You know how it is."

Eddie is an institution here. He is a sort of liaison department between the locale and the army. His parents were pioneer Finnish residents of this community. He was educated in the Aberdeen public schools, and sailed for France in 1917. He speaks three languages—army, civilian, and Finnish—and this talent enables him to see three sides to every question. Officers of newly arrived outfits call on Eddie upon their arrival. Word has gone abroad that he can show them the lay of the land.

"How I figure it," says Eddie, "it's little things that don't seem important that really are important. And if you want to take the time to do them you make things easier for people. I tell these fellows they're lots better than we were—and see what we did!"

I had the pleasure, not so long ago, of seeing how Eddie does things. I was in his store when a young lieutenant came in followed by a sergeant and several "men." An expression of acute anxiety was common on all their faces. "Do you know where I can get a plumber?" asked the young lieutenant. "Those shower baths won't drain, and the colonel is coming down for inspection tomorrow."

Eddie got a nice smile on his face and came out from behind the counter and said: "Now, son, there isn't a thing about that job that you can't do yourselves. The chances are that the drain pipe comes out from beneath the bathroom. But if you can't find it there, just start digging a shallow trench around the house and you'll come across it. Follow the pipe to the septic tank—that's a wooden box. Your problem is that the system was built for thirty baths and you have a hundred. You'll have to build a bigger tank. Look around and find some boards. No, sir, there isn't a plumber for miles around."

The men hung on every word he said. And then they went off and built the septic tank. "They never knew there was such a thing," Eddie explained in their defense.

Then there was the problem of fires. An army truck dumps a load of dripping chunks of wood before the cottages. The custom was to attack a chunk with an axe and cut off a slice when you need one—or that was the custom until Eddie changed it. "Now see here, fellows, you've got to put that wood under cover, and cut it up. The first thing a self-respecting man does is to get a supply of dry wood."

After a week or so when the stoves clog up, Eddie explains the mystery of ashes. "Now see here, fellows, you've got to dump ashes from the ash compartment; it isn't like gas."

Eddie has rescued startled jeeps from the clutch of high tide, mixed lotions for sunburned hides, dictated love letters with a winning punch, fed lost souls at the family table, loaned money for a present for "mom" on Mother's Day, and assured at least a hundred and fifty men that salmonberries are edible, and that, no matter how good your intentions are, there is no use digging for clams in dry sand.

━━

When the colonel came down, grandly followed by a staff car, it was Eddie who stopped the triumphal entry into the village before it even got started. He stood in the middle of the road and held up a finger and looked solemn. The colonel's car stopped, and the staff car stopped, and the driver of the colonel's car leaned out and said: "What do you want?"

"I don't want you. I want the colonel," Eddie said. So after a minute the colonel got out of the car and followed Eddie into an empty hall where there was an old pool table without a cover, and a few chairs, and that was all. And Eddie said: "Colonel, look at this. If it was fixed up, the boys could have a nice recreation room here. And wouldn't you rather have your boys here than down at the beer hall?"

The colonel pulled out a little black book and wrote something in it. He put the book back in his pocket and said: "Is there anything else?"

Eddie said: "No, colonel. You can go now, colonel." So the colonel went.

And that is how we got the canteen.

The Vanishing Victuals

August 1, 1942

I DON'T KNOW ANYTHING about the gold standard, and the changeling propensities of the dollar—being worth so many cents when you go to bed at night, and turning into something else again before the sun comes up—but when carrots suddenly begin acting queer, why then I am concerned. It's pretty hard to set your teeth in any facts in this present chaotic world—even hard to find any facts to set your teeth in. But when you suddenly discover that you can't even set your teeth in a carrot, nay, that it is all but impossible to find one to set your teeth in, why then you begin to have that queer feeling (mentioned in the Bible, I believe) that one gets in trying to maintain a firm stance on shifting sands. For carrots have begun to shift about, and turn up their noses, and to insist on running around with the avocado class, and it is as if the world moved under my feet.

When the vegetable wagon arrived this week, my good Italian friend was extremely apologetic, and more or less distracted—really more than less, as being Italian, he has a gift for distraction in the higher sense of the word. Before I even stepped into the truck he handed me a greengage plum to sample (a most unusual procedure) and I saw at once, even before I saw that there were no green onions, that something was the matter.

One of the few gifts I have is the gift of knowing when a man is troubled. One glance at Rossitti and I knew that things weren't quite right. Apprehension rode his shoulders like a monkey on the back of an organ grinder, and at the same time I had the curious feeling that he was trying to protect me from the full force of some blow which was about to fall, and which would strike with less violence in the vicinity of a crate of avocadoes in the rear of the truck, and toward which he seemed bent on leading me.

Now it is one of the principles of economics with me to always begin a vegetable buying orgy with carrots, and as carrots are generally on the end of the wagon that is where I stopped. I am not particularly fond of carrots—but neither am I particularly fond of going to bed, or of second cousins, or shampoos, and yet what would life be without any of those things? You just about have to have sleep, second cousins, and shampoos—and carrots. So I said at once, "Where are the carrots?" and having said it I realized instantly that I had hit the nail of disaster on the head. Rossitti kind of shriveled up. His shoulders drooped, and his hand, bearing a beautiful avocado (large enough and hard enough to bomb Tokyo), dropped to his side and he looked at me with a sort of terror in his eyes. "There are no carrots!" announced Rossitti in a whisper.

As if to prove it he dived into a carton and came up with two withered yellow roots and held them at arms length. "Only these," he said sadly, "and they are without price."

"Like pearls?" I asked.

"Yeah," said Rossitti. "Something like that. You can't get anyone to dig carrots . . . I guess that's what's the matter."

"Any green beans?" I asked, to change the subject.

Rossitti went into sort of a convulsion, in which he suffered some sort of acute Italian vegetable wagon blues. "No green beans," he said.

"Skip it!" I said. "I'll take some beets."

Ah! Smiles! Gesticulations! Action! (with accompanying approving gestures) Rossitti dived into a crate of hard green apricots, where no one would ever look for anything (not even an apricot) and produced two beets tied together en-bunch. He held them up for my admiration. "I have save these for you!"

We admired them together. "That," I said indicating a great bulbous ruddy globe, "is the largest beet I have ever seen in my life! And the other one is . . ." here breath failed me, but I took another breath, "the other is . . . why, it's a perfect little marble, isn't it?"

And so we parted on a high note of confidence between producer and consumer. I went into the house bearing the big and little beets. But I have known carrots all my life, and suddenly not to have carrots was too much for me. I sat down, more or less dazed. Then into my consciousness there came words that I had read recently, or heard recently in the helter-skelter of radio-newspaper-magazine commentary which is the salt without meat of our daily lives—someone had said that the American people will get enough to eat, but they will not get the things they are accustomed to eating.

Somehow I can't help believing that there is more rock-bottom truth in that statement than in any other news of the week. And while wisdom may once have come out of the mouths of babes, who knows but that it may now come from the mouths of vegetable peddlers. I sat thinking of these things while Rossitti chugged on his carrotless way. All in all, life is pretty interesting, interesting down to the last carrot.

Ducks—Donations—Dogs

August 15, 1942

SUNDAY WAS A GRAY, blowing day, and although I hate to say it, there was a feeling of Fall in the air. My neighbor came to the back door and said, "Get your boots and come on, there's a duck in the stream."

I got my boots and put on an old coat and followed him through the brittle wild grass, and the stunted willows, down to where our miniature river meanders seaward. We weren't breaking any game laws, as the duck we were after belonged to him—a large Muscovy that had gotten out of the pond and refused to come back.

When we reached a bend in the stream, we saw the duck on a partly submerged log only a hundred feet or so away. We stood on a little plank bridge and my friend took aim. Just then a couple of soldiers stopped on the bridge to see what was going on. "We are shooting a duck," I explained. As an afterthought and without any particular reason, I added, "Mr. Dortch always hits them in the right eye."

At that instant, my neighbor fired his gun, and the duck fell dead. One of the soldiers retrieved it for us. It had been hit in the right eye!

—

What is known locally as a "high fog" has prevailed down here for days on end. The wild blackberries came and went unpicked in the drenching rains of July. Now the rambler roses are drying on the picket fences, and the wild roses, which show their subtle pinks best against the gray fog, have passed their prime. For the moment, there are no birds about, and even the bees have taken themselves elsewhere. There is a conviction down here that bees cannot be kept commercially as they are said to die from the effects of the spray used to kill insect pests in the cranberry bogs.

—

A girl wearing a sky-blue slack suit and carrying a freshly pulled cabbage (lock, stock and barrel) in one hand and a cucumber in the other hand made a pretty sight coming through my gate one day last week. I had barely thanked her and admired the cabbage, when there was a knock at the back door and another good neighbor came in with a fine piece of salmon. To consummate the deal, I handed out a loaf of warm bread to the bearer of the cabbage and a dish of green apple sauce to the giver of the fish.

The barter system has much to recommend it. Vegetables, fruit, fish, clams, and homemade bakings are circulated up and down the road here. If you have a little more of something than you can use, you might proposition some other gardener for a few ears of corn. It isn't necessary to have met your neighbor socially to pull such a thrifty deal—at least it isn't necessary down here.

Leave it to the buck privates to devise ways and means of defeating the censorship so painstaking]y set up by their betters. When an outfit is pulled up by the roots and hurried off, they know not where, it is understood that if they are to embark for the theater of war, no letters can be sent during the period they are awaiting transportation, and until they are safely on the other side. But the other day an army truck snorted up to the village store, and a hurried "sarge" dumped a small shivering dog into the dust in front of the store. "I'm supposed to leave this dog here," he announced cryptically, and drove on.

"Pinocchio! Why it's Pinocchio!" people exclaimed. The small dog crawled forward on its belly, thumped its tail in the dust, and took a lick or two at a friendly boot. Everyone gathered around and stared, and patted the dog, and some of them got a tear or two in their eyes. For Pinocchio was a letter that everyone could read. When the 00th Battalion was called out one night a couple of months ago, destination unknown, it was agreed that if they sailed—in which case it would be impossible to write—the dog would be sent back. The arrival of Pinocchio would indicate that the boys had reached their battle station.

Well, Pinocchio is here now. His bed and board are paid for the duration by company funds. Explicit directions have been left as to what to feed him and what not to feed him, and he is to be bathed frequently and dried in a warm room. When that happy day comes when the war is over, it is the intention of his masters to claim him in a glad reunion. What a day that will be!

Chronology of 1942

August

1 Local police and FBI agents round up more than 80 Japs, Nazis, and Italians in New York City and Philadelphia.

8 Six of eight Nazi saboteurs executed in the electric chair at Washington DC. Two others (who turned state's evidence) sentenced to prison.

10 Marines land in Solomons. Navy raids Jap Kiska positions in Aleutians.

14 German military begins march on Stalingrad.

19 Ten thousand Allied troops, mostly Canadians, supported by British Commandos and a few score U.S. Rangers, raid Dieppe, France, for nine hours. Casualties heavy on both sides. Overhead 1,000 British planes engage the enemy.

21 Japs attempt to retake Solomon Island positions. Repelled by U.S. marines.

Houses—Hawks—Harvest

August 22, 1942

"**LOOK AT MY NEW STOVE**," the shoemaker called as I walked by his house. I went into the cottage he was fixing up for rent. The new stove was really a secondhand stove, but it had been polished within an inch of its life and shone with a burnish which can only be achieved by getting right down to the metal and going to work. He took off the lids and exposed the grate and the interior workings. Not an ash, not a fleck of dust, obscured the metal workings of the shoemaker's stove.

But what really intrigued me was the built-in sink. It stood in one corner of the brown weathered room, enclosed in shiplap boards painted a lovely deep pink. This charming decorative touch had been accomplished without the aid of one of our better house and garden magazines, you may be sure. The shoemaker used pink paint because he liked it. It hadn't occurred to him to conform to 1942 conventions and have it all white. He wasn't trying to "express his personality" either, and the last thought in his head would have been to attempt the artistic. But unconsciously he had done both, and the result was refreshing. You just couldn't help liking a man who liked a pink sink, could you?

Another surprise awaited in the bath house where the dim interior was flanked on either side of the door by two long benches of rough planks painted maroon.

———

There is a dead spruce which rises out of the bogs and stands remote and ghost-like against the backdrop of the forest. On gray days the flying clouds skim through its topmost branches, and in clear weather a scraggy gray hawk rests from his circling on one of its out-jutting snags. From this perch, he is enabled to see everything that is happening round about. To the north he can see the Westport light, and to the south he can watch the surf roll into Willapa Harbor. He knows what is going on in the forest to the east and the ocean to the west. But particularly he knows what is going on in the young alders, the salmonberry brush, and the blackberry vines along the cranberry ditch where the young birds are hatching.

Having lined up a promising kill, he leaves his perch, flaps in a lazy circle for a few turns, and then pounces earthward. Immediately, a flight of small fighters rise from the brush and do battle. Sometimes they pursue him back to his perch, taunting him, and getting at him from above and below simultaneously, so that he arrives the worse for many a sharp peck on the head. He sits for a while on his snag gritting his bill and breathing fire through his gills before he sallies forth again. But I shall witness this amusing spectacle no more. The hawk's tree has disappeared!

Directly across the road another bleached grandfather of the forest, which reared its white skeleton against the sky, has also disappeared. Can you guess why? I couldn't, at first—not until someone told me. Well, it seems that the old white trees were landmarks which might assist the enemy. Who would ever have thought that those old trees, dead and forgotten, should come to life as sinister allies of the enemy!

A sidelight on the falling of the tree was that the soldiers who felled them were so thrilled with the new sport that they went about beseeching the neighbors to permit them to cut down any tall spruces that happened to be about—alive or dead.

———

I walked down the beach to see the fishing boat that had come ashore. She had broken up and lay in five scattered sections of flattened bleached red boards on the wet sand, except the prow which had apparently sailed gallantly on and had her nose in a sand dune far up the beach. Her backbone had broken loose and lay partially buried in the sand with a few broken ribs sticking out. Where she had broken, the edges of the boards were paper thin. The fragility of these craft, broken and beached, gives me the same sad feeling some hunters claim to feel when they walk up and view the body of the deer they have shot—the thing that was so alive had, when you get right down to it, so few defenses.

———

At 4:30 o'clock this morning, I was awakened by a series of house-shaking thumps which turned out to be a load of wood arriving. After the driver had pulled out, I went out and closed the gate. I had the nervous feeling that I should, perhaps, padlock it as I had paid fifteen dollars for the load.

This afternoon there comes from the vicinity of the shed the comforting sound of axe strokes as the wood is split and put away. Somewhere beyond the dunes at the water's edge the chug-chugging of a dragsaw can be heard as some thrifty soul prepares against winter with a driftwood log. Beyond the clump of sand pines, the monotonous thudding of another axe penetrates the fog which still stands above us without budging, as it has for days. Things have that melancholy remote look that grays the land before the wild geese come. It won't be long now until the frost is on the pumpkin and the fodder in the shock—only it won't be here. Yesterday I harvested my bean crop and wish to put it on record for statisticians concerned with victory gardens that I produced for my country sixteen beans—eight black wax, three green wonders and five Oregon giants. I also wish to report that I have in captivity one zucchini squash vine which has fulfilled the promises of the seed catalogue and actually has a squash on it, and one Hubbard squash, which, while it has nary a nubbin on it, has out-stalked Jack's bean stalk.

Penalties—Parlors—Products

August 29, 1942

ONE OF THE PENALTIES of being a kitchen critic is that I have become self-conscious about my kitchen. Time was when the kitchen was the least of my worries and it was my policy, once a meal was over, to depart from the scene of confusion and blithely close the door behind me. And having closed the door, it was as if the room no longer existed, and I could concentrate on the much more interesting forepart of the house where, having arranged some flowers on the window ledge to my satisfaction, and piled the current magazines (with the prettiest covers on top), I could settle down and enjoy the blissful world of unreality.

Those days are gone—and forever, I'm afraid. Whether it is because all America has become kitchen conscious and feels rebuffed if not invited immediately upon arrival to inspect the cupboard and see where you keep the dish pan, or whether it is that having set myself up as a kitchen critic I have become sort of a semi-public bureau open for inspection twenty-four hours a day, I do not know, but the fact remains that my kitchen must now be taken seriously and—well, it is awful! How can I peel potatoes, scatter flour, and wash dishes in a room subject at any moment to enemy attack? Literal-minded friends, acquaintances, and even strangers have come to the house, spent a few uneasy moments on the edges of their chairs and then burst out with, "Can I see your kitchen?" Heavens!

━━

Once all respectable houses sported a small box-like room near the front door known as "the reception room." What a woman saver that was! How secure grandma must have felt when, upon the dinging of the doorbell, she left the clothes drying above the range, dishes in the sink, and an apple pie in the making and, slipping out of her voluminous apron, she made for the front door and shunted the caller into the smug banality of the reception room. There seated on a creaking-backed settee in front of a long mirror, the visitor was enabled to glean no more, no less, of the domestic debacle than a silver card tray that needed polishing, or a potted fern the worse for wear. You could visit such a room and leave the premises knowing (mercifully) less about the inhabitants than you did before you came. If in those days a visitor had risen from the settee and demanded to see the kitchen, why—well, imagination simply quails!

My kitchen is not a modern one. The wood-burning stove sifts ashes. The sink is in a corner, and the linoleum in pieces. The only grace I can give it is to keep it in a sort of static order—get it all set for inspection and leave it just as it was when I used to live there—like Washington's bedroom at Mount Vernon. But in the meantime where am I going to cook, and scatter my lettuce leaves, and sift my flour, and wash my dishes? I have racked my brains but the only solution that comes to mind is so expensive that I doubt if I can accomplish it—I must have another kitchen, a second one. It must be modern and gleaming and so wide awake that it will never be caught napping with its hair down, bread rising on the oven door, and a disheveled tea towel lying in an attitude of abandonment on the drain board. Its chromium and porcelain must reflect only white disdain. It must be located near the front door. And it must not give away by so much as a fleck of dust or a ghost of a crumb of bread the double life of a kitchen critic.

———

During the recent meat shortage, even the army felt the pinch; at least that part of it which is stationed down here did. No meat arrived for five days and the boys lived on macaroni and spaghetti during that time. Then fate took a turn for the better and a load of calves' liver got through the lines—at least it was considered a turn for the better until it became evident that fate had outdone itself—there was calves' liver enough for five days. At the end of the third day, the boys began falling off like flies, and at the end of the fourth day they gave up the ship and bought the local butcher out of beef steaks.

The Kalaloch Cow

September 5, 1942

EVERYTHING WAS FINE at breakfast. The little pines were motionless on the dunes, drinking in the sun. The fog backed out to sea and lay down like a good dog, and it looked like a fine day. I had my hand on the cream pitcher and was about to have my morning's cereal with cream from our neighbor's Jersey cow, when my boyfriend spoiled everything. He said: "Do you remember the Kalaloch cow?" I put down the cream pitcher, picked up my coffee cup, and sat back in my chair and tried not to remember the Kalaloch cow. But it was no use. Breakfast was ruined. Having once known the Kalaloch cow, it takes a long time to get over it. Even when I remind myself that there never was a cow at Kalaloch, I still can't get over it. Even when I call my wandering imagination sharply to account and remember that I never even laid eyes on the cow, it still doesn't help.

There were no cows at Kalaloch because there was nothing there for cows to eat. There is the greenness of forests there, and the false verdantness that sometimes lies over glacial moraine, but no grass. There is no grass at Queets either, but there was a

Chronology of 1942

September

2 John McCloy, assistant secretary of war, says 500,000 American fighting men and technicians are now abroad.

13 Selective Service Director Maj. Gen. Hershey says married men with children face draft in '43.

14 New type Nazi stratosphere bomber reported flying over England on reconnaissance flights at 40,000 feet.

16 U.S. 19,000-ton carrier *Yorktown* reported sunk on June 7 during Battle of Midway.

23 Tobruk attacked from sea while British mobile units raid Axis African positions 500 miles behind lines.

cow there. Down at the river's mouth among the backwash of drift logs and water, a man and his wife had squatted on an abandoned homestead, where there had once been pasture, before the river tore it up. The woman came in a creaking old car to announce their arrival and the fact that they had set up a cow and wanted to sell milk. As we had had only canned milk for months we eagerly subscribed to the cow, and sat back to await the first of our daily quarts. When she brought it three days later it was so thin and blue that we would have given up then and there, only the woman herself looked so thin and blue that we hadn't the heart.

The pasture would improve with summer, she said, and they were trying to repair the bridge across the slough so that they could get out every day with the milk. So we kept taking the milk, but each day it had less of vital earthiness about it and more of—was it the sea? Anyway it changed before our eyes from a thin blue to a thin green. We cringed to see it. The pale smattering of cream across the top of the bottle, it seemed to us, must be produced by some fearful grinding of gears of the poor starving animal, and we could not bear to contemplate it. We gave the milk to the dog, but he accepted it with a disinterested lap or two and turned away.

Every three or four days there would be no milk delivery at all, the bridge, or was it the cow, having broken down. Then, horrors! The milk itself began to contain awful mementoes of the struggle going on. One day I found a pin feather in it. I picked it out of the dog's dish, and tried to assure myself that things were going well; they had, at least, ducks or chickens. Then it occurred to me that I could go and see for myself how things were with the Kalaloch cow. But I couldn't get near the place. Acres of driftwood logs and a surging arm of the high tide shut off the never-never land where the homestead lay at the river's mouth. The small boy who went with me in the hope of seeing his first cow was vastly disappointed. We followed the ruts made by the old car across the gravel bars to where the bridge planks lay scattered along the slough, and gave it up.

Now the milk began to come less often, and we would never see the woman or hear the car, as she made her deliveries at night. In the morning the phantom quart would be resting on the doorstep. I never touched the milk now, save to dump it out and wash the bottle, and replace it on the doorstep with the life-saving ten-cent piece in the bottom. It was during this phase that I found the grizzled hair in the milk. It was a short black hair, sort of piebald black and white, as if the head that had grown it had stayed black by sheer determination, and then suddenly given up the ghost.

I wanted to be angry the morning I found the beer bottle cap in the bottom of the bottle. I tried to be angry. "Look here!" I said, "We have been feeling sorry for them, and all they are doing is sitting down there and drinking beer." But my boyfriend called to my attention that the beer cap was rusted, so that they couldn't have had beer for a long time anyway. Nevertheless I made up my mind to speak to the woman. But she never came again. The bottle stood on the doorstep until a spider used it to anchor his web, and the autumn rains filled it and the ten-cent piece lay fathoms deep.

In the Spring when I ventured near the Queets gravel bars I saw the skeleton of an old car lying beside the slough. "Whatever became of those people, who had the cow?" I asked at the inn. Nobody knows. They must have "pulled out" they said.

So that is why I can't eat cream whenever I remember the Kalaloch cow.

Comings and Goings

September 12, 1942

Some will choose the tortle shell,
And others like the white so well.
Let them choose from this or that,
But give to me my old gray cat—
Poor pussy! Oh, poor pussy . . .

THE SUN WAS JUST COMING UP over the spruce tops when I went out on the dunes to a miniature glade surrounded by five small pines. I dug a hole, not very large, in the dry sand. Then I went back to the shed and got my old gray cat. Under his chin, I tucked the only possession he had in this world—a tiny bell on a frayed yellow ribbon. I pushed the sand over him and scattered the withered grass and the pine cones where they had been before I dug the hole, so that the place would be familiar again to the quail and the chipmunks, and to Claude Furbottom himself, if by any chance in the scheme of things he should be cognizant of his favorite lurking place. The back door is visible from this dell, the woodpile and the chopping block, and the sandy hollow under the broom bushes where my neighbor's hens dust themselves on warm afternoons. Also the sea can be glimpsed, and the wild beach grass where he loved to play that he was a tiger in Africa.

Here indeed, I thought, lies a creature who brought nothing into the world and took nothing out of it except a ten-cent store bell and a scrap of ribbon, and yet, the backyard which was so alive is now dead. We are no longer aware of the beetle and the ant, the arrival of a bird on a bough, the stirring of a mole under the sand, the popping of the broom pods under the sun, as relayed to us by the faithful wireless of our cat. There is no one to call our attention to the catkins of the wild grass by sticking an approving nose in a pollened tassel, and winding an affectionate tail about the clump, while looking at us as if to say, "It's pretty wonderful, isn't it?" No one pads with the tread of a miniature panther across the roof shakes at night, or sits beside the chimney pot staring with benevolent tolerance at the moon, and yet alert withal—who knew at what instant a mole might not burrow to the surface of the celestial countenance!

A whole miniature world which was created for us has vanished with one small creature, into the earth. "Well," say our friends, "that is the way with pets."

═══

On a lonely stretch of beach where a lagoon lay exposed by the low tide, a solitary figure stood. As I came near I saw it was a gaunt angular man, with the trousers of his store suit rolled up. The sleeves of his blue Sunday shirt were also rolled up, but the rest of him was as neat as a man can be who wears a starched shirt, white collar, tie, tie clip, sleeve garters, and horn-rimmed glasses, and who has the general air of having come from the bookkeeper's desk in the rear office of some small, soot-ridden industrial plant, which has managed to get a toe hold in the city backwash, and reached the precarious stage of security where an occasional employee gets a week's vacation with pay.

He was leaning on a new crab rake, and was absorbed in a small blue pamphlet which he studied with knitted brows. At his feet a freshly caught crab lay on its back, clawing rhythmically at the air. As I came alongside he looked at me over the rim of his glasses, and then glanced with a worried expression at the crab, then back to the book again, fluttering the pages, and finally straining his eyes on the rear cover.

As I was about to pass by, he cleared his throat and said: "Excuse me! But I wonder if you could tell me . . . it doesn't say here, and I don't want to break the law, but . . ." He held out the pamphlet, marking a sentence with his thumb. I took the book—it was a tide book—and read the line he indicated: "Do not

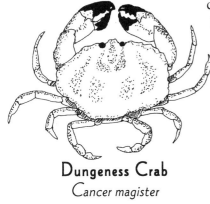

Dungeness Crab
Cancer magister

take female crabs." While I wrestled with this unadorned dictum of the fisheries bureau, he coughed with embarrassment, and shifted the crab rake about nervously.

I looked down at the protesting monster at our feet, and my instinct for the preservation of the law almost betrayed me into an exclamation of dismay. But I remembered in time that he might not get another crab, and after all this was quite an important vacation, and whoever starched that blue shirt ought to have something to brag about to the neighbors when he got home, so I withheld my fire. "Why, let me see," I said, and I bent with an authoritative gesture over the creature in question. "Why, it's a male!" I exclaimed. "A female only has six legs, you know," I said, adding invention to just plain lying. And I went on my way, warmed by the happy feeling that I had done a good deed. But darn those little books anyway! How is the stranger in our midst to know what they mean—do not take female crabs indeed!

Traveling—Tinned Foods—Itinerants

September 19, 1942

My neighbor, she of the sky-blue slacks and the giver away of home-grown cabbage, returned from Los Angeles this week by bus. Trains were to be had only by giving thirty hours' notice of intention to travel, and then only by proving that you had some essential war reason for getting yourself somewhere else. She didn't have any essential reason for getting somewhere else, except the essential reason common to all of us now and then, of getting home. And yet her journey south had to do with the war—she drove a newly hatched navy lieutenant who couldn't drive his car to a port of embarkation.

"Heavens!" everyone said when they heard the lieutenant couldn't drive a car. "How can he drive a ship then?" But I stood up for him. "He'll probably make a very good ship driver," I said, and I told them about our pioneer captain, the late Tom Stream, who, when ashore, used to pilot his automobile with equal ability on the pavement, the sidewalk, and the parking-strip, but always managed to reach his destination. A man who knew every nook and cranny of the seven seas ought to know what he was doing was the way people looked at it. And he did. You can see where the term, "Give her a wide berth" originated. I don't know just what makes a good sailor a bad car driver, but it seems to be one of the well-established traditions of the sea.

My neighbor's bus trip was not uneventful. Three buses bearing thirty passengers left Los Angeles, and in Southern Oregon hers broke down, and stayed down for nine hours. At night they arrived at a town where the only hotel was filled, and the driver hauled up before the closed bus terminal, switched off his lights and showed every intention of going to sleep. But the passengers put up such a cry that he was forced to call the manager out of his bed to come down and open the station, which he did very grudgingly, so that they spent the rest of the night under cover at least.

At Portland she was informed that unless she wanted to go to Seattle or Vancouver, B.C., she couldn't continue on her way, but would have to wait ignominiously until a bus load of small fry was collected for small way ports. Just when that would be, she was told, was one of the things that time and tide would decide. Whereupon she rose up, flung caution to the winds, split intimidation asunder, and made a right hearty scene. "See here!" she said, "I've been on this bus three and a half days, and I'm not going to spend another three and a half days getting home. You have to pass through Olympia and I'll get off there." And she did. If anyone has any friends or relatives who have come up missing on a trip from California, they'd better look for them in the Portland bus terminal, is her advice.

———

Gradually, the last of the tin-canned food is disappearing from our grocer's shelves. For a while there was a flurry of glass-packed food, but now little cellophaned packages of aerated goods are appearing cautiously on the counter, and one of the least of these is dog food. I got a package of the metamorphosized hash (it is now pellets), soaked it in water, and offered it to a local bird dog, one of those growing boys who is always hungry. He took a mouthful of the mixture and backed away shaking his head, opening and shutting his jaws painfully, and going through all the gestures of one trying to dislodge a jawful of caulking glue—and was still engaged with the first mouthful when darkness overtook the experiment. I'll say this for the new product; it certainly has staying power.

Had the great good fortune to get someone to work a spell on the wood pile this week. He arrived in a bright pink automobile, and went to work with a gusto that belied his small size and his seventeen years. He had worked everywhere in the country, from Tennessee to Oklahoma, he told me, and wasn't above taking forty cents an hour, although he confided to me that he expected to be getting $1.30 an hour before this war is over. I didn't ask him how he figured it down to the last cent that way, but I wish I had.

While he worked, I noticed that a woman of about thirty-five years, or so, was waiting in the car. "Is that your mother?" I asked. "No, it's my girl," he told me. After he had worked an hour and twenty cents' worth, she called him off the job, and they went away to spend their ill-gotten gains. The grapes of wrath certainly grow on a long vine, don't they?

War Stories

September 26, 1942

NOW THAT OUR ARMY down here is leaving the civilian houses and preparing to take possession of permanent barracks, many a householder has had the opportunity to see the inside of his beach house for the first time in months. I have talked with many of these citizens who either loaned or leased their summer homes to Uncle Sam. I have seen them enter their domains with a proud air of the proprietor motivating their eager steps—and I have seen them emerge a few moments later, stagger to the nearest log and collapse, clutching at their throats and staring about with wild eyes.

And after a few minutes I have seen them rise up, take a long breath, square their shoulders and walk away just as proudly as they came—but with a new kind of pride. It has suddenly come to them that they have sacrificed a beach house to their country. It isn't like losing a ship exactly, and yet it is something like that, after all. The tide of war has surged, not only to their very doorsteps, but right through the house, and it has left havoc in its wake. But it is all part of the pattern of ultimate victory. When you have given a house to the cause, you are entitled to a new kind of pride; you are nearer to understanding the problems of men who lose ships and cargoes. You are nearer to understanding the meaning of war. You are part of it. You belong to a new and select brotherhood with a monument commemorating your sacrifice standing by the roadside where all may see—your beach house.

Oh, the roof is still on, and the foundations are intact, or almost, and it stands in the same place but—well, the floors, the door jambs, the stoves, the bedsteads, the chairs and tables have taken a hard pummeling. Put thirty boys (or fifteen, if it is a fifteen-boy house) under one roof for five months to bang their gun butts on the floor, drag their trunk-lockers about, patter to the bathroom in hob-nailed boots, and hang their dripping raincoats on the wall, and you are bound to—well, it wouldn't take Sherlock Holmes to tell you that somebody had been there. The big bear, the middle-sized bear, and the little bear multiplied a hundred times have sat in your chairs, eaten out of your bowls, and slept in your beds. And how! You expected that of course. But where are the dishes, the clock, and the mirror? Where are the pictures, and the clam shovel, and the bathroom faucets? Where are the porch steps, the radio, and the electric plate? Gone! Gone with the war!

Time changes all things. Some day the household gear can be replaced. "I tell myself," I heard a woman say, "that someday I'll be proudly pointing out to visitors that place in front of the fireplace where they chopped up the load of wood, and telling how we gave our beach house to the war."

"When I first saw the inside of my house, I thought the Japs had been there already," another citizen said to me. "But then it couldn't have been any other way. Take 20 or 30 boys, now . . . it's nothing, really nothing! I'm glad I could do it."

━━━

A local logger did a spell of work for the army down here. When he had finished, he sent his bill to the headquarters at Portland. Among the items was one for $110 for moving a donkey two miles. Back came a protest that $110 was too much to charge for leading a donkey out of the woods. Our logger wrote back a technical explanation and in due time received an O.K. for his claim. Under the officer's signature was written in pencil: "I'm the jackass that kicked about the mule."

━━━

"Did your mamma go to the soldiers' dance while daddy was away?" a local mother-in-law is reputed to have asked her grandchild.

"I'm not supposed to tell you," replied little Lulu. "It's a military secret."

Animal Story

October 3, 1942

GOT HOME FROM a shopping trip the other afternoon, and was carrying my bundles into the house, and trying to appear unself-conscious in my new suit and hoping the neighbors wouldn't be too impressed, when one of them leaned over the fence and said, "Hey! Would you mind coming over and helping me shoot a skunk?"

"Does it have to be shot this minute?" I asked somewhat brusquely. And I stood with well-tailored dignity and looked severely at the ruddy face of my neighbor which loomed like a dimly burning Chinese lantern through the willows by the fence.

"Well, it ought to be," he said. "It's in a trap, and it has dragged trap, chain and all, under the house. I want you to pull it out, and I'll shoot it. I can't very well shoot it under the house, can I?" I could see reason in that all right. I told him I couldn't very well pull out a skunk in my new clothes, but that I would change them and join him pronto.

In the house, while taking off my finery, I tried to decide what to wear for the occasion. "What does one wear to shoot a skunk?" I called to my boyfriend.

A shower bath curtain would be just the thing, he told me, but I compromised on an old gingham dress, a pair of clam digging shoes, and no stockings. I bound my fresh finger wave in a bath towel turban and set forth to the skunk pull.

My neighbor had hung a canvas curtain over the woodshed door. I was to stand outside the curtain, pull a piece of twine, which in turn would pull the chain, trap, and skunk from underneath the house. He would stand inside with his gun, and shoot the animal. It was as neatly arranged as a major operation.

I took up my position and pulled gently at the string—gently because the wounded animal might tear away from the trap, with the usual conventional ending; the one which my neighbor wished to avoid at all costs. I pulled. I felt delicate quiverings and jerkings on the end of my line as if there were a small fish there. By the time I had got the chain under the canvas, I was cautioned to hold it steady, which I did. My neighbor fired, the quivering ceased. There was no anticlimax. The evening air blew freshly from the sea.

We congratulated each other on the success of the operation. There is even a proper technique for shooting a skunk, I told myself as I walked home by the path. But as I turned the corner of my house the dank unmistakable odor of skunk rose up from the ground to smite my nostrils. It surged about my own back door in choking waves. Inside the house it seemed to come up through the floor boards. That is queer, I thought; not a sign of skunk where we shot one, but here the air is almost unbreathable. A minute later another neighbor who lives farther down the road came in to say that she was feeding her chickens when she heard a shot, and on the instant the air was redolent of skunk. As we stood at the front door, a girl across the road called to us that she feared her dog had scared up a skunk, and could we smell it across the road.

Intrigued by this mystery I returned to the scene of the crime. In the dusk I saw the freshly killed skunk hanging tail down from a clothes post. He was large and beautiful, with a tail almost as long as a fox's brush—and odorless. The air about my neighbor's house was as fresh as the sea.

"I'll tell you what I think," he said after I had told him of my breath-taking experience at home. "That fellow I killed had a lot of friends and relatives running about, and when they heard the shot, they registered a vote of protest . . . that's the only thing I can figure."

The following day an eager-eyed school boy came to my neighbor's house and asked to borrow the skunk. "I just want to take it over to the schoolhouse to show the kids," he said.

"Son, you can have the animal," my neighbor told him. "If you skin it, you will have a nice pelt." So the boy put the skunk in a sack, and went off with it. In the afternoon I saw the sack in a sunny place against the schoolhouse wall. When the school bus left for North Cove, boy and sack went along. I have no way of knowing just how his prize was received at home, and whether the skinning was accomplished without a vote of protest by the skunks of North Cove. But I would like to know.

War—Art—Agriculture

October 10, 1942

A FOUR-YEAR-OLD BOY of my acquaintance pumps his tricycle to the post office and fights for his parking rights with the drivers of army jeeps and trucks. When he looks out of his front window, he sees patrols crossing the dunes. From his back door he sees squads of soldiers drilling on the road. Sometimes he takes his wooden gun and drills with them, very solemnly. The other morning he shot a Jap.

His mother was awakened by the thud of Maerick's bare feet as he ran to the window, and the sound of his voice in imprecation, as he grabbed his wooden gun. "It's those damnable Japs!" he exclaimed. She got out of bed and looked out the window. "Yes, there they come over the dunes," she said, as she is a modern mother and believes in entering into the spirit of things.

"The hell, they do!" yelled her son in an excited voice. "I've shot them!"

———

Some soldiers down here are spending their off hours picking cranberries. A few of them remember the hospitality they have received on the bogs, and are attempting to show their gratitude during the severe shortage of manpower. Three of them came to the store for a coke after their first morning on the bogs, and it was their opinion that their brothers in the New Guinea bush were having an easier time of it.

On the bogs the cranberry pickers are scattered in irregular colored patches over the russet landscape. So absorbed are they, so slow in their progress over the miniature orchards, that from a distance they seem to be creatures grazing on the land.

Cranberry picking is something like reading a book. The page consists of a strip some five feet wide marked off by white cords extending in the distance. Each picker has a strip to read, and his progress depends on how fast he cares to read. His absorption in his task is so intense that, like reading, he becomes unconscious of everything but what lies under his eyes. In a little while, he sees nothing but the luminous green light which penetrates beneath a million tiny leaves. The spider-like stem of the vine is so heavily weighted with red globes that it is a constant marvel that anything so fragile can bear so much. Surely, sooner or later you will come upon one of these eight-inch trees which will have done what could have been expected of it, and produced five or six offspring—but you

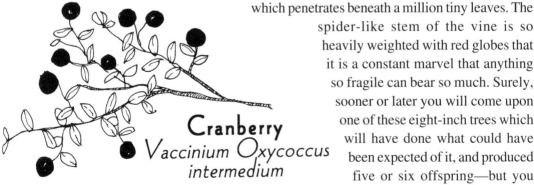

Cranberry
*Vaccinium Oxycoccus
intermedium*

never do. The cranberry vine counts its children by the dozens. A family of forty, or sixty, or ninety berries is the custom.

Picking is really a pleasant job. There's not much talking. The only sounds are the dumping of full baskets into the nearby long boxes for the sorting shed. Once in a while a picker rests on his haunches and watches a "V" of wild geese move majestically southward, or a flock of crows on reconnaissance. Many things which seemed important before you started picking lose their importance, and things which disturbed you once seem far away and unreal. But the cranberries are real. These fragile vines are tough enough to hold you to earth. You have the feeling that if you hang on long enough, and hard enough, the world will adjust itself into those nice little squares and triangles and colored patches with names on them, like it used to have in the fifth grade geography.

——

No clams are to be dug this winter. This is a queer time for the State Fisheries Department to set its teeth in the wheel of clam propagation, isn't it? If I were a chamber of commerce, I would find out why, when groceries threaten to be scarce and tons of home-dug clams would lessen the carting of tons of produce to the beaches, the fisheries department should suddenly show its fangs. Why does our economic system always, when pinched, reach around and take a bite out of its own tail?

Education—Sanitation —Astronomy

October 17, 1942

HAVE A NEW BOARDER—name of Rafe. He is a young sprout from the backwoods. He came to the door one morning dressed only in a pair of gray and black striped jeans, and barefooted as the day he was born. But he was clean, and he had a nice smile, and such an ingratiating way about him, when he asked if there was any spare food about the house, that we took him in. He is no beauty. He has the largest ears I have ever seen on one cat, but he is willing and eager to learn and sheds the daily rebuffs that life offers like a duck's back sheds rain.

Until he came to us, he had never heard of indoor plumbing or running water—or seen a skyscraper or a railroad train either, for that matter. The kitchen sink was what intrigued him most. For the first few days, it gave me quite a turn to come into the kitchen and find Rafe sitting complacently in the sink polishing his face and hands. I could see the advantage of the position all right. He could keep one eye on the ice box

Chronology of 1942

October

3 U.S. army troops, supported by navy, occupy Andreanof group of the Aleutian Islands, between Jap-held Kiska, and Alaskan Dutch Harbor.
   Office of Economic Stabilization created by the President to stabilize farm prices, rents, wages, and salaries.

17 U.S. troops arrive in Negro Republic of Liberia.

20 Total of 530 Axis submarines announced destroyed by British and U.S. navies since war began.

24 British start African campaign to drive Axis out of continent.

25 First U.S. air raid on Hong Kong destroys Kowloon docks.

26 Naval officials announce that aircraft carrier, *Wasp*, sunk off Solomon Islands on September 15; serious fighting continues on Guadalcanal with heavy Jap losses.

30 Nazi conscription of Belgian labor for work in German factories protested by Belgian exile government in London.

and the other on the stove, and thus miss nothing of importance that happened to be going on. But sinks simply weren't made for cats to sit in, and so for several days we fought out the issue. I finally won out by turning on the faucet. He gave up the ship.

Introduced to the niceties of a woodshed sand box, he agreed instantly that it was a good idea. It hasn't worked out so well though. He took to it too enthusiastically. It will suddenly occur to him, when he is playing in the dunes half a block away, that he has a nice sand box at home and he will come flying to the back door to be admitted to it. At two o'clock in the morning he will scamper on the roof and suddenly think of that sand box and set up a fearful and persistent whine. There is nothing to do but get up and let him in. If I am a bit late in answering his summons, he casts a glance of anguished incredulity in my direction as he shoots by me to the sand box. If, after introducing him to civilization, I should attempt to explain that there is such a thing as being too civilized, you can see what a hypocrite that would make me. I can't very well tell a growing boy, just at the formative period, that I expect him to be a little gentleman by day and a little alley cat by night, can I?

However, the experiment is an interesting one, involving as it does the age-old question of inheritance vs. environment. The waif taken into your home will either adopt your ways—or he will answer to the call of the old Nick in his blood. There is no telling which it will be until you have tried it. Rafe, it seems, is one of those souls destined to make the most out of the advantages offered him. At this very minute he is sharpening his claws on the davenport cover as if to the manner born.

———

The curtains had been pulled and the fire lighted, as it was a starlit night with a hint of frost in the air. I sat reading the last page of a mystery novel when I saw the glow of a flashlight at the front door. One of my neighbors and her husband had come to tell me that "there is something happening out at sea."

I put on a coat and followed them. We went by a path, feeling our way with the dimmed flashlight to a house on the dunes. It was unlighted, and we fumbled our way through chairs and tables to the attic stairs, climbed them and went out on a porch where you can see the ocean.

The owner of the house was a dark blob in the night. "Right over there," he said, and pointed. I saw the darkness of his arm against the stars. I looked. Was there something like a Roman candle shooting distantly and faintly against the horizon? For a long time, we watched. A report had been made to the authorities. There was nothing for us to do. If something was happening, we would not know about it. And yet we stood with our hearts in our throats.

How many civilian watchers on this coast are staring westward tonight, I thought. In lonely outposts, with the vast sea and the vaster firmament, they pit their little wits against infinity. Always conscious that the nearby army and coast guard are doing a better job of things, more than a little self-conscious about his place in the scheme of things, and inclined to joke about his unimportance, the civilian watcher clings to his post. In his heart he knows that if his diligence is responsible for saving . . . well, not a boat load of American boys, perhaps, but a cabin boy, say, he will have done something very worthwhile for his own soul. In the meanwhile, there are the stars to look at.

October Days and Nights

October 24, 1942

"ENJOY FOR ME the sea and the fog and the winds that whistle and roar over the dunes and make their own wild music among the pines . . . and write about them," a reader's letter says.

Things haven't commenced to roar here yet, but you can see every day that the ocean and the land are getting ready for their winter's tussle. Already we have had one high tide which snatched away the clumps of beach grass, rolled logs and debris into the soft sand and retreated, leaving a white chaos of foam glistening in the October sun, and enough old iron exposed—automobile fenders and small craft engines and whatnot—to build a gunboat.

There is no watching the sunset from the shores these days. The army herds all amateur beachcombers inland before the sun has set. They come reluctantly like stray chickens that must be shooed back to the coop. When everything is well cleared away, the big light battery trucks can be seen moving to their stations at the water's edge.

From sunset to sunrise these powerful searchlights, at a moment's notice, can pierce the night with a ray of light so fierce that you can read a newspaper twenty-five miles away—or so they tell me.

All day long the wild ducks and the wild geese fly southward, the ducks in quick darting flight over the surf, the wild geese high and majestic over the forest. First is heard a distant honking which, in seconds, becomes a wild confused gabbling directly overhead. Yesterday, I saw a formation disintegrate as a volley of shots came from the direction of South Bay. They fell back like an oncoming wave dissipated by a gust of wind; then reformed into a great elongated V as if governed by some faultless mechanism, and caught up with the beat of the mysterious rhythm which urges them southward at all costs.

The sun sets farther to the south now, and on clear days the long shadows to the north of the pine trees are purple. Purple shadows crouch under the lee of every dune, and the small vegetation on them has turned to dry yellow crispness. In the little swales to landward, the alders and willows are shedding their leaves with monotonous relentlessness, but here and there a mound of gorse has burst into startled bloom, as if there were very little time left in which to get ready for winter.

———

This week I finished piling the wood. I built a small stockade of piled wood and formed a hollow square around the back door. It stands between me and the Pacific. All I need now is an old muzzle loader to be thoroughly prepared for any eventuality. As things are now, I am unarmed. I traded my boyfriend's shotgun for some fine daffodil bulbs last April. I haven't told him about it yet. But I will have to tell him sooner or later. One of these fine days he will lead off with, "Where is the gun oil?" and follow immediately with, "And bring me my shot gun." And I will say, "You know those lovely daffodils . . . not that they have bloomed yet because I got them too late, but they will bloom next year . . . Well, Bill, he's the man who raises bulbs, wanted a gun so . . ."

And that is as far as I have to go because from then on there will be sound effects similar to Fibber McGee's closet—but amplified. And prolonged. You can't get something for nothing in this world. Come Spring, and there will be daffodils.

———

One of my neighbors, an older woman, was awakened from sleep one night by a lost soul from the village pub who insisted on coming into her house. She went to the army for help. She knocked on the army's door and called, "Help! Help!" but nobody answered. So she opened the door and went in. A single electric bulb burned in the hall and cast its unshaded glare—into the rooms to the right and left where the 00th engineers slept like . . . well, anyway, they slept on. She finally aroused one boy, and between the two of them they woke up the house. In their bare feet and with the hue and cry of a pack of hounds, the engineers sped off over the dunes, captured the lost soul, and returned him to his bog. But the next day my neighbor got herself a gun. She said she thought things would be simpler that way in the future.

Sailor's Return

October 31, 1942

A STORM WAS COMING UP. Outside the wind whipped and whistled over the dunes. The long flat-bladed beach grass in the swales and hollows rippled and swished, and you could trace the direction of the wind in its flow, northeastward. The small alders and willows bent like umbrellas which have been turned inside out, showing the gray under-linings of their leaves. On the knolls and ridges the staunch little jack pines dug in their toes, and shook their thick arms at the sky, hunched their shoulders and roared with gnomish laughter. The sky was a formless swift-moving grayness overhead, and to the southwest the ocean thundered and rattled like a racing express. Now and then a pellet of rain struck me on the nose or the cheek as I hurried along to the village store and post office.

Inside the store, the usual habitués sat around the stove; the gentle old man with the well-behaved cocker spaniel, the tall thin man with the slow shy smile, and a sprinkling of restless hip-booted fellows from the bogs, waiting for the mail. Where the magazines are kept in the window, soldiers lolled, turning the pages of magazines with half-hearted interest. They sat on the closed lid of the ice cream cooler holding half-empty pop bottles listlessly in their hands, or leaned with their backs against the candy counter and stared dully in front of them. If they spoke at all, it was to say that this was the kind of weather that they didn't like, that back in New Jersey, or Georgia, or Texas, things were very different. By their manner, they implied that this was a helluva country, but, by and large, they would forgive us for the weather, for it was plain to be seen that we didn't know any better anyway.

That's how things were when the door opened and a sailor blew in. A sailor on this beach is as rare as the almost extinct plover. To have one come in on you unannounced like that amounted to a virtual blow, as if a ladle of hot lead had suddenly been thrown into a bucket of cold water. An impact was what it was, not an entrance. Whereas the atmosphere had been one of lifeless somnolence, it was now charged and vital. The bunch of bananas swayed on the hook; the wrapping paper blew up into the face of the proprietor who was doing up ten pounds of ground beef for the little woman who cooks for a crew of fifteen men down the road; the post mistress, carrying a burden of *Saturday Evening Post*s and *Life* magazines to the counter, stopped in her tracks with opened mouth in a ludicrous, bent-over position. The soldiers bristled and froze like a flock of dusting hens into the midst of a which a hawk has suddenly settled.

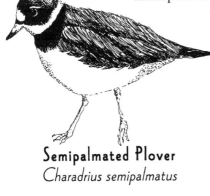

Semipalmated Plover
Charadrius semipalmatus

Chronology of 1942

November

1 Army troops reinforce marines on Guadalcanal; Aussies and Yanks push Japs back on New Guinea; U.S. air force bombs Japs daily on Aleutian Kiska.
   U.S. takes over all short-wave broadcastings for use by the Overseas Division of Office of War Information.

2 To relieve growing coal shortage in West, UMW executive committee authorizes seven-day week.

4 Republicans make new gains: 19 in senate, 42 in the house of representatives.

7 U.S. troops land in French Africa (French Morocco, Algeria) under Commander-in-Chief Lieut. Gen. Dwight ("Ike") Eisenhower to forestall successful Axis invasion which would endanger America.

8 Vichy government breaks relations with U.S. for first time since 1778.

11 Axis forces invade unoccupied France; Italians also land on Corsica.

12 Second naval battle of the Solomon Islands begins.

16 U.S. naval authorities announce crushing defeat of Jap navy in second naval battle of Solomons; 23 ships sunk, 7 damaged, with enemy casualties near the 40,000 mark.

The blue apparition strode to the center of the room, turned on his heel and looked about. Then we saw that his eyes were brown, his skin a shining ruddiness, and that he held his head high. He glanced about the room as if it were a small cove into which he had sailed just to take a look, and then seemingly satisfied, he strode for the door. This was too much. The army stirred in its nest of magazines—you couldn't just let the navy sail in and out on you like this, without scoring a single goal, could you? "Hey, sailor!" a soldier called out. "I've always wanted to ask you guys something . . ."

The sailor turned in the doorway. He looked at the soldier politely. "Yes?" he said, and we saw the glint of friendliness in his eyes.

"Are you fellows," the soldier asked, "allowed to have radios on the ship?"

"We can't have radios," the sailor said. "Or cameras, or binoculars." He opened the door. The wrapping paper rattled again in the gust of wind that came in, and the bananas swayed on the hook. "Or beer!" said the sailor, and his white teeth flashed in a smile. Then he closed the door, and ducked his head into the wind and was gone.

The room resumed its drabness. Life had, somehow, gone out of things. It was as if we had been looking into the depths of a blue sapphire and had been left suddenly holding only a tarnished setting in our hands. Everyone got up and left the post office.

At home I said to my boyfriend, "What was there about that sailor, do you suppose, that stood out like . . . like a flame, a blue flame?"

The next day we heard the answer. Our sailor was home from the battle of the Solomons—alive! And vicariously somehow, sitting there in the village store, we had felt his joy, his keen relish, his profound appreciation of—living.

Pete's Progress

November 14, 1942

ONE OF THE SIGHTS on this beach for the past three years has been to see Pete come out of the schoolhouse. You will be passing by at recess or at noon or in the afternoon and suddenly the double doors of the schoolhouse will burst open and out will come the grades—starched and pleated little girls, small overalled wiry boys—and Pete, looming among them like Gulliver among the Lilliputians; like a shaggy red sheep dog; like a pillar above a multitude. He will stand on the step a moment with the younger children swirling around him like a wave around a rock. He will look off over their heads with a wondering, baffled expression on his good-looking face, before he climbs on his bicycle and pumps homeward without eagerness, but with the unconscious grace of a very well-built young man of seventeen. For Pete can't get out of the grades. It has become almost a legend down here that Pete can't pass.

It isn't that he isn't bright enough or is refractory in any way or hasn't good manners. Pete has all the best of those things with the added charm of a well-scrubbed skin and a burnished mop of hair on the red side and on the curly side too. Furthermore, he has the community back of him. Everyone is pulling for Pete to get out of the grades.

And then—he didn't make it again this year! Everyone was disgusted and indignant.

"What is the matter?" I implored his teacher. "Why can't Pete pass?"

"It's past participles," she told me. "He simply can't get them. And reading too . . . he just stands there and says he knows it but the words just won't come out."

"But he keeps the stove filled pretty well," I said defensively. "And I note he always opens the door for you and picks the younger children out of mud puddles and settles their disputes and . . . and well, I think he should be passed."

18 Marshal Petain appoints Pierre Laval dictator of Nazi-occupied France.
President orders registration of 600,000 youths who reached 18th birthday after July 1.

24 Russian offensive smashes across Don, Germans lose 50,000 men in pincer drive.
Saboteurs sentenced in Chicago: men get death, women 25 years in jail.

27 French scuttle fleet at Toulon. 62 ships sent to bottom of harbor to avoid seizure by Hitler.

26 All war industries continue working while nation celebrates Thanksgiving.

29 Prime Minister Churchill appeals via radio to Italian people, to overthrow their dictator, sue for peace.

"We just can't do it," Pete's teacher said with finality.

"Well, they'd do it in an enlightened community," I said. "It's Pete that's important, not the system. You can't take a healthy ego and run it through the seventh grade for four years . . . subject it to the ceaseless beat of past participles for four years, and expect it to come out alive."

So Pete went away. He went to the eastern part of the state to visit relatives and to rest and prepare his soul for another tussle with the abhorrent participles. And then, wonder of wonders, fate gave Pete a break. Suddenly he was back among us without his bicycle, which he had outgrown. He visited up and down the road and proudly and with quiet dignity, told us of the fine thing that happened to him.

And up and down the road the news traveled even faster than Pete. "Have you heard the news?" people asked each other; and even if they had, they said "no" because they liked to hear it again. And, as they passed the schoolhouse, where Pete had endured his ordeal, they sniffed and tossed their heads in the air and hurried on their way. For the little red schoolhouse has been thoroughly put into its place. Pete wasn't good enough for the schoolhouse, but glory be, he is good enough for Uncle Sam. For the long and the short of it is that Pete has enlisted. He passed his physical examination 100 per cent, and nobody shot anything at him about participles, or asked him to read one of Macaulay's essays with the proper pause for commas, and he is, at last, free! I know a number of young fellows who can decline a Greek verb with the ease of a mechanical monkey going up a string who won't make better soldiers than Pete or better men when this war is over.

———

When I had finished gathering up my bundles at the store, I said: "And I'll take a cake of yeast."

"How many loaves do you make?" asked an interested neighbor.

"Three!" I said with pride.

"Three?" she echoed incredulously. "Why, I bake seventeen loaves at a clatter— three times a week."

All jauntiness had gone out of my step as I made my way homewards. All the wind had gone out of my bread-making sails. I may bake again; may even at some future date accomplish seventeen loaves, but never, I fear, at a clatter; never with the zest of true genius.

Country Life

November 28, 1942

THERE WAS THE FLURRY of departure at the village store Sunday morning. A smart southwest wind was blowing, and the proprietor's car stood ready to take off, while we neighbors stood around and gave him last-minute instructions on our Thanksgiving dinners. The packing company was holding what our proprietor called "open house" in town so that rural merchants would come in and pick their turkeys. For a week past, a homemade sign on a piece of wrapping paper had been pinned to the meat counter informing us that we could put in orders for turkeys. But most of us only bestirred ourselves at the last minute. It is human nature, I suppose, to tell yourself, with self-congratulatory virtue, that you can very well get along without fifty-cents-a-pound turkey this year, and cook a chicken instead, or something else that can be decided upon later. And then, at the last minute, no decisions have been made, and you realize suddenly that you knew all the time you were going to have turkey, and that when you gave yourself the excuse that you were running short of butter and went to the store Sunday morning, it was really so that you could order a turkey. The subconscious mind is a wonder, isn't it?

I noticed that, of my neighbors, the men standing around in their hip boots were like men everywhere else. "Get me the biggest turkey they've got," or "Oh, twenty-five pounds, or so," said the men and turned on their heels and forgot about the matter. And the women too were like women everywhere; they wanted first-class medium-sized turkeys, specifying the poundage down to the last ounce, and giving specific directions covering everything but the color of the bird's eyes—and they took their time about it too.

Our proprietor, looking slightly harassed, finally got his car underway, and all to a successful conclusion; last week we had gasoline rationing, before that we mastered the scrap drive, and heaven knows what will come next! But whatever it is, we will stand together. That's the fine feeling you get from living in the country.

"Did you get some extra coffee?" my good Norwegian neighbor asked as we turned homeward.

"Why no!" I said.

"Well, you should have," she told me. "Everyone else did."

―――――――

I went into my house and into my kitchen and opened the bottom cupboard and looked with satisfaction at my dwindling pound of coffee. It was a sort of symbol of my patriotic response to the national emergency, and it pleased me immensely. Then I opened the top cupboard door and looked at my ten pounds of sugar. I closed the door hastily. "Darn that ten pounds of sugar," I said aloud, because technically speaking I have no right to have it, and morally speaking I have no right to have it, and patriotically speaking I have no right to it. It is what remains of the fifteen pounds I got for canning—and I haven't canned!

Phrases like "ignorance of the law is no defense," and similar dire pronouncements, run through my mind when I contemplate that ten pounds of sugar, and such popular quips as "little man, what now?" fight for supremacy in my consciousness like a song that you want to forget and can't; showing, according to the best tenets of modern psychology, that I have a problem—an unsolvable one. True, I did use up five pounds on some wild blackberries, and my intention was to follow through with some nice jars of summer fruit, and then I couldn't get any. The vegetable wagon, when it arrived after a thirty-mile peddling campaign, was always in a state of complete demoralization, as if it had crossed the African desert under fire. What fruit there was was pretty well shot up. Once there was a small box of pears which escaped intact, but priced at $2.85, and I don't like pears. Not $2.85 worth, anyway. I didn't get them. So what?

Today when I opened my cupboard door and took a surreptitious look at my sugar, a new refrain started running through my brain. And to music this time! You know that song, "Waiting for the Robert E. Lee?" It's a catchy tune, hard to get rid of, once you get it going in your head. Well, today when I looked at my sugar, that tune popped into my head and it wouldn't get out. Only the words were different, but they fitted the tune perfectly—"Waiting for the F. B. I.!"

There! I feel better. All my cards are on the table. And that confounded ten pounds is still in the cupboard—waiting, waiting for the F. B. I. And I'm waiting too; in fact, you can come and get me anytime, boys.

Economics

December 5, 1942

JUDGING FROM THE LENGTH of the want ad columns in the city dailies, the lowest rung on the ladder of desirable employment is general housework. The longest columns and the highest wages are combined in a seductive conspiracy to get someone (anyone) to give a helping hand with the daily grind of cooking, bed making, and cleaning, but not, I notice, with washing. Washing as a bucker upper of servant morale has gone by the boards. Most of the advertisements specify "no washing," but even so, the situation remains critical.

Where are the maids of yesteryear? Well, they're welding, sorting, and assembling in the war factories and saving their money against that rainy day when, if they aren't careful, they may find themselves in other people's kitchens again.

In the meantime, newly acquired skills and heaven-sent husbands may save them forever from slipping back to the bottom rung.

And also in the meantime, women who have employed domestic help will continue to do their own housework.

Experts have written reams on the subject of housemaids. It is pointed out that girls would rather endure the gruelling rush hours of restaurant service—would rather suffer the driving insults of stockroom foremen in dreary city lofts—than the soul-shattering experience of domestic service in the average American home. It is a question which has two sides—both of them bad.

The only solution I can think of at the moment would be to have some hard-headed woman unionize the housemaids, making a college degree in economics a requirement, and raising the job to the dignity of a profession. Make the union hard to get into and thousands would beat a path to its door.

As an economic stroke, it would have a double-barreled wallop—the housewife with one of these professional geniuses in the home could go out and get herself a job (indeed she would probably want to) welding, sorting, and assembling in a factory. Or if nature has endowed her with wits enough, she could go in for job compatible with her training and desires.

As this happy state of affairs is not liable to arrive for some time, my advice to the housewife in search of a servant is to clear the decks, stow all gear, batten down the hatches, and prepare for a long dry spell.

Chronology of 1942

December

1 Gas rationing begins on nationwide basis.

4 President orders Works Progress Administration abolished.

7 Office of War Information reveals 58,307 casualties in first year of war.

11 Approximately 660,000 war workers frozen to jobs in Detroit.

Ways and Means

December 12, 1942

OUR BUTCHER IS a lively, hard-working fellow who only butchers at odd hours—the rest of the time he is occupied with a trucking route. When his wares run low on the meat counter, he stops by, hauls a chunk of meat out of the cooler and cuts it into chops and steaks. He works very fast, giving the impression that he has to hurry and get the meat business over with, and get back to the truck and get going or he and his family will starve to death before night falls. I like to go to the store when he is there as he carries on a running fire of comment on the economic situation, punctuated by well-timed blows of the hack saw on the chopping block.

"What with these new regulations that's coming up," he told me this morning, "we won't be able to trim the meat. The customer will have to take the hide, hair and teeth, along with the butcher."

"What do you mean by that?" I asked.

"I mean that you won't be able to come in and ask for a piece of lean meat, or say you want something without bones in it. We butchers have to buy the bones and fat, and you customers will have to do the same . . . an animal has a skeleton, you know, and fat to cover its ribs, and somebody has got to eat it in the long run, and the way the government figures, it might as well be you . . . leastwise there isn't going to be any pampering about choice cuts. As I see it, there won't be any choice cuts."

As if to prove the last statement, he threw a pile of chops into the show case which were about ten per cent meat and ninety per cent hard, white fat.

"That's the day's catch," he announced as he rolled down his sleeves and put away his surgical instruments. All that was left on the chopping block was a glistening, knotty bone of indefinite shape. I looked at the chops, and I looked at the bone.

"I'll take the bone," I said, and I walked home with the good feeling you have when you have gotten the best of a deal.

———

Went to town this week and spent two hours at the canteen handing out coffee and sandwiches to the armed forces, including a coast guardsman who has written a novel, a six-foot-four-inch Finnish sailor with a booming voice that could be heard in Reykjavik if he really let it go, and a small shivering soldier who refused cake.

"I'm an army cook," he told me, "and I've been on a bus for ten hours. Haven't had any breakfast or any dinner. I'll take a sandwich . . . thank you! . . . and do you know where I can get a cheap room?"

I put a tray of ham sandwiches in front of him and filled his coffee cup. The booming Finn told him where he could get a room for a dollar, and somebody else told him

where there was to be a dance that night. The shivers went out of him. His furlough was looking up. A little warmth, a little fellowship, the order and friendliness of the large pleasant room, and the world began to look saner again to the little army cook. He was the kind of a customer that the canteen was invented for. If he had been the only one who had come in that day, I thought, the project would have justified itself.

Every Man For Himself

December 26, 1942

ONE OF THE BARE FACTS of life on this beach is that we have no butter today. Our three merchants, by dint of trips to town and persuasive arguments with the wholesalers, managed to bring back what amounted to half a pound per family the other day. But before we could lay hands on it, there was an infiltration of enemy troops in cars from town, and they carried our butter away. They also carried away our cheese, our canned milk, and even our matches, and pretty well stripped the shelves. That means that we are without a number of necessary commodities, that our merchants will have to use valuable rubber and gasoline to make another trip to town where they may, or may not, be able to replace the goods.

There are no railroads here. Every ounce of food, with the exception of fish (and this is the slack season), must be brought down here on rubber tires. So when people drive from town to carry back a pound of butter which has already been carried 26 miles, they use up another 52 miles of tire wear, which makes a pound of butter a pretty expensive thing in more ways than one. We are hoping that the butter runners won't raid again, that perhaps next week they will pillage Quinault or White Star or Arctic or some other helpless nonbelligerent. It is a selfish wish, of course.

———

The young lieutenant's wife, who hails from the deep South, is coming over one of these days to show me how to make biscuits. Learning how to make biscuits is a habit I can't break. It is always the same; suddenly, when I am eating someone's good biscuits, I burst forth with, "I wish I could learn to make biscuits," and the reply is always to the effect that they will come over and show me how. So they come over and show me how, and I go right on making bad biscuits. Modern psychology teaches that we all manage to do pretty much what we want to do, in spite of our denials to the contrary—but why I should want to make bad biscuits I can't imagine. Perhaps it's an unconscious desire to remain perpetually in that bride-like state where bad biscuits are inevitable.

———

Old Ivor who lives by himself in a neat little house beside the road has broken into the news this week with curtains in the front room windows. For years he has lived a guileless life in his three spotless rooms, as all could see who passed that way. Daytimes he piled wood, chipped his small strip of hedge, and put coats of paint on the kitchen woodwork, and at night he sat under his unshaded light bulb with closed eyes, listening presumably to the radio. What deep stirrings beneath the surface of that quiet life, what upheavals of the soul have brought forth, at this late date—curtains? And starched lace ones, at that.

The village store and post office keeps a number of luxuries which we are liable to find ourselves in need of such as magazines, liver pills, and writing paper. Last week, they put in Christmas cards, very pretty ones too. But there was a joker in the deck; after they had been unpacked and put on display, it was discovered that most of them bore the inscription, "Merry Christmas to Grandma." I had even bought some and addressed them before I noticed this slight departure from the norm. Well, I said to myself, you were feeling sorry because you didn't have something original so now you've got something original. So what are you going to do about it? So I put them in the mail. Today at the store I noticed that the cards had been sold out. Everyone else must have done as I did, and cast a 100 per cent vote for grandma.

1943

Turn of the Year

January 9, 1943

THE LIEUTENANT'S WIFE hurried over with some news. "We can get radishes, lettuce and early carrots in by the end of the month," she told me.

"Gracious!" I exclaimed, and sat up from the reclining position which, it seemed to me, I had assumed for the first time in months. "Isn't it a little early?" I asked hopefully. But she assured me that it was not. Mrs. B., an old settler here, had told her that it a not a bit too soon.

A wave of tiredness swept over me, reminiscent of aching back muscles. Already I could feel the grittiness of the spade handle, and the tough, grass-ensnarled clods resisting my proddings with the tenacity of live things. I could feel my hoes caked with mud and my fingernails full of it. I knew that I was not enthusiastic about another Victory Garden.

But I was committed nevertheless. In an off moment, during a snug afternoon over a cup of coffee in my kitchen, I had agreed to the lieutenant's wife's proposition that we raise a vegetable garden together. I had failed to tell her that the noble experiment of 1942 had turned out a failure, that my success had been so limited that the five carrots I had managed to raise still blushed unplucked in the row, as it seemed sacrilege to destroy something which it had taken such effort to produce. Unplucked also are eight heads of endive, frozen, so to speak, in their tracks and about as edible as papier maché stage prop fowls. The only satisfaction I ever had from them was when a neighbor leaned over my fence and asked me, "What kind of cactus is that?"

"We'll have lots of turnip greens," said the lieutenant's wife, her eyes aglow, "and some great big ears of corn. We always have lovely corn in Carolina, and . . ."

I put out a placating hand and stood up. I was faced with one of those moments I abhor—throwing a monkey wrench into the machinery of expectation. "Look here," I said, "I have never grown an edible turnip green in all the years I've lived in this country, and seldom have I set teeth in a wormless turnip of my growing. And as to nice large ears of corn, there is a special kind that we raise here, but it isn't nice and large." And I went on to try and explain that a vegetable garden in this country was something that you could get a lot of pleasure out of if you gave your imagination free reign, but as for actual tangible results, they were liable to be disappointing.

But she wasn't listening to me. She was turning the pages of a new seed catalogue, and her eyes sparkled and her cheeks were pink with excitement. Giant red beets, green cucumbers, golden carrots, and white butted radishes flicked before her eyes on the turning pages.

An old eagerness stirred in my winter-locked veins. A desire to have the catalogue in my hands was suddenly irresistible. I bent forward and took hold of the book. "Let me

see," I said, "what kind of black wax beans they've got this year." She surrendered the catalogue and sat down beside me.

"We might as well make out our list right now," she said.

So we made out our list. It was comprehensive, taking in its stride turnip greens, giant corn, and a new kind of squash which has been grown successfully in Guadalajara, Mexico. At the end of an hour we eliminated regretfully a persimmon tree which both our hearts were set on and sat back with every available inch of ground more than accounted for.

The lieutenant's wife stood up. "I think we can begin spading about the first of February," she said.

I considered the idea for a moment. "On the other hand," I said, "I don't think next week will be a bit too soon." Already in imagination I could feel the smooth handle of the spade in my hands, the loam sifting lightly under the touch of the metal, and the warm sun of another spring on the back of my neck. The Victory Garden rides again!

Frosty Weather

January 16, 1943

ALL THE LITTLE rainwater ponds among the dunes sparkled under a coat of ice this morning. I remembered when I raised the kitchen shade that last year it had frozen hard enough for Pete to fall and break his arm in a "skating accident," causing us to feel a New England-like sophistication. "Did you hear how Pete fell and broke his arm while skating on the pond?" we asked each other. It made us feel important, somehow.

At breakfast, Rafe the cat wound himself lovingly around my knees asking for a bit of bacon. "There isn't any bacon," I told him. "And if there were, I'd eat it myself." I gave him a dish of prepared cat food; a war product composed of mill sweepings and fish oil—or it was, until they left out the fish oil. He sniffed at it gingerly, backed away, shook his head and fixed me with a baleful stare. I tried to ignore it, but there is nothing more penetrating than a cat's stare when he puts his mind to it. Not to be outwitted by the animal, I concentrated determinedly on my breakfast, and absent-mindedly buttered my toast with the entire day's ration. Exasperated, I turned on him. "In Paris," I said, "good plump cats like you are selling at a price formerly charged for squab and pheasant. You're lucky to be alive."

He gave me an indescribable look and marched with stiff dignity to the door. I opened it for him with mock politeness. He paused on the threshold and muttered something to the effect that if I didn't feed him better he'd go and chase that robin again.

"Very well, go and chase it," I said, adding a final insult, "You can't catch it anyway." And I slammed the door.

For more than a week now our cat has been pitting his wits against those of a wily camp robber who, I believe, actually enjoys baiting him. Over dune and through dell, behind the wood pile and under the willows by the pond, the hunt proceeds with kitty always losing by a neck. He'll never get that bird, I told myself, and put on my coat, muffler, and mittens and went to the butcher's.

A group of neighbors stood before the counter gazing with awe-stricken eyes at the empty show case. And no wonder; they were beholding a phenomenon rare in American history. "No meat?" they asked, although it was plain to be seen that there was none. "No meat!" said the butcher, standing at bay behind the counter, cleaver in hand, which gave him a sort of heroic air, like a gunner at his post.

Old Ivor, who is handicapped with deafness and an imagination incapable of comprehending a world cataclysm when he sees one, stepped forward and asked for a five-pound pork roast. Immediately, and in chorus, we told him that there was no pork roast. He looked mildly perturbed and after a pause, announced that he would take a beef

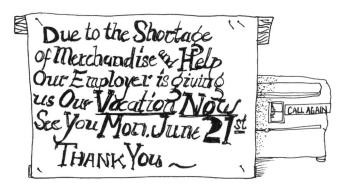

roast. We all jumped on him again with all fours. Baffled, uncomprehending, but seeing negation on our faces, the old Finn turned to the grocery department and asked for a can of pork and beans. The proprietor told him that there was none, but that there was chili. We all moved over to the grocery department and told Ivor how good chili was. We virtually forced chili on him. He took a can and went out the door looking doubtful. Once a week he journeys to the store and buys a five-pound pork roast. It is apparently the mooring mast to which his life is anchored. And now . . .

I arrived home meatless with the dull premonitory feeling that dinner would consist of canned salmon. I was met at the door step by a drenched and shivering animal resembling an elongated and fantastic rat. It was my cat. He had been lured out on the thin ice of the pond by the robin and had gotten the worst of another deal. He gave me what I took for a sheepish grin before he shot for cover underneath the kitchen stove.

———

In the afternoon a neighbor came over to read a letter. But she didn't read it. She told me about it instead. "You know that soldier, the sergeant-cook who baked the cake when the army gave a party for us last year? He is dead in New Guinea. And Jack, the laughing one who insisted on taking coffee out to the boys on beach patrol, is gone . . . Fifteen of them are left. Bill writes from the hospital . . .

———

In the middle of dinner, the window was rattled by four muffled blasts.

"Sounds like depth bombs," I said.

"Why? What do depth bombs sound like?" asked my boyfriend. "Why doesn't it sound like road blasting or range finding? Why depth bombs?"

"Well, it does . . . that's why. Can you eat canned salmon again tomorrow?" I asked, changing the subject. "Or would you like macaroni and cheese?"

———

The setting sun dived into a sea of pink mist, and the first stars crackled in the eastern sky. Jack Frost crept out from his hiding place in the purple shadows beneath the dwarf pines and thumbed his nose at the young moon. I pulled the dim-out curtains on another day.

Mutiny in the Pantry

January 23, 1943

"I GUESS YOU GOT OUT of bed on the wrong side this morning," my grandmother used to say to me occasionally. I seem to remember a more or less frequent use of the phrase as it applied to me. A child is quite literal minded concerning the whimsies of its elders, and as my bed was pushed against the wall and there was only one way to get out of it, that was the side I used. Right or wrong, I had to make the best of it. It was several years later that I broke a shoe lace while the last bell was ringing and the full realization of the phrase burst upon me: to get out of bed on the wrong side simply meant that inanimate objects with which you had to deal in your daily program had conspired to defeat you at every turn and would continue to do so until you fell at length into the exhausted and dreamless slumber which ends the day for sinner and saint alike—unless the sinner has a guilty conscience and the saint insomnia.

Yesterday I got out of bed on the wrong side. The insidious thing about such a day is that you don't recognize it when it comes along. At least I don't. Not at first anyway. But if you are a thinking person capable of understanding cause and effect, and are suddenly faced with effects which have apparently no causes, then you are forced to the conclusion that we live in a mysterious world. When breaking shoe laces, clogging stove dampers, mirrors that jump off walls, and lamp cords that go out of their way to trip you up get together and cooperate with perfect teamwork to bedevil your day, be assured that you are faced with one of those mysteries that man, for want of a better word, has attempted to pass off with a meaningless phrase—getting up on the wrong side of the bed.

I began my day by tripping on the lamp cord. Setting the broken pieces of the lamp aside, I hurried to the kitchen and stepped barefooted into a puddle of melted snow water that had come under the door. Even then I didn't recognize the early symptoms of a diseased day, but went right ahead and struck a match to the kitchen fire. In the bathroom, I found the cold tap on the wash basin frozen up and, oddly enough, the hot tap on the shower. Returning to the kitchen, I was met by a kitchen stove smoking at every funnel and emitting blasts of soot onto my newly painted walls.

At times like these there are a few old friends who refuse to join in the conspiracy against you. The sink faucets, thank heaven, stood by me, and the toaster worked, and breakfast was gotten over without undue incident.

It was at the village store and post office that I got the really telling blow of the day. There were no letters, but my favorite magazine came. I set it down on the counter while I picked out some potatoes and a woman shopper, while my back was turned, picked it up with her groceries and carried it away. I flew to the door but she was already out of sight.

"Where does she live?" I asked the proprietor.

"You go about a mile down the back road, turn left toward the hill, and it is the third house beyond the bridge," he told me.

"I'll take some potatoes," I said, and went home. I faced the bitter knowledge that it was only 11:30 o'clock and I had nine and a half hours of absolutely diabolical frustration before me; unless I called it a day in the middle of the day and went to bed. I have found that I can circumvent the fates by simply refusing to face them and simply giving up and going to bed—sort of turning my other cheek to the wall.

The more I thought of it, the better the idea seemed. So after lunch, which no stretch of the imagination could spoil—crackers and milk—I rolled myself in a blanket and retired from this world. It was then that the big Victorian mirror fell off the wall. I do not know if it was because the wall expanded with the heat or contracted with the cold and the screw became loosened or vice versa, or whether it was because I had attempted compromise and had gone to sleep on the couch instead of actually the bed. Be that as it may, the crash was a fearful clatter and thud as the mirror first hit a chest of drawers and then slithered to the floor. With fear and trepidation (fear and trepidation is a hackneyed phrase which you can well save for a Victorian mirror), I got up and crept toward this latest manifestation of the unseen. The mirror was lying on its face with its thick pine back exposed to the light of the day. Gingerly I turned it over expecting to find the inevitable. But there wasn't even so much as crack in it.

"The jinx missed me!" I exclaimed and bent down to pick up an object that was lying on the floor. It was a flattened and crushed metal tube; my flashlight, which had been fitted the day before with the last remaining battery on the beach.

"Huh!" I sneered, addressing myself to the gods of the inanimate, "you certainly struck at a gnat with a mountain," and I turned and went out to the kitchen to make a cake. In making a cake, I know all the answers beforehand. I can leave out the baking powder, or the salt, and drop an egg on the floor, and burn the thing to a crisp no matter which side of the bed I get out of.

What's News

January 30, 1943

THE COMMUNITY WITHOUT a newspaper would be in a sorry state if it weren't for the feeling, shared by all citizens, that it is a public duty to pass along the news. Tradition has it that every hamlet has a loquacious female who collects

Chronology of 1943

January

4   U.S. Department of War Information announces 61,126 service casualties to date.

5   Death of famed Negro scientist, Dr. George Washington Carver, 78.

6   Pleasure driving banned in eastern states; fuel oil ration reduced 25 per cent.

12 U.S. planes based in Africa bomb Naples, Italy.

23 British enter Tripoli, Libyan capital.

25 Voronezh, big Nazi stronghold, falls to Russians.

26 "Unconditional Surrender" agreement of Casablanca summit meeting announced.

February

2   Last German troops surrender in Stalingrad. U.S. naval forces repel major Japanese attacks in Solomons area.

9   Last Japs withdraw from Guadalcanal.
    Roosevelt orders 48-hour work week minimum in labor shortage areas.

14 Rostov and Voroshilovgrad captured by Russians.

16 Cruiser *Chicago* is sunk by Japs; U.S. navy reports15 Jap ships hit.

20 Dried foods rationed, effective March 1.

26 U.S. flyers raid Kiska in Aleutians.

and disseminates the domestic facts of her neighbors' lives. But I can say with assurance that we lack the highly developed kitchen gossip. There is no demand for intimate information, hence no supply. But there is a forthright and insistent flowing up and down the road of worthwhile things one wants to know—the shoemaker's wife is selling eggs for only 45 cents a dozen, the butcher on the back road has some lamb, the Green girls are going to slaughter twenty rabbits. That is the sort of news we get. It is handed out for what it is worth, and if you act upon it you are liable to have at least a rabbit in the casserole before the day is over.

In the meantime, you have made a little expedition and found that the butcher did have a bit of lamb (which he sold pronto), that the shoemaker's wife is selling eggs for 45 cents when she has them, and that Mrs. A., when she gets enough cream saved up, is going to make some butter. This latter item being news, you go out of your way to broadcast on the return journey. You come home feeling that the day has been worthwhile because of the thoughtfulness of your neighbors and that you have also contributed your bit to the important, even though unprinted, news of the day.

We also have a variety of formal or printed news. The daily newspaper of every large town usually carries a weekly column of rural news covering the crossroads within its scope. We are represented by such a column. Once a week, our rural correspondent takes up a position of vantage at the post office and queries all comers for news. It is the general understanding that nothing of import shall be given the rural correspondent, and this fact is well understood by the rural correspondent herself. When she asks some gent from the back road if he knows any news, they both know that she isn't after that story about how he filled a visitor with buckshot Saturday night. All she is interested in is whether Uncle Eber and "the folks" came down from the cove for dinner Sunday, or if his wife is contemplating a shopping trip to town, and what night they are having the schoolteacher to dinner.

I tried country correspondence myself once. And failed miserably at the job. In my zeal to make news copy of broken fisheries laws, bashed in heads, and casual mayhem, I was met with well-bred, if wondering, reserve and learned before very long that it isn't good manners to write about such things. And it isn't, either. Well-bred news consists solely of the goings and comings, more or less vague, of friends and relatives twice removed, and the eating year in and year out of Sunday dinners. That in a nut shell is the unwritten ethics of rural news.

To digress from that pattern means failure for the rural correspondent. Any deviation from the norm is not only frowned on, nay, it is well nigh impossible. I once chose a lively go-getting fisherman as a source of news. He took his boat out over the bar every day in fair weather and in foul, and things of interest were bound to happen to him. I waited frequently at the dock for Oscar's return from the deep. But he never had any news. He would greet me good naturedly enough, scratch his chin, wrinkle his brow, and finally dig up the information that the Smith boys had a clam bake on Decoration day. Weeks later I would hear him mention casually how, on the day in question, a giant shark had fouled the line around the propeller, and that three coast guardsmen had overturned their boat coming to the rescue, and that the four of them and the shark had spent the night marooned on the North Spit.

"But why didn't you tell me?" I would ask, trying to keep exasperation out of my voice. "It isn't news," he would answer. "But I'll tell you something! Ebba's folks are coming for dinner Sunday . . . "

And that's the inside story of rural news.

Wives and Mothers

February 7, 1943

MY NEIGHBOR CAME HOME from an Olympian visit bubbling with news. "Two officers' wives slept on davenports in the hotel lobby for three nights," she told me. Then one of them had a bright idea; she asked the manager to find out the name of the head of her sorority in town. She would appeal to her to give them rooms. The manager said the sorority sister would be easy to find as she was his wife, but the room question would be just where it was before as she lived at the hotel. However, he called his wife and she called a meeting of the sisters and it was agreed to hand the officers' wives around from home to home—something on the idea of a progressive dinner. When my neighbor left, the officers' wives had progressed to the tenth home and will keep on going until they run out of sorority sisters.

━━

A Spokane woman whose sons had gone to war, leaving her alone in a big house, had her war work set in her lap. She was in a tea room one day when a young officer and his wife came in and sat down at a table nearby where the girl promptly burst into tears. Our Spokane mother, who believes in trying to make religious theories work, went to their table, introduced herself as an old time Spokaner, and asked if she could help them in any way. The young wife lifted a startled face, apologized for her tears, and said that for fourteen days she had walked the streets looking for a place to live. At present, she said, they were living in a basement.

The next chapter in this story is that the motherly woman took the young people home, installed them in one of the big bedrooms, and then went downstairs and cooked a good dinner.

The third chapter is that on the following day the young couple went out and came home with another young officer and wife, perfect strangers whom they had found wondering around homeless. Before the week was over two more strays were rounded up, and the big house was operating again at a 100 per cent capacity. The big-hearted woman who took them all in says she has never had so much fun in her life.

This story was contributed by another of my well-traveled neighbors who got as far east as Spokane. She tells me that the hotels there are full of "Montana Admirals"— new navy men who haven't yet glimpsed the sea.

━━

There has been a big run on glass balls—those Japanese fishing floats we pick up on the beach after a southwest storm, and put in our windows, and use to edge our garden paths, and float in garden pools for want of anything better to do with them. The army is collecting them. The barber, who had quite a splendid display in his front yard, was awakened the other night by a disturbance, and when he looked out the window there was the army carrying away his glass balls. They are, it is presumed, sent home to mother and the girls. No one begrudges the loss very much, although if the war turns out according to expectations they may become a collector's item.

━━

Hogan was sick and took some time off. She also filed for a divorce from her third husband in mid-March. The divorce became final in mid-October.

━━

98

Ration Pains

April 10, 1943

THINGS WERE GOING FORWARD at the rationing board when I went to get my second book. Some thirty people stood in three lines that moved slowly forward toward the counter where three girls struggled with filing systems, telephones, and customers.

"I want something to eat," a very old, very deaf man announced simply and loudly, when he finally confronted one of the feminine judges. His first book had been turned in and whisked away in that mysterious process wherein you turn in Book I and, in due time, both I and II are delivered by the postman. Only in the old man's case things hadn't happened like that. Nothing had happened at all.

The girl leaned over the counter and attempted to explain things. She bolstered her defense with an imposing-looking file to which she referred frequently. She waved papers under the old man's nose, and quoted from the scriptures of red tape.

"You will get your book in the mail," was her final sentence.

"I want something to eat," insisted the old man, but the line of customers moved relentlessly forward.

When my own turn came, after three quarters of an hour, and I was about to present my case, the telephone on the counter rang and a voice from the upper Wishkah wanted to know if it was all right to slaughter a Guernsey calf. By the time that matter was disposed of—it required consultation of the files, and a reading over the phone of highly technical information relative to Guernsey calves, milch cows, hogs, hens, and the right of the OPA to prohibit a man from giving a neighbor a batch of spareribs—another fifteen minutes had passed, during which I clung to the gunnel of the counter with both hands.

"I want my second book," I said when the girl finally gave me her attention.

March

4 Allied bombers destroy Jap convoy of 22 ships.

7 Draft classification "4H" for men between 38 and 45 ended.

11 Lend-lease extension to July 1944 signed by President.

24 Advancing Russians retake Abinsk and other towns near Smolensk.

26 U.S. and British troops advance in Tunisia.

April

8 President moves to check inflation by executive order freezing wages and forbidding war workers to change jobs.

11 A bill permitting the national debt to rise to $210 billion dollars and a rider repealing the $25,000 net salary limit becomes law without President's signature.

17 Bremen and other north German cities bombed by "biggest raid."

21 Japanese execute U.S. flyers.

23 U.S. naval forces occupy Funafuti islands, southwest Pacific.

30 Soft coal miners of United Mine Workers union reject President Roosevelt's order.

"You're in the wrong room," she told me.

In the right room, when I found it, things moved with more dispatch. There weren't many people lined up, and the girl seemed eager to get my "I" book. She took it from me with the promise that it would be returned to me in two days through the mails in company with the new Book II. That was a week ago. To date I have not the books. I haven't got any coffee, or any meat, or any sugar, or any shoes either. I haven't even got a calf to kill. All I've got is a bone to pick with OPA.

I suppose the bone-picking room is the one where I met the deaf old man who wanted something to eat. I shall go back there tomorrow and feast on one of those meaty regulations which the young woman will read to me out of the files. They must be pretty good because, as I was leaving the Finch building that day, I saw the deaf old man sitting on the bottom step and he looked—well, sort of dreamy and strangely happy, as if he had experienced a miracle of some sort.

Could it be that—well, what if there is some deeper meaning to those printed regulations than our crude physical senses recognize? Could it be that we actually get sustenance by having read to us suggestive words like butter, meat, sugar, and cheese? Had something like that happened to the deaf old man? Or am I a little light headed for lack of my accustomed cup of coffee? I could also do with the best part of a roast Guernsey calf. Or a milch cow. Or a flock of fried hens. I'm not particular. I just want something to eat.

City Life

April 17, 1943

"**W**HAT DID YOU SEE in the shops?" a bevy of Easter-minded women asked when I got home from a Seattle visit this week.

I told them that Frederick's had a window of black suits with pink hats, and Magnin's had a window of chartreuse suits with straw-colored hats, and Igoe's had a window of blue suits with both pink and straw-colored hats, and all the little hat shops had hats and hats and hats.

But what kinds of hats? And what shade of blue suits?

I didn't know. As a style scout, judging from the disappointment on the faces of my audience, I wasn't playing according to the rules. It was sadly evident that I didn't even know them. Tentatively, and to reestablish myself in her good graces, I threw down a trial card: "I did see an interestingly dressed woman in a restaurant, though," I said.

Interest revived. What was she wearing, they wanted to know.

"Well," I said, "she had on a mustard and green plaid jacket, kind of loose and low—boyish, a blue skirt, and a sort of tam with rainbow-colored cock feathers worn well back on the head. Her shoes . . ."

"What restaurant?" someone interrupted suspiciously. "Blanc's? The Hearthstone?"

"No-o-o-," I said. "It was a kind of large, empty restaurant; one of those places that are easy to get into because the food is bad, and you can always find a seat."

"Heavens!" someone else exclaimed. But I went right on with my story.

"She had nice blue eyes, and wind-burned skin. She sat down opposite me in the booth. The minute I saw her, I thought of that old song, 'Cheyenne, Cheyenne, Hop on My Pony.' She was from Idaho, she told me. They have a sort of a style of their own in Idaho; no slavish adherence to Hollywood or New York. Her husband works in a shipyard. She says it's all hooey about the big wages; that she has to scrimp and scramble to make ends meet for her family. The men in the shipyards are heroes, most of them, she says. Those fellows with the riveting machines are getting so much dust and acid in their lungs that the army has already rejected some of them. Every day there are accidents, even deaths. She had a piece of pie and a cup of coffee, and when she opened her bag to get her change, she showed me a thin packet of lunch meat for which she had paid 80 cents. You've got to have something to put in those black tin boxes, you know, and as everybody is buying it, the price . . ."

At this juncture, I suddenly realized that my audience was no longer interested in my style talk, so I quit talking.

Outside a tiny cleaning and pressing shop a picket leaned against the wall, sandwiched in one of those signs which read, "Unfair to Labor." Inside the shop a little man sweated over a huge pile of soiled clothing. There was no sign on his shop, only a number on the door, but pasted in the window was a poster showing an exploding merchant ship with the caption, "Careless Words Did This!" I knew somehow, as I stopped to observe the simplicity of this dead-end stage setting, that my sympathies were with the little man in the shop behind the poster.

———

"Last week when we had fine porterhouse and prime ribs, no one had the stamps to buy them," a butcher told me ruefully, "but this week when we've only got ground beef, they are all rarin' for choice cuts. Can you beat it?"

We both shook our heads. There was more to the situation than either of us could put adequately into words.

"I haven't had a piece of red meat myself for days," he concluded, and we parted leaving the missing meat mystery unsolved.

Women at Work

May 1, 1943

"HOW MUCH IS THAT STOVE?" I asked the secondhand man, as I pointed to a gnarled, pot-bellied "parlor" model, badly rusted and minus several of its isinglass eyes.

"Twenty-five dollars!" the secondhand man answered blithely. "And the other one with the missing leg is thirty-five. It's got a new grate in it. You can't get new grates anymore, you know."

"Oh, well," I said, "never mind. I'll look at air-tight heaters. Have you any air-tight heaters?"

"No I haven't," the secondhand man said happily. "The OPA has frozen them. Look here!" he grabbed up a Seattle paper and turned to the classified section. "One firm up there is advertising for a hundred secondhand stoves. You know what that means, don't you? It means that people are going to buy anything they can burn a stick of wood in. What if you can't get oil next winter? What are you going to do? It gets pretty cold in this country, you know."

"Give me that little twenty-five dollar stove!" I cried. And I went and stood posses-sively before it, and glared at an old man who came into the store with a basket of old bottles on his arm, but who might be a stove buyer in disguise.

As I left the store I experienced that gloating, superior feeling that goes along with hoarding. I don't now what I am going to do with the stove. And yet . . . if stoves are going to be scarce, and I have one, and other people haven't, it sort of proves that I'm forethoughted and know how to look out for myself. If the secondhand man turns out to be wrong and we have oil this winter, or if a sudden influx of wood stoves brings down the market, I can always exchange it for a bottle of catsup. It might even be good for a pound of ground round. You've got to be on your toes these days, I can tell you.

I drew a woman taxi driver in Seattle the other day. She switched on the radio market news, and we drove along comfortably listening to quotations on cauliflowers and cab-bages. She told me that by the time she finishes her shift she knows just what she is going to have for dinner and where she is going to buy it.

She begins work at seven o'clock in the morning, comes to her job by bus from an outlying suburb, which entails getting up at five. She goes off shift before dark, as women taxi drivers are subject to indignities from lurid-minded males after nightfall.

There are five hundred thousand and three rivets in a British Wellington bomber. I've always thought that all rivets were great spikes about the size of planking nails but many of these bomber rivets are so tiny that women sorting them use eye-brow twee-zers to pick them up. The English have started a project of farming out rivet sorting and measuring among village and farm women. It's all salvage stuff dropped by riveters on the factory floor. It is swept up, put into sacks, and shipped to the home sorters. It takes two and a half hours to sort a pound of rivets, and the pay is three pence a pound. Only older women are allowed to do this work, as able-bodied younger women are drafted for more arduous tasks. You can see what we're coming to.

Mop Psychology

May 8, 1943

HISTORIANS TELL US that anyone with half an eye could have foreseen the French revolution. That time Queen What's-her-name wondered, at a cocktail party, why it wouldn't be a good idea for the populace to eat cake, as long as it had run out of bread, was the tip off. Right there, says the historians, revolution was born. It is not, they tell us, with blazing letters written on the wall, not with exploding bombs, and a mass whetting of scythes that revolution announces itself, but by some trivial word dropped in a tavern, an angry fire in the eye of some obscure worm about to turn, incidents so unimportant that they fall below the notice of kings, statesmen, and philosophers. But not, of course, beneath the notice of historians. Historians always observe the first feeble beginnings of revolution, and are quick to point them out, which is generally a couple of hundred years after they occur, which for all practical purposes isn't quick enough. In other words, the incident was there, but the historians weren't. The worm turned and nobody saw it. The incendiary word was dropped in the empty beer mug and nobody heard it.

It is with considerable pride, therefore, that I point out to you something which occurred yesterday in Grays Harbor County, and which is likely to assume the importance of one of those "incidents" of history, and which—gaining momentum while we sleep and rushing downward like an avalanche in the night—may overwhelm us and change the destiny of man. I discovered this first premonitory rumbling of a world about to crack in the classified section of a newspaper where the following ad appeared:

> *Strong, husky woman wants work; can do anything, inside or outside. Will do anything—but housework.*

Is that the clarion call of a released and vibrant slave forever freed from the shackles, or isn't it? She isn't, you will notice, simply a woman who doesn't want to do housework; there would be no news for history in stating what every woman knows instinctively in

the cradle. The thing which stands out, which causes icy shudders to go up and down your spine, and makes you gasp as if you had unexpectedly got a lung full of substratospheric ether, is that this woman doesn't ask odds of anyone. She is strong. She is husky. She wants to do anything. And she CAN do anything.

Do you get this picture? Here is a woman who has mastered the bucksaw and the rivet, the plywood panel and the plow, the locomotive and the quarter deck. Through sheer ability as an ad writer, she has made you almost see her; at least I can see her. I can see her driving a caterpillar on North River. I can see her bedding down a couple of Percherons in a big dim barn on the upper Wynooche, after a day's plowing. I can see her crossing the Westport bar with the best of the trollermen on a bright morning. I can see her bending over the lighted chart table as a heavily laden freighter wallows through an Atlantic night, Murmansk bound.

———

History may never know her name, but her battle cry, "Anything but housework," will be carried on the pennons of thousands of women who have learned to build and sail ships, to build and fly planes, to plow valleys and build dams. There will be, you will see, a great mass shift from muffin making to mountain moving. And if that isn't revolution, what is?

If this prophecy leaves you with a sort of all gone feeling, wondering who in heck is going to stay home and make the muffins, why never fear! Someday a hero (yet unsung) is going to come home, throw his briefcase down on the floor, get a firm clutch on the kitchen sink, and challenge the world to pry him loose from his rightful place. How often has my heart not failed me at the sight of a door opening in the morning and some poor wretch being flung out into the rigors of a hard-bitten business day! Taught from infancy to shun the cook stove and the kettle, the mop and the meat grinder as he would the plague, he knows deep down within him somewhere that he is missing the fullest part of life. Someday, as I have said, a hero will rise up and create another incident by inserting in the newspaper some such ad follows:

> *Ex-prize fighter and stevedore, six years before the mast of an ice breaker, feels qualified to tackle housework. Willing to try, anyway.*

Coming Up the Hard Way

May 15, 1943

EVERYONE WHO WAS ON A BUS which came through Fort Lewis on a recent pay day heard the story of what happened to Lieutenant John Doe. The first bunch of soldiers who got on were yelling the details to each other, and as the bus stopped to pick up waiting groups along the road, they were greeted with, "Did you hear what happened to Doe?" And the story was told all over again, whether the new arrivals belonged to Doe's outfit or not. Even if they'd never heard of Lieutenant Doe, they heard of him now—and laughed and whacked each other on the back, and a thoroughly good time was had by all. Civilians, too, appreciated the story, and for a while, as the bus rolled down to Grays Harbor County, where the boys could cash their pay checks and see their girls, it was felt that this was a pretty good world after all.

The story is that the "sarge" was calling company roll on the second floor of a drill hall. Everyone was standing at attention facing the stair wall, the "sarge" with his back to it, when this lieutenant, Doe, came upstairs and without ceremony, and with the peremptory manner of a man who thought much too much of himself, called out, "Sergeant!" Now it appears that it is bad form to interrupt roll call, even "the old man himself" wouldn't think of doing it; so everyone was surprised, not to say chagrined. But before they had time to even feel these emotions, the lieutenant stepped a stiff pace backward and fell down stairs. The "sarge," who hadn't even turned around, kept right on calling the roll. Everyone spoke up real lively, and said "here!" in forthright tones so that they could be heard distinctly above the clatter of the lieutenant falling down stairs. The whole episode, it was felt, was an unexpected and delightful tidbit handed out on the erstwhile cold platter of fate.

The most awful thing that has happened to me in a long time is that someone gave me a grammar. It isn't one of those nice little schoolbook grammars which explains away the English language with the blithe gusto of a vacuum cleaner salesman passing over the innocent mechanisms of a simple tool. No, this grammar is something else; something I didn't know existed. It is so vast and convoluted, so bristling with nuts, bolts, screws, and hair-trigger springs, that once you have gotten into it, you feel like a trapped bear. And you are pretty sure that if you ever get out of it, you will never be the same again.

Beginning with the simple word, *And*, this appalling grammar hacks, chews, and saws its way right through the alphabet, and when it finally comes to the *Whats* and the *Whens*, all you have learned has been pulverized to sawdust.

The really high spot in this symphony of destruction is reached at about mid-stream when the author sets his teeth into the word, *What*. If you have ever baited your hook for a trout and had a whale rise out of the deep and clamp his jaws on your line, you will know how it feels to play about with *What*. It is the most dangerous word in the English language. It is the word that the author spends most time on, and when he has finally defanged it, you are pretty sure you will never (knowingly) use it again. A simple *Which* will be good enough for you—and for me too.

———

I suffered my first major defeat at the age of seven in a spelling bee. It was at the old Central School, with Mrs. Mildred West presiding. A platoon of us faced the fire of words and, as one man after another withstood the shock, and the enemy fire came nearer the end of the line (I was end man), how I hoped to be standing among the brave! The word "cradle" was shot at me. I gave it everything I had—which was one too many *ll*'s. I immediately burst into what I would like to call tears, but which were, I must confess, just plain screams. I was thrown into the cloakroom to sober up, which I didn't do, so was sent home. But I took revenge on society; I have consistently cast misspelled words into the machinery of living every time I took my pen in hand, from that day to this.

The high spot in my criminal career was reached one night when an over-wrought editor turned around (I can see him now, his tired face, twisted and white under the green shaded light) and whispered almost piteously, and with a kind of controlled awe: "If there were ten right ways to spell a word and one wrong one, you'd get the wrong one every time." Sounds hard, doesn't it? But it's easy for me.

Local Geography

May 22, 1943

I HELPED A LOGGING COUSIN* scare up a crew the other night. I had thought it couldn't be done. But he did it. On Monday morning, the trucks, the fallers, the buckers, and the loaders were on the job, having been enticed from their lairs in that strip of territory which lies north of the mouth of the Humptulips and runs westward to the sea and north to Quinault. We covered the best part of a hundred miles—a hundred moonlight miles, with the moon jumping after us from peak to peak of the hemlock turreted hills, first to the right of the road and then to the left, until the map we were traveling over seemed to swing about crazily. The moon—losing all sense of the fitness of things, and certainly all sense of direction—appeared with equal impartiality in the northern sky, the southern sky, and the eastern sky. I like good adaptable moons like that. And good round, cheerful moons, which this one was.

It followed us up the remotest little by-roads where low shake-roofed houses squatted in the clearings. It followed us up creeks and down to the mouths of rivers where nothing was to be seen but a shadowy cluster of dark buildings, where the hollow thudding sound of an oar dropped in the bottom of a boat told that water was near. Doors opened and in the lighted rectangles made by the Coleman lanterns, men stood and talked about falling and bucking. Sitting in the car and seeing beyond the lighted doorways into the rooms, I watched a woman clearing a supper table, a woman holding a child on her lap and leaning forward to turn a radio dial. I could hear—although I was not consciously listening to it—something of the bargaining of the men; it was planned to yard the spar tree out of the cold deck in the morning; the truckers, living aloofly in venetian-shuttered elegance in town (we had spent the day knocking at their doors and disturbing their high-priced Sunday repose), had agreed to arrive at seven in the morning. It was necessary to have a crew ready to load.

We visited a dozen moonlit homesteads, each spaced a dozen lavish miles from the other, and flushed up five men who agreed to come in the morning. We also flushed up numerous cocker spaniels who always arrived panting breathlessly a few seconds after the doors had been opened, and who came into the light grinning and foolish from nocturnal scurryings in the brush—instead of being the proper barking sentinels they were supposed to be.

Finally, nothing remained but to get hold of a loader. We came out on the main highway and turned seaward through a vast bleakness of logged-off land, pricked here and there with triangular wedges of young second growth, black in the ravines and dark green where the moonlight lay on the hills and where the sky, with the memory of twilight reflected from the west, was a dark, unclouded blue.

---

* Giles Hogan.

If it had been as black as pitch, I could have felt the nearness of the sea. Our headlights picked out the Army's "Lights Out" sign, and a soldier waved a warning arm. We swooped down a hill in darkness, turned left, and drove out to the brow of a cliff. Beyond the cliff was the sea, and above the sea, stars. The moon was back where it belonged in the eastern sky.

There were small houses on the cliff and when the engine was turned off we heard the barking of many, apparently leashed, dogs—big barks and little barks. A door was opened. A man stood in the light holding back half a dozen hounds from pouring out of the house. With a swift backward kick, he set them back on their haunches. Then the door was closed and he came toward the car. A match which he struck for a cigarette showed a youngish fellow with dark, long locks which had fallen from a part, and hung on either side of his head, Indian fashion. He tipped his head back and made wide gestures with his arms and showed white even teeth when he spoke.

This was the loader, the winning jack or the losing joker (whichever he should turn out to be) that my cousin was looking for. This was the man who decided which logs were to be placed where, so that the finely balanced load would arrive at the mill intact, instead of rolling off the truck on a sharp curve, an accident, if it occurs, which leaves the profits to the ants and squirrels. From a high perch where he can be seen by all hands, the loader works entirely by pantomime. A sway of the body, a droop of the wrist, a flick of a little finger is translated into tonnage, balance, and proportion by the laboring crew. It is an art which you must be born with, and if you are descended from a long line of witches, why, so much the better.

A loader in full swing is a beautiful sight to see, my cousin told me as we drove homeward. "Except when he jumps on his hat," he added thoughtfully.

"Jumps on his hat!" I exclaimed.

"Sure! A good loader always wears a hat so he can take it off and jump on it. Instead of cussing, you know. Like a mad gorilla."

Chronology for 1943

May

1 Federal government takes over closed coal mines.

11 Churchill arrives in Washington for war conference.

14 Last resistance ends in North Africa.

23 Guerrilla warfare spreads in Balkans.

26 Death of Edsel B. Ford, president of Ford Motor Co., 49.

30 Japs admit loss of Attu.

The moving headlight flickered rhythmically along a wall of hemlock trunks, a dark ageless corridor down which we sped. Against this somber background flowering crab apples and elderberries burst into sudden showers of snowy sparks which dissolved suddenly in the flying darkness. We turned south into softer country and headed home. I thought: I have had the sort of evening you can have only one place in the world— north of the Humptulips and west of the moon.

Making the Most of Things

May 29, 1943

A FISH COP CAME to my cousin's house on North Bay and asked if we knew where he could get a seal hunter. I hadn't known there were any seal hunters left, but my cousins told him there was an old seal hunter not a quarter of a mile down the road. The fish cop, who had looked tired and harassed when he came in, looked relieved. "We've got to kill some of the seal around here before they get all the salmon," he said. "Besides I'm hungry for a seal steak."

"How are they?" we asked.

"I don't know," said the fish cop. "I never ate one, but I've got to set my teeth in some red meat, somehow." He told us that two of them had come through Aberdeen ten days before and, with their combined ration stamps, had bought a pound of stewing beef, a pound of salt pork, some butter and bacon, "not enough to keep one man alive for three days," and that they were literally starving. A man alone in the woods with no home larder to fall back on, and supplied only with what his ration stamps will get him, is at a pretty pass, according to the fish cop. "Great Gosh!" he said. "We couldn't even get beans or potatoes."

The state pays a salary to seal hunters. There was once a bounty on seal, and anyone could hunt them, mail in the scalps, and get paid for them. The trouble was that unscrupulous hunters from Maine and Georgia, Florida and California, made too much of a good thing out of the state of Washington. "There isn't any way of telling what state a seal comes from," complained the fish cop. He shook his head and looked rueful, and went off down the road pondering, I suppose, the short sightedness of a deity who could so easily have made red seals in California and blue ones in Maine, but who hadn't.

A group of townsfolk were huddled at the corner by the Becker building waiting for the red light when three soldiers came along and crossed against the green light. As they stepped on the curb by the bank, one of them looked back and said in loud pitying wonderment: "I guess they think they're on Times Square!"

———

There is something sad about going into one of those beach houses that the army has abandoned. After you get over your peevish amazement at the devastation, you begin to see the imprints of the personalties which have occupied your house. Someone has taken the trouble to make a wooden rod for coat hangers, a delicate bit of carpentry with mitered ends set into small wooden blocks and fastened to the wall with wooden pegs. On a rough bedside table, a row of paper-backed "books" of the Bible are laid out in order, their covers bleached and brittle under the sandy dust. A map of the world on the wall has been embellished by a wide line in red ink showing the shortest distance from Grays Harbor to Texas with the inscription "To God's Country," and an arrow pointing to Texas. One hardy soul has even penetrated into the guest book where visiting aunts and cousins put their Sunday signatures. Leaving several blank pages to separate himself from these aliens (they aren't his aunts and cousins), he has written, "East is East, and West is West," Corporal G. Smity, New Jersey.

These mute leavings of an army which has long since sailed away (armies sail now, they do not march) leave me sad. A line of a poem, known once, but now utterly without head or tail, swims into my consciousness: "Where are you now, whose ways are past my knowing . . . ?" Yes, where are you, Corporal G. Smity? Farther west than ever, I'll bet. And you, Texas? You would probably have to ink a red line halfway around the world to show the way to God's country today. And R. B.! I don't really mind at all, R. B., that you carved your initials in the center of the mantel. (I am also pretty sure that it was you who split wood on the hearth and left your axe prints on the tiles of time). Given the proper tools, you no doubt gave a good account of yourself at New Guinea or Attu. I shall keep these toys of your loneliness.

How We're Doing

June 5, 1943

THE TOWN, LYING IN THE BOTTOM of its forested bowl,* never looked greener or fresher. What with all streets washed, all hedges clipped, all lawns mowed, and all elementary gear, such as plows, spades, and mattocks, stowed away, it appears to be waiting in its party clothes for some event. This being all dressed up with flowering hawthorns, glistening laurels, and every blade of grass in place lends an air of expectancy, as if something portentous were about to happen. All it amounts to, however, is that the citizens, who want awfully to do something real about the war, have worked off the first flush of their futility and are now leaning back on their hoes and lawn mowers to take a look at the crops. Enough energy, enough heart, and enough hours of labor have gone into Grays Harbor gardens to build no mean number of battleships, and an Alcan highway or two.

Everything is going ahead according to plan—cabbages are beginning to head, radishes are getting worms in them, lettuce has reached that stage of crinkly toughness where you can stand and admire it with the neighbors. You might even eat it. Who knows? Much food will result from these endeavors. But it won't taste as good as it would if our boys were here to eat it with us. And who is going to enjoy the clipped hedges, the snowy hawthorns, and the glossy laurels?

Cabbage

With the absence of automobile traffic, silence has settled on the town. Smoke from the mill funnels and burners blows up the river on a stiff west wind. There is a movement of clouds in from the sea, and the harbor glistens in silvery light. From the West Bridge can be seen the tugs and converted fishing boats, dull in war paint. At the new shipyard four ships are on the way, and a new one, launched yesterday, rides at anchor against the incoming tide. Sometimes at night a wakeful citizen hears the sound of winches and the activity that goes with loading ships and getting them to sea before dawn breaks.

In the stores there are many new things to see. Plastic window screens, springless chairs, and davenports made of wood with upholstered cushions. Wooden towel racks and shelf brackets, wooden and paper toys. The jigsaw puzzle has come back. Magazines are thinner, and the morning newspapers later than ever, due, the delivery boys says, to the lack of rubber bands and the necessity of folding the papers three-corner-wise.

---

* Aberdeen.

Working hours are longer, and if, when you get home to dinner, there is meat, you are supposed to exclaim about it. And the cook is expected to tell you how much she paid for it, which always turns out to be plenty. There is something rather breathtaking and stimulating in being able to announce to the family that you paid 70 cents for four cube steaks—to say nothing of $1.25 for four pork chops. Two fried clams in a restaurant cost 80 cents, and up at Bremerton hamburgers are said to be selling for 35 cents.

———

New and older faces are appearing on the milk trucks and delivery vans. Girls have taken over some of the service stations. Old men who haven't had a real job for years now go about with an air of importance again. Small boys with wooden guns hunt Japs ceaselessly. I watched a patrol moving forward through the underbrush at Roosevelt Park the other evening, and I think from the looks of things they got their man. In the Becker building, a very small girl wrestles manfully with the grilled elevator doors.

At noon on Fridays, the silence is broken by a great clamoring of sirens from the city hall—our air raid warning rehearsal. Citizens are cautioned in the newspapers that "if you do not hear the sirens, phone in!" On Sunday mornings the church bells ring. The churches are filled with people. They go to pray for their boys.

Chronology of 1943

June

7   Coal miners of the United Mine
    Workers union return to work.
8   As aftermath of Los Angeles' "zoot
    suit" riots, the entire city is
    declared out of bounds for navy
    personnel.
9   Curtin says invasion danger past in
    Australia.
16 Chinese charge Japs use [poison]
    gas.
17 [British] RAF bombs Cologne,
    Germany.
21 Riots in Detroit between white and
    colored mobs are suppressed by
    federal troops, after more than 24
    hours of disorder. Twenty-nine
    killed, 700 injured.
    Coal miners strike for third time
    since May 1.
23 President Roosevelt threatens to
    draft strikers in essential industries.
30 U.S. forces land on Rendova, in
    Solomons.

Happy Combinations

June 12, 1943

THERE ARE FIFTEEN WAR DOGS stationed with the coast guard on a nearby beach. Each dog has his own house and pen, and his own master. They are fed a diet of fresh horse meat and vegetables. I'd hate to meet one of those unleashed hounds of the Baskervilles coming over the dunes on a gray day. With the distant fog horn snorting, and the mist blowing in, you couldn't ask for a better setting for a murder mystery.

———

Got a fifteen-year-old boy to help with the falling and bucking around the beach house. He is the head of a family of nine brothers and sisters which entitles them to eleven ration cards. They have enough of everything, except coffee for "Dad." They have 1,200 chickens which the children care for, and a fine vegetable garden. Before he arrived in the morning, he had gone to town and loaded up a ton of chicken feed, brought it home, and stored it away. And after he finished his eight hours' work for me, he went out on the beach and caught six perch, by surf casting. When I paid him, he put the money in a proud new billfold, already bursting with earnings. If by some mischance "Dad" doesn't make the bar some night in his fishing boat, Robert will be perfectly capable of taking the family helm. It is good to know that the great American boy (lately almost an historical or fictional character) lives on. I can't help but feel that eight brothers and sisters are a great help to a young fellow who wants to get ahead in the world. Sort of sets him up on his feet.

———

Beachcombing is my favorite sport. Last week I found a long cylindrical metal object which I was sure was a torpedo—until I examined a brass name tag screwed near the detonator which told me that I was looking, for the first time in my life, at "Seller's Safe Seed Planter." You don't

114

come across one of those every day in the week. I wonder if radishes grow better fired out of a cannon like that?

———

A neighbor told me once that he had just finished building a bunkroom with two fancy bunks in it when the tide brought in two fine single bed springs. Saved him a trip to town.

Fighting Words

June 19, 1943

WE ARE GOING AHEAD so fast that we daily use words which haven't cooled off enough to get into the dictionary. *Flak* is a shiny new word, coined by our fliers, which has been wholeheartedly accepted by headline writers to describe an atmospheric condition induced by smudge pots, anti-air craft fire, and a little fog thrown in for good measure. A whole new vocabulary is being born with flight. Words which are now no more than a gleam in the eye of a bombardier are due to be spoken familiarly by all of us in time. When the army and the navy get through with them, we will take these new words and twine them in the hair of our popular fiction. Many a short story hero is going to have to penetrate a lot of *flak* to get his best girl—and when he gets her, he is going to be cast into uncertainty because of the flakish look in her eye.

I remember how the waiting fictioneers seized upon the word *camouflage* after the allies got through with it in the last war. They took it like a school of fish rising to a single bait, and you couldn't pick up a magazine without being camouflaged at least once on every page. Writers went in for such sentences as: "Her downcast eyes were a camouflage which baffled him."

For the present, our new words are used in their original sense; the hero walks home through a blackout with quickly beating heart. But when this war is over and his girl turns him down, he will go into a blackout. A good title for an old suitor would be *a dim-out*. Or a dim-out might

be a dead gangster. The ultimate usage will depend on which type of magazine gets there first.

Just why words of war are transposed into words of love is more than I can figure out; unless, perhaps, they are synonymous of two poles, with love on one end and war on the other—and a lot of flak in between.

———

We are participating in a mass geography lesson the like of which has never been seen on this earth. And thanks to radio, we are learning to pronounce as we go. Roughly speaking, I'd say we learn about three new place names a week, and we have covered in our scope some of the best jaw-breakers of all time. This week's lesson was fairly simple—Pantelleria, Lampedusa, and Linosa.

———

We've got some picturesque language of our own right here in Grays Harbor County. While white-washing the wood shed, the neighbor's boy told me that, "When Dad was out in his fishing boat yesterday, three mole-hill breaks swelled up around him . . . he thought for a while he couldn't make it."

If you have ever been in a small boat and had the ocean slowly heave up into a crestless, green dome of might right in front of you, then you know what a "mole-hill break" is. I hope I never see one in the flesh. But I'm glad to know the name of the thing.

———

A nephew about to enter a New England college has been informed by bidding fraternities that he will be taxed three ration points every time they entertain him. There'll always be a New England, won't there?

———

Have unearthed two local superstitions on the make. One is that our cold, blustery weather has been cut loose from its moorings by bombings in the Aleutians, and the other is that the dark-colored, fatless beef we buy isn't beef at all but horse meat. I don't pretend to know much about the weather. But about the meat—for years I have bought that dark-colored, fatless product on the beaches where it is known affectionately as "swamp beef." Comes from those dun-colored cattle on the salt marshes. And tastes pretty good if you give it a handicap of three or four hours.

Peace Talk

June 26, 1943

IT'S GOOD TO HEAR that a number of the soldiers stationed here have gotten so fond of us that they plan to come back after the war and get "a little place." I've talked with some of these young men who yearn for a little place in Grays Harbor country and with others who have more ambitious plans. One young fellow says he's coming back and building a big icing plant at the Westport fishing dock. Sort of hold the stakes while the fishermen and the canneries are having their annual price argument. Another says he wants to come back and run for sheriff. "I've always wanted to be a sheriff," he said. He's asking for votes already. Some of these boys will see opportunities that we've missed. And because experience hasn't taught them, as it has us, that some of their ideas are impractical, they'll make a success.

Montbretia
Crocosmia crocosmaeflora

Tooling with Food

July 3, 1943

IT LOOKS, AS FAR AS FOOD is concerned, as if the general public is caught in the bight of the line and is going to stay in the bight of the line until congress and the president get through with their tug of war. If Mr. Roosevelt wins, we will pay subsidies to the food industries (taxes to you) for selling us something—and if congress wins, we will buy and pay for what we can afford (and lay our hands on), and let the devil figure out some way to keep labor pacified. If wages are to be kept down, the cost of food has to be kept down, says the president, and the only way we can do that is to pay the producers some hush money so they can afford to sell cheaper food to labor and keep labor pacified. Labor's got to be pacified, says Mr. Roosevelt, but just why it's got to be pacified when nothing else on the face of this earth is pacified he doesn't say.

Congress, on the other hand, has indicated that, if the president wants to pacify labor, he will have to figure out some other way than taking the pennies out of the pockets of the folks back home. The folks back home are beginning to realize that any business deals they sign up for will have to be paid for by their sons when they get home from the war, and to ask the boys to go and fight for us and then come home and pay up for the groceries we ate while they were away is a bit stiff, isn't it? Perhaps it's better to leave labor unpacified. None of the rest of us are very pacified. And we're not asking anyone else to pay for our potatoes, either. The average citizen with a modicum of wits is sure of just two things, (a) this war is going to cost him all the spare change he can get together, and (b) he will not starve to death in America.

———

Where Is Our Missing Meat?

"Don't swallow all that hooey about the meat going to the soldiers," writes a correspondent from camp. "No steaks yet! And it isn't going to the boys overseas either. Officers returned from combat fields tell us you're lucky to get to eat in combat for days at a time. You have 'K' rations or vitamin pills a good share of the time."

The Texas and Southwestern Cattle Raisers Association reports 78,170,000 head of cattle on United States ranges where there were but 67,000,000 before the war, and 20,000,000 little pigs are due to be born into the 105,000,000 national pig clan this summer. But it's against the law to slaughter them; and unless somebody invents a method for getting some corn out of Uncle Sam's regulation-locked cupboard, they are liable to die of starvation.

"You get some very strange mixtures slapped on your plate in the army," writes a neighbor's son. "Today, for example, I had fish covered with tartar sauce and that was covered with dessert which was strawberries. Some of the likelier combinations which result when we line up with our plates are mashed potatoes covered with orange jello, combination salad sprinkled with pork gravy, and stew with prunes a la mode. One of our better combinations, guaranteed to make four out of five men bolt for the door with pale faces, is chocolate pie decorated lavishly with stewed tomatoes.

"After dinner the mess sergeant blows his whistle and we sit at attention and listen to him lecture on how much food is being wasted in the army. We get a complete resume, or inventory, of the shameful overflow in the garbage can, when it is plain as the nose on your face that the food is wasted before they give it to us. If it doesn't stop, I'm going to write to Mrs. Roosevelt."

Joe Takes Time Out

July 10, 1943

I met Joe on the beach bus. He was a big, rangy fellow with a distracted air and sad dark eyes. "Just let me out anywhere when you come to the ocean," he told the bus driver. Then he sat down beside me and told the story which follows.

"I'M A WHOLESALE GROCER from Eastern Washington. I haven't got anything left to sell in my warehouse, so I'm going down and look at the Pacific for a couple of days and see if I can figure things out. I'm what the newspapers, and the public, and the OPA calls the middleman. I'm the fellow that's supposed to be scalping the farmer and gypping the public, and throwing monkey wrenches into the adolescent dreams of those briefless lawyers and college students back in Washington. Every time some squirt who has just packed a coon-skin coat away in moth balls has a bright idea that doesn't work out, it's the middleman that's to blame.

"Did you know that the food business is the hugest business in the world? My father was a wholesale grocer, and his father before him. I started in the warehouse at the age of ten. Had all the practice before I got the theories in the Harvard School of Business. Knew all about Time and Place Utility before I read it in a book getting the can of tomatoes from the cannery in Ohio to the construction camp at Boulder dam along with coffee from Brazil and pepper from the Orient. A middleman couldn't exist if he didn't serve a purpose. In normal times, I keep 4,500 items and grades of commodities on my shelves. In order to do this, I myself must, at times, employ a broker. I wouldn't use him if he wasn't of use. Just like you wouldn't use the middleman if he wasn't of use. How would you like to have to sit down every year and figure out where your salt was coming from, or any one of the hundreds of items you use just to keep house?

"The wholesaler figures all that out for you. But he has to figure it out in a big way in the West, and that's what you can't get over to the boys in Washington. There are no great wholesale houses on the east coast—just little peanut businesses every ten miles or so apart. They are stocked up when they have ten cases of corn flakes. Out here, where the distances are so vast, we buy 1,600 cases at a time. That's a carload. We have to. Our wholesale houses are spaced about a hundred and fifty miles apart. People buy differently in the West. Why, did you know that back east in big cities people run to the corner store three times a day, and come home with a small can of milk, a quarter pound of cheese, and three eggs? That's the way they buy back there. Out here, it's different. When a farmer has to drive from thirty to ninety miles for his bacon, he wants to carry home more than half a pound.

"Well, I'm all out of blue stamps. My shelves are empty. The canners are begging to get rid of their pack, get it out of the way so they can get to work on something else. But

Chronology of 1943

July

1   Rendova taken by U.S. forces.
5   Russians launch offensive on 160 mile front; U.S. navy battles Japs off Solomons.
12 British capture Syracuse [on Sicily].
23 U.S. troops enter Palermo.
24 Americans take Marsala, Trapani.
25 Mussolini resigns, King Emmanuel assumes government.
28 Fascist party dissolved.
27 Italian peace negotiations begin.

I can't buy it and relieve them. I've used up my stamps. Haven't got enough for a carload of tomatoes. 'Get a few cases, then,' Washington says. Well, I tried that. Along with three other wholesalers. We bought a carload, and by the time it had spent three days unloading on a siding at Portland, and a couple of days on a siding at Spokane, and detoured over to my warehouse for another three days before it went on to Tacoma, we'd bought the most expensive carload of tomatoes on record, besides balling up the transportation system generally.

"Just to give you an idea of what we have to face— I've been handling canvas work gloves for thirty years. Men need them in the woods. They need them on farms and in construction camps, in mills and factories. My quota was used up. I wrote to Washington explaining that I needed canvas gloves badly, and that they were essential to speed production. Some guy wrote back saying that OPA had forethoughtedly set up a bureau to deal with lack of funds and enclosing a bunch of forms for me to fill out, 'Hell's bells,' I wrote back, 'do I have to prove I'm broke to get a batch of canvas gloves?' I wrote a hot letter, all right. I told OPA they ought to clear the decks of all those bright boys who were obstructing the national way of doing business, and send them into the army. I got an answer back from Prentiss Brown himself, calling to my attention that the personnel of OPA was subject to draft just like everyone else. 'Why in hell don't they enlist then?' I wrote back.

"So now I haven't any canvas gloves. I haven't any groceries either. But I have a nice letter from Washington. It says do I know that in case of an invasion and the resultant confusion in transportation, people are liable to starve unless we wholesalers keep an adequate supply on hand at all times, and that it is my patriotic duty as a public-spirited American to see that there is sufficient reserve for such an eventuality. Those bright boys are good at thinking up whose foot the shoe will fit when the pinch comes. Whenever I try to figure out a way to stock up, I get a letter reminding me that there is a thousand-dollar fine and imprisonment for hoarding. I'm just a middleman—with one foot in McNeil Island and the other in the grocery business.

"Well, I'm not broke. But I'm not doing business. And I'm not going to bite on any subsidy bait either—like a salmon on a tin minnow."

When the bus reached the dunes, Joe got out. He said he was going to try to relax and enjoy himself and let OPA figure things out. He said he knew at least five other middlemen who had laid their cares on the knees of the gods in Washington, locked their warehouse doors, and departed for the great open spaces.

Changing Times

July 17, 1943

WHEN I WAS A GIRL, you could travel all the way to Seattle in a [railroad] chair car filled with women and, if no one knew anyone else, you would not hear one word spoken, except a formal "Thank you," for opening the Women's Room door, or an "I beg your pardon, I'm sure," if you tripped over a high-buttoned kid shoe; although you weren't likely to do that, as women kept their feet to themselves in those days. Ladies didn't cross their knees, use their chamois skins in public, or speak to strangers. With their chins elevated above their boned collars, they kept their eyes at a strictly impersonal level. As I remember it, there were only three well-bred things a lady could use her eyes for—she could stare at the water cooler, look at the milk cans on station platforms, and read the *Atlantic Monthly*.

As a child, I made a trip to Seattle in the smug confines of a chair car. It was during the time they were hunting for the famous bandit and desperado, Tracy, who had escaped from Walla Walla and murdered I know not how many men, terrorized housewives, and thrown the countryside into such a state of panic that small dogs and children hid whimpering under beds, while grim-faced posses searched the western counties. The hue and cry of one of these posses crossed the railroad tracks beyond Tacoma and halted the train. The chair car was full of "ladies," (men preferred the smoking car) and not one word was spoken during those exciting seconds when the bandit himself might have been expected to jump aboard the train and present himself in our midst, revolver in hand. Finally, when the train got under way, one dowager, without much breeding, no doubt, exclaimed "Gracious me!" She was answered by reproving stares and the rustle of many *Atlantic Monthlies*.

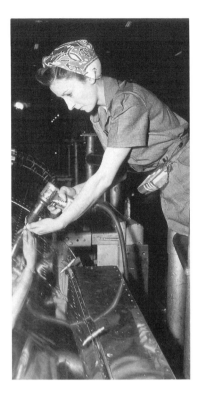

Things are different now. A nice little woman with a tweed coat and an eager face sat down beside me at a lunch counter this week and asked, before she was fairly seated, "How's the pie?" I told her it was good, and we launched into one of those stimulating conversations perfect strangers enjoy today.

"I'm a colonel's wife," the little woman told me. "I live at Vancouver barracks. I took all the first aid and home defense courses but I got tired of not being able to use any of it, so I went to the Kaiser shipyard and learned welding. Right now I'm out recruiting. Men are being drafted out of the plant by the hundreds and women have got to do the work."

When I asked what luck she was having on the Harbor, she said "Not much. The Boeing plant is going to absorb the women here. It's the same in all the coast towns. Next week I'm going into the middle west where there are no defense plants. Welding's pleasant work. A woman can make over $50 a week. We have plenty of housing over there. And nurseries for the children."

I asked if Mr. Kaiser was going ahead with his million-dollar nursery. She hesitated and said, "Yes . . . but there is some opposition. Some people seem to think the idea is communistic. Some think we borrowed it from Russia. But that's silly, isn't it? If it's a good idea, and we don't use it, I mean. The Russians borrowed our engineers and mechanics to show them how to use machines. They didn't refuse our tractor plows because they were an American idea. We've got to be like them and use anybody's ideas that will win the war. They showed us women can do manual work if their children are cared for. And it's a good thing, because women are going to have to build our ships. They've got to."

Other Ways Than Ours

July 24, 1943

THE PROBLEMS OF TRANSPORTATION being what they are, our boys are not going to bring home as many souvenirs as they did after the last war. Another reason is that as a nation we are more grown up and are not so easily thrilled by the sight of enemy helmets, iron crosses, bolo knives, and foreign cutlery as we once were. But you can depend upon it that our boys will bring home ideas—if they are good ones. A pretty custom was introduced to Aberdeen last week by the wife of one of sailors who was stationed at Honolulu. When it rained, she took off her shoes and walked through the streets barefooted. They do that in Honolulu where it floods when it rains. Makes for nice-looking feet, too, our sailor's wife tells me.

———

Read a neighbor's letter from Australia the other day. Two boys from western Washington met there in a bar. One is a flight officer and the other an officer in the army transportation corps. They hadn't known each other here, but they knew many of the same people. They had spent their youthful summers on our beaches, knew the fishing dock, the skating rink, and the dances at the tavern on Saturday nights. "We talked," wrote the flight officer, "until my ship hopped off at four o'clock in the morning . . . about the people and the houses . . . even about the dogs, and the cats, if there were any. We laughed until we cried. But we cried more than we laughed . . ."

So now we know what they talk about over there. They talk about us. And they cry more than they laugh. And so do we . . . so do we.

Defending Democracy

August 7, 1943

WENT OUT ON THE DUNES and took a good look at a barbed-wire entanglement. The wire is stretched in rows like a series of parallel fences, and between the fences it is rolled in waist-high loops, like those early Spencerian circles you learn to make when you first take pen in hand in the third grade. Only, instead of being flat

Chronology of 1943

August

2 Race riot sweeps New York, resulting in death of five negroes, and injuries to 500.

6 Americans occupy Munda, in Solomons.

13 Gasoline ration in Midwest and Southwest reduced from four to three gallons per coupon.

18 Resistance ends in Sicily.

21 U.S. and Canadian troops occupy Kiska.

24 Quebec conference on war plans ends.

25 British Admiral Mountbatten made chief of Allied Southeast Asia command.

and one dimensional, as in a drawing, the loops are in circles like a cowboy's fancy work with a lariat. When the end of the right-leaning row of loops is reached the process is reversed and a left-leaning coil is doubled back over the first, just as you used to do when you really got going good with the back-hand stroke. The result, when done in wire, is a barricade that even a house-to-house campaigning congressman couldn't penetrate.

───

On the beach I met a coast guardsman with a war dog. The dog, a black, short-haired mongrel with tan jaws and drooping hound-like ears, sat down and grinned and thumped his tail on the sand when I came abreast of him. "I'm supposed to beat him when he does that," the guardsman (six foot three in dungarees) told me. "But I never do."

"But I thought they were awfully fierce!" I exclaimed.

"They all are. Except this one," the guardsman said with an inflection which sounded suspiciously like pride. They strolled comfortably off down the beach, a boy and his dog.

Was saddened to read in the newspapers that when the war is over, the war dogs will be destroyed, as their training has made them unfit for domesticity. I hope that the dog lovers of America will see that this is never done, and that the dogs are retired to some peaceful haven to live out their allotted span.

───

"The only thing I've got to tell my grandchildren so far," a soldier on leave told me, "is that I was the sole passenger on a troop Pullman [train] all the way from California." Troop Pullmans are made up of three tiers of bunks, undecorated with either blankets, curtains, or porters. As it was 138 in the shade when my friend left camp, he peeled off his clothes and took the bunks one at a time in an original cooling off process invented on the spot. "When one got too hot, I climbed into another. Boy, was that luxury."

Problem coped with and solved by Hostess House personnel: A young girl came all the way from the Atlantic coast to join her soldier-husband, only to find that he had been shifted to an unknown station. She arrived by bus with nothing but the clothes on her back (a taffeta dinner dress which had been cut off at the knees), 25 cents in change, and a white flower in her hair. Hostess House went into executive session, called all army camps within a radius of several hundred miles, found the husband. They then bought a ticket for the young wife and put her on the bus, along with a five-dollar bill. It all goes to prove what I have always suspected—that love will find a way. . . Even in a second-hand dinner dress. Even with 25 cents clutched in its hand, and two thousand miles to go. Even through the well-groomed "gun fire" of charity. Some of my neighbors have expressed surprise that anyone would have the courage to accomplish their objective in a taffeta dinner dress. But I think they missed the point. Anyone can travel in a dinner dress, but it is a rare soul who can take time out, under such circumstances, to pin a white flower in her hair. A woman who would do that is liable to do most anything, like becoming the mother of a second Genghis Khan. That is the rub about America. Or the glory. It depends on your point of view.

Where to, Utopia?

August 21, 1943

I HADN'T KNOWN that Utopia was the ultimate goal of the human race until I read one of those reports from Washington where the best minds are staying awake nights planning a new and better world. What we are striving for, according to the philosophers and economists, the humanitarians, and the prophets, is to "free man from drudgery." This aim, which has been unanimously accepted by the sages as the solution to the troubles which harass this world, has my whole-hearted endorsement. And I'm not a sage, either. I didn't have to burn the midnight oil, or submerge myself for years on end in the dark tide of world economy, or nose about on the ocean bed of history to find the missing clue as to what's the matter with the world. I was born with the clue in my teeth—no work! That's the answer.

Drudgery, says my dictionary, is ignoble and wearisome toil. You wouldn't think anyone would care much about it, would you? And most people don't. The trouble is— and it is what keeps the professors awake long past bedtime—that while most people don't like to drudge, they have no objection to other people drudging, in fact, they rather encourage it. They not only encourage it, but they rather insist on it. And having insisted on it, and gotten people to drudging, they bear down real hard and are loath to consider a world free from drudgery. The sages are going to have a hard time with these people, but they expect to win out in the end. Education is the answer, they say. If you are one of those human beings who can sleep nights knowing that some coolie is toiling over a mountain pass with a grand piano on his back, you can, say the sages, be educated out of your complacency. If you can eat and enjoy eating while other people live and die without ever having had a square meal, why, you can be educated to a degree where a beefsteak will turn to ashes in your mouth at the very thought of some poor fellow in India sitting down to a cupful of rice after a twenty-four hour shift on one of those spiked couches they go in for down there. If that isn't an ignoble and wearisome way to earn a few sous, I don't know what is. We've got to learn that it is savage and barbarous for us to permit such things, the professors have decided.

Drudgery—other people's drudgery—has got to go. Of course if we want to carry our own pianos, or fritter away the summer mining our own coal, that will be our own business. The minds which have planned the new world have taken cognizance of the fact that it is human nature to want to do a little puttering about.

They have also taken into account the strange fact that there are on this earth people who like to drudge. Just what causes the idiosyncrasy has never been determined. Whether they are a hangover from that generation which found virtue in such phrases as "by the sweat of your brow" and "honest toil," or whether they are the victims of a meaningless excess energy observed, at times, throughout all nature, is not known. It is known, however, that these people love work and, like the bees which gather more honey than all the bees on earth could use, they love drudgery for drudgery's sake. You find their prototypes in the animal kingdom among the pack rats who bend their energies to carrying decks of cards, moth balls, and rusted button hooks to their lairs. To those humans afflicted with that sort of St. Vitus dance, the sages will offer the education cure; they will be taught that it is vulgar and undignified to store away more honey than they can eat, and that there is no more virtue in a round of futile meaningless tasks than there is in a pack load of rusted button hooks. In the New World, so brightly envisioned by the sages, these poor drudges will be released from the squirrel cages and their splendid energies diverted to more humanitarian tasks than that of bringing home all the bacon.

Released from drudgery and prohibited from hoarding, we will have a lot of time on our hands to improve our minds, look at sunsets, and go to ball games. Life will become really worth living. As to who will bring home the bacon, while the professors don't actually say, they imply in a roundabout way that, if there is any bacon in the picture, YOU will bring it home. "But," you will say, and reasonably, too, "that brings us right back where we started from—to drudgery!" Well . . . it does, sort of. Frankly, I admit my own disappointment at having the great New World scheme debauch in a dead-end street like that. Could it be, do you think, that they don't consider it "ignoble and wea- risome toil" for a man to rustle his own grub? Or . . . perhaps we won't even have to eat in the New World. It begins to look like it, anyway.

Chopping Wood

August 28, 1943

WHEN HE ISN'T FISHING with his father, Robert comes over and helps me with the wood pile. He swings the axe with an easy stroke, making not too much of a task of it, while I sit on the door step, and we visit. This week he told me how come Grandpa gave up kidding Pa about fishing being an easy life.

Grandpa, said Robert, always used to kind of sneer and look superior when Pa talked about the hardships of salmon trolling. There wasn't no more hardship to it than going after cat fish in the Tennessee River, Grandpa said, except it was easier because you didn't have go up and down in a straight line, but could go every which ways. Grandpa allowed as how Pa fished because it was a lazy man's life, and because he wanted to get away from Ma and the kids all day. So the day after the war started and Pa couldn't get any help on the boat, Grandpa said he'd go out and take a crack at it himself.

It was kind of rough out there, and while Pa was below tinkering with the engine, he heard a yell come up on deck, and there was Grandpa clinging to a hatch cover a couple of hundred yards astern. A big mole-hill break had come aboard and taken Grandpa and the hatch cover, and all, right along with it. Grandpa was bellering like all get out, and calling out that he was a gone man. But Pa threw him a line, hauled up alongside, and went to work getting Grandpa over the gunnel, which was something Pa can't figure out how he ever done, because Pa is a little man, less than five feet six, and Grandpa weighs two hundred and ten pounds and is fat as a porpoise. When he got him on deck, they had to come in, and couldn't fish any more that day because Grandpa said he was getting pneu- monia. He ain't never gone fishing again. And he ain't never said another word about fishing being a lazy man's life with no hardships to it. He just stays home and helps Ma with the kids—won't even go down to the dock to watch the boats come in.

———

When Robert had finished telling about Grandpa, he set the double-bitted axe aside, and sat down on the chopping block in an attitude of polite attention. It was now my turn to contribute something to the entertainment. When someone tells you about their

127

Grandpa, it's the polite thing to tell them about your Grandpa. In a community practically without books except a few moulded copies of Robert W. Chambers left over from the whalebone age—any little tale is accepted gratefully, and stored away in that cupboard of the mind where it becomes one more drop in the bucket of human experience.

I didn't tell Robert about my Grandpa, though. I told him about Grandma. I guess it was the neat row of piled wood, and the fog blowing in swirls down from the dunes, that made me think of the sod walls of Ireland and the gray day Grandma saw the fairy.

When Grandma was a girl, I said, she and her brother were driving to a wedding in a gig. A gig is a high cart. You drive along a lane which is banked at the sides with high sod walls. They are so high that even from the gig you can only get a glimpse over the top, now and then, to see where you're at.

They were driving along when suddenly the horse shied to one side of the road and stopped dead, with his ears thrown back, and trembling all over. Grandma looked to see what had caused the fright, and there, on the opposite wall, was one of the Little People— that's what they call fairies there. They have lived in Ireland since time began. What probably scared the horse, and what certainly made cold chills go up and down Grandma's spine, was that the fairy was sitting halfway up the wall in an easy position with one leg crossed over the other, but he wasn't sitting on anything—just air. He was no more than a foot in height and, in the instant before the horse leapt forward again, Grandma saw straight into his eyes, and it was like looking over the rim of the world and into the awful abyss of time.

Whenever a fairy is seen in Ireland, it means that something terrible is about to happen, so Grandma went on to the wedding with a sad heart, and pretty nervous and unstrung, foreseeing tragedy as she did.

Well, after the wedding the groom led the bride out of the church and helped her on her horse. But when he let go of the bridle and turned to mount his own horse, the bride's horse suddenly reared up on its haunches and bolted off. The groom got on his own horse as soon as he could and followed. And everyone else jumped on their horses and into their gigs and followed, Grandma's brother included. But the bride's horse outran them all. He disappeared with the speed of light, over the horizon. All the rest of that day, and the next day and the next, they searched the countryside, but they didn't find the missing bride. They never found her. The groom rode into the north country and was gone for weeks hunting for her, and while he was gone, Grandma's brother got in his gig and went looking in the south country. He never came back, but met some woman and settled there. Grandma never saw him again. That's what comes of seeing a fairy in Ireland.

Sea Changes

September 4, 1943

I SPOKE THIS WEEK of my intention to cut down a tree which casts a green gloom into the interior of my house, but the neighbors rose up as one man and vetoed the idea. The tree, a Monterey cypress, doesn't cast any gloom in the neighbors' houses, which are the best part of a block away, but that doesn't make any difference. I am not to cut down the tree. Just on general principles. If there is one thing you can't go wrong on, the neighbors seem to feel, it is that you should never cut down a tree. When I called to their attention that their own trees were down, the neighbors said that was different—their trees had blown down. After they had gone off across the pasture, with the long strides and the upright bearing of people who have done a worthwhile deed, I went and sulked in the gloomy interior of my cypress-shaded domicile. I have been made to feel that my cultural education is sadly lacking. Furthermore, I can't help but be aware of the fact that I am, in some vague unexplainable way, inferior—I am not the sort of person whose trees blow down.

———

When they aren't trying to keep me from cutting down the old cypress tree, the neighbors are busy filling galvanized wash tubs, old wash boilers, and scrub pails with Himalaya [black]berries, which are ripening now in the small clearings along the road and beyond the pasture. At least the men neighbors are busy. Their preoccupation amounts to feverish activity. The women neighbors don't seem to care so much. They have lots of wild blackberry jam put away, and that seems to be as far forward as their imaginations can stretch. The men, on the other hand, are acutely aware of impending famine at the village pub where one bottle of orange gin stands in lonely splendor on a once populous shelf, like an austere headland above an unfriendly sea.

I first got on to this state of affairs when I said cheerfully in a neighbor's kitchen that there seemed to be an awful lot of jam making going on around here, only to be met with cold stares and a request for any old crocks that I might have lying about the shed. An old copper washing machine which sagged on three legs out behind the tool house has mysteriously disappeared.

Wine produced in sunspot years, says this week's *New Yorker* magazine, is noticeably better than other vintages.

———

The vegetable garden has a ravaged, weary look, particularly the carrot patch which has contributed more than its share to the inevitable stews which follow on the heels of red ration stamps. The Hubbard squashes, which resented being put over by the fence, have apparently changed their minds and burst into belated golden bloom. But it is too late. Summer is over.

In the warm hollows back of the dunes the black broom buds are popping in the sun. But beyond the dunes, the sea and the sand have suddenly come to life. In summer the sand sleeps in warm soft mounds, and the ocean dozes, breathing lightly against the shore. Then comes a day when the northwest wind arrives. Overnight everything is changed. The beach is swept clean, the miniature hillocks have vanished, and the sand moves in a steady gray migration southeastward. If you listen you can hear it beat with a tiny purring sound against your shoes, and once you have stepped forward your tracks are obliterated. Where there was roundness and softness, there is now hardness and relentlessness. The ocean has lost its misty-eyed look and is intense, alive, blue with icy white trimmings. Over against the outer jetty the white surf breaks and flashes, while against the shore sudden treacherous arms reach in and snatch away the small islands of beach grass, the bits of dried driftwood, the bottles and rusted cans, the bleached red and green planks which were once fishing boats, and the bits of battleship gray planks which were once ships. Here and there the foam is stained a rusty brown—clam boil, my fisherman neighbor calls it. Other more scientific-minded people say the stain comes from disintegrating kelp beds, but I am inclined to hold with the theory of my fisherman friend. I haven't the slightest idea what clam boil is, and neither (I find after questioning him) has my fisherman friend. We simply like clam boil better than disintegrating kelp, and that's all there is to it.

Infiltration of Culture

September 11, 1943

MY NEIGHBOR WAS WEEDING her garden when a soldier leaned over the fence and asked, "What're you doing in there?"

"I'm weeding," she told him.

"Weeding? What's weeding," he asked.

"Why, pulling up weeds," she said.

"Well, what's weeds? That's what I'm trying to get at."

"These are weeds. Right here by the cabbages." And she indicated the weeds.

"Listen," he said, "Cabbages are white."

"Those are cabbage plants," she said. "Haven't you ever seen a vegetable garden?"

"Never have," admitted the soldier. "But I bet you've never seen the New York Giants, have you?" And he went whistling off down the road—the complete metropolitan.

———

Another New York boy saw his first live chicken at Westport a few weeks ago. He was entranced. He bought himself a chicken, built a pen beside the barracks, and spent his off hours tending it. Kindly townsfolk contributed several more chickens which were immediately named (regardless of sex) for famous baseball players. Shortly after the Sicilian invasion, he shipped overseas. The post fell heir to the flock—including Babe Ruth and sixteen downy rookies.

———

I went with an officer's wife to look at a painting job a soldier was doing in the kitchen of her newly rented house. When she told the soldier that the color was too bright, and that she wished he'd put a little more white in the paint, he said, "Listen, Sis! That's the way it come out of the can, and that's the way it should be. The fellows who made this paint know their business."

When she still insisted that she'd like a paler color, he set his brush down carefully on the edge of the can, turned around and faced her. "Listen!" he said, "Have you ever seen a big league game?"

"No," said the officer's wife.

"Huh!" said the soldier with a shrug of the shoulders that said plainer than words that he thought so. And he picked up the paint brush and went ahead putting on the vivid paint—just as it came from the can.

———

Across the road a big circular saw hangs suspended by a rope from a pine tree. A sledge hammer lies in readiness in a sand hollow at the foot of the tree where the Rhode Island hens wallow in the sun. Down the road where a trail forks into the woods, an iron kettle hangs from a low limb, with a short length of iron pipe dangling alongside. Further on an iron triangle is tied to a

Chronology of 1943

September

1 Japs withdraw air base from New Guinea.
2 Allied forces invade mainland of Italy near Reggio Calabria. The exchange ship *Gripsholm* sails with 1,310 Japanese, to be exchanged for 1,250 Americans at Goa, Portuguese India.
8 Italy surrenders unconditionally; Stalino, steel center, falls to Russians.
9 British troops take Taranto. Greatest Allied [air] raids strike northern France.
10 Germans seize Rome.
11 Allies take Salerno, Italian fleet surrenders.
14 Salamaua falls to U.S. and Australian forces.
16 U.S. casualties total 105,205, OWI reveals: 20,104 dead, 28,226 wounded, 32,905 missing, 23,970 prisoners.
20 Army and navy chiefs of staff ask full draft quotas, and state delay in drafting fathers will prolong war.
23 Shoe ration stamp becoming valid November 1 must last six months.

gate. I don't know how many of these homemade air raid alarms are set up hereabouts, but from what I've seen, I'd say we are prepared to the best of our ability to warn the continent of an invasion, should one occur. A tocsin sounded on that old circular saw might be heard around the world. Also we have the man who might go down in history as a runner-up on Paul Revere—I mean the fellows delegated to ride forth and beat the triangle, thump the kettle, clang the circular saw, and arouse the countryside generally. I don't know who holds the job, but it's probably some versatile guy like the ex-jazz band player down at the dock. He's seen a big league game too—if anyone wants to know!

———

When the Captain moved his family into the new house, he moved his lettuce plants too. The lettuce plants are less than an inch high and it is almost the middle of September. I went and leaned over his fence, while he was transplanting the lettuce, and asked him if he'd ever seen a big league game. He said he hadn't, that he came from California, and that's why he was planting lettuce in September, not because he'd never seen a big league game.

Harvest Moon

September 18, 1943

ONE THING MOST OF THE WORLD is doing in common these days is getting up early in the morning. Several people I know have got acquainted with morning for the first time in their lives. And while they don't agree with my trite contention that it is the best part of the day, they are, nevertheless, willing to admit that it isn't half bad; morning bestows its own benefits and rewards—for one thing, you get to see the sun come up, and for another thing, you can hear the early radio programs. After you have listened to a few of the sunrise broadcasts, you can't help coming to the conclusion that some of the bright boys, whose job is to awaken you with gentle words and soft music to the pleasures of early rising, have managed to tumble into the studio barely a leap ahead of John Barleycorn. "Give your daughters to Uncle Sam," one such fellow pleaded this morning at 5:45, adding, I thought, new life to the bond drive slogan which during the previous week had begged only for dollars.

A nearby lookout station on the dunes, which is guarded at all times by two soldiers, was attacked by "the enemy" at four o'clock the other morning in a war game. The "enemy," led by a sergeant, found the two soldiers asleep in their bunks. "What the h—!" bellowed the sergeant. "Don't you know you're supposed to be on guard?"

The soldiers explained that they had been "killed" by an earlier enemy patrol.

"Yeah! Killed in your beds, I suppose," sneered the sergeant.

"No," said one of the soldiers, "We were shot and fatally wounded while on guard duty—but we managed to crawl to our bunks to die." And they pulled the blankets back over their heads.

The dunes here constitute a miniature mountain range which controls, believe it or not, our immediate weather. Last night the sun went down in a thick bank of murky fog, in which zoomed, unseen, a busy and angry bomber, and sounds of machine-gun fire echo back and forth in the fog bank like thunder in a cloud. I crossed back to the lee side of the dunes to see a magnified harvest moon coming up over the rim of a cloudless world. I followed a sandy lane through moon-etched pines to a farm which is exhibiting the biggest potato ever grown on the beach. It was raised by a man who has also raised one of the biggest families hereabouts, and who has also raised a big flock of huge white rabbits which played and gamboled like spring lambs under the moonlight. Rabbits and children were cavorting together. It was such a fascinating sight that it was hard to turn away and give proper attention to the potato which, to give it its due, will have to be boiled in an outsized dish pan.

Luncheon Party

September 25, 1943

PROMPTLY AT NINE O'CLOCK on Friday morning the master plumber drove through the gate, cut a circle around the pasture, backed the rear of his panel truck against the terrace, unloaded a battery of wrenches, set up a tripod, hauled out a length of pipe, tossed out half a ton of nuts and bolts, and said, "Lead me to that stove that needs new coils."

I took him into the kitchen. He stood back and surveyed the stove, sort of getting the feel of the thing. Then he said, "Girlie, if I was you, I'd take this thing outside to do the job." And he picked up the stove and took it outside, lingering in the doorway, with the thing clasped to his bosom, to watch a flight of wild geese stream southward.

"Kind of early, aren't they?" he asked.

"Yes," I said. "They've been flying south for six weeks now."

"Is that so! Means a hard winter when the geese fly south early, doesn't it?"

"Yes," I said, "Say! Aren't you going to put that stove down?"

"Excuse me!" he exclaimed. And he put down the stove. I took a full breath. I instinctively hold my breath when I stand chatting with someone with a stove in his arms. The master plumber took the top off the stove, bent down and looked at its interior. "If I was you, girlie," he said, "I wouldn't put all that pipe in the firebox. I'd sort of bend 'em over the oven."

"All right," I said.

"Give you more room for wood."

"So it will."

"O. K.?"

"O. K.," I said, and he set to work.

It was a pleasure to watch the complicated coils evolve from the length of pipe, with, of course, that extra fancy loop over the oven. A few neighbors gathered, and stood about admiringly, looking into the interior of the truck, which was a complete small workshop, and contained, I am sure, every known size of nut, bolt, and wrench. Tools lay scattered everywhere, but each was returned to its particular place after it had been used, and we saw that there was an ordered plan amid the chaos. In no time at all the coils were installed, and the problem of hitching up to the water tank in too small a space was solved. The master plumber grinned good naturedly when we exclaimed at his ingenuity, and we gathered, from a few words he let drop, that a man who had spent sixteen years fitting steam pipes into the bowels of battleships, and who had put new innards in a gun boat which blew its top, off Singapore in 1908, ought to be able to rig up a little dish-water in a domestic dory. To discover that our master plumber was an ex-navy steam fitter was the high point of the day.

"Let's have lunch," I said, and put a blue checked cloth on the terrace table, and we sat down—neighbors and all—to coffee, sandwiches, and a rare bottle of beer contributed by a neighbor for the personal use of the master plumber. Conversation was purely professional.

"The point is," said the master plumber, waving a cheese sandwich in the general direction of the house, "that plumbing is like the heart. If it stops, everything stops." He looked from face to face to see whether the point had sunk in. It had. "The most common thing the matter with plumbing," he continued, "is what people flush down it. My! What I haven't been called in to fish out of people's plumbing." A reminiscent look came over his face, and he shook his head. "Tooth brushes. Bath towels. Tinker toys. Cakes of soap. You'd be surprised what I've fished out. Soap is the worst. It gets away from you. You can't put your hands on it. You know what soap's like?"

We all said we knew what soap was like.

"Let me tell you one thing. Never flush down a cake of soap. And diamond rings! You flush a diamond ring, or a set of teeth, or a pearl necklace down the plumbing and where does it go?"

"Where does it go?" we asked as one man.

"Right into the main trunk. That's where it goes." We shuddered mentally over the vision of diamond ring lost forever in the uncharted waters of the main trunk. "It's a funny thing about plumbing," he continued, "it's a lot like doctoring. Some kid'll get the earache at breakfast, and they wait until two o'clock the next morning to call the doctor out of bed. Plumbing's the same way. I'll be damned if they're not always calling me out all times of night. And when I get there, I find that Junior threw his father's shaving soap down the thing when he got out of bed in the morning. Wouldn't that get you?"

We said it would. The master plumber looked at his watch, got hurriedly to his feet, stowed away his gear and said good-bye. "Next time I'll tell you why you shouldn't ever try to fix your own plumbing," he said, and started up his motor.

"How's that?" we called.

"It's like doctoring, too," he yelled back, as the car lurched forward. "Just to give you a hint, you wouldn't ever try to take out your own tonsils, would you?" And the master plumber's truck shot through the gate.

Men Must Work

October 2, 1943

MY FAVORITE FISHERMAN is going out of business. He came in yesterday, sat down, stretched out his long Norwegian legs, put his white starched fisherman's cap on the fireside bench, and just sat there with a bewildered grin on his face.

"What's the matter?" I asked.

"I'm quitting fishing," said my fisherman friend.

"Why!" I exclaimed. "My goodness! You just got your new boat not so very long ago."

But he didn't bite on that bait—just sat there grinning foolishly.

I tried again. "Didn't you have any luck with the tuna?" I asked.

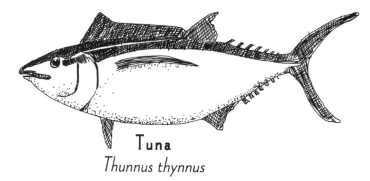

Tuna
Thunnus thynnus

"Not much," he said. "We lay out there, sixty miles off shore, for eight days, and only fished one day out of the eight. Too rough. We just lay below with thirty-foot rollers going over us, and the boat rocking like one of those celluloid toys you push over and it stands on its feet again. We had so much water on top of us that the only difference between us and a sub was that we don't have a periscope. Then she calmed down and we took on about a thousand pounds, and came on in for fuel. Burned up six hundred gallons, we did."

"Oh, well," I said, "you can make up for it next time."

"It isn't that," said my fisherman friend, "that gets my goat. You've got to use gas to get fish. It's that confounded OPA. I get 35,000 gallons and I have to sign my name three hundred and fifty times—once for every hundred gallons. And when I get in, instead of getting home for dinner and getting a hot bath, I have to sit down and figure out deductions and percentages on my deck hand, and allowances deductible from the cargo, besides prove I'm the owner of my own boat and not some Jap spy that's sneaked into port . . . What's funny about that?" he asked with quick suspicion as I attempted to hide an impolite grin.

"Nothing," I said. "Nothing at all." And I smoothed out my features, determined not to let my mind play with the picture of a Japanese spy disguised as a six-foot-three Norwegian. "Go ahead," I said.

"It takes a man all night to figure out what I've got to figure out. But that's all right. I'm willing to do it. But last night when I got in, there was a new regulation waiting. A man's got to sit down now and sign, not for every hundred gallons, but for every five. How many times does that make? Five into thirty-five thousand . . . No, sir! I won't do it. They can have my boat. I'm a fisherman, not a bookkeeper. Do you know what I'd like? I'd like to take that bunch back in Washington for a real boat ride—not just a glide down the Potomac. No, sir! Eight days wallowing in a heavy surf, with nothing but a sandwich to eat, if you can hang on to it, and the engine rattling around like a monkey wrench being shaken up in a paper carton. That's the boat ride I'd like to give them. And when they got back, instead of climbing out on the dock, I'd make them sign seven thousand gas tickets. That's what I'd do. And when they got through with that and wanted their supper, I'd make them read all those regulations they sent me. Three brief cases full! Without head or tail to none of it."

He reached for his white cap, pulled it over his brows at a more than usually dour angle, and stood up. "What I can't figure out is what they're trying to do to a man," he said. And the look of puzzled wonderment appeared again on his face.

"Say, Chris," I asked, as we walked to the door. "How do you cook a ling cod?"

"You scale it, and split it, and salt it down overnight," he told me. "And in the morning you cook it up and have it with boiled potatoes for breakfast. I'll try and pick one up for you next time I come in."

I didn't exclaim, as I might have: "I thought you were through with fishing!" Chris has been getting through with fishing for fifteen years now. But when the "fleet" puts out to sea again, when the gull-like bodies of the white boats lift and shudder at the impact of the first roller that sweeps in from the bar, my fisherman friend will be right up among 'em, heading due west, along with the rest of the boys who go down to the sea with a ballast of OPA regulations battened down in the forward hatch.

An Open and Shut Case

October 16, 1943

DID YOU EVER ASK YOURSELF what kind of a person you are? What distinguishing marks have you that set you apart from the common herd? If a novelist wanted to put you in a book, what would he seize upon as outstanding and characteristic so that he could, in one short sentence, preserve you forever, alive and kicking, for posterity?

I have asked myself that question. And answered it. I am the kind of woman that people always come in at my back door. Starting from that premise, and working both ways, a novelist would have me in a nutshell. Why I am that sort of person, I am of course unable to say—it's a rare thing in this life to get an objective view of yourself, but to have to tell why I am what I am is beyond me. People always enter my house by the back door. They never use the front door. When they leave, they leave by the back door. They never leave by the front door. Such are the facts.

At first I was inclined to attribute my outstanding characteristic to the vagaries of architecture—the house I set up housekeeping in had its back to the street. But since that time, I have lived in houses which face the world with front doors more smugly front-doorish than any in the block, and campaigning congressmen, visiting ladies, and Fuller brush men have fought their way under dripping clothes lines, snagged their nylon stockings on the currant bushes, and tangled their ceiling mops in the power lines to get in at my back door.

I admit that there are kitchens which are fun to come in at. Batches of cookies are still warm on the table, loaves of bread stand on the oven door, and a pound of butter and a knife wait invitingly on the ledge, a cat purrs behind the stove, a canary twits in a cage, a geranium blooms on the window sill. But I don't have that kind of kitchen. I have the other kind. Furthermore, I am not to be found, except at rare intervals, in my

Chronology of 1943

October

1   Allied forces take Naples, 22 days after landing at Salerno.

3   Australian troops capture Jap base at Finschhafen, New Guinea.

10   Yankees win World Series, defeating Cardinals, four games to one.

11   Censorship of weather news is lifted.

12   National Labor Relations Board rules that labor unions have a moral responsibility not to strike in wartime.

13   Italy formally declares war on Germany, by action of Premier Marshal Badoglio.

20   The 48-hour week for war industries is extended to 30 more localities.

29   U.S. and New Zealand troops land on Treasury Islands, in Northern Solomons.
     Jams and jellies are placed on rationed list.

kitchen. And neither is my cat. We can't use it. We've got to keep it slicked up for visitors. We've got to do all our purring in the parlor.

I haven't sat supinely and let this happen to me. I put up quite a fight to change my character. Perhaps if I make the back door look like a front door, I told myself, they won't use it. So I built a brick terrace in place of the back porch, put in a glass door with a white painted bench beside it, an iron umbrella stand on one side and a potted box tree on the other. I moved the garbage can around to the front door and set the cat's dish in a realistic attitude alongside. It didn't work. The day arrangements were completed, friends arrived for tea via the back door, and we had just gotten into our cups when the front door was shouldered open by the fuel man who entered the living room with an oil barrel on his back and the butt end of a hundred-foot hose in his hand. He took the curse off the day for me, however. I greeted him with a pleased grin. It was the first time the front door had ever been used, except for putting out the cat.

My kitchen is seven feet wide and ten feet long, and by the time you get a stove and a sink and cupboard in it, and have opened the door for callers, there isn't a thing to do but turn your back on them and leave them to fight their own way into the living room, following your retreating back. After you get into the living room, which is almost thirty feet long and half as wide, you can turn around and see who's arrived. I never know who I've got until they're standing on the hearth. Thought I had the ladies' guild the other day, and when I got 'em inside, it was the county engineers looking for the Northwest Passage. I was expecting a girl to dinner the other night and when I got her to the table, it was a fellow from North Cove wanting to know if this was the place that had the Coleman lantern for sale. It's disconcerting.

Other people have front doors and people use them. They're born that way, I guess.

Annabelle

October 23, 1943

ANNABELLE IS A POOR NAME for a dog, if you ask me. But that's what the neighbors named her. She was left on my doorstep one morning. I fed her. The neighbors named her. They got tired of hearing me come to the door and say, "Here, Doggie, Doggie!" I guess. So they came over and said, "Here, Annabelle." So now I say, "Here, Annabelle." But it doesn't do any good. Annabelle won't come, no matter how much you say "here" to her—just rolls on her back, waves her big feet in the air, and sticks out a long red tongue which would do credit to an anteater. But if I say, "Don't come, Annabelle," and start to the clothes line, Annabelle always comes. She likes to play tug-of-war with the stockings and towels. If I say "don't come," and start to the village store, Annabelle always comes, trotting in the middle of the road, causing passing motorists to give me dirty looks, and derailing an occasional jeep. At other times she will accompany me like the wolf that went to grandma's with Red Riding Hood, unseen and unsuspected in the brush by the side of the road. I don't know she's there until she pops up in the village store and gets tangled up with the butcher as he comes from the cooler with a side of beef in his arms. When he curses and wants to know who in tarnation's dog that is and I pretend not to know, Annabelle comes and licks my hand and follows dutifully at my heels as I leave the place. If she didn't always come away with an ear of corn in her jaws, or one of the butcher's wife's galoshes, her art would be more telling.

She is, I believe, part fox terrier and part police. She has the hide, coloring, and jaws of a wolf, the ears, eyes, and tail of a terrier. Her outstanding characteristics are digging and skulking. Let me plant some daffodils or tulips, and before the sun sets Annabelle has unearthed every bulb. She goes about daffodil digging with the zest of a child at an Easter egg hunt. And after she has got them all dug up, she sits down and chews them to bits. When we walk to the beach, she doesn't come along with me like any common house dog, but instead slinks from dune to dune, taking advantage of the shadows, and crawling on her belly through the open hollows, so that I do not see her from the time we leave the house until we have arrived at the shore, where she will suddenly spring at me out of the tall grass and take a bite out of my new Kress stockings.

When the milk man and the laundry man come to the house she does not bark and nip at their ankles in the conventional manner, but bleats as if she had been struck and crawls under the house. She does the same thing when visiting neighbors arrive, so that they come in, apologetic and red about the ears, explaining that they did not kick my dog. Even those who named her Annabelle! But let a stranger with a double-bitted axe come into the pasture, and Annabelle runs and licks his hand, fawns upon him, and asks him in for a drink.

"Isn't it fine that you have a good watch dog down here!" a visiting relative exclaimed, seeing Annabelle for the first time.

"Yes," I lied. And I reached down with the intention of giving her a pat on the head. She immediately rolled over on her back, threw back her head, and emitted a series of anguished, high-pitched yips, as if she had been suddenly smitten with the pangs of strychnine poisoning.

"My goodness!" exclaimed my relative. "Why, the poor little thing! Do you think you are feeding her all right?"

"Oh, I think so," I said. "If what it says on those packages of prepared dog food is true, she is eating better than I am."

"Well, something is wrong," said my relative looking down on Annabelle, who had ceased to yip, and was moaning softly through clenched teeth.

My relative, overcome, turned her back on the pitiful sight. Instantly, Annabelle shot to her feet, sprang forward and with a lightning-like slash of the paw, rent my visiting relative's stocking from knee to heel. It wasn't a Kress stocking, either.

Now—has anyone got a wolf, or a cobra, or a gorilla that they want a good home in the country for? Because if they have, I might be able to make a deal with them. If they will take Annabelle, I mean.

Big Game

October 30, 1943

REFUSED THE OFFER of a nice venison steak last week, and have gently put off two neighbors who proffered steaks this week. I like deer meat if someone else cooks it. One of my neighbors said his deer steak was delicious— garnished with meadow mushrooms, a bit of onion, and a whiff of garlic. After I had had my own dinner of wieners, I rather wished that I had gone in for deer steak. While doing the dishes, I picked up a label, in fine print, which had been attached to the wieners and read it. It was then that I wished I'd stuck to deer. Wieners, said the label, are composed of the following ingredients: Beef, Water, Pork Fat, Beef Cheeks, Beef Hearts, Pork Head Meat, Pork Diaphragm Meat, Beef Tripe, Pork Stomachs, Pork Spleens, Salt, Sheep Tripe, Corn Flour, Refined Corn Sugar, Flavorings, Sodium Nitrate. I don't like sodium nitrate. Never did.

———

I know what land mines sound like, now. A platoon went out and planted land mines in the dunes the other day—spent the whole afternoon peppering the dunes with them. Then, at sundown, another platoon went out with the avowed purpose of removing the mines—without exploding them, if possible. But it wasn't possible. At nine o'clock the first devastating explosion rattled the windows, and my dog emitted a tremulous wail, and shot under the couch. After that it was just one explosion after another until twelve o'clock, when, I suppose the boys ran out of ammunition. (I have no way of knowing how many they removed without exploding them. But I do know that if I were on practice maneuvers and it was a question of exploding or not exploding, I would explode. Sort of a hangover from Fourth of July, I guess. And I suspect the army felt the same way.)

An exploding land mine sounds like what I imagined aerial bombs sound like. Only I imagined wrong. Land mines are not to be mentioned in the same breath with aerial bombs, according to an authority I consulted the following morning. "Land sakes, Lady!" exclaimed Gunnery Sergeant Debrovitch, when I asked him about it, and he shook his head pityingly.

"Well," I said. "I thought they sounded like aerial bombs."

"Your chimney didn't come down, did it?" he asked patiently.

"No," I said.

"And your windows didn't bash in?"

"No."

"Or your ear drums bust?"

"No."

"Well, then you know they aren't aerial bombs. See!"

———

These mornings I have the kitchen fire going before daylight. A crackle of gunfire comes from South Bay where the duck hunters, by some sixth sense, know the legal grayness that is sunrise from the illegal grayness that abounds before sunrise. A covey of grouse, tame as hens, spends the day in the rain-devastated vegetable garden, picking happily at the unripened tomatoes, and sharpening their beaks on the winter cabbages. I have stripped the last (and best) small nubbins of golden bantam corn from the withered stalks. Up on the hard sand of the dunes, a doe and her fawn have left fairy footprints along the edge of the willows, where they strike through the sand. Is that a special kind of willow, I wonder, which continues to grow after it has been covered with thirty feet of dune, enabling you to walk through its topmost branches? The evergreen huckleberries are black with fruit, "the which I never saw the like," as Mr. Pepys says. The wood, which I piled no less than three weeks ago, has become the winter abode of earwigs—papa and mamma, and millions (looks like) of baby earwigs resting up for the spring offensive. From across the way comes the slow, easy rhythm of my neighbor's bucksaw eating into a driftwood log.

Huckleberry
Vaccinium ovatum

———

My vote for the Heroine of the Week: The woman who hurried into the post office to-day, a little breathless and with wisps of hair clinging to her damp forehead, and who exclaimed, as she rolled down the sleeves of her gingham dress, "I've just canned two bears!"

Rioteer

November 6, 1943

THAT SERGEANT, the one his men called the General down here because he walked the legs off them, used brass polish on his chevrons, and rode to work in a jeep in which he sat so importantly that second lieutenants used to salute him—that sergeant is now a captain in Italy.

Arnoni had a lot of things to do to get to be a captain—more than most men. The army was willing to let him be a sergeant all right, but when he applied for officers' school his record showed that he had once incited a riot in a union row in New Jersey. Officer candidates are asked to tell what qualifications for leadership they have shown in civilian life. You've got to have leadership to lead a riot, but if you get arrested the army doesn't want you. So, for the best part of two years, Arnoni had to be content with putting all that riot-leading energy into being a sergeant, while back in Washington his application for officer candidacy—with the black mark on it—was scanned and re-scanned by men in urgent need of officers for the backbone of a fighting army.

So Arnoni stayed a sergeant. The soldiers were living in civilian houses here then, and they chopped wood in the living rooms, broke windows, drank beer after supper, and straggled to their posts in the morning. But not Arnoni's soldiers. Their wood was piled the minute an army truck dumped it in the yard. A chopping block was set up in the yard and every day a man was detailed to chop wood, wash windows, sweep out, and keep the home fires burning. The unfortunate soldiers chosen by Arnoni for this job became so proficient that they were known throughout the day of their travail as "mother," and neighborly women made up a batch of red calico aprons and sent them over to the victims of Arnoni's system. They wore them, too, with a sort of bitter humor, and it was a nice sight, on a frosty morning, to look over and see a khaki-clad "mother" with a big ruffled apron around his middle dumping out a bucket of scrub water.

Other soldiers in the area walked to their post of duty in a straggling line, in groups of three or four, like boys going reluctantly to high school. But not Arnoni's boys. They marched. They snapped to attention in front of the house with all their gear on their backs, shouldered their guns and their fox hole digging shovels, and marched off over the dunes—they resembled, in the care-free, far-flung landscape, a moving engine. Arnoni went with them dark, glittering, pressed and polished. And, presumably, muttering curses under his breath, as he was never heard to shout an order. Everyone looked very unhappy. Including Arnoni. Everyone wanted Arnoni to hurry up and get assigned to officers' school. Including Arnoni.

If the men had to be moved some distance away, they rode in trucks. But not Arnoni. The trucks would come, and everybody would pile in and, just as they would think that Arnoni would have to pile in, too, a jeep would drive up and Arnoni would step in, sit in the back, and be driven to the works. It was while being driven in a jeep that young officers would mistake him for a colonel or something, and salute him. That's when they started calling him the "General."

Finally he was assigned to headquarters. Headquarters occupied a cluster of summer houses down the road which boasted a tennis court, painted porch furniture, a Dalmatian dog, officers' mess, visiting ladies, and a general air of easy goingness. But not after Arnoni got there. Arnoni introduced the mother system. The place was thoroughly cleaned up. The yard was raked. The gate posts were whitewashed, the dog chained up, a guard posted, and visiting ladies kept at bay. A young officer who tried to get home via the back fence early one morning was stopped by the guard and made to go around and come in by the whitewashed gate. Arnoni was doing his duty. It was all according to regulation; certainly there was nothing about his conduct that ever faintly suggested the leader of riots. No one even thought of such a thing. But they did begin to think at headquarters that Arnoni was too good for the job he was doing. That officer candidacy was revived again, and everyone put in a plug for Arnoni. There was only one place for him to go, and that was to candidate school. So they got the appointment for him. After he went away, the gate posts fell down again, the dog ran wild, and more people came to dinner at officers' mess than regulations permitted but *c'est la guerre*.

In due time, word came back that Arnoni had been commissioned a second lieutenant. Then word came that he had sailed to Africa as a first lieutenant. Then word came—well, it seems that Arnoni landed on the beach at Salerno in charge of a herd of tanks. They came ashore in the second wave under heavy fire. There was a lot of confusion, and the colonel told Arnoni they better stay right where they were until things cleared up ahead—perhaps all night. But the old riotous blood was running in his veins again; or perhaps it was the blood that made order out of chaos back at officers' mess. Anyway, Arnoni got his lines straightened out on the beach and then—he moved forward. You see, it was against or-

Chronology of 1943

November

1 Federal government seizes 3,000 coal mines in which strikes are halting production.

2 U.S. marines invade Bougainville Island in northern Solomons.

4 RAF planes drop more than 2,000 tons of bombs on Dusseldorf, Germany.

6 Kiev, capital of the Ukraine, retaken by Russians.

7 British Eighth army advances in Italy, taking eight towns.

13 Interned Japanese at Tule Lake, Calif., stage another demonstration.
U.S. war expenditures from July 1940 through October 1943 total 138 billion dollars.

19 Greatest [air] raid in history blasts Berlin, dropping 2,500 tons.

20 January draft call to be twice as large as War Manpower Commission estimated.

23 Another huge air attack smashes Berlin. One-fourth of the city said to be razed.
Makin Island, member of Gilbert group, is taken by U.S. combined forces.

27 Marines take Tarawa, one of Gilbert Islands, after "toughest fighting" in their history.

30 British Eighth army bursts through Nazi lines in Italy, approaching Rome.

ders, so I guess he incited another riot all right, in that quiet way of his. Arnoni's tanks crashed right up to the front and kept on going. And back on the beach, where the colonel had told him to stay, the colonel was killed by an exploding shell. And now Arnoni is a captain.

It wouldn't surprise anybody here if he really came home a general. It certainly wouldn't surprise any of his old outfit. And it certainly wouldn't surprise Arnoni.

About that old rumor of his having incited a riot—well, everyone knows there was never any truth in it anyway. He might have organized, and engineered, and directed a riot, but he never incited one. That isn't the way Arnoni goes about things. His riots are well-thought-out riots, in which everything proceeds in an orderly manner toward a well-conceived objective. Right now his objective is Rome.

What Every Woman Knows

November 13, 1943

WHEN HISTORY WRITES about the era in which we are living, it will come to numerous conclusions. Every phase—economic, political, domestic—will be taken up and discussed by authorities of another, and distant day. What problems were we faced with? And how did we solve them? Time will pass and generations in the distant future will see us only dimly in the well of time. They will try to understand us, to put us together again, like the bones of a prehistoric monster, in an attempt to find out what made us tick. I wonder what they will think of the permanent wave.

As I write this, the Nazis are in full flight from the Ukraine. I ought to be in high spirits. But I am not. My hair isn't curled. We have shot down in the Mediterranean 3,645 enemy planes and damaged 3,000 others since the American and British landings in North Africa. But on Monday morning, November 8th, I woke up to find that my permanent wave had given up the ghost and that my head resembled, on inspection, a peeled seal. (There isn't such a thing as a peeled seal, but the alliteration is good, and describes how I feel. And how I look too. Only I look worse than a peeled seal because seals don't wear collars for the dank wisps of their lifeless hair to fall over.) Is there anything uglier, or more disheartening, or more stubborn, or more spirit quenching than the good straight hair nature gave you, when it reverts back to the wild?

I am wondering about what future generations will think of the permanent wave because I wonder if they are going to do anything about it. I had hoped, in my igno-rance, that something would be done about it in my time. But recent investigations have

IF YOUR CURLS GO

DINGLE DANGLE

MACHINE AND HAIR

ARE SURE TO

TANGLE

DON'T GET SCALPED — COVER YOUR HAIR!

dispelled any such hope. Even to discuss the subject, you must begin with the premise that the permanent wave isn't permanent. I don't know what your dictionary says about permanent, but mine defines it as "continuing or enduring in the same state, or the like, without marked change; not subject to alteration; lasting; abiding; fixed; constant." You don't have to use a dictionary to prove that a permanent wave isn't any of those things, but it's just as well to be authoritative. The permanent wave, then, is not permanent, it never has been, and it never will be.

The Egyptians thought up the permanent. They wound their hair on wooden sticks, wrapped it in henna leaves and buried their heads in the hot sand to bake the curls. The only difference between that method and the one they use today is that they now leave out the hot sand.

The permanent cut a wide swathe before it got back to the Egyptian method. When it was revived during the last World War, operators used to wear big pockets in their aprons to slip the odd charred curl in when they were unwinding the frizzed heads of their victims. The customers weren't told that they had lost a curl or two, here and there, but were left to find it out at leisure. The ultimate in perfection then was a cooked frizz that you couldn't get a curry comb through. If it didn't all come off when you brushed it, it was considered a success. Since that time, the profession has been busily engaged in getting less and less curl into the hair and less "lasting, abiding, fixed, constant" staying power. They get to give more permanents that way. And, whereas you used to look like a peeled seal every five months, you now look like one every three months. Pretty soon, they will have it so you will look like one once a month, and shortly after that the permanent wave will have vanished into the limbo from whence it came. It won't happen in our time, though. It has taken the permanent twenty-five years to reach the peak of production, and it will take it another twenty-five years to decline. That is a more optimistic prognosis. After that time, you can start burying your head in hot sand.

I have just made the interesting discovery that while my dictionary has the word "permanent," it doesn't have permanent wave. It has pompadour, marcel, water wave, crimp, curl, char, bleach, and frizzle. Evidently Mr. Webster thought that was enough. He didn't approve of permanent waves. Mrs. Webster had to go around looking like a peeled seal, probably. And after looking at her for a while, he sat down and wrote the dictionary. It goes to show how a woman, when she is her sweet unpermanented self, can inspire a man.

Away with the permanent wave then. But not, heaven help me, until I have another.

Polish the Kettle

November 27, 1943

I READ ONCE ABOUT A MAN who, when he had something on his mind, used to go out and curry his horse. I do the same thing. I haven't got a horse, but I have a copper tea kettle. When I get mad enough to gnaw nails, and there is no hapless friend or relative about for me to bite, I get out the brass polish and go to work on my tea kettle. At the end of a couple of hours' workout, it shines like a roan stallion.

I don't polish it very often. Don't get mad often enough to keep it in good condition. When the time comes for me to go after it, the grime is fathoms deep. Nobody would know, on looking, that it was copper—nobody but me. And I never look at the kettle unless I am mad, although I use it every day.

Polishing an old copper tea kettle is not a simple job. I begin by spreading old newspapers on the kitchen table. On the newspapers I put the kettle. Then I reach up on the shelf and get down a can of metal polish, carefully read the directions, and set to work hopefully. Nothing happens. The metamorphosis promised by the polish manufacturers does not occur. It has never occurred. But somehow I keep hoping that it will. Like one of those solitaire games you can win once in a thousand times.

The next step, then, is to put away the metal polish and get down the salt and vinegar, make a mash of the same, and apply with ferocious energy. If you keep up a furious tempo you will, in due time, strike copper. Once you get a glint, the thing to do is to grab a chisel, or a piece of steel wool, and go after it (over hill and dale if necessary)

148

never losing sight of it until you have trailed it to its lair. You can then take it up by the scruff of the neck, dip it in a bath of hot soap suds, dry with a soft cloth. It will shine like the morning star.

Yesterday I polished my copper kettle. I had returned from a four-mile walk to the butcher's with my weekly ration of ground round, had placed it on the porch bench while I unlocked the door. I turned around in time to see my pup, with the slim packet in his jaws, disappear under the house. I would have liked to polish the dog. I polished the kettle instead. Life is just one compromise after another, isn't it?

———

The willows and the alders have lost most of their leaves. The brake ferns, instead of turning to sodden blackness overnight, as they do in a rainy fall, have turned to amber brittleness against the dunes. The sky is blue, but fog hangs over the surf and there is a great heaving whiteness as far as eye can see. One of the simple pleasures I look forward to, along with the neighbors' children, is to run up on the dunes and watch the blimp pass by.

It patrols south, on a more or less irregular daily schedule. We hear a sound like someone running a rusty sewing machine in a distant room, and we know the blimp is coming. We see it first sticking its nose out of the fog north of the jetty, where, so slowly does it move, that it appears to be standing still. And it is, almost. There is always a current of air sucking into the harbor at that point, and the blimp has a hard time not to turn tail and come into port. Its engine rattles louder and faster, it swings about and

Sword Fern
Polystichum

swoops landward, but by turning its back to the sea, it manages to sidle down the coast broadside. You gather from watching it that it is the intent and purpose of the pilot to stay at sea, if he possibly can. But if there is any kind of a wind, he can't. He blows ashore like an inflated top, bobbles up and down, stands on his nose and then on his tail, and progresses in a series of landward swoops. The other day he came down so close that we could see the whites of the eyes of the sixteen, or so, crew members in the under-slung carriage. We children don't wish any one any bad luck, but if there is going to be a forced landing we want to be there to see it—one without any casualties, of course.

Classified Funnies

December 4, 1943

AN OLD-TIME NEWSPAPERMAN, the late William Irvine, advised me to always read the classified section of my daily newspaper. That's where you will find the news behind the news in the small community, said he. And I have read the classified section ever since. And many a good lead have I got. We are, of course, no longer a small community, but even so, given only the classified section of my daily paper, I would be pretty well able to deduce how things are going on the home front. And on the national front, too.

According to the classified section, we are, at the moment of writing, a community in desperate need of beauty shop operators, hotel clerks, bellhops, and waitresses. We are in need of old ladies (no age is too old) to sit with small children while their mothers work at essential war jobs. We want washing machines, electric irons, tractors, and bicycles. We want to rent furnished houses and apartments. These are the services and the things we want to buy.

But what are we offered? We are offered (in the For Sale column), herds of cows, teams of work horses, bowling alleys, bulldozers, cornets, and wardrobe trunks—and, oh yes, pigeons! Those are the things we can buy. You can see at a glance that the law of supply and demand has gone off the beam. Multiply the above findings to cover innumerable communities throughout the land and you can see that—well, we are a country with not enough bicycles and too many pigeons, no bellhops and too many bulldozers, not enough old ladies and too many cows. It's a bad state of affairs all right.

But it isn't as bad as it might be. You may not realize it, but the best news on the classified page is that about the pigeons and cows. Over in Europe, they don't have pigeons and cows on their classified pages—not even workhorses. Not even dogs. Not even canaries.

We have, it appears, enough to eat. We can't ride bicycles, or get our hands on a bulldozer, and nobody has time to bowl anymore or to play a cornet. Is that so terrible?

The government had good news for us this week, too. OPA is going to throw some canned pineapple into the ring. And the war department is going to release for civilian consumption 30,000 horse harnesses and 60,000 wooden mustard spoons and any number of plated silver tea sets. That ought to take our minds off nonessentials, hadn't it? Just figuring out what you could do with 60,000 mustard spoons would take your mind off anything. It takes my mind so far off that I have a hard time to get it back again.

The classified section is good sane reading. It is reality. You know what's happening. My favorite characters on the page are those hounds that are forever getting lost. If a week should pass without that ad in the lost and found section, then I would worry. "Lost," it reads. "Two black and tan hounds on North River." Those hounds, to my knowledge, have been getting lost every week for twenty years. If they're not lost on North River, they're lost on the Little Hoquiam, or Quinault, or the east fork of the Humptulips. They've been lost on the Neushkah, the upper Wynooche, the Satsop and Chehalis. They come up missing on John's River one week and play a return vanishing act at Eleven o'Clock Creek the next. They're the losingest hounds I ever heard about. They ought to be in the funnies. Two black and tan hounds who can't stick their noses out of doors without getting lost are really funnier when you come to think about it than 60,000 wooden mustard spoons. If they ever take those hounds out of the lost and found column, I'm going to cancel my subscription.

The Next Best Thing

December 11, 1943

WELL, NOW, HOW WOULD YOU LIKE a nice Japanese family to move into the house next door? You wouldn't? The people back in Freemont County, Iowa, feel the same way. This week, when the War Relocation Authority tried to lease a 600-acre farm for three American Japanese families, the neighbors from miles around gathered at the school house and said no. They said it in telegrams to Congress. They said it in the newspapers and on the radio. And they will keep on saying it. But whether

it will do any good or not remains to be seen. It didn't do us any good when we hollered about the administration deducting the Olympic Peninsula timber from our state bank-roll.*

But to get back to democracy—it seems that we have 70,000 loyal Americans that nobody wants. They don't look like our hide-bound conception of Americans—the kind Abraham Lincoln's phrase, "free and equal," makes you visualize. They aren't as tall as the Lincoln type. They're a different color from the accepted standard. Their legs are bowed and bandied. But they are American citizens. And that's to their credit. It has taken the rest of us thousands of years to get to be Americans, but the Japs—who were a tribe of diapered aboriginal fishermen when Commodore Matthew Perry let them out of their economic Pandora's box back in 1854—have beaten evolution to the draw and got to be Americans in less than a hundred years. It's the first time evolution has speeded up its tempo since the dawn of time. The rest of us took a long time to lay off savagery. Civilization was won by the discipline of centuries. But the Japs got to be civilized by putting on little frock coats and glasses and learning to rattle off the preamble to the Constitution.

Perhaps the people of Iowa are a little nervous about that quick-cooking brand of civilization. Perhaps they have a sneaking suspicion that freedom and equality are only

---

* Olympic National Park, some 900,000 timbered acres, was established in 1938.

meaningless mouthings in the throats of these little puppets, and that if the tops of their skulls could be taken off you would find, neatly stenciled in the top of each one of them the trade mark "made in Japan." Civilization isn't something you can learn in twenty quick lessons.

We've got these Japs on our hands, the "loyal" and the disloyal, some tens of thousands of both brands. They are expert, it appears, at raising vegetables, populating islands, and importing shoddy and imitation commodities. If we keep them and assimilate them in the fullest sense of democracy (and democracy has only one interpretation), we are going to come out a shorter-legged race in the end, with a jackdaw-like proclivity for reciting preambles to the constitutions—and not the haziest understanding of what it's all about.

The question will have to be decided some time. But before the people are given a chance at it, WRA* is going ahead on the principle that we shall assimilate the Japs, whether we want to or not. And a good place to begin, thinks WRA, is back there in Iowa.

Just to find out for myself what the people really think about the subject, I went out and asked them. Jim, my neighbor, was cutting up a pine log when I tackled him with the problem. Said he: "I don't want no Japs anywhere in this country, least of all in Iowa. Why, I was born in Iowa. It's a fine state. So are the people. If they've got to give six hundred acres of land to the Japs, let them have Hyde Park. That's what I say. That'd show 'em, wouldn't it? You know what I mean—if the Japs are good enough for Iowa, they're good enough for New York." Jim picked up his ax, gave a ferocious look around the dunes. "They hadn't better none of 'em come here, either."

My other neighbor, E——, was sitting in his kitchen weaving a fish net, his big figure upright in a straight-backed chair, his fingers busy with a reel of twine. "Wa-a-l," said he, with deliberate rumbling throatiness, "there's only one thing to do and that's to load 'em up on boats and take 'em out over the bar and . . ."

---

*War Relocation Authority

December

1   RAF and U.S. bombers continue massive raids, hitting Dusseldorf region.
    Ration of meats reduced 30 per cent.

3   U.S. plane output for November announced as 7,789.

6   Roosevelt, Churchill and Stalin meet at Teheran, Iran, reach "complete agreement on measures to crush Germany."
    U.S. naval task force raids Marshall Islands.

7   Biggest U.S. battleship, the 45,000-ton *Wisconsin*, is launched.

14 President Roosevelt, returning from conferences, visits Malta and Sicily.

15 American planes raid Greece.
    U.S. heavy bombers smash Jap base on New Britain Island.

16 Prime Minister Churchill stricken by pneumonia.
    German bombers sink 17 United Nations merchant ships.

17 American Sixth army lands at Arawe, on New Britain Island, southwest Pacific.

"No! No!" I exclaimed. "You've got to have a practical plan. You can't do that."

"Wa-a-l," he considered, "then you'd have to do the next best thing. Take one of those islands we're getting over there and put 'em on it. And put that feller that wanted 'em to wash the farmers back in Iowa along with them. That's the next best plan."

Having extracted the opinions of the entire male populace down here, I went home. I had gone out to find out what the people think. And I have found out. I wouldn't be a bit surprised if Iowa feels about the same way.

Blundering Through

December 18, 1943

IN CLEARING SOME LAND between my house and the dunes, I uncovered a prehistoric mound of "square faces," the bottles that bootleg liquor was sold in during prohibition. It is said that the sense of smell is the one which best jogs memory back to a sort of sensual reincarnation of the past. But I don't know. . . Anyway, just to look those bottles caused a tingling sensation in the tips of my fingers, my head swam lightly for an instant, and then I felt that paralytic clutch at the base of the brain, which followed swiftly upon the heels of a nip from a square face in the black days of prohibition. There was, however, no reminiscent odor. I picked up one of the bottles and sniffed it. There was nothing but the smell of dead leaves and rotted earth. I don't like the odor of ether, but just the sight of an ether can doesn't throw me off my base. It just goes to show what horrors must have been locked up in those square faces. The timely purchase of two distilleries by the states of Oregon and Washington precludes, for a time at least, the return of the square face. I got my shovel and buried the bottles under a mound of sand where they will stay, I hope, to puzzle the scientists and mound diggers of the future. I wonder what they will make of them; not the truth, anyway. In March 1926, a long, low, rakish boat washed ashore here and lay wallowing in the shallow surf. There were seven dead men aboard, and a cargo of square faces. When it had been ascertained that the men died from sampling their own wares, they were buried, and the bottles reluctantly emptied and thrown on a heap under the dunes. The name of the boat was *The Milkmaid*, the prettiest name for a bootleg ship that ever I heard.

Was on the beach with my dog one blustery day this week. We were sitting in the lee of a bunch of beach grass smoking our cigarette when we were surprised and puzzled to see a soldier creeping toward us on all fours. He was in full war regalia, and being one hundred per cent furtive that way, he sort of sent a chill down our spine. When he came up to us, he said he was in the midst of a war game, and was on the lookout for some other guys who were supposedly creeping toward him from the other direction. Whoever saw the other fellow first was supposed to let loose with a blank cartridge—just like cops and robbers. He had hardly got through telling about the game when my dog gave a joyous bark and dashed in a beeline to the dunes which (by city measurements) must have been four blocks away, and routed out the "enemy." Everybody was a bit embarrassed, and doggy and I got off the beach. I couldn't help thinking that small trained dogs might do a pretty good job for Uncle Sam. I have since learned that they are being trained for that very purpose for our island warfare in the Pacific.

═══

My fisherman friend came in a while ago and asked if I would join the Roosevelt for King club. Said it would save the taxpayers a lot of money every four years to give Roosevelt the decision, as long as we know it's going to come out the same way anyway.

═══

My forthright neighbors are willing to let Major General Patton, Jr., go on fighting the war for us if he'll promise not to go to hospitals and slap sick boys on visitors' day. The

155

New Yorker magazine, which goes a little deeper into the matter, says, "We advise Old B. and G. against climbing into a tank and single-handedly engaging Marshal Rommel in another tank, as he once announced he was eager to do. Not a calm, ice-cool cookie like Rommel, who wouldn't get cross with a jammed machine gun."

———

The girl next door, who went to California last week to say goodbye to her sailor son, writes that she shared a section with a soldier, a sailor, a sixteen-year-old mother and a very damp baby. The boy insisted on standing four hour watches with the baby, and they were all pretty well damped off by the time they got to San Francisco. There were several other babies in the car—all going down to say hail and farewell to their non-pre-Pearl Harbor fathers.

1944

Changing Times

January 1, 1944

NEW ENGLANDERS PRIDE themselves on the picturesqueness of their coastal fishing villages. The stubbornness with which the natives cling to the ways of their ancestors provides pretty material for magazine illustrators—the pump beside the kitchen sink, the red checked tablecloth, the ruffled window curtains parted to admit a view of bobbing dories manned by sou'wester-clad fishermen, and in the distance the white Gloucester-type fishing boats pulling out to the banks.

An illustrator could get some picturesque shots for a story on the Westport dock, but once he had followed his fisherman home he would have a tough time getting any of that prized New England atmosphere. The first thing a fisherman's door bumps into when you open it, down here, is a big glistening electric ice box. The eye travels across an expanse of inlaid linoleum to an electric hot water heater incased in its cylinder of white metal, and from thence to the double enamel sink set flush in the plastic kitchen counter. I was surprised when visiting one of these typical domiciles recently to see that a typewriter had been added. It looked efficient, but certainly not picturesque, on top of the blue metal breakfast table.

"For goodness sake!" I exclaimed to my fisherman friend. "I didn't know you ran a typewriter!"

"I've learned how," said he. "If you had to write seven reports to the government every night of your life you'd learn to run one too."

———

During the storm, a falling tree took down the power line early in the evening and dimmed out the fun at the general store and skating rink. The proprietor lit some candles in the kitchen, built up a fire in the range, and invited the boys and girls in, to—no, not to pop corn. He dumped three sacks full of ration stamps out on the table and set them to sorting them, after which coffee was served.

———

You know those advertisements put out by the railroads—"Don't travel unless absolutely necessary. Let a serviceman get home for Christmas." A young fellow stationed in Florida, the husband of a business girl I know, had a fifteen-day furlough at Christmas and planned to come home to say goodbye, as his next post will be on the other side of the Atlantic. Halfway across the continent, he had to cool his heels for five days at the station of a mid-western town, while the sisters and the cousins and the aunts of the country went home to grandma's for Christmas. He managed to get one day at home. At the same time, the Associated Press released the photograph of Miss Rita Stearns, who won a free trip to New York as the winner of a "Why I Swoon at Sinatra" contest.

I have heard it whispered that, beginning along about the middle of January, it's going to be impossible for auntie and uncle to go to visit grandma, and that the government will forbid the railroads to transport Rita the next time she wants to go and read a fan letter to Frank in person. This will be pretty hard on Frank and grandma. The only other solution of the transportation problem I can think of is to postpone the war. Or shoot Rita.

Chronology of 1944

January

1   Russians move to within 27 miles of Polish border.
3   Twenty-eight men and two women are indicted on sedition charges.
11 Roosevelt asks for National Service act.
15 U.S. orders C.I.O. to end strikes in defense plants.
18 Two new Russian offensives are opened.
20 Army allows induction of loyal Japanese-Americans.
22 British blast Magdeburg in 1,000-plane raid.
27 Leningrad cleared of Nazis.
29 World's most powerful battleship, the 45,000-ton *Missouri*, is launched
30 Hitler in speech anticipates defeat.

Clams

January 8, 1944

HEARD ON THE RADIO that a group of women consumers have organized themselves and written to OPA to ask why there is such a shortage of common clothes for growing children and such a surplus of $30 women's blouses, satin housecoats, and black chiffon nightgowns. Kind of looks as if there weren't any real family men on OPA, doesn't it?

A neighbor brought me three shaggy manes not long ago. This mushroom, an ivory, fleece-covered cone, is so delicate as to almost shatter at a touch, and yet he told me that it grew so profusely in a clump under the edge of the road that it had lifted the pavement.

When we got through talking about mushrooms, we talked about clams (there's an awful lot of talking about food these days) and Joe said that once when he was working on a road job over back of Bay City, they bulldozed a big fir root out of the way, and underneath they found a great mound of clam shells. The engineer on the job dug down and found stone implements and ashes. The Indians had had a clam bake there before the fir tree took root, which must have been "at least before Columbus discovered America," said Joe. The engineer was a scientific-minded fellow so he scurried around and found an old Indian who came and looked at the mound and nodded his head and said yes, they used to have those parties when he was young. They used to bring canoe loads of clams in and dump them on the bank and invite their friends from the east. It took many days to get enough clams. Sometimes one week, sometimes "two-week." Once (after a two-week dig, I suppose) everybody got sick and died, and clam bakes went out of style. In the high ground over against the hill a populous burying ground bears out the story.

All Quiet

January 22, 1944

WHEN A GOOD SOUTHWEST GALE starts blowing down here, the first thing you do is inspect the kerosene lamps and take a look at the stock of candles. Then you can settle back and wait for that inevitable moment when the electric current fails—because it always does. Off go the lights. Off goes the radio. You light the candles, throw a log on the fire. The wind spurts down the chimney with a roaring sound, sending occasional puffs of smoke into the room. The candle flames flicker. Between gusts, you can hear far down the beach, the roar of wind and sea winding up for another punch. That's the way it was Sunday evening when my neighbors from across the road came to call. Firelight glistened on hip-boots and galoshes, trickles of water dripped from oilskins and sou'westers, and drops from shaken garments sputtered on the fire, as my neighbors took off their things and settled themselves before the hearth.

"I'll be gol-darned if those English aren't scared to death for fear we won't elect Roosevelt again," said my fisherman friend, refusing a cigarette, and producing a brightly banded cigar from the pocket of his green and black plaid jacket. "I don't see how as they'll be entitled to have much to say, once this thing is over. Look at us . . ."

"Did you try that cake recipe?" my fisherman friend's wife interrupted brightly.

"Look at us," continued my fisherman friend. "Now we're starting to stick our nose into Russia's business with Poland, I'll be gol-darned! Are we going to stop and have an argument every time Russia crosses a border? What's it of our business? Let Stalin alone . . ."

Western Sandpiper
Calidris mauri

"I put white icing on mine," my fisherman friend's wife said.

"Take India," said my fisherman friend. "Did you ever ask yourself . . ."

"How about a cup of coffee?" I interrupted rudely. I was not in the mood for taking India. I have tried to take India. But I can't. I flew to the kitchen and rattled the coffee pot. I lathered a loaf of French bread with butter and garlic, popped it in the oven, got out some cold salmon. We ate without India. When they left, the candles had gutted out and so had the storm. A watery quarter moon etched the flying clouds in the western sky as I said goodnight.

"Neighbors are gol-darned nice to have," I said aloud, as I brushed back the embers and put up the fire screen.

———

There is bad news for collectors of those hand-blown Japanese fish floats commonly known as "glass balls." For months none have been found on the beach. But yesterday after the storm, I found a glass ball. It was made of slick brown beer bottle glass without a flaw, and on its slightly flattened bottom it bore the name of a well-known glass manufacturer. A neighbor picked up a clear glass one of strong-looking, pyrex-like glass which had the maker's name running in a circle around its middle. They were about as interesting as a carton of empties: I'm afraid the day of those pretty glass bubbles—blue, lavender, sea-green, and emerald—has passed.

———

A young naval officer was telling about a dinner party at the commandant's house, and the commandant's gracious wife. "How old is she?" someone asked. "Oh, she has quite a bit of mileage on her, all right," said he.

———

The army gave us back to the Indians this week. For two days and two nights there was a great rattling and rumbling as the artillery moved out. Today most of the barracks are deserted and civilian caretakers have been installed. Even my fisherman friend admits to the slightly edgy, nervous feeling which we have all experienced on being left suddenly on our own. It's the way you feel after an illness on the day the trained nurse goes home. The only piece of defensive equipment in this neighborhood is an old circular saw, hanging from a pine tree across the road and the mallet for pounding it in case the Japs arrive. And, silly as it sounds, we have all gone and checked up on it—to see if the mallet is handy and the rope that holds it strong.

Various Dinners

January 29, 1944

A LETTER RECEIVED from the South Pacific contained the following paragraph: "We had a marvelous Christmas dinner, which the steward's department put on with elaborate detail and great effort to please. The bright spot of the day was having about 70 soldiers aboard as our guests, and somehow it made it seem like Christmas to see those boys put away the food. A meal like that to them was paradise. One boy sat down at the table covered with a clean white cloth, rubbed his hands over it and said very quietly, 'I didn't think I'd be alive to celebrate Christmas this year.' This is a very lonely fight in all respects. Money is the smallest item of expense, and all the glowing headlines of your great victories and progress, while they are mostly true, fail to mention the cost. And I don't mean in dollars and cents."

———

Recently my California sister and brother-in-law entertained some Russian naval officers at dinner. "They are awfully attractive, up-and-coming, bright people," she writes. "Only one of them could speak much English, but you never heard so much laughter. We had the Smiths, too. They laughed at the name Smith. Mr. Gneisen explained, 'Pardon me, but in Russia we learn to read English and always in the book there are only two people. Meestaire and Meeses Smeeth. For us it is hard to say *t* when followed by *s*, so we must try very hard.' Then he held up a book as if reading and said in a high, sing-song voice, 'Meestaire and Meeses Smees 'ave gone to Tehicago. Meeses Smees 'as a new pocket book. Meestaire Smees 'as a black pencil.' He put down the book and said, 'We are overjoyed. At last we 'ave met zis Meestaire and Meeses Smees.'

"Their language is something! There is a subtle little *y* sound in so many words. Stalin is Stal-yin (almost stallion, poor fellow), Leningrad is Len-yin-grad, and all the endings change three or more times. For instance, one match is one spichka, two matches are two spichki, and so are three matches. But four or more matches are called spichek. As in French, most of the dirty work goes on far back in the throat where you can't see how it's done, and it would take years to perfect the succession of hisses and whispers that is the Russian language."

House and Garden

February 5, 1944

MY HOUSE IS a weathered-shingled affair, with white doors and window casings. It is also a one-story affair, and should really be called a cottage. I don't call it a cottage, however, as most of my neighbors' two-story houses (and in one instance a three-storied house) are called cottages. The word cottage in this vicinity means a fairly upstanding house, and that lets me out. I've got to fall back on the word house, although, according to fairy tale standards, I live in a cottage.

My house resembles a lanky tabby cat squatted on its haunches, with its snoot to the road and its hips backed into the dunes. The kitchen is in the nose, and the living room takes up the main body of the animal. Two sleeping rooms get what elbow room they can in the narrow wing made by pussy's forelegs. The interior is white-washed, and there are yellow cotton sash curtains at the windows. There is a fireplace of whitewashed brick, a couch covered in red calico, and an old black leather wing chair which needs a cover badly and which, if it

Chronology of 1944

February

1 Chinese advance in northern Burma.
3 Marines capture Namur and other islands in the Marshalls.
6 U.S. army takes Kwajalein atoll in the Marshalls.
16 War Relocation Authority (WRA) transferred to department of interior.
   Heaviest bomb load yet dropped hurled on Berlin by British bombers.
17 U.S. naval task force attacks Truk, main Jap base in south Pacific.
18 Selective service orders farm workers reclassified.
19 Japanese cabinet reorganized, following attack on Truk.
23 U.S. naval task force strikes at Marianas Islands.
24 All of western New Britain passes to American control.
29 Stalin offers peace terms to Finland.

survives the war, it is my intention to cover with green corduroy. Pictures are anything I happen to like at the moment. They are clipped from magazines and thumb-tacked to the wall. My bookshelves are fast filling up with a collection of the Buck Jones Rides Again variety of literature, contributed by well-meaning neighbors.

When city visitors are getting their first glimpse of my interior, I always stand defensively by and interpret it for them. "Well," I say, "If there's one thing you can't say of my place, it's that it's cute. I couldn't bear to live in a place people called cute."

So far I have succeeded pretty well—a hundred per cent, in fact. No one has ever called it cute. Not even those of my friends who don't have any other word in their vocabularies for describing a small house. They just look and say nothing. Or else they tell me about somebody's house that is cute.

One nice thing about having a house that isn't cute is that my fisherman friend doesn't feel intimidated by a verbosity of things when he comes to my house. And neither do his sisters or his cousins or his aunts. They suggest, these neighbors of mine, that it would be nice sometime if I sealed the walls with plywood and varnished it to a nice glisten, and put a good grade of inlaid linoleum on the floor and got myself a blue plush davenport, and a Maxfield Parrish or two. But these things can wait, their attitude seems to say. It seems to say further that, being the kind of person I am, I will undoubtedly arrive at the prosperous state where I can have all those things, but if I don't—they will like me anyway. And so they stretch their legs out easily before the fire and we talk about fishing.

———

I said to my fisherman friend, "I see where you fellows went up and promised the Chamber of Commerce [in Aberdeen] that you would patronize the new fish fleet base there a hundred per cent."

"Aw . . . that's just newspaper talk," he told me. "How's a man going to tell what the bar looks like if he's squatted on his rear in the Wishkah River? And the ebb tide? She don't always go according to that little book. There's things you don't understand. Then too, when you're outside, it's just as easy to run into the Strait of Juan de Fuca as it is into Grays Harbor. And if you've got a big boat, a shark boat, it's a toss-up whether you go into the Golden Gate or run into Ketchikan. You've got to be sea minded to get the picture. We come into Westport because we've got our homes here. We like to live here. What would we go to Aberdeen for? One reason a man's a fisherman is he doesn't care whether he ever sees a movie or not. And another reason is he doesn't like getting bumped about by a lot of traffic. No ma'am, we'll dump our fish right here, and they can take it or leave it. What I'm trying to say is that if it's movies or buying things, it's just as easy to go where they're bigger and more of them. See!"

— and Pursuit of Happiness

February 12, 1944

I RETURNED YESTERDAY from my annual trip to town. I go to town oftener than once a year, but I always refer to the journeys as annual trips. They have all the earmarks of major attacks and disordered retreats. A woman who ought to know tells me that it is easier to go from London to Paris than from the beach to town and back—and shorter if you take a plane. At least it seems shorter than climbing on the local bus.

The return trip is what gets you down. I carried an overnight bag, a suit box, a slippery package containing three salt herring, and various other small parcels, stockings, grass seed, hair pins, fresh rolls, light bulbs, vanilla, and books. I arrived with everything but the herring which I would rather have any day than hair pins, having discovered only recently that boiled salt herring and potatoes with their jackets on are a pretty good dish. You can't buy fish down here anyway. If a man gets a halibut in his net he has to throw it back into the sea. OPA thought that one out. And if you dig a clam you get shot at dawn. (Thought out by the State Fisheries dept.)

For the first time since Pearl Harbor, there wasn't a soldier or a sailor on the bus. We carried quite a load though—deep-sea fishermen who had spent a short furlough in town due to rough weather "outside." By eavesdropping I discovered that one of them had been fined $250 for being trapped off North Head with a nine-pound halibut in the hold. Mr. Ickes announced last week that, what with the submarine menace removed, the fishermen wouldn't have the slightest excuse for not producing a bumper crop in 1944. I made bold to speak to my fellow passengers about Mr. Ickes' statement, and the consensus of opinion was that if the government would loan them an outmoded submarine or two to clear OPA inspectors off the wharf they might make the grade. They said they had thrown overboard enough tons of small halibut to feed Grays Harbor County.

A big bushy cat, of the dark tortoise-shell variety, has appeared from nowhere and is seriously considering making his home with me. He comes down from the dunes in the morning, sits under a huckleberry bush, and stares at the house for a good couple of hours. One of these days I expect him to knock on the door and ask what I charge for room and board. One of the advantages of living with me would be that he would be near to a yellow tabby who lives across the road. She is a widow, I gather, and the mother of five, but I have seen him giving her languishing looks. The most determined suitor I ever knew was a black cat on the Hoh River named, oddly enough, Little-Bear. He used to walk the seven miles to Ruby Beach to call on his girlfriend.

Local Gossip

February 19, 1944

ANNABELLE, THE SMALL DOG the army left on my doorstep, has a new home. At Christmas time, I took her to the veterinary for a thorough checkup, and left instructions that he was to do all that was necessary to prepare Annabelle for an uncertain future. Then (and feeling like a dog myself), I put an ad in the local paper offering to give away an army mascot to anyone who would call and convince the vet that a good home was available. Shortly afterward I received a card from the vet saying that everything had worked out beautifully, including a nice new home for Annabelle.

On my last trip to town, I called on him to find out the details of the transaction, which were as follows: Thirty-two people wanted Annabelle. One prospective customer telephoned from as far away as Neilton. On the third day, the vet called up the local newspaper and said, "For the love of Mike, cut out that ad. I'm being besieged."

"I gave her," he said, "to a nine-year-old boy. I had treated an old Pomeranian at various times which belonged to the boy and which was blind and almost helpless, as it was eleven years old—two years older than the boy. The father had wanted to put the old fellow out of his misery, but the boy wouldn't hear of it. So when the father saw the ad about Annabelle he brought the boy to see her. They took to each other like ducks to water. Boy and dog went home together. And the next day the father brought me the old blind Pom. Chloroform is the humane thing in cases like that."

I turned to go. And then I had an idea. "What kind of dog was Annabelle?" I asked.

"Well, ma'am," said the vet, "I've been in this business thirty-five years, and I've never seen anything like her. She is part police, all right. But I'll be darned if I know what the rest of the fixture is."

"Do you know what I think?" I said, "I think she's part mole. She'd rather burrow than eat. Dug herself a series of underground passages she used to run around in."

"Maybe so," said he. "That would account for her wonderful coat. She was a pretty thing. I'd almost a mind to keep her myself."

━━━

I didn't know it was St. Valentine's Day until Gloriabelle* came to see me. I saw her crossing the pasture with a red card heart in her hand, and then I knew. She came in, her hazel eyes dancing, and handed me the card she had made in school. I gave her an apple and a banana, and we sat down and had a stimulating visit.

"Did the cow have her calf yet?" I asked.

"Not yet. But Mom is watching her. The other cow went off and had hers in the woods. We couldn't find it for three days. Pop went out looking for her, and Mom went out looking for her and they couldn't find her. And one night when they got home, there she was in the yard with her new calf soaked to the hide. Mom is watching because she doesn't want our other calf to get wet."

"It was wet enough Sunday to soak half a dozen calves to the hide," said I.

Gloriabelle smiled politely. "Yes it was. My Uncle Nat and my Uncle Ed came running across the pasture with their coats over their heads. Their tires had given out down the road and they had to run for it. Mom was on the porch and saw them coming. 'You'll never make it, boys,' she yelled. And they came flying up on the porch laughing and breathing loud and then—the sky fell." Gloriabelle sat back in her chair smiling, and pleased with herself, particularly over her complete mastery of the phrase "then the sky fell." I laughed too. It is fun to watch a child cut its first narrative tooth.

"And then," said Gloriabelle sitting up, and putting the final flourish on things, "we had fried rabbit for dinner."

---

*Robert's sister

We, the People

February 26, 1944

THIS COMMUNITY IS THOROUGHLY DASHED this week (and there are going to be a lot of thoroughly dashed communities throughout the land) over the way the army pulled up stakes. It wasn't the departure of the warriors (Lord love 'em) which caused the local citizenry to stare with dumbfounded eyes, but the super-boy-scout way they cleaned up camp when they departed. It's got us wondering whether we haven't made a dreadful mistake all these years to let little Willie belong to an organization which is taught to destroy all signs of human occupation before it leaves Camp Cloudtop. There was more—much more—than met the eye in that burning-up-the-paper-plate business. And how!

To present the facts without further ado: Our army, on the day it moved from its numerous barracks here, built the customary boy-scout bonfire and burned several hundred feet of plywood, thirty-five desks, numerous tables and chairs. Wood which was lying about was carted to the bay and dumped in the water, along with a batch of soap dishes (some of which had never been unpacked from their original wrapping) which bore on their bottoms, when examined by astounded [war] bond buyers, a price mark—30 cents. And were the self-same soap dishes you can get in any five-and-dime for 10 cents, say the local financiers.

When the blow struck (men work a year here to accomplish a plywood-lined home), citizens retired within doors and pulled down the blinds to think things over. When they came out of their houses, they were madder than when they went in. "Just think!" wailed one woman. "There were enough desks burned up for every high-school boy and girl in town."

A leading citizen—she happens to be a woman—who runs a mercantile business, said, "The pity of it is that that bonfire cost more than the bonds sold here would pay for. These people have denied themselves actual necessities to pay for them." They feel rebuffed.

Another cause for worry is the coal pile. For months, the army trucked in coal, and there is a pile the like of which has never been seen before. I can't estimate how much coal there is, but it covers several city-sized lots and stands twenty hands high. The popular belief is that there is enough coal in that pile to heat every home in Westport for five years. Is the army going to make a bonfire out of the coal pile? That's what's worrying people.

Then there is the incident of the shaving mirrors. When the empty half-mile of barracks stood stripped and ready for final inspection, a fire-eating colonel (so the neighbors say) came over from Fort Canby and pounced on the shaving mirrors. The young lieutenant who had been left in charge of demolition had forgotten to clear away the shaving mirrors. The colonel blew out his cheeks, pounded his chest, and read the riot act to the lieutenant. The mirrors vanished.

"I suppose things like that are going on all over the country, and people don't know about it," the woman who had protested about the desks said. "But here the people lived right in the army compound. They saw things. That is unusual, I suppose."

———

Yesterday was cloudless, and the ocean, when I climbed the dunes, basked without a ripple. There was no surf, only a white penciling of froth near the shore in which a crab boat bobbled. On the horizon, a dirigible snoozed southward. In the sky a coast guard patrol plane winged lazily northward in the lee of a couple of gulls.

On the dunes, the willows—that variety which has its roots in the soil thirty feet beneath and comes through the sand to let you walk through its topmost branches—came out this year with orange-colored buds which burst here and there with white popcorn. In the marsh beyond the road some pre-Pearl Harbor frogs croaked—I don't recall hearing frogs since 1941. Perhaps we will have spring again.

Also, Robert came over to borrow the clam shovel.

"It isn't even clam season," I warned. "Remember. Twenty-five dollars fine and thirty days in jail!"

"I know," said he, "but I'm awful restless. Seems as though if I could just dig a clam, I'd feel different."

"Well, you've only got a few days to wait until the season opens," I urged.

"I know," Robert said. "I'll try and wait. But if you'll just give me the shovel . . ."

So I gave him the shovel.

One of these days we'll have a law prohibiting birds from singing until March first.

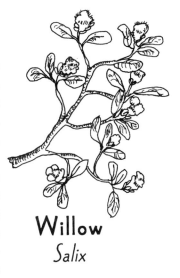

Willow
Salix

Things to Think About

March 4, 1944

A PRETTY SIGHT THIS SUNDAY was the fishing fleet wharf with the best part of a million dollars' worth of deep-sea craft tugging at its moorings. It was a gray, overcast day with a stiff northeast breeze, and a great surf on the bar, so the big shark boats came inside and ranged up in imposing rows alongside the trollers and crab boats. Everything plopped and creaked and groaned, and there was such a heaving of spars and masts as to make you dizzy. General house cleaning was going on, and you glimpsed the red and blue checked tablecloths of sumptuous galleys through the opened cabin doors. Net lines were unwound from their cables to dry, and stretched clear to the end of the dock. Over to the west, beyond the sand spit, great heaves of white surf piled up against the outer jetty.

"Is this prettier than Fishermen's Wharf in San Francisco, or isn't it?" I asked a merchant seaman.

"This is one of the prettiest sights in the whole world," he told me. "And I don't mean because it's home, either."

The old coast guard station house near the dunes by the lighthouse has been torn down. For nearly forty years the white, sloping, red-roofed house has been a focal point of interest and beauty on the beach. I went over to watch John Carstens and helper at their

final job of taking up the big 8x8 piers of the foundation. They were new and clean as if they had just been laid. But John had paid the $10 salvage price the government asked and the place was his. When I asked him what condition he found the house in, he said, "I have never seen a better built house. She was braced and double braced."

"Why didn't you move it to another location, what with houses so scarce?" I asked.

He shook his head ruefully. "They don't allow you to do that," he said. "You've got to tear it down."

"Well, I'll be gol-darned," I said. "Can you beat that?" We stood looking at each other for a minute, saying nothing, while we chalked up another score against an unwieldy, non-workable, hide-bound, red-taped, moss-grown dictum of bureaucracy.

Bonfires—Dogs

March 11, 1944

DOWN THE ROAD toward the "Y" two nice straight lines have been run, denoting the boundaries of a piece of property. A man and a woman, obviously town people, are commencing the exciting job of cutting a new home out of the virgin underbrush. Brush has been slashed away along the tautly stretched lines, and put on a pile which will grow ever bigger, and one of these days there will be a bonfire. If there is a more stimulating or ambition-stirring odor than that of a clearing fire, I would like to know what it is. To get this heavenly aroma, you must have alder and willow, the root of a spruce tree, heaps of brown bracken, cuttings of salal and, if possible, a top dressing of cedar bows. Touch a match to the above combination on a late spring afternoon, and, if you have by any chance begun to feel old, you will feel young again. A clearing fire is an experience you can share with your ancestors way back to the beginning of time. It's something people of the Pacific coast can enjoy—clearing land which has never known the imprint of a human foot, perchance, until, ax in hand, you step from the road, shove aside the salmonberry brambles, step over a rotted, moss-covered log, and take possession of your very own piece of this earth.

Yes, they have bonfires in other parts of the United States, but I notice they call them rubbish fires; they are, I gather from the garden and household magazines, composed mostly of privet hedge clippings, and worn-out galoshes. There is no fine, stimulating, home-building, future-planning aroma emanating from a fire of worn-out galoshes and a dank pile of winter's leaves raked from a concrete areaway. There's no crackle in it. No headiness.

Chronology of 1944

March

8 Record raid on Berlin made by 2,000 planes.

14 Draft deferments for men 18 to 26 in essential industry ended except for "key men."

15 Russian army crosses Bug River.

19 Advancing Russians enter Bessarabia.

21 State department announces that it will have no dealings with the Vichy French government.

26 Russians reach Romanian border.

28 Stephen B. Leacock, 74, internationallly famous author and economist, dies in Toronto.

30 Palau Islands, 1,600 miles south of Japan, attacked by U.S. navy.

Well, there's room for thousands of clearing fires on this rim of the Pacific, and the odor of pioneering will not fail in our time.

Canada and the vast forests of Siberia remain to be tapped. I have had more than one young man say to me lately that after the war he'd like to go over and take a look at Siberia. They may never do so, but if they continue talking about it their sons, and the sons of their sons, will build clearing fires in Siberia. A pioneer is a fellow who likes to be a leap ahead of things.

━━━━

Shortly before the army moved out, and before we knew it was going to move out, I was approached by three local ladies who asked me (because I owned a typewriter) to write a letter to the colonel and ask him to ask the boys not to bring any more dogs down here. The community was suffering from a plague of dogs. Every outfit which came in brought along half a dozen dogs, and turned them loose in the town. They were not allowed in quarters, with the result that every householder found himself the owner of one or more dogs (three in some instances) and the chance to choose more from the unabsorbed canines which roamed loose through the streets.

Well, the letter was never written because overnight the army moved away—and so did the dogs. They really were somebody's dogs after all, it appears. As the trucks moved out, Rover and Red, Pete and Blackie, Wolf, Zero, and Slats were snatched aboard and taken along to face the uncertain future with their masters. They are today probably roaming the streets of some other town, where they will eventually inspire the ladies thereof to write letters to colonels. One or two of them will, if properly stowed away, arrive overseas where they will be quarantined and released to their outfits—after some other writer has written an appropriate column about a boy and his dog.

Home on the Range

March 18, 1944

MOST ARTICLES ON HOW TO have a victory garden start you off on a bright spring morning, amidst a twittering of birds, with instructions to "first spade your ground." I have read numerous articles lately—have even dragged out last year's garden articles—and I have yet to find one that tackles the subject with any but the most conventional curtain raiser—blue sky, bird chorus, glistening dew, and you (in freshly laundered slacks, a gay kerchief over your finger wave, and a song in your heart) blithely spading.

All right, boys, what about that evergreen blackberry vine? The one that grows between the garage and the fence where you want to plant the cucumbers. Don't pretend you don't know what I mean, either. If you are gardener enough to write about gardening, you've had an evergreen blackberry in your past. And you didn't spade it up either. You can't get within striking distance of the heart of the thing, what with its ten-foot-long, flesh-gouging tentacles scoring you across the shoulders and saw-toothing across your insteps. I know because I've got one. And it's got me down. Every day I go and look at it. Occasionally I have struck at the thing with a long-handled hoe. And it has struck back.

There's nothing I can do about it until the manpower shortage eases up. A really comprehensive garden article should begin: First get your fallers and buckers—.

———

I am happy to report that my old black leather wing chair has been lashed into a green corduroy cover, and looks as fit as a stout matron in a new corset. I had intended a rather casual slip cover—something within my scope, which is limited, I assure you—when my fisherman friend came in. Just as I was adjusting my handiwork. He sat back and watched my fumbling tuggings. In a moment, he was down on his knees smoothing the material, and in another moment he had gone to the dock for a piece of line and a net needle. And boy! Did he lash that cover to the mast!

After an hour's stitching, he stood back and considered the job with apparent approval. "She won't give now," he said.

"She sure won't," I said. "If she does anything, it won't be give. She'll explode. That's what she'll do."

I haven't sat in her yet. I'm afraid to. You never saw a more thoroughly covered chair in your life. Seaworthy. That's what she is.

The Mayor's Parlor

March 25, 1944

SOME MONTHS AGO, I told of the little English woman who was found roaming the streets of Aberdeen in search of "the mayor's parlor." She had some business with the mayor, and in England the mayor's office is known as the mayor's parlor. Well, as it turned out, the mayor of Aberdeen didn't have a parlor. Business had to be done across a shiny oak desk in the forbidding presence of a lot of dark metal filing cabinets. I remember experiencing a feeling of regret that the mayor didn't have a snug little parlor to entertain the foreign visitor in. Imagine my delight, therefore, when I discovered this week that the mayor of Westport DOES have a parlor. Yes, ma'am, we've got a mayor's parlor down here. And it isn't a parlor to sniff at, either. It's a parlor that you wouldn't be ashamed to entertain Mrs. Roosevelt in, or the prime minister of England, if you want to get right down to brass tacks. But I'm getting ahead of my story, which is how I happened to get into the mayor's parlor.

I got into the mayor's parlor because Mr. Frank Hill, a public-spirited citizen of Aberdeen and Hoquiam, came down here as a representative of other public-spirited citizens to see if it would be possible to salvage for public use any of the equipment of our army cantonment before it is junked and destroyed. The *piece de resistance* of the investigation is the water system, including a great storage tower, which, if this water-less community could get its hands on it, would be useful in establishing an icing plant to help preserve the million dollars' worth of fish we land down here each year.

"Will you introduce me to the mayor?" asked Mr. Hill. So I said of course I would—just as soon as I found out who the mayor was, I'd introduce him. So we went and found out that the mayor was Mr. McDonald, and we went to his house, where I introduced myself and Mr. Hill. We went in and sat down and Mr. Hill said to Mr. McDonald he'd come down to get a few facts. Mr. McDonald looked portentous. And I looked at the parlor.

Mayor McDonald's parlor is delightful. It is papered in a sky-blue grass cloth, carpeted with a two-toned blue, deep-piled carpet, curtained with gold brocade, peppered adequately with upholstered barrel and wing-type chairs, and has, to divert the eye, a modern walnut three-decked glass cabinet filled to the brim with a collection of figurines. While Mr. Hill was asking Mr. McDonald if it was true that the contractors kept on building the water tank after the army had abandoned the camp, and kept on with their job of laying a reputed $75,000 worth of sewer pipe, I sat enjoying the mayor's parlor.

All the time there was a sort of whirring, churring noise going on—sort of a warm comfortable sound—and suddenly Mr. Hill looked startled and quit talking and said, "What's that?"

Mr. McDonald said it was the motor of the electrically driven fan on the oil heater. We admired the oil heater, which was a nice big one, giving off lots of heat. Mr. McDonald said it sure was a honey. "I'm telling you, you can stick your finger up that flue anytime and you won't find a bit of soot on it," said he.

Mr. Hill asked if it was true that one of the contractor's specialists on the water tower project had said that as soon as they got the tower painted, they were going to tear it down. The mayor replied that he understood that when a contract is two-thirds completed, the rule is that the contract can't be canceled, and that the project must be finished. "So they can't tear it down until they get it painted. That's the general understanding."

He offered to take us over to the army compound and introduce us to a man who lived inside the gates and could give us an eyewitness account of the army's extravagant doings. So we all got up and left the mayor's parlor and went out into the gusty night.

"There she is. There!" said Mr. McDonald, and pointed to a vast, dark blot which loomed overhead among the pines. "That's the water tower."

"They've certainly got good roads in this camp," said Mr. Hill, as we rolled along the expensive, perfectly engineered highway which curved in and out, for the best part of a mile, among the trees.

"Yes, sir," said the mayor. "Those gravel trucks was running down here for months. Night and day. The army certainly does things up brown when it does 'em. Take that water tower . . ."

But I heard no more. I was tired of towers. I closed my ear to the discussion. I was also disturbed. I had written about the army burning up some plywood and desks, and here delegations were coming down to investigate hundred thousand dollar contracts. I had shot at a gnat—and brought down a water tower. I wished acutely that I was back in the mayor's parlor. When it comes to big business, you can leave me sitting by a nice, warm, churring, electric-fanned, oil-burning stove, with my feet on a blue velvet carpet.

To Bee or Not to Bee

April 1, 1944

I HAVE, I REGRET TO SAY, become the custodian or curator (or whatever the term is) of a bee. And unless I do something about it pretty quick, I am well on my way to becoming the keeper of a bee. I don't mind temporary custody of a bee, but to become an out and out keeper of one is something else again. Once you have

Chronology of 1944

April

2   Russian troops enter Romania. American planes bomb Austria.

4   House committee reveals that the federal government now owns one-fifth of the land area of the continental U.S.

5   Wendell Wilkie withdraws as Republican presidential candidate after defeat in Wisconsin.

10   Odessa falls to Russians.

13   Allied troops halt Jap drive near Kohima, in India.

18   Major league baseball season opens.

24   Mrs. Sarah Jane Swanson, 113, said to be the oldest American-born resident of the U.S., dies in Chicago.

26   Federal troops take possession of the Chicago plant of Montgomery Ward Co. by order of FDR when the company refused to obey his order to recognize a C.I.O. union.

27   Fifteen workmen die of suffocation while repairing naval ship in Portsmouth, Va.

28   Secretary of the Navy since 1940 Frank Knox, 70, dies in Washington, D.C.

29   A thousand U.S. bombers raid Berlin.

30   Japan's mid-Pacific base, Truk, is raided for 35th time.

set yourself up as a keeper of a bee, you are, I have discovered from avid reading, responsible legally for the bee's social welfare, and for his comings and go-ings-on within a one-mile radius of your home. If my bee, say, chooses to swarm on old man Pullen's bald head down at the Corners, it is up to me—with the aid of every device within my power—to try and dissuade the animal out of the old boy's whiskers and to return said bee to its rightful domicile. Also I am supposed to provide, in case of a hard winter, enough sugar to the amount of some unheard of number of pounds, to keep my bee, and his progeny, from starving to death. Also (although it isn't in the bee book yet—but it will be), if my bee produces honey, I have to immediately apply to the OPA for a set of forms to fill out, and commence a daily correspondence with Washington. If I wring a profit out of him, I must add it to my income tax. So you see why I don't want a bee.

But I have one. The fact that he broke into my house and now lives there will not be taken account of by the authorities. I've got a bee, haven't I? "All right, let's get a look at your books." That's OPA's attitude. And the attitude of the bureau of internal revenue.

I first saw my bee on a warm February day. He was nosing about the eaves of the house, banging up against the shingles, and even a child could have seen with half an eye that he was determined to get inside. Sure enough! In a short while, he came in through a knothole in the ceiling, strafed around over my head for a time and made an exit through the knothole. He was a big black and yellow fellow, and seemed, at first sight, as he zoomed across the back of my neck, to be about the size of a Boeing bomber. Further acquaintance with him, how-ever (and a natural feeling for truth), forces me to state that he really isn't that large—something more in the nature of a closed fist in size, with added wings. In flight, as he takes his daily constitutional between the dinner table and my desk, he sounds like an electric riveter sign-ing off on the hull of a battleship. You know how you say of a boy, "He is all boy"? Well, my bee is all bee. One hundred per cent.

Daytimes he goes off about his business (which I can only hope is something worthwhile and legitimate), but he spends the nights at home. If it's a warm night, he stays in the attic, but if it's cold, he prefers to stay in the living room; in which case I have to remove him bodily, as he appears reluctant to go to work on frosty mornings. This I do by enclosing him tenderly (an assumed attitude) and respectfully (the real McCoy) in an old sweater and depositing the whole on the door step, leaving the little fellow to blast his own way out of the woolly labyrinth. This he does with the effort of a caterpillar tank fighting its way through a cotton field. Released, he takes off with a beautiful backward, up-zooming flight, not yet mastered by man. When he has reached an elevation of 15 or 20 feet, he pauses for the merest second, turns his turret guns on full blast, and heads into the breeze.

He makes about five flights a day, returning to his attic where the ceiling boards amplify his goings and comings. Sometimes I catch a glimpse of him hovering about the eaves on these return journeys, but look as I will, I can't see that he has any cargo aboard. But it is there, all right, stowed deep in the hold. Once he came in very low, and so burdened down that he had a hard time lifting himself to the level of his hangar door in the eaves. He made a leverage of whirring wings and lifted himself by sheer unmitigated guts and determination. The battle took seconds and several times he slipped back like a helicopter in reverse, and I feared he would crash.

———

Having gotten a bee of my own, I took a little pain to find out what the encyclopedia had to say about him. What I read was good, bad, and astounding. "The Humble-Bee (Bombus) is a genus of social bee," said the book. (Pretty good encyclopedia I've got, isn't it?)

"Humble bees do not form communities so large as those of honey bees . . . seldom more than two or three hundred occupying one nest (that's the bad part).

"Humble bees differ from others in their females existing together in the same community without seeking to destroy one another." (That's the astounding part.)

In rebuttal, let me say that I do not advise rushing rashly into bee keeping. A bee is a responsibility. I was having a good gossip with the milkman at the gate yesterday morning (he is trying to sell his chickens off. Can't afford to buy feed for 'em) when I suddenly threw up my hands, let forth a yell, and started running toward the house.

"What's the matter?" he called after me.

"Oh nothing," I called back over my shoulder. "I forgot to put out my bee."

Crime in the Country

April 8, 1944

WE ARE TAUGHT NOT TO ENVY our neighbor's good fortune, or to covet their worldly goods. But, so help me, sometimes self-discipline breaks down, and I find myself frankly covetous of my neighbors' goods.

To covet, says my dictionary, is to desire; to long for; to crave, especially something belonging to another. And if you are covetous, says the same book, you are inordinately desirous; avaricious. It all sounds pretty black, doesn't it? And it is. It's even blacker than it sounds. There are depths and shades of blackness to which you can descend, once you have started coveting. Once you really let yourself go all-out with inordinate desire for something-belonging-to-another you will, unless you nip the thing in the bud, find yourself a thief. You will, if opportunity offers, lay hands on, possess yourself of, and bear away the inordinately desirous object. And blacker yet, if opportunity doesn't offer, you will create opportunity and, in the dead of night and the dark of the moon, TAKE what you want.

It was along about February that I first started coveting my neighbor's goods. I would go to sleep thinking about my neighbor's goods, and wake up thinking about my neighbor's goods. Every night I would think longer about them, and I would begin thinking earlier each morning. Finally the covetous night grabbed the tail of covetous morning, and they merged—into irresistible impulse. I jumped out of bed (it was early yesterday morning), got furtively into my clothes, slunk out the back door and made my way to the tool shed. Hastily grabbing up the implements which I would need, I dumped them in a wheelbarrow. There was a pair of canvas gloves on the bench, and I put them on. The sun was poking its first yellow finger over the misty horizon when I opened the gate and started down the road toward my neighbor's pasture. I swore, under my breath, at the confounded noise the wheelbarrow made on the graveled road. In spite of all I could do in the way of muffling the sound—running over the new dandelions and the moss patches at the site of the ditch—I still sounded like a piece of county road machinery. "My kingdom," I muttered to a startled robin, "for a rubber-tired wheelbarrow!"

Early morning is very nice. It is enjoyable even on a thieving expedition. Over against the pine woods, the pussy willows had burst into yellow, lacy bloom. The brown

Salal
Gaultheria shallon

salmonberry stalks were sporting their first tufted red and green bowknots. Wild straw-berries spread neat, flat doilies by the ditch, and in the shadow of salal patches lilies of the valley showed their first translucent leaves. Three quail, caught red handed in the pea patch, ran across my bow. I turned into my neighbor's pasture. The grinding sound of the wheelbarrow turned to a soft creak, as we humped over the clods and tussocks. I had reached the scene of the crime.

My neighbor, I knew, was not at home. His ax was still impaled in the selfsame pine knot, where it was stuck when I cased the joint the night before. His car, half in and half out of the garage with one rear tire flattened, was just as it had been since his gas gave out on Saturday night and when, calling upon God and waking the neighbors, he had kicked the rear tire flat, and walked off into the night. "Gone down the beach for a few days to get a hold of himself," the neighbors said. His cow, the one which got caught in the bear trap, was dead. But he had other cows, I reminded myself. Many of them. Over beyond the marsh he kept a whole herd of cows. Why, the man was rich! He wouldn't miss what I had come for! what I envied, what I coveted. I took the pitchfork from the wheelbarrow and, with a song in my heart, I began scooping up the gold of the pasture.

There will be vegetables in my garden this year. Vegetables for everyone.

Alone—by the Telephone

April 15, 1944

WAS MADE ALL ELATED this week by the arrival of Mr. Mumaw with my long-promised telephone. If you're not on the rural line you're sort of out of things in the country. Another thing—if you haven't got a telephone, you're liable to suffer from long spells of quietude. But once get one of those big varnished boxes, with its outsized bells, on your wall, along with a projecting shelf for writing things down and a crank for calling the rural operator, and quiet flies out of the window—never to return.

So when I saw Mr. Mumaw coming across the pasture with a telephone and dragging a reel of wire behind him, I went to the door and welcomed him with hearty words. I had ordered the phone a year ago, but those old hand-cranking instruments are hard to get. But now he had got one. I was a little disappointed to see that the one he brought was not the deluxe gay Nineties model of my dreams. It was smaller, with fewer gadgets on it. The bells were the discreet modern kind, small, black, and inconspicuous,

and not the big shining, cup-sized, nickel, dinging kind which announces, with whole-souled shrieking din, to subscribers for fifty miles around that someone is on the line. If those bells don't turn out to be lusty, I thought, I'm liable to miss something. What if I'm out cutting broom brush when Mrs. X calls the store to see if they've got any pork and to say that she is making doughnuts. And in the mornings when my fisherman friend calls the dock to ask if "it's still bellerin' off the North Spit." What if I don't get in on that? And all the discussion about whether it's right for M——'s wife to serve on the school elections board again and rake in another easy five dollars for the fifth consecutive year, and is this a democracy or isn't it.

"Do you think I can hear it ring outdoors?" I asked a little doubtfully.

"Oh, yes," said Mr. Mumaw. "You'll get used to it."

I went back to my tasks while Mr. Mumaw strung wires, bored a hole in the side of the house, rattled across the roof, and went about installing a telephone generally. In a little while he will be finished, I thought, and—well, life will begin. The bell will ring, I will take down the receiver, lean a comfortable elbow against the wall and listen. And in a short time I will know all. All there is to know on this beach.

I thought of the pleasure I had with a rural telephone on the Olympic Peninsula. Particularly at Kelley's ranch. Roy, a big, barrel-chested, six-footer from Oklahoma who worked there, had, as his particular job, the answering of the telephone. Whenever it rang, no matter whose number, it was the custom to take down the receiver, listen to the conversation, and throw in whatever enlightening, contributory information that came to mind. Roy was chosen for the job because he had the right kind of voice. When Roy bellowed "Hello-o-ooo!" you could hear him in Oklahoma without a telephone. That's the sort of voice you need on a rural line.

"Hello-oo, Mrs. Winn," Roy would roar. "Did I hear you tell Mr. Smith that a green sedan with a Missouri license just crossed the river? That'll be that schoolteacher we're expecting from St. Louis."

He would turn from the phone and tell Mrs. Kelly she'd better build a fire in the room off the sitting room as the schoolteacher's wife had an attack of asthma. He'd got it by listening on the phone earlier in the morning when the party stopped at the Humptulips store for some cough drops.

"And that guy that went over to the North fork this morning got a good catch of trout, so we'll be having fish for dinner," Roy would add, for good measure. "You better mix up a little tartar sauce."

And now I was to know again the convenience, the joy, of intercommunication as practiced on the rural telephone. Mr. Mumaw wound the crank and got the rural operator at South Bay Bridge. "There!" he said, "she's installed." He gathered up his tools and started for the door.

"Wait a minute," I said. "You didn't tell me what my number is. How many bells do I answer to?"

"Oh, you won't have to worry about that," he said. "This is a new line we're starting. You're the only party on it. There will just be one bell—and that will be yours. There won't be any other customers on this line until after the war."

Wild Life

May 6, 1944

WHEN THE SUN HIT around to warm the west side of the house one day this week, a swarm of bees came and cased the joint. A place under the eaves, where a missing shingle gives access to a snug little hide-out between the two-by-fours, was the objective of a thorough research by the bees. I would have given the nook over gladly, but they (like so many groups who get the upper hand) seemed unwilling to grant me any privileges whatsoever—particularly the one of working in my own garden. When I tried to spade the patch alongside the house, they zoomed around angrily making threatening passes at my ears and the back of my neck. I went and called in Robert, my fifteen-year-old neighbor (and the only available male hereabouts) for a consultation.

Robert stood looking at the bees for a long time. Then, "Those are tame honey bees," he said. "They are a new colony from somebody's hive, and they're looking for a home."

"Well, darn those people that turn their bees loose on other people," I said. "Why can't they build a hive for their own bees?" I was pretty mad. I've had other people's cats and other people's dogs to take care of. And now if I didn't watch out, I'd have to take care of somebody else's bees.

We swopped at them for a while with poles and brush, trying to discourage them. We finally soaked rags in fly spray and poked them under the eaves. This made the bees angrier than ever, and Robert and I had to run for our lives. We went into the house.

"Dad and Mom had bees in their bedroom wall last year," Robert told me. "They finally had to tear down the wall. They made so much noise buzzing and humming, and started in so early in the morning that Dad and Mom couldn't sleep."

After this bad news, it was a relief, when we went out later, to find that the fly spray had worked. The bees had gone.

The next day Robert came over again. He stood looking at me dolefully for some time. At last he said, "You know those bees? They're back over to our house. Mom wants to borrow some fly spray."

Yesterday (and by now this begins to sound like one of those repetitious children's fairy tales), Robert came over and told me they had gotten rid of the bees, but that they were then raising Cain over to Grandpa's. Grandma was trying to hang out the clothes, but had to give it up. And could he have some more fly spray?

Today, when I returned from the village store, Robert was waiting for me at the gate. "You know those bees?" he said.

"Yes?" I said.

"They're back in your eaves."

Man vs. Nature

May 20, 1944

THE FATHER OF ROBERT, my fifteen-year-old neighbor, isn't a very big man, but he is a good fisherman, owns his own boat, nine children, two cows, several hundred chickens, and a "place," over on the edge of the swamp. He isn't much for drinking, but once and a while he stops for a glass at the local tavern, to rub elbows with other men of the deep, and pass the time of day in that strange offshore jargon which is the language of his trade.

"Dad isn't a very big man," Robert told me, "only five foot three. But when he sits up on the stool he's almost as large as the next guy."

Well, according to Robert, Dad was sitting up amongst 'em at the tavern the other night and the boys were saying what they thought about things in general, and Dad disputed something a big six-footer sitting next to him said. The big fellow looked down his gills at Dad and said with lofty condescension, "And may I ask who you are?"

Dad drew himself up to his full five feet three and said he was the master of the *Dolly M.* "And may I ask who YOU are?" said Dad, putting a fine edge of sarcasm on the words.

"I'm the master of the *Sea Bride*," said the big fellow in a such a loud, proud voice that everyone set down their glasses to lean over and look along the bar.

The next morning when Dad got down to the dock there was this *Sea Bride*. Eighty feet long, white as a gull, and breathing on water like an eager bird ready for flight. Dad dived down into the hold of the *Dolly M.*, and stayed there until the white bird sailed. The *Dolly M.* is forty feet long, with a teak and mahogany cabin and the best engine Dad could buy. He got to thinking that he was pretty proud of her. Or had been, until he saw the *Sea Bride*. She is swift, too, as a little tern. So Dad started up the engine and put off in the wake of the *Bride*. And when they came to the bar, Dad cut straight off across the spit, instead of going around, like they do in rough weather. Some of the other boats tried to follow him, but gave it up, including the *Bride*. Dad didn't have any ballast in the *Dolly M.*, so it was rough going. She shipped a sea or two and shot to the crest of each foaming break, but she kept her nose nor'nor'west and arrived off Split Rock ahead of the best of them.

"When Dad got home that night," said Robert, "he was just as cocky as ever."

=====

My fisherman friend came over not so long ago, looked uneasily about my whitewashed living room and allowed that I'd "better caulk up these seams." Up until that time, I had been blissfully unconscious of the cracks in my boarded walls. But if a man's going to feel nervous in the room, as if the sea is liable to leak in and swamp him, it's up to me to do something about it. I have, therefore, acquired a putty knife, putty, patching plaster, and enough resolution to make this place seaworthy before the equinoctial storms strike. When I come up out of the hold, along about September, this will be different place, one you can ride out a gale in.

Chronology of 1944

May

1   Pulitzer prize for novels awarded to Martin Flavin for *Journey in the Dark*. Musical comedy *Oklahoma* wins a special award for authors.

3   Most meats are removed from rationing. Steaks and beef roasts are principal exceptions.

7   Allied forces in Italy turn back German counterattack near Anzio.

9   Sevastopol, Black Sea naval base, falls to Russians.

11   New draft regulations defer most men over 26.

16   George Ade, famous humorist, dies at 78 in Kentland, Indiana.

18   Cassino, Nazi strongpoint in Italy, falls to Americans after long seige.

20   Communist party votes to disband as a political party, but to continue as an "association."

28   Allied bombers strike at German synthetic oil plants in Leipsig area.

31   Synthetic sugar is produced at the University of California. Process is too expensive to be practical at present.

What Every Sheriff Knows

May 27, 1944

A SHINGLE TACKED TO THE DOOR POST of the square, shingled cottage bore the legend "Sheriff," and a shiny black panelled truck was parked outside. I felt a little silly when I knocked. Here I was disturbing an arm of the law on Sunday afternoon. And about nothing. It had seemed like something until I stood on the porch, but now for the life of me, I couldn't help but feel that the sheriff would know instantly I was a foolish and over-imaginative woman. And treat me accordingly. I am a foolish and over-imaginative woman, I said to myself. And, furthermore, all women are foolish and over-imaginative to sheriffs, so why should I even bother to come here and tell a man something he already knows. Just what is it you have come for, I asked myself severely, but before I could formulate a good answer to my question, the door opened and I found myself in the sheriff's living room.

It was a nice big room. Not gay, but comfortable, with a radio going full blast, and an odor of pot roast coming from the kitchen. The sheriff, a square set bring-back-your-man sort of fellow, stood looking at me out of noncommittal hazel eyes, and a weather-ear cocked in the direction of Fred Allen and the radio. The insignia of his office, a gun in a holster, lay on the table, and fulfilled its function of impressing me with knee-quaking awe. He didn't say a word, but stood looking off over my head, and I knew it was up to me to lead with my ace.

"Is it true," I burst out, "that someone shot at my neighbor when she was taking the cow to pasture this morning?"

The sheriff didn't answer. Just stood looking off over my head. The old give-a-woman-enough-rope-and-she-will-tell-all technique.

It worked. I was started now, and nothing could stop me. "The neighbors say," I rattled on, "that after her husband went to work this morning and my neighbor was putting the cow out, she was shot at with a twenty-two," I added with proud technicality. "The shot came from the barn, because when she turned around she saw the barn door swing shut. So she ran in the house, got the children, put them in the car and drove down here to find you . . ."

The sheriff looked concerned. The Fred Allen program had come to an end. He strode to the radio and turned it off. He took a couple of turns up and down the room. A slow grin came on his face. The how-to-soothe-the-imaginative-woman expression.

I gave him something to work on. "If there is a murderer running around here, I want to know about it, I . . . I'm afraid . . ."

"Now, now!" the sheriff said. "I don't think there is anything to be afraid of. We went down there and looked around and we can't find a single footprint."

"Didn't one of the neighbors pick up an exploded shell?" I challenged.

"No, no!" the sheriff said. "There wasn't anything like that. We didn't find a thing."

"Well, what was it then?" I almost sobbed. "I don't want to sit down there at night, being afraid . . . I . . ."

"Sit down," the sheriff said gently. And he pulled up a chair.

I sat down, breathing hard.

"Now listen," he said. "It wasn't anything."

"But the shot," I wailed.

He seemed to consider. I've got him there, I thought. He can't get around that shot. Other people heard it too. My neighbor's mother for one. I hadn't heard it myself. But perhaps I had, now that I came to think about it. When I was cutting kindling, hadn't I heard something that caused me to pause, set down the ax, and listen? It must have been the shot.

"You can't get around that shot," I said.

The sheriff sighed, and sat down in a chair, facing me. I'm going to get at the truth now, I thought triumphantly.

"The truth is," said the sheriff looking straight into my eyes with that gentle but firm expression that you use when you tell a child about the fallacy of Santa Claus, "that there was no shot."

"No shot? What . . . What was it then?"

"Just another . . . Just a foolish, imaginative woman," said the sheriff. "And a barn door that banged shut in the wind."

185

Live and Let Live

June 3, 1944

ALL THOSE FANCY-LOOKING BUGS the garden articles tell about have arrived. The curlicues are being snipped off the peas, the spinach is being devoured (in a lacy cut-work pattern), young corn plants are disappearing bodily overnight. I have built a Chinese wall of poison pellets around the radish bed, but it does not hold back the thundering herd.

"You know how it is after a mild winter," my neighbor said, matter of factly.

I don't know, of course. But I can see that I'm going to. I'm thinking seriously of giving up beets and things and going in for bugs. I came flying out of the cabbage patch yesterday all excited with a black and white striped beetle. "Look," I exclaimed, "here's that very bug they had the picture of in *Life* magazine three weeks ago. I'm pretty sure it's an American corn crick, or something."

I put it in a bottle of alcohol, labeled it, and went back to the garden in search of a Bolivian potato borer, or something. I've got everything, I'm pretty sure, including the exquisite little green and orange Patagonian cucumber cruncher (or something). And— but I don't want to announce it too soon, not until I get all the known varieties labeled—I've got some new bugs heretofore unknown to science. Isn't that exciting? I'll get to name them. And they'll get good American names. I never did like giving foreign names to local bugs. No, ma'am! It won't be long now until you can read about the North Pacific parsnip parer, the Grays Harbor County cabbage crimper, and the North River radish riveter. I tell you we've got everything in this country, and lots of it. I'll have to do a lot of planting. Good seeds are getting scarce, but I have determined— and I don't think I can fail—to feed those bugs. Build a better mouse. . . No! No! I mean, build the best garden you can and the bugs of the seven seas will beat you to the onion patch, or something like that.

"Do you know what President Roosevelt said about the fishing business?" my fisherman friend asked.

"No," I said, "I don't."

"Let the old men and the young boys do it, is what he said," replied by fisherman friend. And he burst into hollow Shakespearean laughter, and went away pawing the air.

NOTICE TO MARINERS, reads a Coast Guard sign on the door of Lars Anderson's barge and goes on with "UNEXPLODED DEPTH CHARGES. It has been reported that a group of ten depth charges have been dropped in a zone approximately 15 miles west of Willapa Bay lighthouse. Do not handle in any way. Get them out of your nets at once—"

Or let the old men and the young boys do it for you.

Business as Usual

June 10, 1944

TURNED ON THE RADIO at 6:45 Tuesday morning and got D-Day. I wasn't looking for D-Day—had long since given up hovering over the radio, and I don't ordinarily get up at 6:45. But a little bird woke me up on Tuesday morning. A couple of weeks ago I had, in weeding, inadvertently put a handful of grass on the window sill. The grass dried, the bird came to get the grass for a nest, and that is how I happened to get out of bed so early on D-Day.

"Blast that bird," I said. He scratched and fluttered against the glass and when I thumped on the pane, he flew to a nearby bush, waited until I had closed my eyes in hopes of sleep, and returned to scratch and skitter at the window, which, architecturally speaking, lies athwart my left ear. There was only one thing to do, and I did it. I got up, went outside and moved the bird's 2x4's nearer to the theater of operations. Or what I thought was nearer. Anyway, I got them off the window ledge. Then I came back in the house, turned on the radio and got the news which rocked the world.

———

On the dunes the wild peas are blooming—heavenly blue, and a pale haze of lupine is spreading over the pasture. The wild blackberry vines are studded with white stars. This ought to be a good wild blackberry year, my neighbors tell me, what with being so wet, and all, this spring. I have begun harvesting my vegetable crop and had for dinner last night some mustard spinach which has all the fine flavor the seed packet said it would, interlaced with a stringy toughness of stem the like of which I would have found impossible of mastication, had I not raised it with my own fair hands. As it was, it was the best mustard spinach I ever ate. I also brought to the table three icicle radishes, only two of which had worms in them.

———

Robert, my fifteen-year-old neighbor, is now my sixteen-year-old neighbor. He came to tell me, with pride, that he had reached man's estate. The OPA and the child labor

Chronology of 1944

June

4 American troops enter Rome.

2 War Manpower commission announces that it will take over "absolute control of all male workers over 17 to check turnover in essential industries."

6 Invasion of continent begins with landings in Normandy [D-Day].

8 Allies in Italy capture port 38 miles north of Rome.
   "G.I. Bill of Rights" clears congress.

13 Allies advance into northern France, reaching point 15 miles inland.
   Democrats lose majority in the house with the election of Rolla McNillen, R-Illinois.

17 Chinese take Kamaling, Burma.

23 Week-long German robot bombing reported by British.

25 American tank units enter Cherbourg.
   146 killed and 1,000 injured by tornado that swept over parts of Pennsylvania, West Virginia, and Maryland.

26 Russians capture Vitebsk and Zhlobin.

28 Republican convention nominates Thomas E. Dewey, governor of New York, for President.

29 A serum to prevent measles has been developed, and will be available soon, the Red Cross reveals.

laws can no longer keep him off a fishing boat, and he goes out with the trolling fleet on Monday. He'd like to get in the navy right now, but has one long year to go before he can get to "Farragut, Idaho," which is the beginning of things to come—if you are a sixteen-year-old boy.

"In the meantime," said Robert, "I'm going to run the legs off that fishing boat."

———

Made my spring shopping trip to town this week, where I defied temptation at a farm equipment store and didn't come home with half a dozen yellow puff balls which entranced me. Chickens, I reminded myself, don't always stay young, yellow, and cute, but grow leggy and squawk, get in neighbors' carrot patches, and bring the feed man to your door each month with a bill in his hand which, if I can believe the neighbors, averages in this year of our Lord to a sum which would have fed a team of Percherons when grandpa was a boy. At the market, where I lunched, the waitress told a worthy burgher who asked for banana cream pie that, "There's only one piece left, and it's got the head tore offen it."

Is it the war which is causing us to lay about like that with language? Oh, for the return of those happy days when pies didn't get their heads "tore off"—and if they did, it wasn't mentioned. Not at the table, anyway.

———

My fisherman friend is reshingling his roof, and I must say I never saw a more awkward man aloft. He slips and slides all over the place, cascades down gutters with hair-raising abandon, and has given his wife the nervous jitters. "The trouble with him," says she, "is that he forgets that he won't be going into fifty fathoms of water, when he falls off."

Down on the Farm

June 17, 1944

SPRING HOUSECLEANING on this sandy, pine-studded peninsula is a ritual which has not changed its form for fifty years. There are no vacuum cleaners, electric waxers, and other complicated devices of the devil to obstruct, confuse, and confound you when you set about setting your house in order for summer. Armed with a bucket of whitewash and a can of good white hull paint, purchased at the dock, you go over your old board walls and window casings. The floor is scrubbed and, if more elegance is desired, you dip a mop in melted wax and hot water and end up with a fine dull shine under foot. You give the old Boston rocker a fresh coat of barn red paint, hang the starched, yellow cotton sash curtains at the windows, put an armful of wild blue sweet peas in the glass bowl on the fireside table, and get on with the business of living.

It isn't quite as simple as it sounds. Before you can whitewash, you've got to locate your whitewash brush. It's always been borrowed by the neighbors, and when you go for it, they have loaned it to other neighbors who have, in turn, given it to someone else. This gives you an opportunity for a good visit around the neighborhood, and you come home the richer for a cup of coffee, the gift of a pint of porch paint, and a broader knowledge of world affairs. "The way to keep weeds out of your carrots," the woman across the road told me, "is to bury the fertilizer in a trench underneath 'em. If you leave it show, the weeds will come." And "I make a good floor wax by melting up a slab of

Wild Sweet Pea
Lathyrus rigidus

paraffin in a quart of kerosene," the wife of my fisherman friend told me, as I went the rounds in search of my whitewash brush. My fisherman friend took the whitewash brush, nicely cleaned and dried, from where it hung suspended between two nails on the shed wall and gave it to me. "How's everything over at the farm?" he asked, turning his back on me to hide a pleased grin. "Everything is just fine," I said, with dignity. If he wants to make fun of me because I managed to raise a radish, I thought, I can't help it. I took the brush and went home, determined to make a go of the farm, fisherman friend or no fisherman friend.

———

My garden lies in a sunny place over against the dunes. First come the telephone peas climbing a neat row of crab apple brush. The brush has sprouted and if I don't get peas,

I may end up with a crab apple hedge. Next in line come the winter onions, evidently a very snooty variety, as they are leaning backwards to get away from the peas. Thirty-six potato plants (a vegetable without any complexes whatsoever), gaze innocently into the face of the sun, followed by cucumber and squash vines. Here, it seems, I've done the wrong thing; the big, friendly, elephant-eared squash is lurching over into the cucumber patch with a fatuous grin on its face, and the cucumbers, holding their meager skirts above their bony ankles, are running the other way—with sneers on their faces. The beets and the carrots, while they don't exactly eat out of the same dish, live beside each other with well-bred toleration, say good morning to each other if they chance to meet on the front steps, but never chat over the back fence. The beans are a poor ragged family who live on a bleak ridge across the ditch, a sort of tenement suburb of the fashionable corn skyscraper section. The end of the garden is an international melting pot where I planted parsnips and petunias, pole beans and morning glories, dill and dahlias, helter-skelter.

June . . . on the Dunes

June 24, 1944

ROBERT, MY SIXTEEN-YEAR-OLD NEIGHBOR, came over this morning and said Mom said not to buy any beef this week as Mrs. S—- had sold her withered old cow, Flossie, to the butcher.

"The warning comes too late, Robert," I said sadly. "Flossie has already gotten into the frying pan. I had her for dinner last night. Had is probably the wrong word though," I said. "Had at her, would be better. That steak, except for a ravelled stretch or two on the beach head, is still intact."

Robert looked distressed, like one does who gets there too late with bad news, but I comforted him. "I'm awfully glad you told me," I said. "Now I know that it was from a respectable cow of good reputation in the neighborhood and not, as I feared, a hunk of water buffalo."

I felt better. I'd been more than a little peeved at having walked two miles and spent ten points on what was to have been a treat. But now to know that it was Flossie I'd bought cheered me up. Besides I always buy named varieties of products whenever possible. Robert went away after assuring me he'd let me know when they took their veal calf, Jitter Bug, to the butcher. Jitter Bug, somehow, doesn't sound any too good either.

Have gotten so expert with patching plaster and putty knife that I am in demand for patching cracks. Was called out twice this week to operate on defaced fireplaces. Fireplaces which brick masons have given up are my specialty. I find myself falling naturally into the role of a master mason—letting the customer do all the dirty work like spreading canvas, mixing plaster, and getting the stage set for the job. When, with my brightly gleaming putty knife, and when my audience has become so hushed you could hear a pin drop, I step into the arena and with the deftness of a matador pick up a glob of plaster and apply the telling stroke to a crumbling mantel breast. So as not to spoil the effect, I depart immediately after the operation, striding from the scene without the banality of words, leaving my audience spellbound. The effect is somewhat marred by the nonappearance of a surreptitious ten-buck bill pressed into my hand as I leave the premises—-in return of course, for five minutes of my life's blood translated into stone.

——

Was appointed a committee of one to call in the sheriff and report the theft, from this community, of a heating stove, three gold velvet davenport cushions, one electric pump, and divers other whatnots.

"Have you got any clues?" the sheriff asked.

"Like what?" I wanted to know.

"Like the other night when Mrs. Wilkins' chickens were stolen. All I had to do was follow a trail of feathers over to the army camp where I found six soldiers and their wives frying chicken."

"I see what you mean," I said. "No I haven't got any clues. Stoves don't have feathers on them, unfortunately."

I was disappointed with my interview with the sheriff. Too much reading of mystery stories has led me to build up an altogether false conception of the art of crime detection. I've got to get back down to earth, criminally speaking. Even a child would know instinctively what the sheriff had to come two miles to tell me—no feathers, no stove.

——

Black smudges of oil, which last winter tarred the surface of the sandy beach, have gathered themselves up into little balls and blown up into the soft sand. Here, if you step on them, you must remove the adhesive stuff from your shoes with turpentine and much rubbing. There has been no oil on the beach now for months.

——

Also, my neighbor down the road has removed the iron kettle and hammer from his gate post, but our other air raid warning siren, the circular saw hanging from a pine tree across the road, still stands. Wild roses now bloom in the sandbagged gun emplacement pits. The bags themselves have rotted and the sand has sifted from them. Strands of

Honeysuckle
Lonicera japonica

rusted barbed wire sag listlessly from lichen-covered posts. By ones and twos the discharged wounded are beginning to drift back home. In England, one columnist writes: "Trainloads of wounded are already beginning to pass through summer England, festooned with its dog roses and honeysuckle . . . The red cross now shines on the side of trains going past crossings where the women, shopping baskets on their arms, don't know whether to wave or cheer or cry. Sometimes they do all three."

Under Dog

July 1, 1944

I READ AFRESH the new price control regulation: "Ceilings will bring prices on apricots, plums, sweet cherries, Italian prunes from 15 to 35 per cent below last season's prices." Then I went out to the gate to meet Tony and his vegetable truck, determined to wrench some fruity tid-bit from him for which I would not have to mortgage my soul. I visualized in particular cherries. If he tries to pass off those 35-cent-a-pound cherries on me again, I told myself, I'll read him the regulation. But he fooled me. He didn't have any cherries. Didn't have any fresh fruit whatsoever. Not even an Italian prune. I paid 88 cents for four withered beets, a cucumber, four dehydrated tomatoes, and six Lilliputian lemons, and crawled back to my fox hole. That's how I learned that the war isn't over yet.

I don't blame Tony. Whenever the little threadbare man rattles and chugs into the yard on his frayed tires, I experience a feeling of warm gratitude. If it weren't for Tony and his indefatigable determination to drive a 60-mile route peddling fourth-rate vegetables, I would do without green things several months of the year. I am aware of the fact that he surmounts almost impossible difficulties and frustrations to arrive at my door with a few sketchy gleanings from the bottom of the economic barrel. It's only once and a while that he has a big break, like last week, and gets out on the road a leap ahead of an OPA regulation with a plumb like 35-cent-a-pound cherries. When the regulation catches up with him, he settles for no cherries at all. It was the same with strawberries. I haven't even seen a strawberry this year. He started out with a few boxes once, but they were all sold before he reached me. On his next trip, when I asked for strawberries he shook his head. "Those regulations," he said, and rubbed the back of his neck and looked as if something had bitten him. So today when I said, "What! No cherries?" Tony answered, "Regulations," with the promptitude of a smart child who has the answer ready even before the teacher gets the question out of her mouth. I had to be content, but as to what he means by regulations, I don't think either of us has the foggiest idea. I tried prodding him once to see if I could stir up a mental image of regulations, but all I got was something to the effect that "nobody wants to pick strawberries when he can get twelve dollars a day doing something else. Regulations!"

Natural History

July 8, 1944

LEONARD, MY SMALL NEIGHBOR from the back woods farm, was seen to hot foot it down to Gramp's early yesterday morning. A minute later Gramp was seen jumping off the back porch with his six shooter in his hand, and cutting back across lots to the farm. I waited for the sound of a shot, but there was none. I learned later that a big black bear had made a few passes at the bee hives, but had been driven off by the mother of Jitter Bug, the veal calf.

———

Just at sunset a coast guard boat came in from the sea with a couple of fishermen on her deck. The boat anchored, the men climbed into a small dinghy and came to the dock.

"What happened?" I asked a fish truck driver, who went about his business of heaving boxes of iced fish on to his truck.

"Their boat turned over off the bar," he told me.

The two men climbed up on the dock—a tired-looking little fellow in dungarees, and a tired-looking big fellow in dungarees and a watch cap. Someone said, "Hello, Bill," and the big fellow nodded and climbed into a waiting car. The little fellow followed. A woman sitting at the wheel said, "Hello, Jack" to the little fellow. The car drove away. I couldn't help but think that if a movie director had been present and had seen what poor technique these heroes of the deep use he would have had a stroke.

Archaeology

July 15, 1944

"**T**ELL ME WHAT YOU DO with your spare time," some sage has said, "and I'll tell you what manner of man you are." I don't pretend to give the exact phraseology of the seer, but that is about what he meant. Anyhow, if he had been around this week, he would have, no doubt, foreseen that I should come to no good end.

It was a nice gray, blowing day when I took my spare time in one hand and a hoe in the other and hied forth to the dunes to squander away the hours in a pursuit which would win, I fear, nine votes out of ten in a "Dull Things to Do" contest. The fact that I had fun shows, I realize, what manner of woman I am. But I can't help it. I'll probably do it again—take time by the forelock and throw it away in useless frittering, when I might have made it my slave to accomplish some worthwhile project.

Sand Verbena
Abronia latifolia

The sort of thing that gets you somewhere in the world, I mean. Because what I did with my spare time didn't get me anywhere, rightfully speaking, but instead set me back thirty or forty years.

Arrived on top of the dunes. I walked to a large mound, overgrown with blooming sand verbena and bleached sand grass. Climbing to the top, I carefully inserted my hoe and extracted a cracked, old-fashioned, wide-rimmed soup plate, with a blue design on a white ground flecked with tarnished gilt. An aroma of clam chowder seemed suddenly to permeate the air, the kind of chowder I had eaten from this very sort of plate at the age of twelve, which, as everyone knows, is the epicurean age, if there ever is one. Rather breathless, I set the plate aside, and went to work determinedly. I had struck pay dirt with the very first prod of the hoe; beneath me in the mound lay the refuse dump, abandoned these many years, of the old beach hotel of my childhood. I bent down and picked up a brass lamp wick holder, green with age, and recalled on the instant a huge whitewashed room, a fire roaring up the chimney, lighted lamps, candles on the mantel, a white fog brushing against the windows at the end of day. And through the opened double doors at the end of the room, a glimpse of long tables covered with white cloths, and rows and rows of blue- and white-rimmed soup plates steaming invitingly. Beneath the clams and potatoes, the onions and salt pork, once you had finished your chowder, would be a few gritty flecks of sand.

My next find was a wooden box containing old shoes. This sand is dry, roofed over by vegetation. The old shoes came from the box in a dry crumbling block and fell apart in my hands. Pointed-toed shoes with high buttoned tops. Black tennis shoes, the sporty foot gear of the day. Patent leather shoes, with cloth tops. An old gray spat with a rusted buckle. Why should I think suddenly of straw sailor hats, black derby hats, mustaches? And horses! The chink-chink of harness as the stage coach rattled from the dock and the sudden silence as the horses' feet sank in the sandy road. The sweaty smell of the straining horses as the big yellow coach with its daily batch of guests—be-gloved ladies in sailor hats with traveling rugs on their laps, be-derbied gentlemen with up-flaring mustaches, smug little girls in "Peter Thompson" suits, small boys in knee-length pants scuffling, prodding and squirming—rolled through a two-mile stretch of pine woods to its fashionable destination.

Under a stratum of old broken stoneware—washbowls, pitchers, chamber pots—I struck bed rock. Persistent scrapings with the hoe revealed that I was standing on the boat deck of the old hotel range, red with rust and disintegrating back to elemental dust. A gleaming object lying near the gaping chimney hole proved to be a silver metal soup spoon. I picked it up and, scraping the sand of ages back over the old range, I turned homeward across the dunes. I carried also a half-pint whisky flask of lavender glass, colored by the sun and sand of thirty years. It recalled nothing. I experienced, when I held it in my hands, only a feeling of irritated exasperation—things had gone on back there when I was twelve years old that I had known nothing about. I hadn't had a drink out of that bottle!

As for the silver spoon—the large, dog-eared, generous soup spoon of the day—I think, when I go walking again, I shall bury it where I found it, neatly in its place in time and space, where memories are best left lying.

Chronology of 1944

July

3 Minsk falls to Russians as they sweep into Polish territory.

6 Robot bomb casualties and damage in southern England are admitted to be serious.
A fire in the main tent of the Ringling Bros. Circus in Hartford, Conn., causes deaths of 167 persons, mostly women and children.

9 British and Canadians enter Caen, France, anchor of German lines for weeks.

11 National League team wins the All-Star game, 7-1, in Pittsburgh.

14 Army reveals that there are now 196,941 war prisoners in the U.S., 146,101 being German and 50,278 Italian.

20 Democratic convention in Chicago nominates Roosevelt for fourth term.

21 Sen. Harry Truman is nominated for Democratic vice presidential candidacy.

27 Six Nazi bases, the most important being Lwow, fall to Russians on various fronts.

28 Brest-Litovsk captured by Russians.

30 Allied "break-through" registers large gains in France.

Crop Failure

July 29, 1944

THERE OCCURRED THIS WEEK one of those minor tragedies which fall so low in the emotional scale that they are not even recognized by the sensibilities even after the eye has perceived them, and pass from the range of consciousness without even causing a ripple, to say nothing of not even raising a tear. Indeed so callous is the average mentality, that it is almost instinctive, nine times out of ten, to burst into a good hearty guffaw when confronted by an event which passes beyond the range of common understanding. At least I have found it so. This week I have been sadly pained, and my grief intensified, when seeking the sympathetic ear of friends and neighbors in what, to me, was a real loss. I have been greeted by shouts of laughter or, what is harder to bear, cold indifference when I recounted to them the sad details relevant upon the death of Hubbard, my squash.

Even yet I am in no condition to write about the tragedy. I go about button-holing people and muttering inanities. "Did you ever see a finer squash?" I ask. And when they want to know what squash, or whose squash, I say, "My squash, Hubbard. He's dead, you know." And I go gulping off, holding my ears against the unfeeling laughter which seems to be the single reaction of lesser souls.

It was in April that I planted Hubbard. I first prepared a super trench, filled it with fine loam and super fertilizer and then, opening the packet of seeds, I spread them on the ground, and choosing the very plumpest one, I planted it, destroying all the rest. There was to be only one Hubbard. And I had ambitions for him. I had heard somewhere about a squash which got into print with a weight of 200 pounds and a girth of eight feet. And from the day Hubbard first stuck his nose out of the ground, and his two elephantine ears, I groomed him for the championship. Nothing was too good for that squash. I put him on a special diet of equal parts of all the best commercial fertilizers diluted in water. He drank lustily from the garden hose hours on end. And how he GREW! At the age of three weeks, his leaves were the size of turkey platters. Soon he stretched out two nine foot arms and opened five big yellow eyes. With a start in life like this, I thought, he'll weigh 210 pounds if he weighs

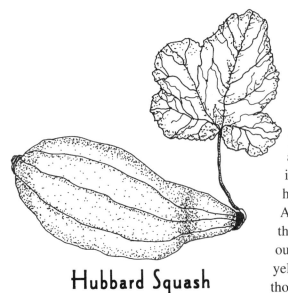

Hubbard Squash

an ounce. And then the neighbors for miles around will come to look at him. There'll be much talk. He'll get in the paper. I'll have established a reputation for horticulture. I'll be an authority. Oh, the things I planned for that squash! And the pleasure I got from watching him grow; his first step—right over the radish bed, and his second step into the corn patch. And how good natured he was, with his big foolish elephant ears.

Well, he is gone now. It was on Monday morning that Joe—arriving five days before he said he ever possibly could, and at seven o'clock in the morning—came to lay the pipe for the new septic tank. I didn't know he had come until I went into the garden. A yawning trench was cut through the plot at right angles, exposing the bare bottoms of an innocent row of beets, and on top of the embankment of up-flung sand lay Hubbard the squash, his bare feet parched by the early sun, his long arms inert and dangling, his yellow eyes closed.

Smothering a sob, and violent words, I lifted him gently, filled a bucket with water and lowered his toes therein. It was too late. He shrivelled visibly before my eyes, and in less time than it takes to tell about it, he assumed the aspect of a quantity of limp spinach—yards of it. Hubbard was dead.

Later, when I questioned Joe at the scene of the crime, he told me that by digging the trench where he had, he had saved my valuable potato crop. "And you know what you can get those things for?" he said, indicating Hubbard with the toe of his shoe. "Sixty cents apiece!"

"Oh, yeah!" I said hotly, putting everything I had into the expression. "Not my squash, you couldn't," I said.

"Eleven cents a pound at the most," continued Joe, following the thought pattern of those gifted souls who are born knowing the market price of intangible values. And, as if to settle the argument once and for all, he clumped a length of six-inch sewer pipe, which he carried on his shoulder, down upon all that remained of the heir presumptive to the squash championship of Grays Harbor County.

Time & Tide

August 12, 1944

ROBERT, MY SIXTEEN-YEAR-OLD NEIGHBOR, came to see me Sunday dressed in a new store suit, complete with shirt, necktie (the first I have seen him wear), and new shoes—the fruits of toil on the tuna banks. He and his father rigged up their small crab boat and went out with the best of them, due west, until even Mount

Rainier vanished over the shoreward horizon. They were gone four days and saw, I gathered, some pretty wonderful and interesting things the nature of which Robert refused to any more then hint at. "Anyway," he said, "you don't have to worry about the Japs ever landing on these shores."

When I asked if he ever ate fresh tuna he look at me pityingly and said he had, and that if I didn't know how to cook it his mom would tell me. Later I went and got Mom's recipe: clean and skin the fish, bake in a slow oven for an hour (to render out oil) separate the chunks of good white meat from the dark (the dark is edible, but "don't look so nice," Mom says), and place on a bed of good onion-seasoned bread stuffing, and bake for one hour, "or until done." (You can take that "or-until-done" any way you want to. It's what Mom said and what all the best cook books of my younger days used to say, but in my experience it's one of those unhelpful phrases which might better be left out of the language—to say nothing of being left out of cook books. Puts too much responsibility on the cookee.)

———

Toward the end of the day I went up on the dunes and sat beneath a stunted, wind-racked fir. Roughly speaking, I had spread before me like a map some twenty miles of beach. The semicircle of ocean reached north and south, darkly blue under the blue sky and greenly black where it moved under cloud patches. From end to end of this expanse, flying low over the breakers, the whale birds flew northward. For the two hours I sat watching there wasn't a single break in their assembly line. Like a swift narrow stream they flowed above the sea, until to my bemused gaze they became, not birds, but a silver line being reeled in by some giant in the north. As I write, the relentless flight continues.

Today, and tonight, and tomorrow night, and for many days to come, that gray stream will move northward above the surf. There aren't that many birds in the world, I once told myself, after watching the phenomenon one August several years ago. About that time the coast guard thought so too. They followed the flight in a swift boat for four days and unraveled the mystery. The birds took them on a wild goose chase which circled some five hundred miles of Pacific Ocean and cut in again toward shore. It's all a lot of hooey about the birds having a pressing engagement in the Arctic; they're just putting on a big one-ring circus. And I know now, when I watch them, that I am seeing the self-same birds today that I saw yesterday. But why they play follow-the-leader, and on such an extensive scale, no man knows. One scientist who observed a similar flight has suggested that the birds once migrated to some lost Atlantis which, ages ago, sank under the sea, and that the annual flight is an inherited race impulse, meaningless and futile, now.

Whale Bird
Red Phalarope

198

Rewards of Toil

August 19, 1944

IT IS THE CUSTOM of middle-western writers, I have observed, to describe, sooner or later, a field of growing corn, which they are unanimous in praising. In one instance which I recall, the writer went so far as to say a field of corn was the most beautiful sight in the world. Having been born and raised in the shadow of an evergreen forest, I used to feel sorry for those writers who went into ecstasies about corn; they couldn't ever have gotten very far afield, I thought, certainly never to the Pacific coast. But now, I don't know—I've got a corn field of my own (thirty-six plants) and I'll have to admit corn has got something.

My corn (I'd better call it a patch and not a field) grows in three straight rows alongside the living-room windows; and from the day I planted it, until the present moment, it has gone through all its paces with a dispatch and an esprit de corps which I have observed in nothing else in nature—unless, perhaps, when watching a lady Moose's drill team in full cry.

I planted the corn for fun; simply as the bold gesture of an inferior-complexed soul, sort of an other-people-have-corn-why-can't-I affair. I never expected it to grow—not very high anyway—but just to rattle a few leaves in the wind. So that I could wave a superior hand and intone, "there is my corn patch" to visitors in passing. But to my surprise and delight, those thirty-six seeds have come through 100 per cent and now stand like a well-disciplined squad of seven-foot-tall soldiers, every man with a golden fez on his head, and three ears of corn under his belt.

Historically speaking, corn was not first introduced to the old world by Christopher Columbus. My encyclopedia (published in England in 1886 and whole-souledly all-out for England) debunks that idea with the revelation that some corn grains were discovered at an earlier date in a cellar in Athens. The book does, how-

August

1. Resistance in Tinian Island in Marshalls ends.
2. Turkey breaks diplomatic relations with Germany.
   Strike of Philadelphia transit workers is referred to President.
6. Philadelphia street cars and busses operate under army control.
   Newly developed calculating machine that will solve problems in higher mathematics is announced by Harvard University.
10. Guam conquered, giving U.S. control of all important islands of Marshalls.
14. Strike of midwestern truck drivers ends, following government seizure of lines.
15. A second Allied invasion force lands on southern French coast between Marseille and Nice.
16. Army ends censorship of soldiers' reading matter.
19. U.S. tank units reach suburbs of Paris.
20. Southern France invasion force enters Toulon.
30. Navy reports the construction of 65,000 ships of all types since September 1, 1939.
31. Romanian capital, Bucharest, is entered by Russians.

ever, grant that we have corn in America: "The unripe grains, slightly roasted, burst and turn inside out, assuming a very peculiar appearance in which state they are a favorite article of food of the natives."

=====

Two neighbors, who had been walking in the quiet, dewless night, came to the door and said, "Come!" excitedly. So I went with them across the pasture where a symmetrical young pine tree stands by the gate. It was about church-Christmas tree in size, and what they wanted me to see—and what I couldn't fail to see—was that it shimmered in phosphorescent light. It was a dream tree, illuminated from within, apparently. Every needle glowed. "Saint Elmo's fire," pronounced my neighbor with proud approval, as if he had invented it. St. Elmo's fire, I find on looking it up, is a brush or star of light, which appears on the tops of masts, spires, or other pointed objects, and signifies, when it appears on the masthead, that the sailors have nothing to fear from the storm. There was no storm the night we saw the illuminated tree, but it was unduly warm and still, as if heat lightning might be playing over the horizon.

=====

Received this morning the mail a list of farmers' bulletins available to us country folk. Makes me feel important. Am I annoyed by the Rough-headed Cornstalk beetle? Do I want to shoe a horse, brand a beef, fight a fire, dock a lamb? All I have to do is write to Uncle Sam and he will send me the proper booklets. There are seven hundred to choose from, and I am urged to choose five. "Hints on how to skin a mountain lion" ought to make pretty good reading, for one.

Things to Come

August 26, 1944

DURING THE PAST FEW WEEKS, I have witnessed a heaving and shifting about of the people living along these dunes which may reflect a national run to cover. The time has arrived, if I can believe the well-nigh breathtaking decisions of some of my neighbors, when a man can get a glimmering of the immediate future—like seeing a sun-topped dune appear suddenly above the underbrush trail—and make plans for getting out of the woods. We have all had our noses pretty much to the grindstone. We have been a pretty well-disciplined, well-regimented army of civilians. But now, my neighbors seem to feel, Uncle Sam is likely to turn us loose before very long and let us scramble for ourselves again, in which case it behooves every thoughtful citizen to find some place to hole in. In the economic return-to-reality campaign it will be up to each individual to dig his own fox hole. So he had better begin keeping his eyes open and make a dead run for it, once he gets the go-ahead signal. At last that is how I interpret the strange doings of my fellow citizens hereabouts.

Our shoemaker, who has resoled (and re-resoled) all the shoes on this twenty-mile strip of beach bought himself a little repair shop in a town in the east end of the county.

Our barber, who cut the hair of the cranberry growers at Grayland in the morning, and went to Westport and shaved fishermen's beards in the afternoon, has bought an interest in a small factory in the northern part of the state.

Our beer hall proprietor, who served in the navy in the last war and the coast guard in this one, has come ashore, sold his beer business, and is buying a 400-acre range to run beef cattle on.

A former town businessman (and all the friends he can recruit) are busy as bees clearing land down the road for the greenhouse business he always wanted.

This week a well-cared-for old sedan drew up across the road, and a retiring brakeman (thirty years aboard a freight train) got out, climbed the dunes, and took a look at the hundred-foot strip of land abutting the Pacific Ocean which, of all this vast continent, belongs to him, and where, God be praised, the tide arrives and leaves on schedule, and without the help of man.

A young fellow, fresh from the wars, has bought himself two acres of blue-ocean-view to the south, and a young sailor at sea has an option on a block of land to the north. A city man has sold his lumberyard and bought himself a place here where he can set up a jig saw, make gadgets for the neighbors for fun, and fish for the food of his soul. Eager-eyed strangers—young fellows discharged or on furlough, and odd fellows with the first change they have had in their pockets for years—have suddenly appeared at the fishing-fleet dock where they hang about looking with loving eyes at the boats. (The expression on the faces of certain men when they look at a boat can only be described as loving). I have heard that the same expression is to be observed in the eyes of some men when they see a good horse, but I cannot vouch for it, as I haven't ever seen a good horse myself (much less a good man looking at a good horse).

This change and movement which I have described portends something; but just what it is I am not qualified to say. Granted that it is felt that the war is about over, what then of the "brave new world"? The world of widened highways, pink plastic villas, modified Roman baths, perfumed chinchilla blankets, air-wafted transportation, robot-cooked meals, and effortless education? Do my neighbors, picking out their little fox holes, expect such things? They do NOT!

Furthermore they don't even want them. I have cross-questioned some of these about-to-be pioneers of a new day, and find them, down to the last man, peculiarly apathetic about tinted bathroom basins. Our barber, a skeptic, told me not to believe everything I read in magazines. He is a man who instinctively suspects ulterior motives back of everything. "It's all just a lot of pictures," he said. "They've just got on to how to use colored ink and so they make everything pink." Our shoemaker seemed vaguely uneasy about the possibility of plastic shoes, however. If it comes to plastic shoes, he'd be put out of business. My fisherman friend hauled up a thought from the depths of his consciousness. "Hells bells!" he said. "No man can eat more than three meals a day, or sleep in more than one bed at night can he? There's too many THINGS in the world already. Everyone's dragging too much ballast. I don't see how they can take on any more."

As to our railroad brakeman, he who is about to retire after his thirty-year stretch, I watched him walk the boundaries of his new domain and saw the light on his face when he finally stood on his westernmost dune looking seaward, and I gathered somehow that that bit of ground under his feet will be enough for him. If a rainbow-colored, plastic cabana, with liquid-cooled drive, air-cooled sleeping compartments, nonstop vacuum air cleaner schedule and automatic dinner service, ever rises there, I will be more than surprised. I think there was an idea, not a gadget, at the end of that thirty-year dream he had.

How to Write a Column

September 2, 1944

ALMOST EVERY DAY you read about the heroic deed of some war correspondent who managed, amid the din of shot and shell, to stick to his typewriter and, at great risk to life and limb, get out his story for the newspaper. I've thought quite a lot about those boys and girls today. All that stuff they write about their difficulties just sort of rolled off me like water off a duck's back. Until today.

It was shortly after eight o'clock this morning when I put a clean sheet of paper in my typewriter, set the dictionary handy, and sat down facing my western window, which gives upon the quiet sun-topped dunes. There was no sound save the distant purr of the sea, the sough of wind in pine tops, the occasional faint scramble of a chipmunk across the roof. But before I could finish a sentence, there were sounds of commotion outside. A caterpillar truck and a logging truck, with much screeching of gears, drove into the yard, two men and an Irish water spaniel leapt to the ground and began tossing (the Irish water spaniel didn't, of course, toss anything) timbers and cables, blocks and other tackle to the ground. "We've come to haul that shed up for you," bawled one of my neighbors.

"It won't take any time at all," bellowed another neighbor. And as if to prove it, he threw a lasso over the shed, scaled the kitchen wall at a leap, threw a haulback (or whatever it is) over the chimney and called, "Let 'er go, Joe."

With that, Joe chugged up the caterpillar and let 'er go. There was a screeching and ripping sound, as my house strained at its moorings, and finally all but came out by the roots. A short consultation was held between the bridge and the fo'c'sle in voices which would have outridden an eighty-mile gale, punctuated by a high keening sound from the Irish water spaniel who had got caught, somehow, in the bight of a line.

It was decided to take time out to cut down the old pine tree. This was done forthwith, and the crash of the falling giant caused my typewriter to slip a few heart beats, for (and I don't want to appear immodest) I was still trying to stick to my guns. This determination on my part was further complicated by the arrival of a gentle, hard-of-hearing neighbor who came to put in a long-distance call on my telephone, and who managed to talk at length, unperturbed, while three more pine trees came down around our ears. The haul-back was then rerigged; again the caterpillar charged through the underbrush, and again the Irish water spaniel yipped, although this time he wasn't caught in anything.

About this time, my family of chipmunks, who have a snug home underneath the eaves, decided to abandon ship. Papa, leading the way, came down the side of the house headfirst, followed by mamma, and two infants so new that their thin fur coats were still damp. This pitiful exodus disturbed me, and I was glad when, a few moments later, it was decided that the chimney couldn't stand the gaff and that a pine might make a better spar tree.

"A good stalky pine is what we need," roared Joe, sticking his head in at the window and taking a quick look about the room. His eye lingered speculatively on the underpinnings of the dining table. I made some com-

Chronology of 1944

September

4 Finns and Russians cease fighting in truce.

5 Russia declares war on Bulgaria.

6 Army announces demobilization plans. More than a million men will be discharged when Germany is defeated.
Seventeen processed foods removed from ration list.

7 Britain lifts black-out regulations, considering menace from air conquered.

11 American First army pushes five miles into German territory.

12 Romania granted armistice by Allies.

13 Russians reach border of Czechoslovakia.

14 U.S. Third fleet attacks Cebu and Negros islands of the Philippines.

15 Nineteen coal mines are seized on the President's orders.

16 Second Quebec conference ends. Plans for quick finish of European war and of marshaling of forces for Japanese front are made.

19 Finnish armistice signed by Russia and Finland.

28 Ration controls removed from all farm machinery except corn pickers.

30 Birth rate for 1943 increased, census bureau says.

ment about it being a little late for pines. Joe withdrew his head and another ear-splitting conference took place, after which all hands laid off for lunch.

During the intermission, Robert, my sixteen-year-old neighbor, came in. He told me that "Mom" had gone to town to buy school clothes for her brood, and if she called on the telephone, would I tell her that he guessed she'd better get his shoes a size larger after all, and could I lend him the wheelbarrow. While I was getting the key to the tool house, the Irish water spaniel which had come in with him remained behind and ate up my sandwich. All but the lettuce, which he left licked clean in the center of the rug.

Lunch over for the working crew (war correspondents missed theirs), the second phase of the battle began. The men fell back into what had once been a small pine wood and making the most of what cover remained, lashed their tackle to a stump, and supported by their motorized armament, stood their ground until the shed, giving up with unexpected suddenness, threw down its guns and lurched, in exhausted surrender, against the house. The impact caused a shower of dry whitewash to settle over the floors and tables, dislodged numerous spiders from my rafters, and impelled the Irish water spaniel to fly in at the front door, his tail between his legs, and yipping as if he had been kicked. He hadn't been kicked, so I kicked him.

Then I went to my typewriter and destroyed the clean page I had put there in the morning, and upon which was written the single sentence: "If there is one thing you can be certain of in this uncertain world, it is quiet in the country . . ."

The Ghost Ship

September 9, 1944

JOE WAS REPAIRING the fence at the top of the dunes when he yelled down to me that there was a fishing boat in the surf. I hurried up, and sure enough, there was a small boat broadside in the trough, her decks awash, and all but her mast disappearing as we watched. Then she surged to the surface once more, glistened, complete and whole, in the bright sunlight for a second, and then, once more, vanished. We stood for a long minute, looking down from our high perch on the place where she had been. Then I headed for the telephone and called the coast guard. "There's a small fishing boat in the surf down here," I said. Then I added: "I think she's gone down."

Several neighbors gathered and we ran to the beach in a body, following on the heels of Joe, who preceded us at a fast trot. On the beach, we could see nothing, as there was a high surf, although the day was clear and bright. "Are you sure you saw a boat?" the neighbors asked. And we said yes, we were sure, she stood out as plain as day, as if she had been painted there in the clear light.

Soon we saw the coast guard coming around the jetty, a dark, high-powered little boat that went forward through the surf like a prancing horse. We would see her for a second above the waves, then she would vanish, only to appear a pace or two farther ahead. She was followed by a smaller white boat which we later learned was the pontoon boat, and came right abreast of us and cruised up and down just beyond the surf. Both boats seemed to be caught at times in the long surging rhythm of the sea, and were carried forward in great running leaps. They searched for a couple of hours, running as far inshore as they dared. My neighbors began to lose interest and departed one by one. My fisherman friend, one of the last to go, gave me a wry look and said, "I guess you seen a yeller belly. Them whales often come into the surf and sport around." Then he went home over the dunes, leaving me alone with my delusions. I sat down with my chin in my hand, and thought about how I'd called out the coast guard, used up a lot of valuable gasoline, caused men to risk their lives, and lost caste with the neighbors all because I couldn't tell a whale from a ship.

On my way home (I sat there until close of day), I picked up a new canvas glove with a smear of grease across the palm, and a little further along on the wet sand, a sort of mechanic's coat. It was made of yellow cotton drill and smelled overpoweringly of oil. I took them with me for purposes of rebuttal, although I realized that a spar or a mast would have been better. A hatch cover would have been best of all. My fisherman friend could, of course, laugh off the glove and coat as being beside the point; but a freshly painted hatch cover could prove that I'd seen a ship and not a whale, as not even the whales of my fisherman friend (and he's seen a lot of unbelievable things in this ocean) have taken to wearing hatch covers.

At home, my injured feelings were somewhat mollified by a call from the coast guard. Their truck drove into the yard, and a young fellow came in to ask me a few questions about what I'd seen. Joe had finished his fence and gone home, so I had to stand the inquisition alone. I told the young man what I'd seen and then he asked, "What color was the boat?" and I said, "Yellow."

The minute I'd said it, I could have bitten off my tongue. I hadn't thought until that second what color the boat was. I was glad my fisherman friend wasn't present. "Also," I said hurriedly, "it had a mast."

He appeared to believe me. He said that a forty-eight-foot fishing boat had capsized about a month ago at a point directly opposite this beach, and that the owners were anxious to salvage her before she came ashore and broke up.

For a number of days now, at low tide, a tug with a derrick has cruised about inshore, dragging, I presume, for the boat. I spend most of my time sitting by myself on the dunes, watching and praying. If that boat doesn't come to light, I am as good as done for. Or if a yellow-bellied whale comes to light, I am done for, too. I am avoiding the neighbors. Every time I meet them, they get big grins on their faces and call out, "Well, have you seen the phantom ship lately?"

205

More Mysteries

September 16, 1944

WHAT I THOUGHT was a fishing boat in the surf last week—and what the neighbors declared must have been a yellow-bellied whale—came ashore south of the jetty and turned out to be a boat. I have been taken off probation and reinstated in the tribe. Next time I "see something," and come flying down from the dunes to give the alarm, there will be respect in their eyes, not skepticism. Anyhow, I am no longer asked if I have seen any phantom ships lately. I have tried to be modest and not overbearing about my victory. I couldn't refrain, however, from saying to my fisherman friend when I met him on the road, "I see where the hull of that yellow-bellied whale of yours came ashore down the beach."

───

While I am sitting at my typewriter, the earwigs are busy eating the silk off my ears of corn. I got up this morning and looked out on my corn patch, and it looked queer somehow. Then I saw that the silk had vanished from the ears. I went outside, opened up an ear, and there were the earwigs, snug as bugs in rugs. What to do? There was nothing in my garden book, *Your Vegetable Garden*, publishers: Union Oil Co., which covered the matter. I had to resort to my 1886 encyclopedia. And after resorting to it, I found that I didn't want to kill earwigs. I hadn't the heart. The female E., says my book, "sits upon her eggs and hatches them like a hen; also, she gathers her young ones around her and under her in the most affectionate matter." Also: "No instance has ever been authenticated of an E. entering the ear of a human being. It is curious how extensively prevalent the notion is. The E. gets its name from the shape of the wings (the hind ones) which when fully opened are the shape of the human ear; and from the circumstances it seems highly probable that the original name of the insect was 'earwing.' The injury which it does to field crops is probably more than compensated by the destruction of multitudes of smaller insects as thrips, aphis, etc."

You see! When you get right down to facts, there isn't really anything much the matter with earwigs. And they're so affectionate. Who am I to separate mothers and children? No! They can have the corn patch. And besides, I've run out of arsenate of lead.

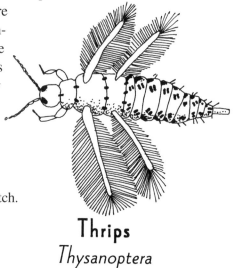

Thrips

Thysanoptera

Weatherman

September 30, 1944

EVERY MORNING MY NEIGHBOR crosses the pasture, cuts through the pine woods, and climbs the dunes to "see what she looks like out there." He takes a good, long, thorough look, I judge, because he is sometimes on the dune tops for a good fifteen minutes. When he comes down and makes off homeward, those of us who weren't born with the gift of weather prophecy call out to him, "Well, what's she look like out there?" And he calls back, "Well . . . she looks as though she might be clearin' a bit." Or he may say, "She's a bellerin' up off the north spit." If she's a bellerin', we grab up a big supply of fireplace wood, and think about completing the caulking job on the north side of the house. If she's a rollin' around down there, we decide to dry the clothes in the house. And sure enough! Pretty soon the southwest wind plays a prelude on the loose shakes, and rain begins to fall.

My neighbor doesn't, of course, "take a look at 'er," just to oblige us. The day's prophecy is a byproduct of the serious business of deciding whether or not to take out his fishing boat. Just what calculations that entails, what pros and cons, what weatherwise yeas and nays, I do not know. He can see a twenty-mile strip of beach from the dunes, and an indeterminate quantity of ocean stretching to the horizon. I can see the same thing, but I can't make head nor tail of it. My neighbor not only makes head and tail, but he makes a "she" of 'er.

Sometimes, hidden in the furze, I have been able to observe the prophet at close range as he stands motionless for minutes looking out to the horizon. He isn't concerned apparently, with the conditions in shore. At such times, I have envied him his six feet two inches as I have the feeling that his height enables him to see many leagues beyond my ken. That, and the intent gaze he concentrates on the dim, gray demarcation line between sea and sky, makes me impatient with my limited sight. Oh, to be able to count the fishes in the sea! To be able to look over the earth's rim, as my neighbor does, and see whatever it is he sees out there.

The seance over, he turns, pulls a moss-green felt hat over his eyes, and descends the bank in long strides, followed by a curled-tailed dog with a mean eye, and heads for home at slow cruising speed. We can't tell from his pace, which is always deliberate, what she's like out there, not unless we ask him. And we believe what he tells us. We plan our days accordingly. This neighbor, who first saw the light of day in the upper reaches of the Blue Ridge Mountains some sixty-odd years ago, is our man of the sea, hereabouts. He looks like a mountaineer. His dog looks like a mountaineer's dog. His house might have been picked up bodily—flag-eared gables, pine scrub, and all—and transplanted to its site in our midst. But ever since the 17th of October, 1933, my neighbor's word about the weather has been the law in this community.

It was early in the morning of that October day that I opened my kitchen door to throw out the ashes and saw something I had never seen before—my neighbor, followed by his wife, his son, and his two curled-tailed dogs, streaking single file through the pine woods. "You better git to the pasture," he called out. "There's a big blow comin'." Just then the top of a seventy-foot pine beyond him cracked with a sound like a rifle shot and sailed off lightly through the air. I grabbed up a dozen eggs—just the sort of thing you do when the house is on fire—and streaked after him. Back doors and front doors opened to let out the last of the summer cottagers. We just made it in time; a few seconds later, the porches were smashed and the doorways blocked by dozens of fallen trees. As I hot-footed it to the pasture, the rifle fire of snapping tree trunks sounded on every side. In the pasture there were no trees, except a small clump of cypresses under which the ground rolled like water.

For a time, we felt safe. To be out of range of the trees was a relief. Then the wind which had blown from the east shifted suddenly to the west, and the tops started blowing off the dunes. The sky was darkened with wet, blown sand, which pelted our skin like buck shot, and made breathing difficult. "There's only one safe place," announced the prophet. "That's that tie house." The tie house was built staunchly from a deckload of railroad ties which had come ashore from a wreck many years ago. It stood at the edge of the pasture. The owner was absent, but we broke the glass of the kitchen door and entered. From the windows, we watched while hundreds of dead sea birds blew down over the dunes. Their small bodies clustered like leaves against the fences and along the ditches, as if left by the receding tide. I saw sea gulls making valiant efforts to return to the dignity of flying right-side up, only to be borne onward, their feet clutching spasmodically skyward. All that day and night, the storm raged. At night we lit candles, rifled our absent landlord's cupboards and, with the help of my dozen eggs and a pot of coffee another cottager had abandoned ship with, we ate our supper. At the head of the table sat our prophet. He had gone out once and tried to climb the dunes to "get a look at 'er," but had given up. He came back to report that, "No man could live out there." Later we reclined on couches and in chairs, as no one cared to brave the second story. I roused myself once, I remember, to call everyone's attention to one of the curled-tailed hounds holed up for the night in the center of the dining table. He was curled snugly about the guttering candle, on our absent brother's wife's best hand-crocheted doily. Then, I think, we all fell asleep. All, I mean, except our prophet. I'm sure he stayed awake to see what "she" was a-going to do next.

Getting Ahead in the World

October 7, 1944

MY FISHERMAN FRIEND stopped by the other evening and recounted some of his adventures while "bottom fishing," which is a newly developed industry here. "There's strange things in that ocean," said he. "There's things hauled up in our nets even scientists never see." He told of a little "tree" about four feet high of translucent red, plastic-like substance, delicate as fine wire, and so tough a man couldn't break a single branchlet with his bare hands. He told of a lance-like creature nine feet or more in length with a flat body glued to the ocean bed, and capable, it would appear, of harpooning a whale. On a recent trip, his boat was an object of interest to a sea elephant, which is a creature with a snout. "And a body," said my fisherman friend, "about as big as this room." That was all he could tell me about it as they "got out of there in a hurry." They didn't want to risk being banged by that much bulk.

Out beyond these shores there is a current of water as blue as the bluest sky; even in stormy weather, and under an overcast sky, it is blue. So clear is the division of this current from the darker ocean that the edge, particularly in some places off the Columbia River, is almost knife sharp. When I asked how many miles offshore the current lay, my fisherman friend answered that it "Might be nine hours out, might be twelve hours out." It's a good thing to know, isn't it?

——

When I asked my Blue Ridge Mountain neighbor the purpose of a tower of scaffolding which soars above the chimney tops of his shake-roofed domicile, he replied: "Well . . . I started to put in water and along come the first World War. And before I could git goin' again, along come the second World War. I'll be gol-darned if a man can git anything done around here."

Chronology of 1944

October

1 Calais, French channel port, falls to Allies.

3 Siegfried line breached at Uebach by U.S. Fifth army.

4 U.S. bombers raid Borneo oil fields.

5 Strike of Detroit maintenance workers, affecting 33 war plants and 50,000 workers, ends.

6 Russians cross Hungarian border.

7 Peace conference at Dumbarton Oaks, N.H., ends sessions. A general framework for peace and security agreed upon, it is announced.

8 Wendell Willkie, 52, Republican presidential candidate in 1940, dies in New York City.

9 St. Louis Cardinals win World Series, 4 games to 2.

11 East Prussian border reached by Russians.

17 U.S. troops enter Aachen, important German border city.

18 War Production board announces that it has permitted 1,110 manufacturers to resume civilian production.

20 American forces under Gen. MacArthur invade Philippines, landing on Leyte Island.

23 De Gaulle recognized as head of French provisional government by U.S. and other United Nations.

25 U.S. and other United Nations resume diplomatic relations with Italy.

26 U.S. navy meets and defeats huge Jap fleet between Philippines and Formosa.

Good Hunting

October 21, 1944

AT A QUARTER TO SIX Sunday morning I sat at the breakfast table. It was dark yet outside. The yellow sash curtains were drawn. Candlelight gleamed on the red-checked tablecloth, the rolls, the coffee cups, and the ruddy face of Deputy Sheriff McArthur, who sat opposite me, shaved, uniformed, holster on hip, cap on knee, flashlight on table, and a cup of steaming coffee in hand. When you call out the law at five o'clock in the morning it is only courtesy to tender a cup of coffee—and besides, it is fun. I mean it is fun after the sheriff gets there. When something tugs and wrenches at your bedroom window in the dark which precedes the dawn it is not fun.

The noise that got me out of bed at five o'clock was nothing to the shock I got when I switched on my flashlight and got a glimpse of a black object, which might have been a head, protruding through the window opening. I flew to the telephone and got the sheriff out of bed. I had closed the bedroom door behind me when I fled the room, so, knowing that the law was on the way I armed myself with the fireplace poker, and sat awaiting his arrival. I told my story as coherently as I could when he came in. He listened a moment and then went into the bedroom.

"There are footprints here all right," he called.

I went in and peered over his shoulder to where his flashlight played on the sill. There were footprints all right—neat little paw prints. "Have you got a cat around here?" the sheriff asked.

"No," I said. "At least . . . Yes, there's a cat around here, but it isn't my cat."

The sheriff turned from the window. "These cats live in the woods all summer," he said, "but when cold weather starts they begin looking for cover. A cat is a nice thing to have. Why don't you get yourself one? I thought I saw one as I came into the yard."

"Was it a black cat with one yellow cheek?" I asked.

"Some such color," he answered.

"How about a cup of coffee?" I asked, changing the subject. If I must have a cat I don't want it to be that yellow-cheeked cat. And yet . . . I can't get over the uncomfortable feeling I've had ever since I first laid eyes on that animal that some day it WILL be my cat.

━━━

Over coffee McArthur told me that he presented some confiscated clams to an old age pensioners' home recently, and that the following day the woman who runs the place called up and asked him never to bring any clams to the house again. The old gentlemen, she wailed, had all insisted on having the chowder prepared different ways—some with pork, some with bacon, with and without thickening—and finally each and every man had risen up and demanded to cook his own.

McArthur, who served on the North Beach front before he invaded this peninsula, also told me that when a tea shortage threatened immediately after Pearl Harbor an old Indian showed him thirty acres of a low-growing evergreen bush which the older Indians have used for tea since the dawn of time. And it IS tea, McArthur says.

Tea, says a not-too-old issue of *Life* magazine, resembles a wild laurel found in the Pacific Northwest.

I parted with my new-found friend just as a huge red sun came up over South Bay and the calm dawn was punctuated by a barrage of gun fire laid down by duck hunters. A flock of crows flapped in disordered panic above the willows for an instant, and then flew off, swearing in loud voices. The crow, in my observation, is the only creature who seems to get an actual, sadistic pleasure in telling man what he thinks about him. And the vocabulary they've got!

━━━

With a fine early start on the day I climbed the dunes to watch the white surf turn to fire as the sun struck it. The east wind was blowing and a veil of spindrift moved above each breaking wave. Lured to the beach I collected an armful of bark. This bark, churned and ground from logs in distant river booms, is finally cast up in good stove-sized bits on our shore. It arrives with nicely bevelled edges, heavy with salt, and makes the finest bed of coals I ever turned a steak on. It is also much favored for holding a fire but is frowned on in some quarters as being a burner-out of grates. If you've got a nice, new, white, enamel covered stove you don't want to burn bark in it. But I haven't. I've got a small, black, tough, little galley stove without a nerve in its body. Its grate may be burned out, but I wouldn't know a burned-out grate if I saw one. My little stove takes to bark as a duck takes to water, as a ship takes to the sea and a wild goose to the storm. And it bakes wonderful buckwheat hotcakes these crispy fall mornings.

Taken for a Ride

October 28, 1944

MRS. **TILLEY IS THE CITY CLERK** of Westport, so that's where I went to register—at Mrs. Tilley's home. It's lots nicer to register in someone's home than in a stuffy office somewhere. Mrs. Tilley's house might have been torn right out of a page from *Better Homes & Gardens*—two-toned carpet over everything, mirror above mantel, overstuffed chairs, and glistening walnut dining-room set. At the dinner table (I went at seven o'clock) sat two model children; a starched little girl in a pink hair ribbon, and a boy with a washed face and combed hair were finishing a dessert which couldn't have been anything else, in that pictorial setting, but jello. And it was jello. The little boy held out his bowl and asked for more. I wish the editors of *Better Homes & Gardens* and the jello people could have seen at first hand, as I did, just what their advertising dollars are doing for the American way of life. They would be encouraged no end, during those dark hours which all idealists know, and would have felt in a flash, just as I did when I first saw Mrs. Tilley's menage, that America is fast hastening toward a state of affairs where every home will have two-toned carpets on the floor, glistening walnut dining sets, and boys and girls who eat jello and ask for more.

———

Having come, in a matter of seconds, to certain definite conclusions relative to the literal interpretation of the printed word as practiced in Mrs. Tilley's parlor, I sat down at her immaculate desk and on the form which she pushed under my nose wrote down the number of years, months, and days I have lived on this earth, that I was born in the United States of America, that I am not a naturalized citizen, that I have never been convicted of a crime, that I did not reside in Washington prior to 1886, when Washington was a territory, that I own property, have committed no treasonable act against the flag, and have lived in this precinct one year, three months, and twenty-two days. Feeling slightly guilty, and as if I hadn't told all, I handed the pen back to Mrs. Tilley who—or was it my imagination?—seemed to feel the same way about things.

———

Released, I hurried down the darkening road, my spirits rising as I took a lungful of unstandardized Pacific air. I made bold to hail Sheriff McArthur, who was driving my way in the Black Maria, and beg for a ride. We rode a pleasant two miles, the headlight flashing in and out among the pines on the curving road, and the searchlight, with which the car was equipped, exploring the side roads and sand trails where thieves and evil doers might be lurking. Where an overgrown trail leads from the highway to the back of my neighbor's farm, we picked out a small black and white skunk who leapt from the ground in sort of a whirling dance and was unable, it appeared, to escape from McArthur's pursuing light. As we neared my gate, he turned the flash on my weather-beaten cottage lying snugly against the dunes. It stood out with its rim of summer chrysanthemums and second-growth marigolds in intensified light, surrounded by a dark halo of shadowy dunes and pines. I smiled approvingly at it in the dark. Here was the "property" which I had testified to owning on the registration form, and which had risen up to give me face in Mrs. Tilley's parlor when all else seemed to be conspiring to make me out a low order of person with a natural tendency to commit felony, hanker after treason, lie about my middle years, and withhold secret knowledge of territorial activities prior to 1886—all for the avowed purpose of claiming citizenship. As it was, I felt that I had gotten in under the wire only by a nose, and a rather dubious nose at that. But not—I reminded myself happily as I crossed the pasture—a nose without property. Inside my four walls I turned on the lamp, lit the fire, sat down and stretched my feet toward the blaze. The moment was propitious, I realized, for self-congratulation; for an unpleasant second or two, there in Mrs. Tilley's parlor, I was afraid I wasn't going to make the grade. As to what I will do with my ballot, now that I have one: I will vote for a state of affairs where all who want two-toned carpets can have them, and all those who don't want them won't have to have them. And the same thing goes for jello every night for supper because it is good for you. And it begins to look . . . But pardon me! My time is up.

Buck Fever

November 4, 1944

THIS IS THE TIME OF YEAR when every other neighbor you meet on the road says, "Could you use a piece of venison?" And you say you've already got a piece but thanks just the same. At least that's what I say. I haven't got a piece of venison, and I don't want one. It took me three weeks last year to cook up the generous gifts of friends, and this year I'm all venisoned out.

The best place to pluck a wild duck is on top of a sand dune. Pick a high dune in the center of an extensive waste of sand, and if there is a stiff wind blowing from north or south, you can go ahead and let the feathers fly. If the wind is to landward however, beware—the feathers will come home to roost in the eaves of your house. I have tried to figure out a way to pluck a wild duck without getting feathers in my ears, and I have about come to the conclusion that it can't be done. But when a neighbor asks, "Could you use a couple of wild ducks?" I always say yes. And I don't mention that I already have several couples of wild ducks at home in the cooler.

We are the better down here for the advent of a meat wagon—a glistening, red-painted, refrigerated traveling butcher shop, which honks a mellow, coach-like horn at the gate twice a week. Yesterday the young fellow who drives it gave me a lift to the village, and I was surprised on climbing into the cab to find a shotgun leaning up against the seat. Every once in a while, the young fellow told me, he gets a duck. We slowed down to watch a flight of wild geese string across the sky, but at a height well beyond the range of our armored truck.

———

Have harvested my crop of winter potatoes. From thirty-six plants I got four cartons; enough to last all winter. The largest—there were a few really potato-sized ones—I put in a box on the porch in plain sight of any visitors who may arrive. The lesser or marble-sized ones, which constitute the bulk of the crop, I have stored away out of sight. It is my intention to present them to unsuspecting neighbors, using the old venison gag— "Could you use some new potatoes?" All those who avail themselves of the offer will be given, free of charge, a sample packet of the New Victory Garden Midget; patent applied for.

———

Robert, my sixteen-year-old neighbor, having been kept home from school this day in the interest of the family wood pile, was observed by this correspondent shortly after lunch escaping, under cover of the north pasture fence, to the dunes—shotgun in hand. From the sound of things—I can hear his gun blasting away down on the beach— hunting must be pretty good. He won't dare take his kill home, so it is quite logical for me to predict that before nightfall there will be another duck or two in my cooler. Strange indeed are the workings of nature.

Turn of the Year

November 11, 1944

NOW THE COWS, which in summer time obey the herd laws, are turned loose on the road, and wander in unrestrained glee, eating the rambler roses off the fences, and shredding the lower limbs from the poplar trees which stand in the lane. The chickens from the farm at the edge of the marsh come every day to dig up the crocus bed, and one white hen, a gentle lady-like creature of undeniable breeding, has even come to the back door and asked for a donation of cracked wheat for the hen's welfare drive she is conducting. I gave her a couple of handfuls, explaining at the same time that it was hard for me to get, as I had to carry all supplies from the village two miles away on shanks mares. She clucked with sympathy and said that she wouldn't be asking for another donation until the next morning. She comes regularly now, and the question is: Am I going to have a garden or a hen? Joe, who was fixing up a batch of leaks on the roof, said there wasn't any question to it—he'd bring along his twenty-two next time he came and we'd cook up something. Later I saw him feed her some of his luncheon sandwich. That was days ago and Joe still continues to contribute to Henny Penny's fund. When I ask him where's his twenty-two, he laughs as if he were hearing a worn-out joke.

"When you get to know something, it's different," he philosophized yesterday.

So I guess I won't have any crocuses next year.

———

Our sheriff did yeoman service in the storm, election day, picking up all beach strays and taking them to the polls. Among those picked up by the Black Maria were two old ladies who didn't know what county they were in (they were in the wrong one) and a Finnish gentleman who had undertaken to walk to the next precinct, a distance of seven miles, so he could vote for a Finnish candidate he insisted was on the ticket there. We were finally set down at our proper station, and filed in before the election board, wet as dogs. Here the village ladies sat authoritatively, pens in hand, and gave us our ballots. A pleasant steam arose from a kettle of stew athwart a stove made of an oil drum. Soothed, somewhat, we went into the booths and set down those rows of little crosses with which we hoped to change the pattern of the world.

———

Call for Bids on Westport Gear
by Army Engineers at Seattle
From *The Grays Harbor Post*, November 11, 1944

> *The office of the Pacific Division, U.S. Army Engineers, has announced through the Seattle Real Estate Sub-Office that the War Department will sell three (3) groups of installations located near Westport, Grays Harbor County, Washington, in what is known as Westport Cantonment Area, more definitively described as follows:*
> *Water supply and distribution system consisting of supply tank with fittings and tower, 60,000-gallon capacity, pump house, 8 x 8 feet with Fairbanks Morse Home Water System complete, pump house, . . .*

Chronology for 1944

November

4   All German forces driven from Greece.

7   Nationwide elections held. President Roosevelt reelected by 53% of popular vote, winning 36 states. 20 Democrats and 13 Republicans gain Senate seats. Democrats elect 242 representatives, and Republicans 185. 18 Republican and 13 Democratic governors elected.

11 U.S. planes sink eight Jap warships.

14 British bombers sink *Tirpitz*, famous German battleship, in Norwegian port.

16 Great Allied drive launched on 300-mile front from Holland to Vosges.

18 Special committee on wartime living reports to President that rise is 29% over January 1, 1941, level.

20 French troops reach Rhine River in plunge through Belfort gap.

21 Lieut. Gen. Patton leads Third army in drive 23 miles beyond Metz.

24 B-29s bomb Tokyo factories from base in Marianas, 1,550 miles away.

29 U.S. Third army attacks forts at Saarbrucken, Saarlautern, and Merzig.

30 U.S. planes sink 10 Jap transports and three destroyers, drowning 4,000 near Leyte.

Beach Business

November 18, 1944

SPENT MY OFF HOURS last week planting five hundred Croft lily bulbs, or what are commonly called Easter lilies. The sandy soil having been found well-nigh perfect for lilies, every man jack of us decided to make a lily industry safe for democracy. It seems that before Pearl Harbor we imported twenty million bulbs annually from Japan to the tune of five million dollars. My Italian neighbor, Tony Ceslev, went to work on the idea early in the game and succeeded this year making *Time* magazine and $9,000. The bulbs are harvested in the late summer and fall, and sold to greenhouses to force into spring bloom. The groundwork has to be done "in the field," if you can call a sand lot a field.

After one week's experience with five hundred bulbs, I am, of course, unable to speak authoritatively on the subject, but I did get a glimmering, after four days on my hands and knees, that the Japs undoubtedly earned their five million dollars. You go about planting by digging a six-inch trench, sprinkling in a bed of peat, and setting each bulb (they are about the size of hazel nuts) on a little mound of steamed bone meal. Then you cover them up and scour the neighborhood for barnyard fertilizer with which to cover the bed to a thickness of one inch. When you can't find the barnyard variety you come home and order the commercial kind, delicately known as chicken peat. There is nothing to do after that but to sit back on your haunches and read a pamphlet called "Croft Lily Insects You Should Know." Which is all right with me. I'm looking forward to getting to know a new bunch of insects. I'm all fed up with corn borers and potato beetles, and badly need some stimulating new contacts.

My neighbor across the road who cans choice crab legs and whole razor clams, re-turned last week from the industrial front where he went to the mat with OPA, the Pure Foods and Drugs Administration, the lieutenant-governor of the state, and the state's attorney. If you could see his little shake-covered cannery you would know that that was a pretty big order for one backwoods canneryman to take on. He had been experi-menting around with canning gray fish, got four hundred cases of good luscious product in the cans, sold it, and was all ready to ship it out when these "administrative vul-tures"—to quote my friend across the road—descended upon him and demanded that he label his product "Shark Meat." After spending a sleepless night, he got up the next morning, put on his store suit and drove to meet his adversaries, armed only with an old copy of the Encyclopedia Britannica. It was a very ancient Britannica, but it said that gray fish were fish. And it didn't say they were sharks. This pronouncement took the enemy off guard; they shoveled hastily around among books and papers but were un-able to produce anything to the contrary. It seems that no one has provided the state and the Pure Food Administration with the proper precedent for changing the names of God's creatures overnight and it was reluctantly admitted that "gray fish" it would have to be. And "gray fish" it is. And very good too—I dumped a can of it into green peppers and onions browned in butter, folded it into a cream sauce, and baked it in the oven under a crust of cracker meal. The first order of this new product was purchased by one of Seattle's big department stores.

———

As I walked to the village I witnessed a right pretty sight—two burr-voiced Norwegian fishermen had spread out along the high-way for a hundred feet some lengths of heavy rope cable which they were splicing for a drag net. The straight stretch of road made an ideal, level, work table on which to fabricate the intri-cate "line," of which, even after they attempted to explain it, I could make neither head nor tail. It isn't every place where you can turn a corner in the lonesome pine woods and find fisher-men at work. I wish more people would bring their chores out on the highway. During the gasoline shortage, when so many people have to walk, it would lighten up the scene considerably to turn the corner and come upon a quilting bee, say, or some one of the other manual arts in full swing. Since coming upon the net-makers, I'm for making more and better use of our pub-lic highways.

Club Night

November 25, 1944

I HAVE JOINED A CLUB. I've never been much of a club person. To be really truthful about the matter I haven't ever belonged to a club, but have gotten such knowledge as I have from social column accounts of organized, decorous, gatherings where papers are read by well-groomed women who later sit down to dessert luncheons lighted by pink or lavender candles, as the case may be. Somehow, clubs didn't sound very vital. It was the dessert luncheon clause, I suppose, which discouraged me—if the papers had ever published anything about a club that sat down to a good, rare roast beef dinner I might have been interested. But they never did. So I was pretty gun-shy when invited to join a club down here. If I let myself in for pink and blue tapers at my age, I thought, it's a sure sign I'm slipping. So I asked if I couldn't attend a trial meeting as a guest.

My neighbor called for me at seven o'clock on Monday evening. It was raining hard, and my freshly curled hair unrolled into dank locks as I ran across the pasture and climbed into the tonneau of the darkened car. We drove down the road and turned off into a byway through the pine woods, and eventually, after many false turns and one stall on a bridge over a slough, we arrived at a barrack-like building which loomed darkly in the night and from the chimney of which there issued a welcoming shower of sparks.

We hurried inside and I saw that we were in an abandoned army kitchen. A coal fire glowed in an immense coal range, and about it, rubbing their hands above the stove's hot surface, were many members of the club. Others were seated on benches around the great oblong tables. There was no sign of roast beef or any other collation. But there weren't any tapers either, and I was delighted to see my fisherman friend among those present, and numerous friends of my fisherman friend.

The meeting opened without any ceremony whatsoever. The subject under discussion, I gathered, was the razor clam, and whether he should be dug only when, and where, the State Fisheries Department decreed, or taken, as it were, on the run and at any time of day or night by crab fishermen, who use him to bait their crab traps, and others on the beach. When it became apparent that no one was going to read a paper on Ralph Waldo Emerson's poetry, or give a review of a Doubleday-Doran current best seller, I sat back and enjoyed myself. During the part where state biologists presented graphs showing how digging had depleted the clam beaches I snoozed cozily beside the coal stove. But when Dick Strong got up and told about what he saw one night on the beach when he was hiding out from the clam cops, I sat up and opened my eyes. It was during the depression and he was breaking the law to feed his family, he said. He would run out with his shovel, dig a few clams, then run back and hide behind a log. He heard a peculiar noise, like someone walking. And it was the clams! They would come in with a wave, anchor themselves and hang on. When another wave came they would let go and move forward again. The receding surf, among the hundreds of advancing clams, made the thudding noise, he said. And since that night, he said, he hasn't had much faith in the state biologists' theory that clams stayed put and moved about very little, and just waited around to be depleted.

Razor Clam
Siliqua patula

Old Mr. Hinton from the Cove,* who has lived on the beach for fifty-eight years, also disputed the clam graphs. He said the intervals illustrated by the graphs were too close together in time and meant nothing when compared with the mysterious graphs which nature herself put before men's eyes in her own good time. He said that there had been three such incidents in his fifty-eight years' observation, the first taking place in June of 1894. At that time there was thrown up on the beach, from Cohassett to North Cove, a windrow of clams eleven feet or so wide and three feet deep. Twice since, the same thing has occurred. Mr. Hinton, a staunch, ruddy-cheeked little man with an expression of child-like wonderment in his eyes, shook his head at the state's graphs. They were just so many lines on paper and didn't prove, to him at least, that clams were in danger of extinction. Someday, within the next fifty years, Mr. Hinton thinks, nature will again show her abundance, and give the lie to all graphs by casting up another great sea harvest.

There was something extremely soothing in Mr. Hinton's revelations, and I, for one, am all for giving nature and the clams another half a hundred years before any drastic prohibitive regulations are put in force. Furthermore, I have become a confirmed club woman. As we wound home through the dripping pine woods, took a couple of wrong turns and got stalled on the little bridge again, I discussed with my host the plans for our next meeting.

---

* Probably North Cove.

Chronology of 1944

December

1 Strikes in Detroit and Chicago delay production of B-29 bombers.
2 Nazis withdraw troops from Norway.
   War and navy boards rule that Pearl Harbor commanders will not be court-martialed.
6 B-29s raid Jap bases on Bonin islands. Others hit Tokyo again.
7 Sedition trial of 26 defendants ends in mistrial.
   Prison revolt of 25 Atlanta convicts ended.
8 Units of 77th division make new landing on Leyte, splitting Jap lines.
11 France and Russia sign mutual assistance pact.
13 B-29s hit Nagoya, Japanese aircraft production center.
   War prisoners at Fort Sheridan, Ill., go on sit-down strike; 1,300 put on bread and water.
14 U.S. tank and infantry units reach outskirts of Duren, key to Cologne region.
   Production quotas on machine guns reduced to release workers for more critical items.
15 U.S. Seventh army advances to German border on 35-mile front.
16 Germans launch a surprise winter offensive in the Ardennes Forest against U.S. Third army.
   [Beginning of the Battle of the Bulge.]

Business as Usual

December 2, 1944

I DON'T WANT TO AROUSE any false hopes about a change in the manpower situation, nor, on the other hand, do I want to be caught napping when the tide of human affairs turns back to normal. It's got to begin turning somewhere. And who am I to say that such an earth-shaking event couldn't take place right here in my own backyard? And perhaps it has. Anyway, there was a knock at the door, and when I opened it there stood Robert, my sixteen-year-old neighbor, who—unsolicited, unbribed, unintimidated and unwooed— asked if I had any work to be done! After I showed him the wood to be piled, the fallen pines to be sawed up, and the gutters to be cleared of sand, I came in and sat down all trembly at the knees. It's the first time since Pearl Harbor that anyone has asked me for a job.

Local Improvement

December 9, 1944

THE MOST POPULAR MAN on the beach is a neighbor who owns a cigarette-rolling machine. A path is being beaten to his door. He views with skepticism his present prominence and knows that his days as a man of importance are numbered. Just let a carton of cigarettes appear in our midst and we would abandon him with the alacrity of rats leaving a sinking ship. In the meantime, he keeps the cigarette-making gadget set up on the kitchen table with a newspaper underneath to catch the gleanings, and a broom handy for those unskilled operators who, like myself, put more tobacco on the floor than we do in a smoke. I haven't any opinions on what created the cigarette shortage, but I know from the looks of that path through the salmonberry bushes that it wasn't caused by the hoarding of my neighbors. Everyone who smokes and who has two legs to walk on is using the cigarette machine.

———

As I passed the home of Tony Ceslev, who recently made *Time* magazine and $9,000 pioneering in Croft lily bulbs, he leaned over the gate and called to me to come in. "You can open up some mail, if you want," he said persuasively, biting a hunk from a large banana.

"What mail?" I asked.

"The mail I got. You know—about that write-up. From every state in the union. Everybody wants bulbs. I don't even read about it any more. What's the use?" He tossed the empty banana skin into a compost heap.

"But you can open some if you like."

I said I didn't have time to open letters just then; that I would come some other day and read orders from every state in the union. It didn't sound like a very interesting pastime to me. It was only when I got down the road that I realized I had missed a point of the interview: Why in thunder hadn't I found out where he got that banana!

Night Life

December 16, 1944

MY OLD DAVENPORT got a new cover this week. The red calico print which it wore for ten years simply disintegrated, took to coming off in disconcerting patches on the rears of people who sat upon it, so that it was not unusual to see a visitor leave with a red calico patch on the most prominent part of his jeans—at least that's how my fisherman friend left the house on Saturday night. People don't like it, after they leave a place, to have to stop and pluck pieces of calico off their persons. So now the davenport has a slip cover.

I know there's a war on. All the advertisements in the women's magazines keep reminding their readers that there's a war on and that they shouldn't forget it for an instant and should keep up world morale by using various advertised products such as rainbow-colored nail enamels, non-shrinkable satin slips, and should never go to bed at night unless covered by a hundred per cent rose-colored wool blanket and sheets of the finest long thread cotton. If you're a real patriot, according to the magazines, you'll also buy a little $60 an ounce perfume to put behind your ears, and a $250 trinket or two to clip on the front of your gown. Makes you feel better, and makes everyone you meet feel better, if you show a glint of amethyst or topaz appropriately surrounded by diamonds and refuse to eat anything but Hormel hams.

No one is urged to buy new septic tanks, squander money getting their tonsils out, or build up morale with new davenport covers. All such expenditures are considered, apparently, self-indulgence of the lowest order. So I was feeling pretty furtive when I went to Kress' store and bought the barn-red calico with the pink roses on it. It is made now, and looks, with its crisp full ruffle around the bottom, like something out of a gay Nineties valentine. It doesn't have five cents' worth of pretentiousness about it. It looks like calico. And it IS calico. My fisherman friend will take to it as a duck takes to water.

———

Over across the pasture, beyond the road where the leafless willows stand against their background of spruce trees, a mist of color hangs in the air. It is the sap rising in the willows. The sun, before it sinks into the sea, reaches landward and picks out mauve-sapped willows, pink-sapped willows and willows with bright orange-colored buds spreading their wares on the dune tops. There is nothing as color loving as the winter sun. "Look," says the winter sun, and immediately the dried beach grass turns to gold, the white, red-roofed, fog horn station stands out so vividly you can almost feel it. Above the little wind-bent pines the lighthouse stands tall and strong, its great glass lantern reflecting amber light. The moment the sun has set the golden light fades from the land, and grayness creeps in from the sea. Five minutes after sunset, the lighthouse glows like a hot coal, and the first red flash swings above the pine tops and out to sea. As the twilight deepens, the flashes become intensified, and finally as night settles down the lighthouse becomes the center and focus of night on the beach.

———

I went, one frosty, starlit night, to the dock to take a look at the new tavern. There was the heave and tug of boats at their moorings, and over all, the stars. From the luminous darkness where the dock juts out from its sandy spit, warm air came from the sea, brushed lightly the rigging, stirred softly among the gear and tackle. To landward there was frost. On the dock—while it looked like frost, and the stars crackled overhead— you felt the warm breath of the Pacific about your ankles.

Inside, the new tavern was a glistening box of varnished white pine. There were customers, a fisherman and a coast guardsman having a beer. The coast guardsman, spare fellow of forty or so, with the lined face and alert eyes of a mechanic, was telling the fisherman about the boat he engineered on. "She's fifty-two feet long and with a whale of an engine, she cost the government $100,000," he said. "And she rides so

Westport Lighthouse

rough, there's only three of us to take a turn in the engine room without getting sick. You're wedged in there and after a run with her, you come out black and blue from the hips down." He held his hand out before him to show how "she went." "First she tips this way," he said, turning his hand sidewide with a slow sinking motion. "Then she goes that way," and he reversed the motion. Then THIS way!" He stood up on the rail and shot his arm forward with a lunge. "Or go straight down. That's when it leaves your stomach in your throat. And when she comes up again, your insides stay down in your feet. There's not many can stand it. We get a young fellow in there and with the fumes and all, he gets green pretty soon and says 'You take over,' and beats it to the deck and hangs on the rail and says he wishes he was on a nice, easy-going bomber or something. There's not another ship like her in the world."

"The sickest I ever got," said the fisherman, putting down his glass, "was off Split Rock. We had a holdful of shark livers. It was a warm night . . ."

I didn't hear the rest of the sentence. I left the new tavern in a hurry.

December

December 23, 1944

DROVE TO SEATTLE and back Sunday through the fog-blackened, frost-glazed countryside, and all I can say about the trip is that if someone came in and said do you want to drive to Seattle and back today, or would you prefer to go along on a bombing jaunt from Saipan to Tokyo, I'd rise up and declaim, "Lead me to that bomber!" And without waiting to be led I'd break into a dead heat and make a bee-line for the nearest Boeing bomber.

Robert, my sixteen-year-old neighbor, has settled his Christmas worries. He's decided to take Mom and Dad and eight brothers and sisters to the movies—that is, if he can swing the deal. He had it all figured out once, and then last week, the moths got into the pants of his suit, and he had to work up $9 and tax for another pair. If I get another load of wood and let him put it in, he figures he can make it. We've discussed the pros and cons of all the dilemma and I have decided to help him; but it all depends on Mr. Hazen Holmes, the wood man. Will he give me another load? He isn't supposed to, he says. It's against OPA. I've got wood, and he isn't supposed to bring me any more until I'm down to my last stick. However, when I put it up to him how things were, he said he'd go home and sleep on it. If I get the wood, it will cost me $18.55, and Lord knows what it will cost Robert to take ten people to the movies. Frankly, I don't like these big complicated business deals. I'll be glad when Christmas is over and I can start watching for the first crocus to pop up beside my doorstep. Just between you and me, I've about decided that I like crocuses better than Christmas anyhow. And (it's a mean thing to do, and almost unethical before the first of January) I'm going to announce the arrival of the first pussy willow. It has popped, like a piece of corn, on the tree on the dune top. You might say, almost, that Spring has sunk her teeth in Santa Claus' heels. But that's all right with me.

The "Schoolhouse"

December 30, 1944

SET A BUILDING DOWN in cow-clipped pasture land, give it a background of stretching marsh and misty bay, place a couple of tall, sky-swishing spruce trees in the middle distance and a sprinkling of munching cows in the lee of the white sand dunes which tumble in from the north. And, if your building is one basement and two stories high, with a tower, and made of wind-grayed clapboards with a faded red roof, a double staircase and a general air of having been dreamed up in the Nineties and forgotten these many years, why—well, then you have our schoolhouse. All cut of scale with the little white houses and the bleached slab-sided cottages of the village across the way, it looms in perpetual elegance above the plain, and recalls, if you want to let yourself in for that sort of thing, the day when the town was a resort and not a fishing village; when a great curlicued veranda-ed hotel kept it company; when the stern-wheeled steamers dumped their passengers into waiting horse-drawn stages at the end of the long dock, from whence they were whisked away to Lowery's Hotel or Mrs. King's boarding house where good clam chowder was the order of the day; and where picture postcards could be purchased showing various scenes—the town's fine new schoolhouse, among others—all with the identical caption:—"At the Seashore."

A new, modern, one-storied schoolhouse stands at the other end of the town, and the old building hasn't seen a boy or girl for years. Nevertheless, it remains the important building of the town. It took me a little time to get on to the state of things. I was sitting in the kitchen of the wife of my fisherman friend along about suppertime one evening when she shoved the potatoes back on the stove and said, with what I couldn't help but feel was a touch of envy, "He's going to be late again, I guess. Probably sitting over there at the schoolhouse with his long Norwegian legs curled around a stool."

When I wanted to know what he would be doing at the schoolhouse at that hour, she said, why drinking beer, of course. What did anyone do at the schoolhouse? And she went on to tell me that once [you] let a Norwegian get his long legs curled around a bar stool at the schoolhouse, nothing could pry him loose. Not even salt herring and boiled potatoes for supper.

So that's how I learned about the schoolhouse. There's a beer hall in the basement. It is the town club. If, in the afternoon, you want to get a new crochet pattern from a neighbor and she isn't home, you'll find her at the schoolhouse. Clicking her needles, probably, and sipping a modest glass. At night the place blazes with light, and along the bar the white-capped fishermen sit through the hours, while in the cavernous rear basement grotto, the polka blares from the music box and young and old fling their heels with gusto. Father and son are there; mother and daughter. About the walls a crew, fresh off a big shark boat from the Bering sea, stand watchfully, taking things in. They wear knitted watch caps, and their eyes are dark in their unshaven faces. One wears a gold earring. They bring with them a feeling of foreigners. There is Portuguese blood here. And Indian. And a dark conglomerate brew distilled from heaven knows what chance landings in a hundred years of Pacific landings. Now they stand watching the pretty Scandinavian girls dance the polka. They do not drink beer.

Above the din and brightness of the basement beer hall, the old schoolhouse stands with its sightless, empty windows. Every two minutes, the beam of the lighthouse swings about and brushes warmly across the faded red roof and the tower. Then the stars prick through the empty windows again, and the sound of the sea echoes from the old hollow structure. Down in the basement my fisherman friend unwinds his long Norwegian legs from the stool, adjusts his white peaked cotton cap in the back bar mirror, looks himself steadily in the eye, and runs over in his mind his homecoming speech which is something about why in hell isn't dinner on the table when a man gets home from the sea.

1945

Music in the Making

January 6, 1945

THERE WAS A KNOCK at the door early New Year's Day and there stood Robert, my sixteen-year-old neighbor, and a covey of six of his nine brothers and sisters from the small end of the scale. They followed him into the room. Robert sat down on the davenport and they alighted beside him in split second intervals, like a flock of quail coming to rest on the beach. I tried to divert some of them to chairs, fluttering my apron and "shooing," but they eluded my gesturing hands and circled to rest beside their brother, where they stared at me, large-eyed and speechless, like so many frightened birds on a submerged log. There goes my new slip cover, I said to myself, and Robert said, "Could I use your telephone?"

Immediately, all the birds leaned forward and stared harder than ever, their eyes unblinking, their bodies breathless.

I said Robert could use the telephone. All the birds heaved a simultaneous sigh and leaned back. They looked down shyly at their Christmas-mittened hands, trying to hide the pleasure in their eyes, and waited.

Robert stood up, walked right over to the table by the fireplace and snubbed his cigarette out in the scalloped glass ash tray. Nobody breathed. He walked over to the end of the room where the telephone stood on the desk. All heads were craned. He rang the bell twice and got the rural operator and asked for a number. There was a long silence as we waited. We could hear the faint click-click-click as the operator buzzed the number. Finally Dorothy, the seven-year-old one, could contain herself no longer. "He's going to tell my aunt about grandpa," Dorothy said. And she flashed me a soft, shy glance. "Grandpa isn't my real grandpa," whispered Dorothy. "He's my real grandpa's father. He lives over east of the mountains."

During our whispered conversation Robert stood by his post. We could hear the click-click-click of the buzzer ringing and ringing. It occurred to me that auntie was probably abed, it being the day after New Year's, and even now but eight o'clock in the morning. But Robert told the operator to keep on trying. Pretty soon auntie said "Hello!" in a voice all of us could hear.

Robert didn't say hello or Happy New Year or anything, but went right ahead and delivered his message. He said to auntie: "Grandpa came last night and he wants to take and come over and tune your piano this morning."

There was a protesting, clacking squawk from the receiver.

Robert continued: "Grandpa tuned our piano last night and he wants to tune yours this morning. If he comes over right away, he can get done in three or four hours and get back over east of the mountains."

The receiver clacked and protested some more. It kept on clacking and protesting for quite a while.

Robert listened politely until auntie ran out of gas. Then he went on delivering his message: "Grandpa says he's got to make his trip count. He's got to tune it today. He says it'll take till dinner time. He'll be over right away."

Robert hung up. Everyone relaxed and Dorothy told what they got for Christmas. All the girls got knitted fascinators and mittens—red fuzzy-wuzzy ones—and the boys got jackets. Then there were three games; a grown-up game for the three big ones, a middle-sized game, and a teeny-weeny game for the little ones. Mom's brother came over with his guitar and played it. All the aunts and uncles and children came, and the big ones danced while Mom cooked dinner. And she danced too. With her brother. And he played the guitar while he danced with her. And he danced with Dorothy while he played the guitar. They all played the games and nobody had to go to bed, but could stay up and dance all night. Of course the little ones fell asleep. Right on the couch where the old cat has her kittens.

When Dorothy had finished about Christmas, Robert stood up to go. The covey rose from the davenport, followed him single file from the house, clustered tight on his heels as he crossed the pasture.

The telephone rang. I answered it and took a message for Robert. I said I thought I could catch him if I hurried. I hung up and flew to the door. I could see the file of red fascinators going down the lane. I took a full breath and let go with a high-pitched and raucous "Roo . . . bert!" The fascinators froze in their tracks. "Robert," I screamed, "your aunt says for grandpa to go right on in. She'll leave the door unlocked. She's called away to North Cove. She says you children can go over, too, if you want, and watch grandpa tune the piano."

Written in Sand

January 13, 1945

THE TIME TO BEACHCOMB is right after a southwest gale. Enough sea-drenched bark was cast up recently to stoke the stoves of Grays Harbor County. Here and there a fine clean log has come in, and in no time at all it is discovered by a truck-cruising wood hunter who saws it up and carries it away. I never come off the beach without a sack of bark slung over my shoulder—not a whole sack, alas, as I

Chronology of 1945

January

1 U.S. Third army attacks north of Bastogne against Germans' Belgium salient. In France, the Germans attack U.S. Seventh [continuing Battle of the Bulge]. In the Pacific, American planes raid Luzon and Negros islands in the Philippines.

9 German bulge in Belgium compressed by new Allied gains.

10 Forces under General MacArthur invade Luzon, in Philippines.

16 Seven billion dollars' worth of liquor was swallowed in the U.S. during 1944, not counting bootleg, the Department of Commerce reports, an 18% increase over 1943.

17 Warsaw, Polish capital, falls to Russians.

18 "Somewhere down the line someone made a mistake," regrets Secretary of War Stimson, referring to the bumping of three servicemen from an army cargo plane to make room for a dog. The mastiff was consigned by Col. Elliott Roosevelt to his wife, Faye, in Hollywood, Calif. It had been purchased in England.

20 President Roosevelt inaugurated for fourth term.

23 Russian forces reach Oder River.

28 U.S. First army strikes near St. Vith, Belgium. British advance north of Aachen, Germany.

29 Russians reach a point 93 miles from Berlin. American Third army enters Germany for first time near Oberhausen. French forces also smash across border.

can't manage that. Those small pieces of wet bark are heavy. But they hold a fire for hours. I can walk to the store and back and find a bed of glowing coals when I return.

The charm of beachcombing is bounded on all sides by the elements of surprise—what will be today? And what, once you have picked up your first find, will the second object be? And the third? You may be sure they will be as unrelated to each other as are fish, flesh, and fowl. This is a pretty big ocean and the highway which runs by my door washes the shores of eastern Asia before it turns its warm current across the Pacific and strews our coast with hand-blown fish floats, bamboo masts, and woven mats. Ten to fourteen months it takes to make that crossing, it has been figured out by experiments with messages in bottles. Other more scientific ways exist, I am informed, of measuring the drift and speed of ocean currents, but I belong to the message-in-the-bottle school.

I have never found a bottle with a message in it, but I've found lots of bottles; empty ones. Mostly big Imperial-sized, smoky green glass Scotch bottles. Seafaring men, it appears, simply consider any other size beneath contempt. So regularly are these bottles cast ashore that I have about come to the conclusion that it is one of the conventions of crossing the Grays Harbor bar to get rid of a bottle or two of Scotch outward bound and a further convention to toss the empties overboard once the bar pilot has bidden the captain farewell, wiped his mouth, climbed down the ladder to his waiting tug, and left the freighter headed into the open sea.

On the beach I know what my neighbors miles away are doing. When a drift of red berries comes in in November, I know they are cleaning the cranberry bogs at Grayland. If a green spruce, root and all, comes in, I know there has been high water on North River or up the Humptulips. Here someone has had to throw away a whole case of home-canned salmon in mason jars which didn't seal. And there are signs that a family has moved out—a heap of sand-covered odds and ends; a rusted wash tub, dungarees, an air tight heater, an ironing board, a faded house coat, a child's red slippers, a schoolbook, a dustpan and broom.

After a storm, crab pot floats come ashore—the painted, wooden, bottle-shaped individual markers that the fishermen use to locate their pots. Some are shaped like vases with rounded bowls and long narrow necks. They are painted red, orange, white, and red and white. I have never seen a blue or green one. Those colors would be hard to distinguish at sea. Once I found where a sailor had cut the skirts off his jacket, clean as a whistle. The beautiful blue cloth lay sodden on the sand. A sailor must have been in quite some straits to do a thing like that.

I can tell by the beach that a ship has passed—a cluster of grapefruit rinds, the heart of a cabbage (cut out with a cleaver, along with the best part of the cabbage), a dozen or so onions, potatoes, and lemons, in fact enough good vegetables to feed a family is thrown out of the galley when the cook gets through seasoning his stew. Things thrown overboard at sea, if of the same weight and quality, come ashore on the self-same wave. And times without number I have seen the cabbage, the onions, the lemons, and potatoes clustered together on the beach. I visualize the hurrying cook then and his impatience and how, having got things on to boil, he gathers up with professional scorn these humble leavings and throws them out the galley port.

After the storm today, I found a kidney-shaped dressing table. A few shreds of chintz were all that the sea had left of its full flounced skirt, but the table itself was intact lying there in the drift of logs and seaweed. You can't see a thing like that and not wonder how it happened to be there. In the first place, we don't go in for chintz-flounced kidney-shaped dressing tables on this beach. But someone did! Someone wanted beauty. And elegance. And then . . .

What happened? Something pretty cataclysmic, I guess, in someone's life. As I looked at the little dressing table, I had a very definite feeling that whoever owned it once was far, far away from this beach. I hurried on to where a big rye whisky bottle stuck its nose out of the sand. I edged it up and rolled it over with the toe of my shoe. Imported, it was. And the best. There is something heartening in these big bottles. Shows that life these days on the rolling deep has its light moments.

Starfish
Pisaster ochraceus

The Pipe Dream

January 20, 1945

AT THE DANCE SATURDAY, all the women arrived together in small groups and the men came later—one at a time. Nobody was disturbed or uneasy on that account. They knew where the men were, all right. They were over at the barber shop. On Saturday night our barber keeps his shop open until the last straggling troller has moored. The crew, hurrying in a huddle from the long dock, make for the low, lighted building to landward where steam baths are available. And if there is a dance or "a doings" of some sort, they go from the bath to the barber's. Sometimes on Saturday nights our barber cuts every male head of hair in town and shaves every jowl.

Pretty soon the men started coming in to the dance. The door would open and in would walk a shining fellow fresh from the barber's chair. Then pretty soon someone else would arrive. They formed a little cluster near the door, sitting on the bench or standing facing each other. They would all look up when the door opened and greet the newcomer with congratulatory or facetious quips on his appearance and then absorb him into the group. While the women danced the men stood about and talked about boats. There are long restful silences in these conversations. After a while, someone says, "I see where the *Hilda*'s up for sale." Someone else says, "I wouldn't have her on a bet." This is followed by a chorus of "me neithers," after which another long restful silence ensues.

I sat down by Reg Elbee. His pale, narrow face was expressionless. A hackle of dun-colored hair freshly pomaded sprouted back from his brow, the jagged sweep resembling somehow a shark's fin. His eyes were half closed and he lazed in a pool of smoke of his own making. I sat there until he finished his cigarette, doing all the talking. After a while he put out his cigarette. He said: "The time I appreciated a smoke most was that time I got swamped out there." I asked when that was and he said, "Why that time two years ago. It was in the papers. Not about the smoke I mean, but about me getting swamped. Didn't you read it?"

I said no, I guess I didn't.

Reg said that was funny, because it was in the papers. "Well, what happened" I asked.

"Nothing," Reg said. "Except I was swamped out there. Submerged. There wasn't nothing but the top of the pilot house sticking out. I didn't have a bite to eat. Then up out of the hatch popped this mason jar with my pipe and tobacco and matches in it. I always keep a dry smoke in the galley. I keep it in a jar on a shelf where it won't get damp. So I grabs it and lights up. I was sure glad to see that pipe all right." He stopped talking and reached in his pocket for another cigarette.

"And then what happened?" I prodded.

"Nothing," Reg said.

"I mean how did you get in?" I insisted.

"I just stayed out there. Forty hours. Once or twice I almost give up."

"Where was the Coast Guard?" I said. "Didn't they come out?"

"Oh, they come out all right," Reg said. "They came out once and they couldn't find me. And they come out twice and they couldn't find me. There was a new captain then. He didn't know nothing about this ocean. That's what my brother told him when he got in the second time. The captain, he patted my brother on the back and said it was no use and he was sorry and all. But my brother just shook him off and said to hell with all that. 'Reg is out there,' he said. 'You go and get him.' And he carried on like a demon. So they come out and got me."

"Where did they find you?" I asked.

Reg raised a long arm and pointed toward the door which had just opened to admit our barber and the last pomaded customer of the evening. "Seventy miles due west," he said. He said it louder than he thought. When he said, "Seventy miles due west," his voice rang out so you could hear it all around. Everyone looked at Reg with his arm pointed toward the door. Then they laughed. Someone said, "What's the matter Reg? You having a pipe dream?"

"Seeing that pipe pop up sure made me feel good," Reg said. "Like your dog meeting you when you come home or something. But I'll give you the paper and you can read all about it. Only they left out that part about my pipe. And they left out about my brother. You don't want to dance, do you?"

"No," I said. "Do you?"

"Not if I don't have to," Reg said.

Private Lives

January 27, 1945

THE RAINSTORM FILLED all the roadside ditches and the hollows in the pastures were knee deep. The brook which meanders through the town, cutting through a field here and shooting under a woodshed there, is brimful. Out on the beach the depressions between the dunes are filled with water, and down at the sea's edge thousands of jellyfish have come ashore. They rest where the last wave of the high tide left them, reflecting the blue frosty sky which followed the storm, and they resemble, in the proper light, so many miniature ponds or puddles. They are about the size of dinner plates, and as transparent as glass. I walked for two miles avoiding jellyfish at every step, and not once did I observe a jellyfish with any outstanding characteristics. Occasionally I would come across a pie-plate-sized one, but for the most part they were almost identical in size, and as alike as peas in pods. "What a dull walk," I said to myself, and went home. I couldn't help but feel that if jellyfish had been left out of the scheme of things the world would still continue to turn on the axis.

I saw to it that I arrived at the home of my fisherman friend just about lunch time. When you've got only one ration book, you've got to keep your wits about you. His wife fed us home-baked beans, macaroni salad, smoked salmon, and apple pie. She begged me to stay for dinner, at which time, she assured me, they would have something substantial to eat. My fisherman friend, shored by a heavy surf, was tinkering about the garden, happily engaged in transplanting a twenty-foot pine to a new location only two feet from its present site. The process involved digging a hole you could float a dinghy in. "Why on earth are you moving that pine?" I called out as I clicked the garden gate behind me. "She's off center," my fisherman friend told me. He stood back of the pine and squinted one eye at the front door, then turned slowly about and squinted in the direction of the North Pole. "I'm just lining her up," he said. I didn't ask why she had to be lined up with the North Pole. If he wants to garden by dead reckoning, it's none of my affair.

Yesterday I answered the telephone and it was the telegraph company calling a young wife down here whose overseas husband hasn't been heard from for a long time. I told central she had the wrong number and gave her the correct one. Then before I knew it I found myself doing something awfully unethical. "Is . . . is it good news?" I asked in a quavering voice, knowing full well it was against all the rules—for me to ask or for central to answer. But I have watched the mail truck pass the girl's house for weeks now, and I have seen her as she turned to walk back up the path empty handed, stooping, perhaps, to pluck a withered seed pod from a dead thistle, or to stare for long moments at nothing. Central must have got something of all that from my voice: I believe she did. "It's good news," central said in a glad voice, throwing ethics to the wind. "Everything's fine." "God be praised," I said and thanked her.

The telegram, relayed shortly afterward via rural operator up and down the beach, said the boy was coming home.

Making the Best of Things

February 3, 1945

ACROSS THE ROAD frost glistened on my neighbor's roof and far-ther on, over against the marsh, the bursting pussy willows carried the white color scheme up into the blue sky. Down the road I heard the siren of the meat truck, a mellow, resonant sound with the haunting quality of an old English coach horn. If—instead of the compact little red meat truck—a coach and four should rattle into view with Mr. Pickwick on the box beside the driver and a couple of straddle-legged, loose-jointed coach hounds in hot pursuit, I shouldn't be a bit surprised. Indeed, so coach-hornish is the siren of our meat truck that I never fail to experience a feeling of disappointment when the fanfare ceases and the meat truck skids to a stop beside the gate. The feeling is only momentary, however; I can still revive the illusion aroused by the haunting horn—Mr. Pickwick and his coach and four have vanished, vanished in the direction of the village inn where horses will be changed amid the confusion and clatter of post boys, and where huge slices of juicy beef will be cut from the joint that sizzles on the spit. At that instant—just when Mr. Pickwick is rubbing his hands, stamping the frost out of his boots and advancing with hearty exclamations of approval toward the sputtering spit—phantasy and reality meet on common ground and I advance on the meat truck with but one thought in mind—juicy, dripping beef.

It was then (as I have said in a paragraph, and should have said in a sentence), a sparkling, frost-tipped day when I approached the meat truck with optimism in my heart and five red points in my hand. And determination in my soul. I had company coming to dinner and it was my intention, if I could possibly manage it, not to serve pork hearts. It so happens that, what with but one ration book and the butter crisis at hand, I haven't been able to do better by myself than an occasional pork heart, the only non-rationed commodity our meat truck carries. And the rewards of three weeks of pork hearts I now clutched firmly in my hand—five red points had accumulated.

The young fellow who drives the truck opened the rear door, which drops to make a counter, adjusted the hanging scales and stepped back to give me an unobstructed view of his wares. The interior of a well-stocked meat truck is a pretty sight—rounds of beef, loins of pork, rows of chops, butter, bacon, cheeses, pickles, jars of horseradish. I gazed enraptured. Then: "How many points does beef stew cost?" I asked.

"I haven't got beef stew," the young fellow said. "Only veal stew." And he shunted a pan of white, skin-covered bones forward for my inspection. But I would have none of that. I know that pale anaemic veal; it melts from the bones, leaving you nothing in the kettle but a handful of mah-jongg counters. "Isn't there any beef I can get for five points?" I pleaded.

He hauled things about a bit and finally produced a reddish slab about an inch wide encased in gristle. "What is it?" I asked. "It's flank," our young man said. It was beef so I took it. There were almost two pounds in the piece. And I knew just how I would cook it—cut it up, flour it, brown it, clap it in a casserole with onions, parsley, celery leaves and a nip of thyme. During the last hour of cooking, I would add carrots and potatoes, and top it off with dumplings—the classic recipe for an anonymous piece of beef.

I unwrapped my flank, placed it on a cutting board, got out my sharp little butcher knife, and whisked it across the white fatty covering which encased it. It didn't leave a dent. I put aside my sharp little butcher knife and got out my big sharp butcher knife and sawed sharply at the flank. The white calcified covering remained scatheless as deathless rock. I now had two instruments to fall back on and I fell back on them—the saw and the hatchet. Eventually I reduced the flank to oblong-shaped pieces vaguely reminiscent of something unpleasant which my tired mind, at the moment, refused to name.

Later, when the stony-looking oblongs arose slowly to the top of the gray broth in which they simmered—they had refused absolutely to brown—I found myself humming tunelessly a couple of lines from Gray's Elegy in a Country Churchyard:

> *The curfew tolls the knell of parting day,*
> *The lowing herd winds slowly o'er the lea.*

Tombstones! That's what my stew looked like.

The company came and ate the onions, the carrots, the potatoes, the dumplings. But the little white tombstones remained untouched on every plate—white, mute, remote as untrod glacial ice.

When the butcher's truck came yesterday, I didn't even notice what kind of a day it was. I didn't even go to look at the mounds of juicy beef. "Just wrap me up a couple of pork hearts," I called when I was halfway to the gate. And I stood and let him hand the package over the fence.

For Better or For Worse

February 17, 1945

WE'VE GOT A NEW BUS DRIVER, our third since the manpower shortage started getting blood out of turnips. He's a hollow-cheeked, loose-wristed fellow, so slightly put together that he appears to be about to fly to pieces every time we hit a rut. Viewed from the rear, or passenger angle, he seems to be all flying knees and elbows. His expression is one of acute, tortoise-shell-rimmed abstraction. He is a man, I should say, who drives with his head in the clouds and both feet on the accelerator. And never the twain shall meet.

On his maiden voyage to town he outmaneuvered a logging truck on Snake Hill and left it dangling on the rim of eternity. He treed a convoy of yellow-painted county road machines in the salmonberry brush by the roadside, and beat an army command car across the South Bay Bridge by a neck. At the first stop, down near the beer taverns and secondhand stores, we passengers abandoned ship in a body. We stood on the curb for a minute or two, like a flock of hens dumped out of a battered crate, plucking at our broken plumage, straightening our bent eye-glasses and retrieving bobby pins from down the necks of our blouses. Then, picking up our shopping bags and umbrellas and glad to be alive, we walked the five remaining blocks to our destination.

I had asked a town woman to send me samples of cotton prints as, what with Spring just around the corner, I feel that urge for new crisp cotton house attire which strikes you overnight, almost—even before the virus of the seed catalogues gets into your veins. Today, in the mail box I found the samples. They were neatly pinned to a sheet of note paper with attached explanatory notations. "Exhibit B," said the note, "is made of 'Arlac' which is milk, and which they showed me when I asked for cotton. And who am I to dispute it, though it gave me the slightly uneasy feeling that I am really unprepared to meet the new things. Exhibit C is a collection which, for purposes of simplicity, I shall simply call cloth as I do not know whether it is the flowering of soy beans, the down of thistle, or the stuff that dreams are made of. I also found you a metal dust pan."

Well . . . a metal dust pan is something tangible anyway, something I can set my teeth in.

———

It's going to be great to be able to give up cigarette smoking without any effort, isn't it? When I think of money I've wasted buying loaves of bread that I didn't need, and bottles of hair tonic that I'll never use just so I could wring a package of cigarettes out of the grocer or druggist!

———

"You're not the only one who had worms in your carrots and beets," my neighbor across the road told me. "Everyone on the beach had them last year." Which goes to show that competition is getting pretty keen around here. However, I see from an authoritative article in *House & Garden* that there are now some twenty-four insects the Victory gardener can go in for, many of them new varieties. I think I'll try a few diamond-backed moths this year and a row or so of three-lined potato beetles. I only had the plain kind last year.

Chronology of 1945

February

3 First U.S. cavalry enters Manila.

6 Manila falls to U.S. forces.

7 Most popular songs, according to survey by *Variety*, theatrical magazine, are "Don't Fence Me In," "Accentuate the Positive," "Rum and Coca-Cola," "I Dream of You," and "There Goes That Song Again."

10 U.S. First army gains control of main Roer river dam.
U.S. superfortresses raid Japan from Guam base, hitting Tokyo district in daylight.

12 Decisions of Big Three meeting at Yalta, Russia, announced. [Plans for defeat, occupation and control of Germany, collection of reparations, call for an international organization for peace and security.]

13 Budapest, Hungarian capital, falls to Russians.

17 U.S. troops land on Bataan, outside Manila.

19 All places of entertainment are ordered closed at midnight to save light and fuel.

21 American Thunderbolt planes bomb Berchtesgaden, Germany, Hitler's mountain retreat.

24 Greer Garson receives gold medal as "most popular star in the U.S.," as chosen by Gallup poll.

The Care and Feeding of Insects

February 24, 1945

IF MAGAZINES AND NEWSPAPERS would drop the misleading title, "Victory Garden," from the heads of their horticultural articles and frankly label the columns "The Hope Lives Eternal in the Human Breast Dept.," it would be a change for the better. A vegetable garden, as everyone who has nurtured a codling moth in a cucumber knows, is composed of a mixture of hope, aching muscles, and disillusionment, victory, if any, going to the bugs.

Sunday—a beautiful blue-skyed day—I took my spade and went to my vegetable patch. I dug up and threw away the chard plants. (The Victory Garden book said they would winter over. And they did. And so did the little beetles curled up in the leaves, snug as pigs in pokes.) I dug up and threw away the winter beets—what four-flushers they turned out to be—all top and no beet. The carrots—I guess I planted them too close together—were gross, many-fingered obscene hands. The parsnips were interlaced with black lines from stem to stern and looked, when split in two, not unlike sections of road maps from heavily populated areas.

I threw these winter crops on a bonfire. "Don't put infested vegetables in the compost heap," cautions the Victory Garden book. "Burn them." That dictum deals me out of ever having a compost heap and throws me automatically into the inexpert or bonfire class. (If the day ever comes when I can toss an uninfested turnip top onto a compost heap, I'll give the story to the Associated Press.) Then, with the ground cleared of last year's failures, I plunged a hopeful spade into a clod of crab grass and turned it over—the 1945 Hope Lives Eternal season was off to a good start.

I watched my tall Tennessee-born neighbor cross the pasture at a quick jog-trot followed by his curl-tailed

dog. He was wearing his best green and black plaid mackinaw and his felt hat was pulled low over his eyes. In the background, a plume of smoke rose above the shake roof of his cannery, so that I knew he had left a mess of crabs cooking.

"What's on your mind?" I asked after he had come in and sat down with his curl-tailed dog wound about his feet.

He rearranged a wad of snoose under his lower lip and deliberated a moment or two. He isn't one to waste energy on meaningless words and I saw that he was feeling about for a phrase that would hit the nail on the head at the first whack. Finally he'd got it. "Anybody in the food business these days is a criminal," he announced. "Just a plain out and out criminal. Every time I put a crab in a can I've got to sign four different sets of papers the government sends out implyin' I'm a thief, a skunk, and a scheming profiteer. It's up to me to prove I'm not, but the way they've got it worded I've got to sit up nights to show cause why I shouldn't be in the 'pen.' Well, today I'll be gol-darned if they didn't send another paper for me to sign which proves I'm a liar no matter what I say. I'll be gol-darned if a man can beat it!"

My neighbor sat back and glowered at the fire. Then: "The way they've got it now, with all them bureaus piled up on top of each other like barnacles on a hull, they're going to bog down the whole works. I go out in my boat and get a few dozen crabs and come home and can them and it takes five inspectors to follow me around and five state and federal bureaus to write me threatening letters. I've got to help feed 'em and keep 'em pacified or they'll run me into the 'pen'."

He stood up and spat his cud into the fire. "That's a fine way for an American to live. Isn't it?" he demanded.

I said something to the effect that it was an ill which would end with the war.

My neighbor looked down at me with an expression composed, I thought, of tolerance mixed with pity. "You don't think barnacles jump off the hull of a ship once a voyage is ended, do you? No, ma'am, you've got to chisel and scrape and burn them off. You've got to haul the whole gol-darned government up on dry dock and hack away them leeches and barnacles that's gnawing away on the constitution of the United States. If you don't, your ship's going to bog down. I'll be gol-darned if a man can tell if he's living in America any more."

He stopped talking suddenly, grabbed his hat, and shot out the door and across the pasture. A minute later puffs of heavy smoke swirled above the cannery roof and a shower of sparks from the replenished fire spiralled into the twilight above the pines. The cannery would run most of the night, I knew. And at dawn he would take his crab boat out for another catch.

"A man's sure got to keep humping," I said aloud, imitating the keening drawl of my mountaineer neighbor, "to keep five inspectors fed and five bureaus pacified. I'll be gol-darned if he doesn't!"

Our Lost Battalion

March 3, 1945

THE DAY AFTER PEARL HARBOR, thousands of troops piled into the beach towns along this stretch of coast. This little community of fourteen houses was occupied by National Guard troops from New Jersey which comprised a unit of a division which for reasons of national safety, to say nothing of reasons of self-preservation, I shall call the Umpty-Umpth. The boys moved our furniture into our leaking woodsheds and set up their cots and cook stoves. Then they went out and dug their big guns into the dunes, dug a string of fox holes, strung some barbed wire, and came home for supper. After supper, they spent the long evenings reading our old love letters, shooting darts at our water colours, driving spikes in our mantelpieces and hitting bull's eyes with our willow-ware cups and pitchers. Our ship's clocks, and our particularly ugly wedding gift vases, they probably wrapped up and mailed back home to their girl friends in New Jersey. They ran our electric pumps without oil, bashed in our septic tanks with their trucks, and bucked their wood on our living-room floors. By the time things got safe for democracy again, and we were allowed to return to our houses on the heels of the departing Umpty-Umpth, it looked as if the Japs had been here already.

We spent the ensuing months pulling spikes out of our chimney breasts, puttying up our hatchet-slashed walls, binding the wounds of our water pipes, burying smashed crockery, and hating the Umpty-Umpth division.

In the reshuffling of troops in the reorganization of the new army, we lost track of the Umpty-Umpth. They vanished behind a curtain of censorship and silence, and whether or not they still existed as a unit we did not know. Once in a while, we would read cabled dispatches of incidents such as that of a group of Americans court marshaled for poaching an English estate and we'd shake our heads. "The Umpty-Umpth is in England," we'd say. Or when some taxi driver would be shot in Newport News by a soldier in uniform, we were sure they were in Virginia. When it was reported that five thousand Americans had gone AWOL in Italy and were hijacking transport lines and hitting Romans over the head with black jacks in dark alleys, we thought we had our finger on our boys at last. "It couldn't be anyone but the Umpty-Umpth," we told each other with something akin to pride in our voices. Hadn't the outfit cut its eye teeth on our hearths?

I don't know when our attitude began to change; when we began to admit to each other that we hadn't seen the fire on account of the smoke. But we were listening to the ten o'clock news one night when a correspondent told of an outfit which battled to the top of a bloody ridge in the South Pacific and held it against fearful odds. Men and officers fell like flies, but the remnants of the company slugged their way to the top and in hand-to-hand combat with gun butts, knives, knees, tooth and claw, they gutted and brained every last Jap and took the backbone of the island for Uncle Sam. It had been, said the correspondent, one of the bloodiest, toughest victories of the war.

"It's the Umpty-Umpth!" we exclaimed. "It couldn't be anyone else!" And we had tears in our voices.

"They're fighting for us," we told each other.

"What does a broken cup amount to?" someone asked.

"Or a bashed-in septic tank?" someone said with scorn.

"I hope they had a good time on the money they got when they pawned the electric pump. I wish I hadn't made such a fuss about it. They can have anything. Anything I've got . . ."

After that, we had the Umpty-Umpth in every heroic major engagement.

———

Sunday a small coupe drove into the yard and two soldiers got out and came slowly toward the house. I opened the door. One was a tallish fellow who might have been quite a boy if he'd had a little meat on his bones. He had good shoulders, though, and nice eyes.

"Lady," he said, "I used to live in this house."

"Come in," I said. The other soldier, a small sunburnt fellow, grabbed his arm and heaved him over the doorstep. He stood for a moment looking around the room, taking in every nook and cranny before he sat, lowered gingerly by his buddy, in the chair I pulled up. "This is the house I lived in," he said to the other soldier, as if the other hadn't heard him say it before. Then he explained that he'd got hold of a car and someone to drive it, and the hospital at Fort Lewis had given him leave to drive down.

"You've sure got it fixed up swell," he said. "We fellows always said we had the best house on the beach. There's a swell hollow up in the dunes where we used to take sun baths. You ought to go look at it, Joe," he said to the other soldier. "We used to talk about it sometimes and say how we'd all come back here sometime. But of course we won't be. We won't be coming back."

After they had gone, with the little fellow easing the tall one over the doorstep once more, and the tall one pointing out to the little one the path over the dunes—after they had gotten clumsily into the coupe and turned down the road—I suffered a composite attack of grief and anger which left me thoroughly shaken. "Darn their hides!" I wailed into my starched Sunday apron. "They WOULD all go and get killed. They've never been anything but a grief to me since I've known them."

Even after I reminded myself that I never had known them, I still felt just as bad.

Lights to Literature

March 10, 1945

EVERY ONCE IN A WHILE a writer sits down and writes a paragraph or two on writing. You're supposed to reach the top before you do it, though. But I'm going to write about writing anyway. I can't wait any longer. If all the big boys and girls can blow off steam telling how tough it is to sit down to a typewriter and put one-dollar words on paper, why can't I blow off a little cent-a-word steam?

Let me see now . . . I will begin by saying that writing is hard. All writers who write about writing are supposed to begin by saying it is hard. It's the conventional beginning. There's a convention, even, on how to write about writing. Only you're supposed to say it in an interesting way. So I'll begin again:

Writing, I'll say, is very hard, and feeling about for the right word is about as easy as pulling out your own teeth—you are after a good bicuspid, say, and after prodding around with the forceps you get hold of something and pull with all your might and suffer dreadfully and come up with an incisor or a milk tooth. All that pain for nothing, see. So you've got to start all over again. That's writing for you. That's the way it is.

Now that I've finished saying what I have to say about writing, I'll sustain my argument by a few quotations from national and local authorities:

Says the *New Yorker* magazine: "Many times we have wanted to fold the magazine up; it is hard to remain seated on the low hummocks of satire and humor in the midst of grim events. A satirist at breakfast may get a firm grip on his day's work from the front page of his newspaper only to have the whole thing drop out from under him when his eye reaches the casualty list. He then spends the rest of the day avoiding the typewriter. In wartime the writer almost always becomes propagandist and advocate, and although he may not realize it, he is operating against the grain, for the deepest instinct of the creative person is not to promote the world's cause but to keep the minutes of his own meeting. When the instinct is disturbed, deep emotional and functional changes take place in writers and scare the daylights out of editors, who still face the same old problem of getting out the next issue."

Says my Fisherman Friend: "All the writing in our family is done by my wife. But she's sure slow. She hasn't even thanked my brother for the mackinaw he sent me for Christmas."

Says Robert, my sixteen-year-old neighbor (after reading this column): "You don't get paid for this, do you?"

Says a Local Club Woman: "You ought to come over some night and write up Grandpa Peterson's life. You could make a book out of it."

Says Birdie down at the tavern: "You could make a book out of my life."

Says my Neighbor Across the Road: "If the government doesn't let up making me write all these reports and let me get in a day's work now and again in the cannery, I'll end up in the poorhouse. I'll be gol-darned if I won't!"

Says the superintendent of the Twin Harbor's State Park: "A good article on how we organized the Boy Scouts down here would be timely."

Says Joe: "They'll have to go a long ways to beat 'Three Weeks.'"

Says Reg Elbee: "If you could write what I see when I'm out in my boat! There's things in that ocean they ain't no man ever seen."

Says Mike the Milkman: "If you could just write a good clear note so's I could tell whether you mean a quart or a pint. Just kind of spell it out. Couldn't yuh?"

The ten authorities I have quoted (with the exception of Robert, my sixteen-year-old neighbor, whose reaction was purely negative and beside the point) are agreed unanimously that writing has reached a sorry pass. The conclusion seems to be that there's not enough of it and what there is is the wrong kind. A third conclusion, and one likely to be overlooked by the critical student of contemporary literature, is that all writing should be done by a universally known author named Someone Else.

And until Grandpa Peterson decides to write his own life, that's the way things are going to stay.

Down to the Sea

March 17, 1945

Rᴏʙᴇʀᴛ'ꜱ ᴅᴀᴅ ʟᴏꜱᴛ his boat Monday afternoon. He almost lost his life too, and the boat puller did lose his life. Robert's dad felt so bad about losing the boat puller that there wasn't any room left in his heart to feel bad about losing the boat, although when he thinks that if he'd done things differently, or figured out something else, he might of held her until he got the engine started again, that makes him feel awfully bad, too.

Everyone else feels bad too, particularly about the boat puller losing his life. Robert's dad says he was the best boat puller he ever had. He was a stranger who came here last year, a shy fellow with an 'E' button from some war plant he'd worked in. One of his arms was shrunken a little from infantile paralysis but you wouldn't notice it much. He seemed awfully glad to get the job as boat puller, although he'd never been to sea before. But he made up for it by working hard, and when there was a slack spell with no fishing, he came home and papered Robert's mom's dining room. He slept on the boat nights, but sometimes when there was company they would invite the boat puller over, and he would come dressed in a neat suit wearing his 'E' button. He never said much, but he'd help make the coffee. And if there was wood to bring in or dishes to do the boat puller would get up and go do things like that without anybody ever asking him. He saw everything, that boat puller. And he wanted terribly to please. If the weather was rough, though, down at the mooring basin, he'd never leave the boat at night. "You go, Bob," he'd say to Robert's father, "and I'll stay with the boat." He was an orphan and didn't have any folks anywhere, so he liked to do things for people.

Well, when a man loses his boat everyone goes to see him, like you do when someone loses a brother, so Tuesday morning I went over to see Robert's dad. We passed a couple of fishermen driving out of the yard, and there was only one visitor left in the house—a big broad fellow from the Columbia River. Robert's dad sat by the living-room table with a cup of coffee, and the Columbia River fisherman sat on the other side of the table. Robert's dad had adhesive tape over his nose, and all down one side of his face. His fingernails were all torn off and his hands were bruised black. He is a little fellow with a shock of black curling hair and a gift of looking younger than his thirty-six years. His eyes looked old and tired, and were sunken way into his head.

I said I'd come back some other time and hear about the boat, but Robert's mom said no, he wouldn't quit talking anyway so I might's well sit down and listen. So I sat down and Robert's dad told what happened.

There was a brisk northwest wind, with an average heavy swell when they put in to pick up a crab pot north northwest of the north jetty. A big comber came aboard, and snuffed out the engine. That was at one o'clock in the afternoon. The boat turned broadside to the swell, was sucked down in the trough and took another slug on the jaw which stove in the weather side of the pilot house.

Chronology of 1945

March

6 Cologne, Germany's fourth largest city, falls to U.S. First army.

10 Tokyo hit by 1,000 tons of incendiary bombs in heaviest raid.

12 American troops invade Mindanao Island in Philippines.

15 Bing Crosby and Ingrid Bergman receive Oscars.

16 London area hit by V-2 bombs launched from Belgium and Holland.

17 Coblenz, Germany, captured by U.S. Third army.

21 U.S. Third army enters Ludwigshafen. German troops in rout.

26 Seven Allied armies advance east of the Rhine valley.

"Like having a freight train hit you," the Columbia River fisherman explained.

When the comber flattened out Robert's father saw the boat puller. He was overboard and was clinging to a life belt. He was swept astern, and when the wave rose from the trough once more only the life belt was there.

The boat was completely awash, and drifting. Between rollers, Robert's dad rigged lines wherever he could to hang to, and he bailed like a demon and jumped about like a monkey for two and a half hours. And if he'd had a bigger anchor, perhaps, he might have held her and got her bailed out and the engine started again and gone back after the boat puller. He was under water most of the time. The sea was right up around his nose.

At four o'clock she drifted past the jetty but was caught up and hurled back against the rock. He was thrown free and managed to get a strangle hold on one of the great boulders. The boat piled up almost on top of him. Robert's dad thought he was a goner then. He knew the Coast Guard couldn't see him, and he knew he wouldn't last where he was.

But lo and behold two strangers who had come to the beach to dig clams saw the boat. And they came out and found him. They managed to get him up on the jetty scaffolding and they took him ashore. That was way over on the other side of the harbor. They gave him a drink of whisky and put him in a hot shower. But he couldn't even feel the whisky. They wanted to put him to bed, but he wouldn't go. He said no, his wife was waiting for him down at the dock where she always waited for him to come in. And he put up such a holler that they had to get a man from Copalis Beach to drive him home.

Robert walked part way home with me. He said he was down on the beach digging clams when someone came along and told him that his dad's boat had piled up on the north jetty and he'd thought both his dad and the boat puller were gone.

"And do you know what I thought?" Robert asked. "It's funny the way I thought it. It just come over me all at once. I'll quit school tomorrow, I thought, and go down and get myself a boat and start fishing tomorrow."

Riding out a Gale

March 24, 1945

DURING THE BIG STORM, my neighbor from across the road came over. "Are you still alive?" he roared. I followed his dripping figure into the living room. He was shedding water like a duck.

"I'm very much alive," I shouted to make myself heard above the din of the storm. "And don't forget—if that house of yours ever blows away, you come right over here."

"If this place of yours starts going to pieces, you'd better start hightailing across the pasture. We always leave the door unlocked," he bellowed.

These preliminaries over, we sat down. It is a polite convention down here to pretend that the other fellow's house is going down in the storm—if not in the current storm, why then in the next storm—and to offer refuge in your own shake-roofed, slab-sided rock of Gibraltar.

The wind slugged against the house in long shuddering spurts. Outside there was a noise as if the devil and all his demons were streaking through the tree tops. Then the wailing would die down for a minute and we would hear the thunder of surf and the wind winding up and down the beach for another punch. Rain lashed across the roof, the fireplace chimney rumbled and belched smoke into the room. In the corner, under the ceiling beam, water dripped into a dish pan; I'd already sprung a seam.

"What's she blowing?" I asked, with what couldn't be called anything but a scream.

"She's doing between eighty and ninety miles. More on the beach," replied my neighbor in his best megaphone voice. "Would you," he continued, "call central and see if you can find out if we're ever going to get any electricity around here? Them lights has been out for eight hours now."

I went to the phone and cranked two bells. A pleased-sounding masculine voice said, "Hello."

"I wanted central," I said.

"Now, now!" admonished the voice. "Wait a minute. You haven't even heard what I got to say. I want to buy your boat, that's what I want. If you've got a nice little twelve-ton boat with a thirty or forty horsepower diesel engine, I'll buy it."

I said I didn't have a boat. I said I guessed he had the wrong number, and that I'd hang up.

"Now, see here," said the voice. "Have I said anything I hadn't aughtta? You don't have to go off half cocked just because I want to buy your boat do you?"

A woman's voice came over the wire. "Could you tell me if the mail truck has gone by yet?" it inquired politely.

"It hasn't gone by yet," I told her.

"Say," the pleased masculine voice interjected, "perhaps you'll sell me YOUR boat . . ."

I hung up. "I got connected with the tavern down at the dock," I told my neighbor. "Some fellow wants to buy a boat."

"That'll be Reg Elbee," said my neighbor. "Settin' down there calling Seattle and San Francisco, wearing out the telephone like a rich capitalist. I'll be gol-darned if he can get a quart under his belt without making a general nuisance of hisself."

I told him I'd try to get central in a few minutes. I got the broom and swept a puddle, which had leaked down the chimney, back onto the sputtering fire. The telephone gave an anaemic jingle. I picked up the receiver. "Were you trying to get me?" central asked. I said yes and asked if she knew anything about the trouble on the electric line. She said they were looking for a fallen tree but hadn't found it yet. I told her my neighbor had a whole batch of clams ready for the cooker when the current went off, and she told me that the cooler down at the store had thawed and wasn't it awful, and then a familiar voice broke in:

"I want San Francisco," it said.

"The long distance line's down. I keep telling you," central said.

"Give me Seattle then."

"The line's down, I tell you. I can't get any farther than North Cove."

"Well, why don't you say so? Give me North Cove then . . . anyone 'ud think you didn't care whether business sunk or swum."

"You already called North Cove. Half an hour ago," central said.

"Try Ocosta," suggested the voice.

"That's the schoolhouse," central said.

"Well, what if it is? How do I know they ain't got a boat for sale? Do YOU know?"

"All right! All right!" central said.

I hung up and gave my neighbor the news. I told him they hadn't found the trouble on the line yet, that the cooler had thawed out down at the store, and that Reg Elbee had tried to get San Francisco but had compromised on Ocosta.

My neighbor listened courteously until my broadcast was over. Then he stood up and put on his sou'wester. "If this place starts going to pieces," he roared, "you hightail it across the pasture."

"And if your roof blows off, you streak on over here," I screamed back, just as politely. Then the back door blew shut with a fearful slam.

Man vs. Nature

March 31, 1945

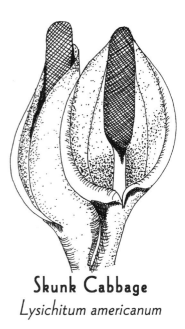

SPRING IS REALLY HERE—the first full-scale cat fight occurred under the house last night. I'm not much moved by the first pussy willow. The first crocus has been known to get here ahead of the first frost. I look upon the first skunk cabbage with a jaundiced eye. But the first cat fight! Well, that really stirs my sluggish pulse. After spending the better part of the night pounding the floor with a shoe and yelling, "Get out of there, you devils," I'm willing to admit that Spring is here.

Skunk Cabbage
Lysichitum americanum

Sunday, an unscheduled high tide swept up over the outer dunes and carried away the end of our sea-going sidewalk. The water raced inland and made a lake upon which floated logs and debris which came flying over the outer dunes like match sticks. If I had a boat, I could row from here to Westport on our new canal.

Several hundred feet of the outer jetty was carried away, and the sea came piling in over the soft sand cutting a cliff-like edge in the high dunes there. I went to see this phenomenon and watched house-high rollers hurl themselves over the rock and shatter into skyward-sweeping spray. The ground shook underfoot.

Across the channel I could see a great gap in the middle of the North jetty where the rock had been torn out—that is, I could see the gap when the white surf wasn't cracking a whip along its length. Several million dollars were spent to make these jetties, and a number of years. And now the ocean comes along overnight, flicks its tail, bares its teeth, yawns, stretches, and goes galloping off somewhere else, leaving us with a couple of jetties that look like old broken-toothed combs, and in a depressed sort of little-man-what-now state of mind.

Down at the dock there is a new restaurant which serves home-made three-inch-thick meringue pies. I hitchhiked down there on the commercial baker's truck, and when he arrived, he beat me into the place and had his fork in the middle of an orange custard before I'd even climbed on a stool. Poor fellow! I hope the experience revived his faith in pie as an edible article of diet.

Chronology of 1945

April

2   U.S. Tenth army invades Okinawa.

12 President Roosevelt dies of cerebral hemorrhage. Vice President Harry Truman takes oath of office as President.

13 Vienna, capital of Austria, capitulates to Ukrainian armies of Russian forces.

16 President Truman addresses a joint session of congress, saying that "we must carry on as Roosevelt would want us to do."

19 Leipzig, fifth city of Germany, falls to U.S. First army.
U.S. Seventh army takes Nuremberg, Nazi "shrine" city.

21 Gloria Vanderbilt marries conductor Leopold Stokowski.

24 Senate extends draft for one year.

25 Berlin encircled by first two Russian armies.
U.N. conference opens at San Francisco.

27 American tanks push across border to Austria and capture Gegenbach.
War Production Board revokes 40 controls over industry, affecting a variety of consumer goods.

28 False surrender report denied officially by President.

29 Benito Mussolini, former Italian premier, is executed by Italian partisans near Dongo, Italy.
U.S. Seventh army enters Munich, birthplace of Nazi party.
Venice and Milan, major Italian cities, fall to U.S. Fifth army.

30 Russian flag flies over German Reichstag building, as resistance weakens.

There are many new faces with the fishing fleet—men who have always wanted to own a boat, others lured by tales of $25,000 bottom fish cargoes—putting their war-earned money into boats. Recently a new man went out and dumped $700 worth of crab pots into a hundred fathoms of water. The pots were equipped with lines for twenty fathoms and will, of course, never be seen again. Another fellow placed his pots inshore in nice calm water, where they reposed until the tide came in and the surf ripped off the lines and sanded down the pots.

There's more, much more, to this easy money than meets the eye. In the first place you've got to know the geography of our ocean bottom, its deeps, shoals, underwater lagoons, and how they shift and change with the seasons and the tides. And in the second place there isn't anything easy in any of it. I've yet to meet the fisherman who can discuss "putting out" or "putting in" over the Grays Harbor bar without getting an expression of deadly seriousness on his face—a sort of reminiscent look with a lot of big green combers in it.

Journey's End

April 21, 1945

LITTLE CLOUDS WERE PUFFING across the face of the sun and their shadows fled before me as I crossed the road to my neighbor's. Shafts of warm sunlight gleamed on the patch of daffodils by the path and warmed the emerald green hillocks of my neighbor's backyard. My neighbor's backyard is not fenced; it is simply a plot of uneven grass-covered ground lying between his shake-roofed house and his shake-roofed cannery, surrounded on two sides by pine forest from which, on this morning, the quail could be heard calling "Tobac— tobac—tobacco" to each other. My neighbor's backyard fulfills the dictum of modern architects that full advantage be taken of the space provided for "outdoor living," and that "functional purposes" be frankly accepted as compatible with "the American way of life." A chopping block with an ax rampant occupies the central, or focal, point and balance is maintained—and functional purposes stressed—by the introduction of a car, in slow process of having a tire changed, canted up on one wheel and propped in place with the butt end of a pine log. A white-painted rowboat, brim full of rain water, lies athwart two mossy hillocks. It has been newly caulked and is now undergoing what my neighbor describes as "getting its seams swole up." Various other objects testifying to the American way of life are lying about the yard in unstudied order—a pile of wire crab pots, a scattering of red and white painted wooden floats, a galvanized tub full of amber-colored clam shells.

I sat down on the edge of the rowboat, and my neighbor put down his ax and stood with one foot on the chopping block. "Did you hear the president's speech?" I asked.*

"It wasn't bad," said my neighbor. "But still—" He hesitated a long second looking out across the pine tops.

"What were you going to say," I urged.

"Waal—" he deliberated. A slow sort of indulgent grin spread over his face. "I'll bet that little man 'ud give the world-and-all not to be in them there shoes."

I went home across the pasture feeling very much better. If my neighbor decides to like our current president, it's going to be much more pleasant around here than it has been for the past number of years.

═══

Our shoemaker is still busy up to the ears and says he hopes the world never gets to the pass again where a man has to resole so many of the same shoes over and over again. The war, to him, has been just one unending tussle with old shoes. He visions peace as a time when he can get his hands on a pair of "new" uppers.

═══

I hobbled to the top of the dunes this week with a young soldier, an infantry lieutenant, with his leg in a cast. He began his military career in Germany and expects to finish it in Japan. He is grateful for the respite the bad leg gives him—really delighted. He'd rather not continue to carry on, but he's philosophical about the prospect. However, when I said I supposed they needed seasoned troops over there he laughed—not bitterly, but with an inflection which I felt only another soldier could understand. "Listen," he said. "You learn all there is to know about war in the first fifteen minutes of combat. All there is to know."

This statement was followed by a silence on both our parts. Then we climbed awkwardly back into the saddle of conventional conversation.

---

* President Franklin D. Roosevelt died April 12, 1945.

Catching the bus home from town I lingered, and was the last to get aboard. I had a bundle of rose bushes in my arms, and didn't want to jab out any eyes. The bus was packed but there seemed to be a bit of space on the rear seat which runs across the back. Anyway a small man sitting there beckoned and the others squirmed over to make room. The small man who had beckoned, and who had a wooden stump of a leg—one of those Long John Silver affairs—politely took off the leg and held it in his lap. He couldn't have moved into the corner otherwise, he explained, as the leg wouldn't bend.

When I went to plant my roses the following day, one of them didn't have a name tag on it so I named it after the little man who had sacrificed his dignity on the altar of politeness. I called it The Complete Gentleman. It's a standard rose too—one of those one-legged ones.

Work for a Living

April 28, 1945

HAD IN JOE THIS WEEK to replace the rooftree which blew off in the storm. One of the fascinating things about this country is the speed with which everything man-made disintegrates—flattens down, levels off, and bleaches to lichen-covered beach color. The window casings of my weathered house, which got a fresh coat of white paint last summer, are already showing the results of a winter's sand scouring, and by next year will have returned to their original bleached gray. My proud new septic tank collapsed under a pond of surface water after our last torrential rain. I broke the bad news to Joe—who will be the man to rebuild it—but not until I'd got a glass of beer down him to mitigate the blow. Septic tanks are always bad news down here—the concrete kind fill up with sand, and the plank ones bog down.

Joe has been busy as a bird dog repairing roofs, untangling rural plumbing systems, and getting fallen trees out of people's electric wires up and down a twenty-mile strip of beach. If you've got a literal mind, you can get a lot of joy out of hearing Joe tell how he installed coils in a kitchen stove, finishing off the job neatly with a No. 2 plug, listen to an accounting of the number of board feet, not counting two by fours, which went into the making of the clam buyer's hut and the ingenious disposal made of the knotty No. 3 boards, along with the poundage of ten-penny nails salvaged for the job from the abandoned bog house on the Heather Road.

The recitation continues until the last nail has been pounded securely into place when Joe, if sufficiently urged and prodded, and after much wrinkling of brows and concentration, attempts to think up a printable fact or two about people—although the chances are ten to one that what he thinks up will be about plumbing. Anyhow, I've got to take that chance.

"What's the news on the beach?" I'll ask.

"Well—let me see," Joe says. "They've about decided to use plaster board on the schoolhouse manual training room. Can't get plywood anymore . . ."

"Yes, I heard that," I interrupt hastily. "Is Bill Brown still under the weather?"

"Yes," Joe says. "The doctor says he's got to take it easy. Quit work and stay around home for awhile."

"That must be awfully hard on him," I say. "He's about the most active man on the beach." (Which is putting it mildly because Bill Brown is one of those giants on the earth—earns his daily bread moving mountains; prize fights and breaks in horses for Saturday and Sunday recreation.) "Sitting around the house doing jigsaw puzzles and playing solitaire is going to be hard on him, all right," I say.

"Oh, he's made up his mind to do what the doctor ordered," Joe says. "He figured out he'd occupy the time learning something, so he bought himself a bulldozer and he's practicing up on it on that hill back of the house."

"You don't say!" I exclaim with delight.

"Kinda keeps his mind off work. Do you know how many yards of dirt a bulldozer can move in a day? When we put the culvert across the North Cove road—eighteen-inch pipe it was—we shoved 'er in with a bulldo . . ."

"Hold it, Joe!" I say, putting up a restraining hand. "That second bulldozer'll have to wait for another day. I can't use more than one to a page; the editor wouldn't stand for it."

And so, the interview ends in mid flight, much to Joe's disgust, leaving out, he says, the best part of the story which was how they hitched up a T-pipe in a wet ditch with a special formula of concrete which wouldn't take any more than a page to tell about.

How to Build a Good Hot Coal Fire

May 5, 1945

WELL, MY NEIGHBORS at Westport have settled the surplus property question. They burned up the coal pile.

The coal, some five hundred tons or more, was left behind by the army when the troops moved out more than a year ago. Barracks were dismantled, barbed-wire fences torn down, a bonfire consumed oddments of furniture, sheets of plywood, and other valuables which my neighbors would have liked to lay their hands on. Everything was raked clean, the watchman was taken off the payroll, and a carpet of brake ferns and infant pines covered the building sites and the drill grounds. But they didn't cover the huge glistening coal pile which the army left behind.

The coal pile stood like a black plateau for all to see—that is, it stood there until last fall when the price of wood went up to $18.55 a load, if you could get it—and then the coal pile began to melt away.

But let me dramatize the story: Dusk was falling on a quiet April evening. Robins were singing their evening songs, the red and white flashes of the lighthouse were becoming more vivid in the deepening gloom, lamplight glowed from the little houses on the grassy hillocks where supper dishes were being done and men were telling their wives how many fish they'd caught and the price they got down at the buying barge. And over at the edge of the pine woods, an old man hummed a thrifty tune to himself as he busily scraped and raked a few shovelsful of coal into a wheelbarrow. It was a historic moment. He was gleaning all that remained of the once prosperous coal pile and was about to settle for good and all the surplus property question, when out of the woods jumped the FBI. (I could have made a better story if the FBI had jumped out of the woods while the coal pile still had some dignity, if, say, the attack had been made on a ten-ton truck instead of on a wheelbarrow, as it stands to reason that five hundred tons of coal wasn't carted away on a barrow. But anyway the FBI got there—at the wheelbarrow stage.) The coal pile had vanished.

The FBI man, a serious-looking young fellow in a fawn-colored overcoat, notebook in hand, jumped out and scared the old man with the wheelbarrow. He said, don't you know this is government property, and how much coal have you taken, and give me the names of others who have taken this coal. And the old man said he hadn't taken any more than what could be seen in the barrow as he lived way down the road and hadn't heard about the coal until that day. As to who else had taken it—the old man turned slowly and looked at the large chimneys from which, with few exceptions, the black coal smoke belched into the night.

The next day the FBI young man made a house-to-house investigation. The coal—what remained of it—was not hard to find. It was not hidden away, but reposed in

254

proud, new bunkers right alongside many a back door where, often as not, a packet of trailing nasturtiums had been planted to enhance its importance. I visited the wife of my fisherman friend shortly after she had been visited by the young man in the fawn-colored overcoat. She was doing a beautiful job of ironing her cutwork centerpiece. She said the FBI man had asked if she had any army coal and she had said yes. She said the coal was by the back

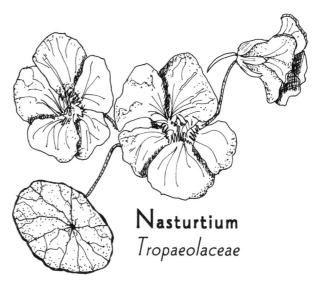

Nasturtium
Tropaeolaceae

door in the new bunker with the primroses planted around it. Many people had planted nasturtiums, she told him, but she'd transplanted primroses, and later on she was going to plant sweet peas around the bunker. There was no reason why you couldn't keep coal neat looking, she told him. He put his notebook back in his pocket without writing anything on it, and said he'd better see her husband and where was he, and she said, why, he was out in the Pacific Ocean, so the young man said he'd come back later.

So that evening he came back. My fisherman friend and his fisherman neighbors, in clean blue shirts and at ease in their deck slippers, were leaning against a pile of lumber in the yard smoking their evening pipes when the FBI young man came back. I watched the interview from behind the starched, red polka-dotted kitchen curtains of my fisherman friend's wife while she brought the supper oysters to a turn on a cast iron hotcake griddle. I couldn't of course, hear what was being said, but I could see the serious, intent face of the young man in the fawn-colored coat, as he stood holding his notebook, poised pencil in hand. Tobacco smoke rose on the calm evening air, and a puppy, rolling over, seemed to have the entire attention of the group of neighbors by the lumber pile. After awhile the FBI young man put his book back in his pocket, got in his car and drove away.

When my fisherman friend had finished his pipe he came in to supper and I asked him what had taken place. He said each man there had said he had coal; but as to who else had coal, they couldn't say. If the mayor and the village fathers, and the deputy sheriff and whole town had contributed to the dissolution of the coal pile they wouldn't have told him anyway, my fisherman friend said.

"Can't he see for himself the coal smoke fogging up out of all the chimneys?" said my fisherman friend's wife. "Why does he have to go around asking people?"

"Well, he's got to," said my fisherman friend. "That's his job. It ain't his fault."

"What did he say?" I asked.

"He said, don't you know that coal belongs to the government? And we said, who's the government? It's us, isn't it? we said. He said, well, anyways, we'd better haul it back again, what we have left. But we said we'd had to use up all our gas getting it and didn't have none to haul it back with. Are those oysters ready yet?"

———

As I walked homeward through the twilight, I passed the site of the missing coal pile. Sprouting brake ferns pushed knobby heads through the black dust. Another week and even the FBI will have a hard time to locate the scene of the crime. And why not, I thought, let the whole issue bury itself underneath the spreading fern? You can't take a whole village into the federal court—or can you? Who would feed the dogs and cats and babies? Who would ring the schoolbell, and pick the wild strawberries, and troll for salmon off Split Rock?

Besides, anyone with half an eye can see that these people are innocent—I doubt if there is a more innocent village anywhere. If I were the government, I would take a tip from nature and blanket the issue—adopt a firm coal-pile-that-wasn't-there-at-all attitude and stick with it.

———

NOTE: Somehow the city of Westport did manage to buy the water tower and water system that was advertised as surplus in November 1944 to avoid having the useful system from the army cantonment torn down.

May Days

May 12, 1945

THE OCEAN HAS TAKEN off its winter underwear and is going around in a misty blue negligee. Clumps of blue wild peas are blooming on the dunes, and the wet sand is strewn with the cast-off shells of infant crabs in various shades of coral and shrimp pink with delicate filigree-like markings in deeper tones. They are barely more than an inch wide, and so fragile that it is difficult to pick one up without destroying it. A crab sheds his outgrown shirt once a year, I believe. So these little red jewel-colored garments must be size 1, unless there is a smaller size which I have never seen.

The loveliest thing I ever found on the beach was the skeleton breast of a sea bird. It was about five inches long and built like a sailing yacht, with a beautiful, breathtaking sweep of keel from bow to stern. It was buoyancy, maneuverability and speed, not captured as the critics say "in marble," but moving and forever free, a feather of time's wing brushing across the face, coming from past pages and hurtling into future eons. Uncaptured flight was what it was, and an ocean conquered.

If I'd ever started out to evolve abstractions on canvas as so many men are attempting to do today,* I should, after viewing that little white flying boat, have put my brushes away forever. Or if I had ever been tempted to chisel white symmetry from stone to make men's souls tug at their moorings I should have put my chisel away in the tool house along with the mattock, the crowbar, and the Swedish hoe—that sea-bird commenced to sculpt his hull before I was a glint in the dawn of time's eye.

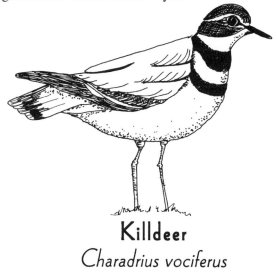

Killdeer
Charadrius vociferus

---

* For example, Robert Motherwell, who was Hogan's nephew.

257

Chronology of 1945

May

1   Premier Stalin of Russia in May Day proclamation hails approaching Allied victory, saying "the collapse of Hitlerite Germany is a matter of the immediate future."

2   A million German soldiers, sailors and airmen in Italy and part of Austria surrender, under unconditional terms signed April 29 at Caserta, Italy.
Berlin capitulates to Russian armies under Marshals Zhukov and Konev.
Allied combined forces invade Borneo.

4   All German forces in northwest Germany, the Netherlands, Denmark, Helgoland and the Frisian Islands surrender unconditionally to British Field Marshal Montgomery.

5   German army group G. comprising 400,000 men surrenders to U.S. General Devers.

6   U.S. Third army advances into Czechoslovakia and Austria, taking Pilsen and Karlsbad.

7   German high command representatives, headed by Col. Gen. Gustav Jodl, meet Allied officers to arrange surrender details at Reims, France.

8   Unconditional surrender of Germany formally ratified in Berlin, ending war in Europe at 11:01 Central European time (6:01 EWT).

One Man's Business

May 19, 1945

MY NEIGHBOR ACROSS THE ROAD came hightailing it across the pasture. He was freshly shaven and shorn, buttoned up to the chin in his green mackinaw and followed by his curly-tailed dog. I could see that serious business was afoot. A smudge of smoke rising above the shake roof of his chimney testified to a banked fire and an hour of freedom while the cooker steamed.

Inside the house he sat arranging the preamble to his speech while he held my eyes with an unblinking gaze. Then: "I'll be gol-darned if they ain't figgered out the worst thing yet," he began.

"They have, have they?" I said. I sat up straight, set my jaws, groaned, and prepared to disapprove heartily of whatever "they" had "figgered out." "What now?" I asked.

"You know," my neighbor said, "when I buy salmon to can I have to take the catch. I've got to take whatever bottom fish come along with it. Like today. To get salmon, I had to take half a ton of bottom fish. But OPA says I can't can the bottom fish. I've got to dump 'em, because I didn't can bottom fish in nineteen forty-three. You've got to have oil to can fish and they won't give me oil, except for salmon."

"Do you mean to tell me half a ton of fish got dumped?" I asked.

"It did," said my neighbor. " And that ain't the worst of it. You can't catch bottom fish without getting halibut in your net. The state fisheries law says you can't take halibut in a net. Fishermen dumped twenty tons of halibut off Grays Harbor in just one day last week."

My neighbor said that he ought, by rights, to go home and put a padlock on the cannery door. He said he'd got a business report through the mail showing how many thousand small businesses were folding up every month—"gettin' gnawed to death by the government," was how he put it.

258

"The trouble with this OPA," he said, "is that they ain't got no laws. Send me a copy of your laws, I said to them, and they said, 'We ain't got no laws. Our law is what we tell you,' they said. So I set up to smoke. If I can't have oil, I thought, I'll mild-cure and put in cans. And OPA they come down and said where is the red points for this fish? And I said they're right up in the National Bank of Commerce, I said. But this process don't take no oil, I said. So they sat back and said, ha-ha and where do you think you're going to get any cans?

"I don't know if I'm going to get cans or not, I said, but I'll tell you who I've asked. I've asked the Congress of the United States. I gathered up all the letters and forms you sent me and copies of all I've had to write trying to get a little oil and cans and I've sent it to the Senate Investigation Committee on OPA. The stuff filled a fish crate. I had to express it. And I sent along a note saying please would they send me some cans so's I can get this fish under cover before it spoils and after that I guarantee to sit down and fill out another fish crate of forms for OPA and haggle and naggle for as long as they please.

"Waal," said my neighbor, "them fellows didn't like it much. They said what did I go over their heads for like that, and it wasn't hardly fair, and didn't I trust them?

"So I said I did it because I needed cans and if we start writing letters to each other it will be too late. The fish can't wait, I said. And as for trusting you I said if I let you run my fish business it'd be deader than a gaffed mud shark in a week."

My neighbor stood up and put on his hat. "I ain't going down without putting up a holler," he said, and shot out of the door.

16 Most popular songs, according to *Variety* magazine, are "Bell-Bottom Trousers," "Dream," "There! I've Said It Again," "Candy," and "My Dreams Are Getting Better All the Time."

21 Lauren Bacall and Humphrey Bogart married.

22 U.S. war and navy secretaries release news on Japanese bomb-carrying balloons, stating that they are of slight military importance.

26 Tokyo hit by 4,000 tons of incendiary bombs from 500 superfortresses.

27 Chinese capture Nanking.

News about Neighbors

May 26, 1945

Rᴏʙᴇʀᴛ, ᴍʏ sɪxᴛᴇᴇɴ-ʏᴇᴀʀ-ᴏʟᴅ ɴᴇɪɢʜʙᴏʀ, is now seventeen. He celebrated his birthday by taking a girl to the senior dance. He bought her a two-dollar corsage, he confided, and when I asked what she wore he said, "Something pink and shining."

Since the event he is a changed man. Spends his spare time between leaning on the fence looking off into space and rushing into the house to play, "Don't you know I care" on the Victrola—and eating his mother out of house and home.

The Late Mr. Holmes

June 2, 1945

Oɴᴇ ᴏꜰ ᴛʜᴇ ʀᴇᴡᴀʀᴅs of living close to nature is that sooner or later you get to know your neighbors as well as your own brothers, and not only do you get to know your neighbors as well as you know your own brothers, you also get to know people who aren't neighbors but who come into your ken disguised as milkmen, oilmen, vegetable men, and what-not. Whereas in towns you know such people only as cogs in a well-oiled service, which leaves milk, say, at the back door mornings, in the country you know these people first as men and only secondarily as milkmen, etc. The milk, or business facet, is only one of a whole, brilliant, many-sided personality which composes that gem of evolution, man.

Take my wood man, Hazen Holmes. In town I would never discover that he isn't a wood man at all. But here in the country I know, even though he spends his days trucking wood from town, that he is really a bee man. He is also a lily man, the father of a family, with a seventeen-year-old son in the navy, the owner of a homestead cut out of the forest. But primarily, and at heart, he is a bee man—a bee man chained for the duration of the war to the driving wheel of a wood truck and eligible, if he once takes his hands off it, for the draft, as he is still within the age limit.

I first got to know of Holmes' bee potentialities when he stopped his truck to look at a swarm of homeless bees which had dug in for the winter in a boarded-up window casing which had been shingled over when the house of my neighbor was rebuilt. Holmes jumped off his truck, sounded about with his ear against the wall, and located the command post of the outlaws in the place where the window had been boarded up. Since that day, he has watched over the "hive" like a father as he intends, when the time is ripe, to capture the bees and remove them to his bee farm.

Holmes stops his wood truck nearly every day now to look at the bees. He has the naturalist's gift for standing motionless for minutes. A few neighbors join him and we all stand looking up at the bees. And indeed it is quite a sight; they have outgrown their window frame and hang in a black, seething mass under the eaves where they spend the night, as there is not room for all to enter the tiny crack which gives upon the hidden window frame between the two by fours. To us amateurs it looks as if the time is more than ripe, but Holmes shakes his head. "Just one hot day'll do it," he says, but he doesn't take his eyes from the swarm for a moment, which leaves us with the uncomfortable feeling that he is only telling us half the truth and that something unforeseen, some bee behavior of an unexpected and unpleasant nature, is about to occur. Also, he has not revealed, except by some vague mumblings about "boring holes" and "blow torches," how he intends to capture the bees. He did ask one question which possibly casts some light on the Holmes bee-baiting technique, although it was more in the nature of a rhetorical pronouncement than a question, as he didn't wait for an answer—it was in reply to my neighbor's rather nervous inquiry about blow torches. "Well, you've got this place insured, ain't you?" Holmes said.

As we stood looking up at the bees, Holmes told how he once housed a clutch of bees in a barrel, a barrel with a glass bottom, and the whole works placed on legs so that Holmes could lie on the ground, gaze upward and watch the bees. He used to spend his lunch hours from this vantage point, and saw the bees eventually fill the barrel. He then clipped the hoops, removed the staves and the sun shone on one big solid, barrel-sized, chunk

Chronology of 1945

June

3 U.S. Third fleet, under Admiral Halsey, raids Japan from carriers.

9 Gen. George Patton and Lt. Gen. James Doolittle return to U.S. and receive ovations.

13 Deanna Durbin, singing film star, marries Felix Jackson, movie producer.

16 Daylight raid made on Osaka. This marks the 77th Superfortress raid on Japan.

22 All resistance on Okinawa ends after bitter 82-day struggle, during which 90,401 Japs were killed, 4,000 captured. American losses were 11,260 killed, 33,769 wounded.

28 All of island of Luzon, largest of Philippines, is liberated.

of honey. It just goes to show, Holmes said, that there's no reason in the world for always having your honey come out in monotonous squares. You can have it any shape you've a mind to.

Warming up to his subject, Holmes conducted for our benefit a sort of original man-on-the-street bee quiz in which he not only asked himself all the sixty-four-dollar questions but answered them—as we were all stumped at the first buzz.

"Do you know how many bee miles are flown to produce a pound of honey?" he asked.

We didn't.

"Forty-five thousand miles!" Holmes said triumphantly.

"How long is the life of a working bee?" was his next stinger.

Nobody knew so Holmes had to tell us. "Eight days! At the end of eight days' flight a bee's wings is so worn and frizzed that the others kill it—they just snip its wings and throw it out of the hive."

"Has man, with all his inventiveness and science, ever been able to make synthetic bee's wax? He ain't," Holmes said. Suddenly he cast a worried glance at the darkening dune behind which the sun had long since set. He turned and sprang into the driver's seat of the wood truck. "That woman at North Cove'll be madder'n hell," he said, as he slammed the door. "She ain't got a stick to cook supper with."

As the truck ground into gear and moved down the drive, I saw that the vital, alive, bee-inspired light had gone from Holmes' eyes. His jaws were clamped and his brows drawn together in the dour frown which is the conventional facial make-up of all men who get home late to supper, but which, in the case of woodmen, is simply the conventional expression—they're always late anyway.

With Holmes the reason is bees.

June on the Dunes

June 16, 1945

IN THE VEGETABLE GARDEN the telephone peas are tall enough for the new kittens to chin themselves on. A shower on Sunday brought snails, licking their chops, into the bean patch. The earwigs are busy on a cutwork project in the nasturtium bed. A mole has engineered a double-track subway beneath my row of beets. As to the cabbage worm and the tomato blight—I fooled them this year—I didn't plant any cabbages or tomatoes. When things get to a pass where I can't out-think a cabbage worm, I'll fold up shop.

───

On the beach I found two red wooden crab floats which I added to a collection I am assembling on the terrace wall. I hang them in a row with the others from the low eaves of my gray shingled roof. I now have, besides the red ones, two orange, one yellow, a white, and a green one with a red nose. They are somewhat the shape of bowling pins, with rounder bases and longer necks, and are used to identify the sunken copper wire pots at sea. Each fisherman has his own colors, and they constitute a sort of a coat of arms. Hanging in long strings from fish houses and sheds, they make a uniquely local decoration when not in use. Sizes and design vary somewhat, and several colors are combined in some instances as, what with the increase in the industry, the boys are running out of plain colors.

Those found on the beach have broken from their moorings in a rough sea, and each one represents a lost crab pot, or fifteen dollars' worth of copper wire sanded down forever with the kelp and sand-dollars on the ocean floor.

───

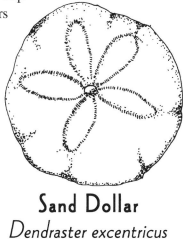

Mandy, one of our grade A seamstresses from town, who promised to come in January and stitch me up some wash dresses has not shown up yet. Word has reached me that she has gone to work for a mattress factory instead. I don't know what to think! I feel rebuffed somehow. When a women finds it easier going to sew for a mattress than to sew for me, why—well, there's an implied insult there somewhere, don't you think?

Sand Dollar
Dendraster excentricus

Getting Ahead of the World

June 23, 1945

IN THE MORNING the east wind blows, the sky is blue, and the rising sun picks out the white fishing boats and the great curls of tumbling surf on the bar two miles north by west of my perch on the dunes. When the little boats, coming out of the harbor, hit the bar, their white hulls vanish for a time in the surf; just as I think they've gone down for good, a white prow heaves out of the chaos, others follow, and soon scores of white flecks may be seen spreading out on the horizon.

In the afternoon, the wind shifts around to the north. A shadow of haze passes over the sea, the horizon dims, the fog horn booms out, the waves turn to tarnished silver. The fog comes down from the north in a thin line, blotting out the shore. It rises imperceptibly from the ground, so that the lower dunes at my feet become miniature mountain peaks, their heads rising above the clouds. All sense of perspective is lost, obscure objects become magnified, and everything assumes a mirage-like unreality. The fog clouds part to reveal a bank of wild roses where none grew before, glassy flashes of light burst through the mist, and a magnified comber looms deceptively almost within arm's length. Up in the air, where the sky should be, you see, for an instant, a fishing boat scuttling in the trough of a wave. The sound of her racing motor echoes hollowly beneath the fog bank.

At the end of day, the returning boats, with the sun behind them, are a line of black buttons sewn on the edge of the purple horizon. In rough weather, the coast guard boat meets them outside the bar. Noses are counted, and when everyone is accounted for, the coast guard leads the way, and with racing engines, they plow in a wild scramble through the churning froth to the safety of the cove. If the wind is right, this pell-mell entrance reverberates down the beach with sound effects similar to those made by a flock of homing dive bombers.

———

Jenny is the wife of Joe. And Joe, as everyone knows, is an artisan without whose skill with the hammer, the pipe wrench, and the trowel, our old gay-Nineties houses would have long since lain over on their two-by-fours and given up their hoary shingled ghosts. To get back to Jenny, however; she lives down the beach in a modern cedar-paneled cottage fabricated by Joe, and she has for rent other, equally neat, pine-shaded, flower-girt cottages nestling in the lee of the dunes. And the news about Jenny's place is that she is doing a rushing business in returned soldier honeymoons. They are boys from all over the country who were stationed here before they left for combat duty, accompanied now, of course, by their brides.

They always begin by telling Jennie that she won't remember them, but that they have remembered her and her little houses which they passed and re-passed when they were anonymous members of sergeant-ridden drill platoons. In Italy, in Germany, on Luzon, they have remembered Jenny's houses; and they promised themselves, if they survived, to return—with wives, preferably—and live, if only for a night, like other free men.

"And you ought to see," Joe told me, "how the young fellow grabs the girl's hand the minute they get here and whisks her up to the dunes. It's twilight when they get here, mostly, and while he's showing her the Pacific Ocean, Jenny puts flowers in the house. Sometimes she slips a kettle of hot chowder on the range—these young fellows don't have an awful lot of money, you know. If I have an extra bottle of beer lying around, I slip it in the cooler, sometimes. Pretty soon we hear them coming down the dunes. There'll be a quarter moon hanging over the pines, and stars as thick as nails on a roof'll be showing up in the sky. Jenny and I only stay long enough to show them where the split wood is kept. Then we go and sit in our garden watching the lights go out in the houses over on the bogs and smelling the cut hay in the shoemaker's pasture."

Natural History

June 30, 1945

A ROSE, which I thought was a briar, and cut back every time it stuck a shoot out of the ground, finally got the best of me and bloomed. And it turned out to be a lovely, old-fashioned, moss-type rose, many petalled, sweet smelling, with clusters of elongated mossy buds. When it bloomed, I understood where we got the term "rose colored."

The bush was probably a survival from the hotel which once stood on this site and which burned many years ago. In the garden an octagonal "summer house" stood at the edge of the pines, and there were roses planted around it. In those days, we'd never even

Rose
Rosa

seen, much less dreamed up, the exotic blooms we have today. A rose was a rose to us, and one of these simple blossoms did very well as a prop when the current visiting tenor, straw hat in hand, sobbed his way through "The Last Rose of Summer" with appropriate rose-ward gestures. These concerts occasionally took place in the garden at twilight, with the little octagon house serving as a stage. After the guests were duly "edified," everyone would return indoors and dance to "Waltz Me Around Again Willie" and "Down Among the Sheltering Pines" played on a tinkly piano until the unholy hour of eleven-thirty or so. Sometimes the modern acetylene plant broke down and everyone had to go to bed earlier. There was a great scurry for candles, a tip-toeing up the stairs and down the creaking corridors. This was considered "a lark." Sounds of furtively dropped shoes would come through the thin partitions, followed by suppressed tinkles from the crockery plumbing of the day, and the squeak of windows being tugged up to catch in the little slots bored into the frame. The damp, heavy odor of the sea hung above the cold sheets, and through the opened windows the North Pacific roared a muffled lullaby. Oh, last, last rose of summer!

Time Marches On . . .

July 7, 1945

WE HAVE THREE NEW PUPS in the neighborhood—a Belgian shepherd has been adopted by the girl next door, and Robert, my seventeen-year-old neighbor over across the marsh, has acquired two hounds in a dicker involving the exchange of a twenty-two rifle and some shells. But whether Robert paid for the hound pups with the twenty-two or the original owners of the dogs, which are twin girls, threw the gun into the deal for good measure is not clear. For the past week, all three pups have yowled all day and most of the night—the Belgian in staccato yaps, the hound dogs in the high-pitched nasal wail originated by the Andrews sisters. Or was it originated by hound dogs? It's hard to say.

———

Robert's father, who lost his fishing boat in the surf last winter, is going to have a new boat. The government gave him the go-ahead if he could find the lumber. Robert's father couldn't find a non-priority stick suitable for boat building at the mills, but he did find two straight beautiful Douglas firs for sale in the foothills near Mount Rainier. They will be cut, trucked to the Chehalis River, sawn into lumber, and about the time the geese fly south again, on some fine November morning, the new boat will cut her eye teeth on the Grays Harbor bar and head west with the fleet.

Robert's mom says life has become worth living again, now that her husband is assured of a new boat. Before that, he was so restless and jumpy that there was no living with him. A fish out of water was nothing as compared to Robert's father without a boat. "A man without a country and a fly on a hot griddle rolled into one," was the way she described him. Now, if he can find the carved teak-wood wheel which was carried off when the wreck of the old boat piled up on the north jetty, he will be a completely happy man. Coast guardsmen from Cape Flattery to Tillamook Bay have been given a blow-by-blow description of the wheel by Robert's father and have been so impressed by the momentous importance of its recovery that there can no longer be the whiff of a doubt in their minds that to abandon the project for lesser game, such as running down an enemy mine, would be nothing less than treachery to the nation.

Professional People

July 14, 1945

THE BIG RESTAURANT on the upper deck of the fish-buying barge hums like a hive. At a horseshoe counter, men wearing knitted watch caps, men wearing white-visored caps, and men wearing just any old hat sit eating roast lamb, broiled salmon, sole, halibut. They come up the stairs from the lower deck or come by the gangplank from the dock. Through the windows of the big white room the blue waters of the cove sparkle, and white boats come swiftly around the little sandspit from

Chronology of 1945

July

5   Entire Philippine Islands liberated and campaign virtually over, General MacArthur announces.

9   Total eclipse of the sun at 7:58 a.m., eastern war time, is visible in path extending from Idaho through Montana and into Canada.

14   U.S. Third fleet battleships shell Honshu island bases, only 275 miles north of Tokyo. This is first direct naval attack on home islands of Japan.

23   B-25 bomber crashes into Empire State Building in New York City. The three occupants of the plane and ten persons in the building killed, 25 injured.

26   Labor Party wins British election. [Clement Atlee replaces Churchill as prime minister.]

31   U.S. destroyer force of Third fleet shells Shimizu, aluminum production center on Honshu Island, Japan.

the sea to disgorge their cargoes on the barge. You can sit with a cup of coffee in your hand and look down on a dripping deck and watch them gaff the salmon from the hold.

One end of the airy room is a ship's commissary stocked with groceries and fishing gear where you can buy anything from loaves of Russian rye bread and Swedish goat cheeses to brass locks and deck paint. The atmosphere of the place is one of well-ordered haste coupled with extreme good nature. The visitor feels that, however enjoyable the scene, he shouldn't linger over long, but should eat and get going. This is a busy world, and thumping feet on the stairs from the lower deck do not permit you to forget it, as a new crew, fresh in, barges into the room and eager eyes search for a place at the crowded horseshoe counter.

Boat gear is being changed over from salmon to tuna. Already word has come ashore that the tuna have commenced to strike. All is happy confusion and great expectations. Yesterday a fisherman told how he'd gone out and picked up forty-four tuna a hundred miles off shore. A big expansive fellow came in, tossed his hat on the juke box with an all-out gesture, and announced to the room that forty-four boats had landed capacity cargoes a hundred miles off shore.

My neighbor from across the road, who was having a quiet mid-afternoon snack of halibut and potatoes with their jackets on, shoved aside his platter.

"I'll be gol-darned," he boomed, "if you fellows won't make four hundred and forty-four boatloads out of forty-four fish before night."

———

Down at the village the wild hay has been cut in front of the town hall—a one-story, red-painted barn—and the names of boys in the service have been painted on a varnished board. There are sixty-nine names, one with a gold star. Beyond the barn the misty plain of the veldt stretches to the cove, and beyond the cove, the sea.

———

A writing friend was giving me some pointers on characterization. "A good way to select outstanding characteristics," she advised, "is to put your subject in an imaginary cocktail shaker, shake well, and pour. You'll find you've got the essence of personality."

"All right!" I said. And I chose a random acquaintance and popped her into the imaginary cocktail shaker. I shook well, took off the lid, and poured. Out rattled six bobby pins, some flakes of plum-colored nail enamel, and a twenty-year collection of bridge scores.

Keeping in Touch with the World

July 21, 1945

MY TELEPHONE is right beside my bed, not because I feel impelled to keep my finger on the pulse of world affairs, but because that's where the rural telephone company put it.

"That's a funny place to have a telephone!" visitors exclaim. But I am used to it now. Besides, I feel pretty lucky; it could have been so much "funnier"—alongside the bath tub, say, or over the mantel. I'm not complaining. As far as rural telephone installation is concerned, I've had a break. There are only a few customers on this particular branch of self-cranking line, and I've learned to sleep through all twelve of them, my own ring included.

When I first got my telephone there were a few local conventions that I had to master, but once mastered, the rural telephone, with all its ramifications, was mine. At first it seemed unimaginative to ring a number fifteen or twenty times, when five or six rousing zings failed to get a response. Anyone with half an ear would answer in self defense after the first round was fired, I thought, so why keep on ringing. So one night, when the phone beside my bed rang twenty-four times, I took down the receiver, just as it was drawing breath for the twenty-fifth salvo, and bawled my irritation into the pregnant silence.

When I'd finished saying what I had to say, a placating voice said, "Listen lady, you're all wrong. Joe'll answer pretty soon. He's down working on his boat gear, and he'll go into the office sometime between one and two o'clock to get a drink of water and he'll answer the phone."

"What time is it now?" I asked grudgingly.

"It's twenty minutes after one already," soothed the voice. "Joe'll come along any time now."

I wound a bath towel around my ears and crawled back into bed.

Zing! Zing! Zing! sang the telephone, getting into the home stretch. Zing! Zing! Zing!

Along about four o'clock in the morning we have fishermen's reveille on the telephone, or what might better be called Waking Up the Boyfriend hour, as the job is generally delegated to a woman friend. If you have a man's welfare at heart it is good form to begin letting him know it at the crack of dawn. And it takes a good hour's ringing to get some of my deep sea neighbors out of their eiderdowns. Or is it bad form to take the bait the first time it is offered? Fishermen are pretty canny—about fish AND women.

Another telephone innovation perfected here on the beach is the general alarm, or the Get Your Man technique. It requires the complete cooperation of everyone on the line, and when played well, with every instrument thrown into the orchestration, achieves its purpose and finds the missing person. The general alarm is heralded by a burst of rings which runs the scale of every number on the line. We had one Saturday night. After playing a number of variations on rings one, one and a half, two, two longs and a short, and three shorts, the bell rang three longs (my number) and I took down the receiver and said, "Hello."

"This is the state park," said the voice. "Is the sheriff anywhere around there?"

"Not that I know of," I said. "I've been in bed for two hours, and if he's around, I wouldn't know it. Why? What's the trouble?"

"Oh," said the voice, "someone just came running over from Seattle, a husband or something, had turned up and was beating on some people there."

I hung up and let the state park tune up on four shorts and four longs, three shorts and one long, five shorts, etc.

The next morning while I was picking blackberries beside the road the sheriff's shiny paneled truck came around the bend. I hailed him. "Did the state park get you last night?" I asked.

The sheriff nodded. He'd gone down to the cabin camp, he said and quelled the riot.

"I put that fellow from Seattle back in his car and sent him back to Seattle," said the sheriff.

Blackberry

Rubus procerus

"What," I exclaimed. "The husband?"

"What husband?" said the sheriff. "I don't know anything about husbands! Fellow was disturbing the peace, and this is a law-abiding community, you know. Are you going to make a pie with those blackberries?"

"No," I said. "I haven't got any sugar. I'm just picking them because I like to pick blackberries."

Sea Gardens

July 28, 1945

LOOKING NORTH, I can see the white fishing fleet putting to sea. Through the gaps in the jetty, left by last winter's storm, I get a good glimpse of the boats before they vanish in the white welter of surf on the bar.

Scientists tell us that a storm on the continental shelf plows up the pastures of the sea and stirs from the bottom rich phosphates, nitrates, and other chemicals which are eaten by plankton—microscopic vegetables and animals—which in turn become food for fish. Where there is no plankton, there are no fish.

Sea fertilizer is most plentiful in cool and shallow northern waters where winds and storms plow up the sea. The vegetable plankton exists only in a narrow layer on or just below the surface in the shallow waters of the continental shelf. Sea plants, like land plants, must have sunlight to grow, and sunlight penetrates only a short distance down into the sea. The vasty deeps beyond the continental shelf provide little or no substance for the salmon, the cod, the tuna, the herring, and their groveling brothers, the bottom fish.

To get back to plankton—innumerable tiny plants sometimes color the ocean waters red, brown, or blue. Red plankton gave the Red Sea its name.

Masses of plankton are sometimes cast ashore. One of the greatest of such masses on record was once cast up on our own Washington coast: a strip of plankton twenty miles long and four to six inches deep.

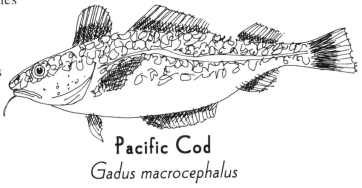

Pacific Cod
Gadus macrocephalus

I gleaned all the above facts from the January issue of the *National Geographic* magazine, and was so enthralled that I flew to my fisherman friend with the issue and insisted on reading it all over again, aloud.

When I had finished, he remained silent for a moment, salting away the meat of the matter. Then: "How long have them plankton been out there?" asked my fisherman friend.

"Forever!" I exclaimed. "You've got a regular Imperial Valley of richness right in your own front yard," I said.

My fisherman friend (he'd been painting his boat) bent down and dipped his brush in a can of copper hull paint. He squeezed off a neat excess drop or two on the rim of the can and applied a gleaming swath amidships beneath the gunnel. "We'll see about that," said my fisherman friend, and went on painting.

But I knew he was pretty well pleased with what I'd read.

———

A high fog has been blowing in over us for days; a fog tinged at sunrise and sunset with the smoke of distant forest fires. I like to pick wild blackberries under a high fog. The ripe ones are not lost in the black shadows made by full sunlight and are easier to find. I pick along the roadside where the county mower has clipped the wild hay and as I progress down the road the small garter snakes leap into the ditch, hurling themselves over the dried hay in one lithe movement which falls little short of flying. The first thing I think of when picking blackberries is garter snakes, and the first thing garter snakes think of when they see me is the ditch. So it all works out satisfactorily.

Since meeting a bear last year, I have confined my blackberry activities to the county highway. I had left the road and gone through the salmonberry bushes following a ripely laden vine, when I was stopped in my tracks by a loud warning, "Wush!" (Contrary to what the story books tell us, bears don't say "woof." They give a long-drawn-out "wush," like an outsized bellows being stepped on.) At the same instant, my nostrils were smitten with an overpowering odor, and a black gleaming shadow crashed off through the underbrush. I crashed off to the county road.

There, when I'd got my breath, I attempted to put my few scattered impressions of the encounter into coherent form for posterity. If I ever write about a bear, I thought, I must remember to say that it smells like an old fur coat that has been worn constantly by several generations of hard-sweating supermen. Wush!

Applied Science

August 11, 1945

PITY THE DULL-MINDED, un-world-conscious housewife. She is so busy running down a stray soup bone, or trying to evolve something revolutionary out of spaghetti, that she seldom gets her nose out of the kettle or her wits out of the ration book. She has, however, got her wits out of the cook book. Cook books, as everyone knows, are purely abstract reading and about as useful in the butterless, eggless, brown-sugarless, coconutless kitchen as a treatise on the fourth dimension. Cook books should be taken out of the kitchen and put on the highest bookshelf along with the *History of the French Revolution, Other Worlds Than Ours*, and the story of the Kimberly Diamond Mines. If a woman is seen to furtively procure a cook book from the shelf and sit reading it over-long with a vacant far-away expression in her eyes, she should be taken at once to a psychiatrist. Schizophrenia is knocking at the door.

Fortunately, most women have faced the facts squarely. The storage cupboards of my friends and neighbors are stocked only with macaroni, spaghetti, waffle flour, saccharine-sweetened syrup, and a powdered cheese composed, according to the label, of "skim milk, salt, sodium citrate, and vegetable coloring." These constitute the rock upon which the housewife builds her weekly menus. Daily, by hook or crook, out in the highways and byways, she struggles to secure some tidbit of meat, bean, egg, or cheese to break the awful monotony of starch. If, at dinner time, she fails to uphold her end of a discussion of the world charter or lets slip that she believes Chungking to be a brother of Chiang Kai-Shek, it is well to remember that her ways are not your ways. If they were, there wouldn't be any meat balls in your spaghetti.

———

Yesterday I dug up and exposed to the light of day a hill of potatoes the size of paving bricks. I couldn't believe my eyes! And the neighbors couldn't believe their eyes. Last year when I dug my crop they came and shook their heads over the niggardly marbles I'd raised. This year, from the self-same seed, the golden dollar, I got gold bricks. They out-weigh and out-girth the big potatoes of railroad fame.

I accomplished this miracle by putting a big wad of hay, dried brake fern, and half-rotted leaves into each hill, and transplanting therein the volunteers which sprang up in last year's patch. I put a shovelful of sand

Chronology of 1945

August

6 Atomic bomb used for first time in war, levels four square miles of Hiroshima, Japan, kills 50,000 Japs. New era in warfare begins.

8 Russia declares war on Japan and begins offensive operations in Manchuria.
President Truman signs U.N. charter, making U.S. first nation to do so.

9 Second atomic bomb dropped on Nagasaki, Japan, razing one-third of city. Total killed 10,000. This bomb was more powerful than one that blasted Hiroshima.

10 Japan offers to surrender provided Emperor Hirohito is left in power.

14 Japan surrenders unconditionally. President Truman announces capitulation of Japan at 7 p.m. General MacArthur is appointed supreme commander for the Allied powers, to make all arrangements on surrender details, and to set up military government.

15 Gasoline, fuel oil, canned fruits and vegetables removed from ration list.

16 Riotous peace celebration in San Francisco ends with 10 dead, many injured, and property damage and losses from looting heavy.

22 Army announces demobilization plan.

(we don't have "soil") over each hill and turned on the hose to wash in a handful of commercial fertilizer per plant.

The neighbors have suggested that I send an exhibit of my potatoes to town to be displayed in the window of the Chamber of Commerce, even offering to take them up themselves. But now, faced suddenly by success and the possibility of world acclaim, I shudder and turn away. It is too late. The desire to stand in the kleig lights of the Chamber of Commerce has withered on the vine of time.

━━━━━

When news of the atomic bomb came over the radio, we neighbors flew from house to house, excitedly turned on radios, and exchanged high-sounding scientific lore, gleaned from long hours with the *American Weekly*, and the Boy Scouts' bible, the *Scientific American*. We were, it appeared, amply qualified to approach the atom on equal ground with the best minds. But the split atom? That was another thing again. But our seventeen-year-old neighbor, a senior in high school, put us right about that. "An atom is in two parts like a pea," he said, "but it's glued together tighter'n anything in this world. And when you split it . . ."

"Bang!" yelled his little brother, a rudimentary scientist of the new or "comics" school of thought.

We all leapt from our chairs. We were nervous and edgy as witches, anyway. Having to grasp the atom in one sitting is hard enough, let alone grasping a split atom. We all gave the rudimentary scientist a dirty look and subsided onto our chairs. A timid neighbor was heard to mutter that it would have been all right with her if the atom had never been split.

My mountaineer neighbor from across the road, who had remained standing, curled-tailed dog at heel, emitted a premonitory clicking of the throat—like a grandfather clock before it strikes. We waited until the mechanism ground into focus. Then, "I'll be gol-darned," boomed he, "if them fellows won't keep foolin' around, and foolin' around, and one of these days they'll blow us all to kingdom come."

After this speech, which was delivered in a fine Shakespearean rumble, and which keynoted the conference, we parted, hurrying home through fast-thickening fog above which the fog horn bellowed its throaty, snub-nosed warning. At home it was discovered that the Belgian shepherd pup, who belongs to the girl next door, and who had not been invited to the conference, had, due to the advent of the atomic bomb and a postponed lunch hour, eaten a hasty pick-up meal consisting of two nightgowns from the clothesline, a length of garden hose, and the current issue of *Time* magazine.

Modern Museum

August 18, 1945

I GOT OUT OF BED the day following Victory and looked about on a new world. Or perhaps I should say I looked about on an old world with new eyes—a four-year-old world. There was a strange sense of unreality about everything. I couldn't quite analyze it at first, not until I went out on my little terrace and took a look at the stringy display of flowers there. "But I couldn't get the seeds I wanted," I said aloud. "It is only a substitute garden." And then, on the instant, I knew what was strange. Everything! All the commonplace things of daily living were earmarked by four years of war. Everything was a makeshift, or a compromise, or something utterly new and unthought-of before 1941. And now, in a trice, overnight, useless, meaningless . . .

As I lifted the clumsy glass coffee jar down from the shelf, I knew that I had always hated it. There will be light-weight tins again, I thought. And I'll be able to get nasturtium seeds again, and carrot seeds that will come up. I felt my spirits mounting. I looked about me with a critical eye. Why, even this tablecloth is blue checked because of the war, I thought, not the red check I really wanted.

At the breakfast table, I sat looking about my pale world, which, while it had harbored me and had been a refuge from world cataclysm, was, however, now fast taking on the feeling of a cell. A cell in which I had been a prisoner. A cell furnished with the necessities and, in instances, luxuries, of life, including food, shelter, and clothing, but a few of which I had a voice in choosing. The phrase "freedom of choice" jumped into the foreground of my consciousness. I rolled it about on my tongue for an instant and then reached out a trembling knife and cut a pre-Pearl Harbor dollop of butter which I spread on my toast. I wasn't struck by lightning, so I took another dollop. I considered the feasibility of cooking one of my three eggs, but thought better of it—reconversion, the morning radio had warned, will not spring fully clothed from the sea, but will toddle in like an infant taking its first steps, and will, naturally, have to grow up before it can pose for the newsreels with a burgeoning horn of plenty in its arms, including a dozen fresh eggs.

I surveyed my domicile with mixed feelings. There was hardly a thing in my small house which had not been touched and changed by war. The broken hearth where the Forty-fourth division* chopped its wood during the winter of '42. The wooden quarter-round substituted for curtain rods, and upon which hung the faded yellow cotton curtains, the best and last that I could get at two stores and, of course, of two shades of yellow. The kitchen linoleum which I paid a fellow from town $28 to lay, which buckled because he'd never laid linoleum before, or got $28 for doing it either. The world map with the smudged section where I tried to follow a son into the South Pacific. The 12 jars of jam I "put up" with my allotment of canning sugar. The radio which works just fine, if you know how to do it—but no one ever does. The brown oxfords which need resoling again. The can of pineapple hidden away on the hat shelf. The photographs, years old now, of boys in bright new uniforms, years old now, too. The faded kitchen aprons, the frayed towels, the teakettle without a lid. The 98-cent alarm clock which has ticked away four war years without ever missing a beat, and for which I have been offered myrrh and fine gold.

These things are symbols of yesterday, a yesterday which is as far away from us today as the remotest planet. There's more to this whole thing than the mind can absorb in one leap, I thought, mixing my metaphors slightly. The thing to do is to occupy myself with the first small task at hand, I decided. And I went and took the battered atlas from the fireside table, climbed on a chair, and put it away on the highest bookshelf.

"One thing I DO know," I said, "I've graduated from the longest, toughest geography lesson in history."

---

* No longer worried about the censor, Hogan identifies the 00th Battalion or Umpty-Umpth Division. The soldiers on the beach were members of the 44th Infantry Division (New York and New Jersey National Guard); after further training in Louisiana and Kansas, the division was sent to Europe in October 1944 and fought in campaigns in northern France, the Rhineland, and central Europe.

Glossary

acetylene plant—Before electricity was available, houses were illuminated by burning a carbonated coal gas from the gas plant, mistakenly called acetylene by Hogan.

aerated goods—A reference to dried foods.

Alcan Highway—A 1,500-mile graveled all-weather road constructed from Dawson Creek, Canada, to Fairbanks, Alaska, for military purposes by U.S. Army engineers in 1942-43. Later known as the Alaska Highway, the road opened to tourists in 1948.

Allen, Fred—A radio comedian.

baby broom—Young Scotch broom (*Cytisus scoparius*).

bar—A bank of sand at the entrance of a river or harbor, which can be an obstacle to navigation. Sand carried by heavy runoff in river settles out when the river's flow is slowed as it meets the ocean.

bar pilot—A skilled seaman who navigates ships over the rough seas of a bar.

Black Maria—A closed panel patrol car.

blackout—A government-ordered nighttime period when all lights must be extinguished or covered so that cities and other habitations are invisible from sea or sky.

blimp—A blimp squadron operated out of Tillamook Naval Air Station on the Oregon coast, to watch for submarines and mines in coastal waters.

blue stamps—Ration coupons for canned goods.

boat puller—An able-bodied seaman working as a deck hand on a fishing boat.

bonds—Civilians were encouraged to buy War Savings Bonds as an investment in America's future. An $18.75 bond matured to $25 in 10 years. Bonds were used to buy weapons for the war: $4 would buy a steel helmet, $80 a rifle, and $20,000 an anti-aircraft gun.

bracken—A large coarse fern (*Pteridium acuilinum* and *Pteris*) also called brake fern.

bucker—The logger who cuts felled timber into shorter lengths for loading onto a train or truck; also called a crosscutter.

Bundles for Britain—A charitable drive to collect food and clothing for England.

canteen—An informal social center where civilians gave out coffee, food, and friendship to off-duty military personnel.

cantonment—The quartering of troops; a group of more or less temporary structures for housing troops.

CCC camp—A camp for Civilian Conservation Corps (CCC) workers. The CCC was established in 1933 to relieve unemployment by putting men to work. Mt. Rainier Lodge and many stone bridges in Washington survive as examples of their work.

central—The human operator in each central telephone exchange.

Chambers, Robert W.—American novelist, 1865-1933; writer of numerous popular novels.

Chiang Kai-Shek—Chinese Nationalist leader.

Chungking—Chinese city.

clam—The razor clam (*Siliqua patula*) is an edible bivalve mollusk, up to 8 inches in length, which lives in the tidal area of sandy beaches on the Pacific Northwest coast.

clam gun—The long-mouthed shovel used to dig for razor clams.

comber—A long curling sea wave.

cutwork centerpiece—An embroidered linen table decoration in which design is cut away so that the table shows through the remaining elaborately edged fabric.

defense stamps—Small denomination stamps were sold individually to be glued into Savings Stamps booklets which, when filled, could be traded for a War Savings Bond.

dirigible—Actually a blimp, see above.

dock—Hogan uses "the dock" to refer to the sheltered harbor at Westport, with piers, pilings, and floating wooden docks.

donkey—A portable steam engine used in logging.

dooryard—An old-fashioned name for the yard next to the door of a house.

dory—A flat-bottomed boat with high sides, sharp bow, and a v-shaped transom, used as a utility boat by fishing vessels.

Doubleday-Doran—An East Coast publishing house; Doran was dropped from the imprimatur in about 1940.

drag net—A large net drawn along the bottom of the ocean to catch fish.

dragsaw—A power-operated saw with teeth slanted to cut on the pulling stroke.

E button—An award for excellence given to a war plant employee by the Navy.

faller—A person who cuts down trees in a logging operation.

fascinator—A knitted or crocheted head covering.

Fibber McGee's closet—When this radio character's closet door was opened, many things fell and crashed onto the floor.

Finch Building—An office building in Aberdeen which housed dentists, doctors, and government agencies such as the Office of Price Administration.

finger wave—A hair style made by dampening hair with water or a styling solution and pushing hair into waves or curls.

furze—A spiny yellow-flowered European evergreen shrub (*Ulex europaeus*).

Gloucester-type fishing boat—A shallow draft fishing boat; the harbor at Gloucester, Mass., imposed a draft not exceeding 12 feet.

gorse—Another name for furze (see above).

Hostess House—A local canteen.

Hyde Park—A village in New York state, home of President Franklin D. Roosevelt.

Ickes, Harold L.—Secretary of the Interior; during the war he was in charge of petroleum, fisheries, and coal mines.

isinglass—A thin plate of mica, used where tempered glass is now used.

jetty—The rock structure extending into the sea from the land at the entrance to Grays Harbor, built to protect the entrance to the harbor. The jetties at the north and south sides were topped with the railroad trestles used to build them. An inner jetty protected the fishing harbor at Westport.

jack pine—A very hardy, crooked-growing, open and picturesque pine tree; most likely a Shore Pine (*Pinus contorta var. contorta*).

John Barleycorn—Whiskey.

'K' rations—A lightweight field kit containing emergency foods and other items for the armed forces.

kelp—A heavy brown seaweed that grows in large floating beds off the coast.

Kress, S. H.—One of the successful "5 and 10 cent" or "five and dime" store chains.

lady Moose's drill team—The women's auxiliary unit of the Order of the Moose wore white-satin-skirted uniforms, marched in parades.

lagoon—Shallow pond or channel left in depressions of sand by the outgoing tide.

loaderman—A logger who operates the machinery for hoisting and loading logs.

McNeil Island—Slang for the Washington State Penitentiary, which is on McNeil Island.

mah-jongg—A Chinese game that uses 144 ivory tiles with elaborate designs.

mill burners—Tall, conical-shaped outdoor furnaces used by sawmills to burn sawdust and wood scraps .

"Montana admirals"—Landlocked sailors working at the Naval Training Center on Lake Pend Oreille near Farragut, Idaho.

Mrs. O'Leary's cow—The cow reputed to have kicked over a lantern in Mrs. O'Leary's barn, starting the Chicago fire of 1871.

myrtle—A trailing or creeping evergreen (*Vinca*), also called periwinkle.

Old B. & G—"Old Blood and Guts," nickname given to General George Patton by his men.

OWI—The Office of War Information handled propaganda and censorship as well as news of battles and casualties.

Parrish, Maxfield—American painter and magazine illustrator known for images of poetic fantasy and romantic idealism and a vivid purplish-blue color named for him.

Pegler, Westbrook—Nationally syndicated and highly opinionated newspaper columnist, usually critical of President Roosevelt.

pennons—Small pointed or swallow-tail flags born by medieval knights on their lances and displaying a personal code of arms.

Perry, Commodore Matthew—The U. S. naval officer who headed the expedition that forced Japan in 1853-54 to open its shores to trade and diplomatic relations with the West.

punchboard table lamp—A prize won at punch-board, a game of chance.

ration books—Books containing coupons called ration stamps good for the purchase of rationed items.

Redcedar—Ancient giant of the coastal forest, Western Redcedar (*Thuja plicata*) and grows tall and straight to heights of 200 feet and diameters of 15 feet.

red stamps—Ration coupons for meat, fish, fat, and dairy products.

Roosevelt Park—An Aberdeen park situated on rolling hillside above town.

route step—A military troop marching with discipline reduced in order to permit singing, talking.

salal—A spreading green shrub (*Gaultheria shallon*).

sand dollar—Shell with star-shaped design left by one of the flat circular sea urchins (*Exocycloida*) that live on sandy seacoasts.

sand verbena—A low-growing plant (*Abronia umbellata*).

Schumann-Heink (Mme. Ernestine) [1861-1936]—An opera and concert singer; a mountain of a woman and one of greatest contraltos of all time, she was frequently heard on the radio.

shanks'mares—Walking on one's own legs.

shark boat—A fishing boat with extra-strong trawling gear suitable for catching shark.

skunk cabbage—A swamp plant with a strong smell (*Lysichitum americanum*).

Snake Hill—The big S curve on old road from the south beaches to Aberdeen.

Sparks, Ned—A slow-moving cigar-smoking character actor who starred in the 1934 film "Imitation of Life," with Claudette Colbert.

Spencerian circles—Children in Hogan's day learned Spencerian penmanship by doing exercises drawing looping rows of circles.

spindrift—Wind-swept salt spray blown up near the surface of the sea.

Timoshenko, Semyon Konstantinovich—A Red Army marshall whose defensive campaigns stopped the Germans.

tonneau—The rear seating compartment of an automobile or limousine.

transom—A small window above a door, pivoted or hinged at bottom.

troller—A boat used in trolling for fish; surface lures with hooks are pulled through the water; on salmon boats, several long booms pivot out and are strung with lines to catch fish.

War Savings Bonds—See bonds.

whale birds—A lot of species seem to have been called whale birds, and to behave as described: red phalaropes, short-tailed (formerly slender-billed) shearwater, or the sooty shearwater, maybe even the broad-billed prion.

Washington Geographical Names

Aberdeen—The largest town in Grays Harbor County, Aberdeen is a lumbering center located on a deep-water port.

Bay City—A small community on the south shore of Grays Harbor on the Elk River.

Bremerton—A city on the Kitsap Peninsula on Puget Sound, site of a naval shipyard.

Cape Flattery—The northwest corner of Washington State.

Chehalis—City in west central Lewis County.

Chehalis River—River flowing from Lewis County northwest to Aberdeen.

Cohassett Beach—Small beach community 3 miles south of Westport.

Copalis Beach—Small beachside community north of Ocean City.

Destruction Island—A rocky 30-acre island 3 miles offshore near the mouth of the Hoh River, location of a lighthouse.

Farragut, Idaho—A large naval training center is located here.

Fort Canby—A fort on Washington's Cape Disappointment designed to defend the entrance to the Columbia River.

Grayland—Community 4 miles south of Cohassett Beach, with many cranberry bogs.

Heather Road—A road in Grayland.

Hoh River—River flowing west from the base of Mt. Olympus and exiting on the west coast of the Olympic Peninsula.

Hood Canal—An 80-mile-long arm of the sea running generally north and south along the east slope of the Olympic Peninsula.

Humptulips—Logging center along the Humptulips River 17 miles north of Aberdeen.

Kalaloch—Small beach community north of the Queets River, pronounced "clay lock."

McCleary—A lumber town 19 miles west of Olympia and east of Aberdeen. In 1942 the entire town was bought by Simpson Logging.

McNeil Island—An island in Puget Sound where the State Penitentiary is located.

Melbourne—An early logging center on the Chehalis River 8 miles east of Aberdeen.

Montesano—Grays Harbor County seat, situated 8 miles east of Aberdeen on the Chehalis River.

Mt. Rainier—The highest mountain in Washington State at 14,408 feet.

Neushkah River—Correctly the Newskah (an Indian word meaning "drinking water") this river enters Grays Harbor on the south shore west of South Aberdeen.

North Bay—The bay extending from the mouth of the Willapa River into the Pacific.

North Cove—A fishing community on Dabkey Slough at the entrance of Willapa Harbor.

North Head—The extreme southwest corner of Washington State at the entrance to the Columbia River.

North Spit—A sandbar near the northern entrance of Grays Harbor that is usually underwater during the highest tides.

Ocosta—A small community on the south shore of Grays Harbor.

Olympic Peninsula—Headland of northwestern Washington State, dominated by the Olympic Mountains.

Quinault—Olympic Peninsula community on Lake Quinault, at eastern edge of the Quinault Indian Reservation.

Queets—Community at the mouth of Queets River on the Quinault Indian Reservation.

Ruby Beach—A Pacific Ocean beach north of Queets on Highway 101.

Satsop—A logging center on the Chehalis River, 6 miles east of Montesano.

Split Rock—Pacific Ocean rock, 1-1/2 miles offshore from Quinault Indian Reservation.

South Bay—South bay in Grays Harbor.

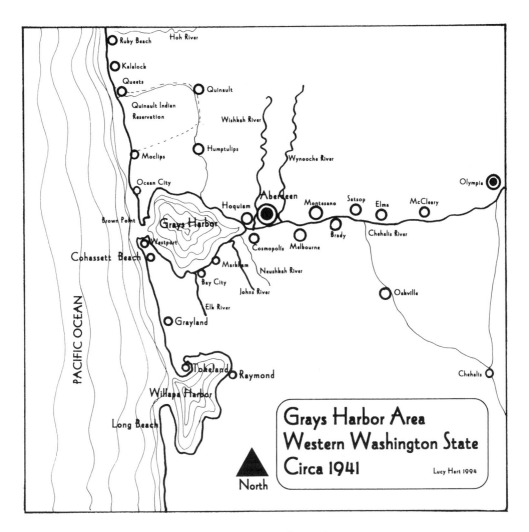

The map shows labels: Ruby Beach, Hoh River, Kalaloch, Queets, Quinault, Quinault Indian Reservation, Wishkah River, Moclips, Humptulips, Ocean City, Wynooche River, Olympia, Brown Point, Grays Harbor, Hoquiam, Aberdeen, Montesano, Satsop, Elma, McCleary, Westport, Cosmopolis, Melbourne, Brady, Chehalis River, Cohassett Beach, Markham, Neushkah River, Bay City, Johns River, Oakville, Elk River, Grayland, Tokeland, Raymond, Chehalis, Willapa Harbor, Long Beach, PACIFIC OCEAN, North

**Grays Harbor Area
Western Washington State
Circa 1941**

Lucy Hart 1994

Strait of Juan de Fuca—A 90-mile-long waterway stretching from Cape Flattery to Port Townsend, separating the Olympic Peninsula from Vancouver Island, Canada.

Tillamook Bay—Oregon bay 50 miles south of the entrance to the Columbia River.

Tokeland—A community on a narrow 3-mile spit at the north entrance to Willapa Bay.

Walla Walla—Rich agricultural center in eastern Washington, home of a penitentiary.

Westport—A small town located on the south spit of Grays Harbor, known for its salmon fishing.

Willapa Harbor—Large shallow bay south of Grays Harbor at the mouth of the Willapa River, known for harvests of oysters.

Wishkah—Small community on the Wishkah River 5-1/2 miles north of Aberdeen.

Wynooche River—A river originating in the Olympic Mountains and flowing south into the Chehalis River.

Annotated Select Bibliography

Associated Press writers and photographers, foreword by Harrison Salisbury. *World War II, A 50th Anniversary History*. Henry Holt and Co., New York, 1989.

Bailey, Ronald H. *The Home Front: U.S.A.* Time-Life Books, Alexandria, Va., 1981. High-quality black and white photos, with commentary by Time-Life writers.

Boeing Company. *Year by Year; 75 Years of Boeing History, 1916-1991*. Boeing Historical Archives, Seattle, 1991.

Bowman, Constance. *Slacks and Callouses*. Illus. by Clara Marie Allen. Longmans, Green & Co., New York, 1944. A lighthearted and informative account of the adventures of two teachers who spent their 1943 summer vacation in San Diego on the assembly line of the B-24 "Liberators" that were bombing Italy. Deserves to be reprinted.

Campbell, D'Ann. *Women at War with America*. Harvard University Press, Cambridge, Mass., 1984. The author recreates the lives of the women of the 1940s, writing from their own perspective.

Cantwell, Robert. *The Hidden Northwest*. J.B. Lippincott Co., Philadelphia and New York, 1972. Readable history with refreshing interpretations and personal memoir about Washington.

Capoeman, Pauline K., editor. *Land of the Quinault*. Quinault Indian Nation, Taholah, Wash., 1990. Tribal history, natural history, logging history, and fishing history. Beautiful pictures and informative, well-written text.

Casdorph, Paul D. *Let the Good Times Roll*. Paragon House, New York, 1989. Social life and customs, 1939-1945. "A chronological rendering of events from newspapers and popular magazines of the period."

Harris, Mark Jonathan, Franklin D. Mitchell and Steven J. Schechter, introduction by Studs Terkel. *The Homefront: America During World War II*. G.P. Putnam's Sons, New York, 1984. "Testaments of American home-front survivors of World War II." Wonderful pictures support each chapter.

Hart, B.H. Liddell. *History of the Second World War*. Perigee Books, G.P. Putnam's Sons, New York, 1982.

Hitchman, Robert. *Place Names of Washington*. Washington State Historical Society, 1985. Includes 340 pages of the history behind the naming of Washington's geographic locations.

Hoopes, Roy. *Americans Remember the Home Front*. Hawthorn Books, Inc., New York, 1977. Portions of various interviews pulled together into chapters, to tell the story of the war coherently. The first chapter includes recollections of early December 1941. This is a thick book, rich in colorful stories.

Litoff, Judy Barrett and David C. Smith, editors. *Dear Boys, World War II Letters from a Woman Back Home*. University Press of Mississippi, 1991. "Excerpts from every 'Dear Boys' column written by Mrs. Keith Frazier Somerville and published in the Bolivar *Commercial* between January 15, 1943 and August 31, 1945 . . . " With a scholarly introduction and a biographical chapter extracted from Keith Somerville's memoirs, journals, and early writings. Mrs. Somerville's columns are full of humor, and provide an incredible amount of local personal detail.

Miyamoto, S. Frank. *Social Solidarity among the Japanese in Seattle*. University of Washington Press, 1984. A "classic study of the Seattle Japanese community in the 1930s" brought up to date with an extensive introduction by the author. A detailed history of the political climate and posturing that led to the executive order.

Morgan, Murray. *The Last Wilderness*. The Viking Press, New York, 1956. Entertaining histories of early Olympic Peninsula communities; Morgan calls it a love story—"I have been in love with the Olympics as long as I can remember."

Morison, Samuel Eliot. *The Oxford History of The American People.* Oxford University Press, New York, 1965. Chapter LVIII On the Defensive, 1941-1942. Chapter LVIV Victory, 1944-1945.

Paulson, Dennis. *Shorebirds of the Pacific Northwest.* University of Washington Press, Seattle Audubon Society, 1993. Highly illustrated with drawings and photographs and detailed descriptions of 78 species of shorebirds seen in the Pacific Northwest.

Schwantes, Carlos A., guest editor-in-chief. "The Pacific Northwest in World War II," *Journal of the West.* Sunflower University Press, Manhattan, Kansas, July 1986. The articles in this special issue cover war industries, the guerilla defense of the Oregon coast, timber in Coos Bay, labor politics, and education during World War II in the Pacific Northwest.

Time-Life. *Life's Picture History of World War II.* New York, 1950. Large-format book with black and white photos and color paintings of the war, and a glossary of wartime personalities.

Tuttle, William M. *"Daddy's Gone to War"; The Second World War in the Lives of America's Children.* Oxford University Press, New York, 1993. Combines a history of social change during the war years with letters collected from adults who were children on wartime homefront describing the impact of World War II.

Van Syckle, Edwin. *The River Pioneers: Early Days on Grays Harbor.* Pacific Search Press and Friends of the Aberdeen Public Library, 1982. Van Syckle, who grew up in Cosmopolis, worked in a mill and in the woods to get through college, then covered the whole scene as editor of the Aberdeen *Daily World* for about forty years. Here he tells about the early explorers, the native Indians, and the white pioneers who settled the area.

Van Syckle, Edwin. *They Tried to Cut it All.* Friends of the Aberdeen Public Library, 1980. An account of the "feats and foibles of Grays Harbor's fabulous forest industry."

Winkler, Allan M. *Home Front U.S.A.: America During World War II.* American History Series. Harlan Davidson, Inc., Arlington Heights, Ill.,1986. A survey of writings and original research. This is a short and useful historical reference to balance against the popular view of the war as found in the Time-Life picture books.

Webber, Bert. *Retaliation: Japanese Attacks and Allied Countermeasures on the Pacific Coast in World War II.* Oregon State University Press, Corvallis, Ore., 1976. Little-known events of the war, including submarine attacks on Pacific coast shipping and Japanese high-altitude balloons.

Webber, Bert. *The Silent Siege* and *The Silent Siege II.* Ye Galleon Press, Fairfield, Wash., 1985.

Weinstein, Robert A. *Grays Harbor 1885-1913.* The Viking Press and Penguin Books, 1978. Collection of photos by Charles Pratsch and others, with some narrative. Photos show Aberdeen was a wooden town with wooden sidewalks before the destructive fire of 1903; chapters on the countryside, the harbor and the rivers, the town and people, the woods and lumbering, and ships.

World War II, Time-Life Books History of the Second World War. Prentice Hall Press, New York, 1989. Another illustrated account of World War II, containing some remarkable prize-winning photos of the war.

Photo Acknowledgments

The editors and the publisher gratefully acknowledge the following for supplying photographs and permission to reproduce them:

Page v: from the scrapbook of Klancy Clark de Nevers. Page i and page 242 (soldiers with football, summer 1941; left to right: Joe, Gil, Fred, Dick), page vi, page xv (Kathy Hogan at Cohassett, August 1949), page xxvi (Kathy Hogan): courtesy of Barbara Hart. Back flap (Kathy Hogan at Cohassett Beach in 1968) and page xxix: courtesy of Lucy Hart. Page xvi and page xxvii: from the collection of Mary Pengra. Front cover (detail from "Japs accept terms"), front cover and page 43 (people in gas masks), page xxii, page xxiii (boy scouts collecting newspaper and cardboard), page xxv (anti-Japanese graffiti), page 7 (soldiers with Christmas tree), page 20 (Eleanor Roosevelt), page 22 (Women's Ambulance Corps with victim), page 37 (canned salmon), page 85 (canteen), page 91 (three young women working in Victory Garden, April 3, 1943), page 135 (woman with cook stove), page 152 (Japanese internee and baby), page 155 (President and Mrs. Roosevelt), page 165 (woman bus conductor and passengers), page 180 (woman on telephone), page 247 (central telephone exchange), page 256 ("It's over in Europe"), page 275 ("Japs Accept Terms"): from the *Seattle Post-Intelligencer* Collection, Seattle Museum of History & Industry. Page 8 (air raid wardens, August 24, 1943), page 113 (launch, October 25, 1942), page 132 (air raid warning center, Aberdeen, August 24, 1943), page 239 (Westport Cannery): from Jones Photo Co., Aberdeen. Page 170 (Westhaven harbor, January 1949): from the *Grays Harbor Post*. Front cover and page iii (women drivers, negative number UW11475), page 17 (woman bus driver, negative number UW2329), page 103 (woman taxi driver, negative number UW2325): from Special Collections Division, University of Washington Libraries. Back cover (ration stamps, fuel oil ration stamps), back cover and page 100 (war ration books), back cover and page 133 (U.S. Defense Stamp Album), page 158 (war ration book and stamps): courtesy of Lucy Hart and the Westport Maritime Museum. Page 105 (Boeing workers), page 122 (woman Boeing worker), page 185 (women with bulletin board): courtesy of The Boeing Company Archives. Page 115 (military dimout zone sign), page 150 (women's bicycle): courtesy of Lucy Hart and Furford's Cranberry Museum.

Index

44th Infantry Division, 276
194th Tank Battalion, Army, xviii
200th battalion, 54, 76, 59, 240, 241, 242, 276

Aberdeen, xvi, xxvi, xix, xx, 2, 36, 112, 123, 164, 174, 237, 280
aerated goods, 68, 96, 277
Agriculture, Dept. of, 39
airplanes, 41; B-17 Flying Fortress, xix, xx; B-25s, xxi; B-29 Superfortress, xix, xx, 216, 220; bombers, 10, 103; patrol plane, 169
air raid, xix, xxii, 113, 131, 132, 162, 191
Alcan Highway, 112, 277
Allen, Fred, 184, 185, 277
army, 16, 25, 34, 42, 84, 98, 142, 162, 168, 172, 218, 255; occupation by, xxx, 69, 111
Arnoni (the General), 42, 144, 145, 146
atom bombs, xix, xxi, 273, 274
Australia, 9, 23, 114, 123
Austria, xvii, 176, 258

baby broom, 40, 277
balloons, high altitude paper, xxi, 259
bar, the, 52, 97, 105, 153, 176, 230, 250, 264, 277; bar pilot, 25, 277
barbed wire, vii, xxii, 123, 192, 240
barber, 201, 232
Barn, the, xxvii, xxviii, xxx
barter system, 58
baseball, 130, 131, 176
basketball, 29
Bataan, xix, xviii, 33, 35, 41, 238
battalion, lost, 240, 241, 242
Battle of Britain, xvii
Battle of the Bulge, 230, 220
Bay City, xiv, 160, 280
beachcombing, 75, 114, 161, 211, 229, 230, 257, 263
beach houses, 26, 69, 111
bear, 143, 272
Becker Building, 111, 113
beer hall, 55, 201
bees, 177, 181; bee keeper, 17, 175, 260, 261, 262

Bendetsen, Col. Karl R., xxv
biscuits, 86
blackberries, 58, 129, 173, 187, 270, 272
Black Maria, 212, 215, 277; black panelled truck, 184
black market, xxiv
blackout, 2, 4, 9, 50, 203, 277
blimp, xxii, 149, 169, 277
Blue house, xxviii, xxix, 265, 266
boat building, 266
boat puller, 244, 245, 277
Boeing, xx, xix, 122, 176
bombs, xxi, 9, 143; depth bombs, 93, 186
bonds, xxiv, xxx, 277; war bond campaigns, xxii, xxiii, 168, 280
bonfire, 168, 171, 238
boyfriend (Hogan's), 63, 70, 76, 78, 93
Bremerton, 113, 280
Brown, Bill, 253
Brown, Prentiss, 120
buckers, 108, 277
Bundles for Britain, xxii, 2, 277
Burma, xix, 23, 163
butcher, 84, 92, 102, 149, 190
butter, 86, 276

cabbage, 45, 58, 112, 130
cake, 38, 104
camouflage, 26, 27, 115
cannery: neighbor's, 239, 258; Westport, 239
canneryman, 207, 217, 244, 246, 250, 251, 258, 274. *See also* neighbor, from Blue Ridge Mountains
canteen, 25, 56, 84, 85, 277
cantonment 21, 174, 175, 256, 277
Cape Blanco, xxi; Cape Cod, xxiv; Cape Flattery, 267, 280
carrots, 56, 57, 90, 129, 189, 237
Carstens, John, 170
cats, 26, 27, 45, 65, 73, 74, 166, 210, 249; Claude Furbottom, 26, 27, 45, 66; Rafe, 73, 74, 92
CCC camp, 35, 277
censorship, xxiii, 24, 139, 241
central, 234, 247, 277. *See also* telephone

Ceslev, Tony, 216, 221
Chamber of Commerce, 164, 274
Channel Islands, 45
Chehalis, 151, 280
Chehalis River, 266, 280
chicken, 131, 188, 214
Christmas, 4, 6, 8, 87, 159, 162, 224, 228, 229; Christmas fleet, xxi
cigarettes, xxiv, 220, 237
CIO union, 159, 176
civilian defense, xv, xxii, 8, 10, 43; Civilian Defense, Office of (OCD), xx, xxii, 19; civilian watchers, 75
Clam Cottage, xxviii, xxix
clams, razor, 16, 73, 160, 165, 217, 219, 246, 277; clam boil, 130; clam buyer's shack (hut), 46, 253; clam chowder, xxvii, 194, 210, 225; clam shovel (gun), 169, 277
classified section, see want ads
club, 218, club woman, 243
coal: mines, 9, 99, 114, 145, 203; pile, 168, 255, 256
coast guard, xxii, xiv, 52, 170, 193, 198, 204, 205, 233, 246
cod, 271
Cohassett Beach, v, vii, xiv, xv, xxvii, xxviii, xxx, xxix, 219, 280
Columbia River, xix, xxi, xxii, 209, 245, 246
comber, 245, 250, 264, 277
Congress, 15, 24, 118, 151
Copalis Beach, 246, 280
corn, 190, 199, 200
Corregidor, xviii, 14, 35, 39
cow, 51, 63, 64, 184, 185, 214; Mrs. O'Leary's, 2, 3
crab, 65, 66, 169, 170, 197, 217, 231, 250, 251, 263
cranberries, xx, xxiv, 30, 41, 50, 72, 201, 230; bog house, 30
Croft (Easter) lily bulbs, xxvii, 216, 221
Czechoslovakia, xvii, 203

D-Day, 187, 188
declaration of war, xx, 3, 139
defense stamps, 51, 277
Denmark, xvii, 258
Depression, Great, xviii, xx
Destruction Island, 53, 280

dirigible, see blimp
dock, Westport, 52, 117, 158, 170, 173, 193, 222, 246, 248, 249, 267, 278,
dogs: Annabelle, 140, 141,142, 154, 166, 167; curled-tailed, 207, 208, 258; hounds, 151, 266; Irish water spaniel, 202, 203; Pinocchio, 59; war, 124, 172
Dolly M, 182, 183
domestic help, 83, 105
donkey, 70, 278
draft, xviii, 9, 64, 79, 131, 145, 172, 183
drag net, 217, 278
dragsaw, 61, 278
dressing station, emergency, 9, 23
dried foods, 68, 96, 277
ducks: hunting, 58, 143, 214; plucking, 213
dunes, the, 123, 154, 200, 204, 207, 211, 249, 265
Dutch East Indies, xix, 9

earwigs, 143, 206
Easter, 101, 216
E button, 244, 245, 278
Eddie, 54, 55, 56
Elbee, Reg, 232, 244, 248
Eleven o'clock Creek, 151
encyclopedia, (1886), 177, 199, 206
England, xvii, 47, 192, 241
evacuation: plans, 9; see also Japanese Americans, evacuation
Everett, 48

fallers, 108, 278
farmers, xxiii, xxiv, 37, 163, 200
farm prices, xx, 37, 74
Farragut, Idaho, 188, 280
FBI, 13, 82, 59, 255
Finch Building, 100, 278
finger wave, 71, 173, 278
Finland, xvii, 3, 51, 163; Finnish people, xxiv, 30, 31, 41, 50, 54, 215
First Lady, xx, 19, 118, 174; see also Roosevelt, Eleanor
Fisheries Dept., State, 73, 165
fisherman friend, 130, 137, 154, 158, 161, 164, 173, 180, 183, 186, 188, 189, 202, 205, 209, 217, 218, 221, 222, 225, 226, 234, 243, 255, 271

fishermen, xxiii,, 25, 182, 193, 269
fishing, xxiv, 52, 61, 127, 137, 164, 170, 186, 188, 204, 207, 225, 250, 268, 271; bottom fishing, 209, 258, 271
fishing floats, Japanese, 98, 161
flak, 115
fog, 58, 272; fog horn, 222, 264
food, 23, 117, 118
Fort Canby, 168, 280; Fort Lewis, xviii, xix, 16, 106, 241, 276; Fort Sheridan, Ill., 220; Fort Stevens, xxi
fox holes, 4, 240
furze, 207, 278

gardening, *see* vegetable gardens
garden pests, 186, 200, 206, 237
gas rationing, *see* rationing, gasoline
General, the, *see* Arnoni
Germany, xvii, 3, 51
Gibraltar, 247
glass balls, *see* fishing floats
Gloucester-type fishing boats, 158, 278
gold star, 268
gorse, 25
government, 239, 266, 258
Grayland, xxiv, xiv, 201, 230, 280
Gray, Robert, xv
Grays Harbor, xvi, xviii, xx, xxii, xiv, 25, 258
Grays Harbor, S.S., xix
Grays Harbor Post, v, xv, xvi, xx, xxx, 215
grocer, 36, 119
guard duty, 133; guardsman, 124
gun, 76; gun emplacements, xxii, 26, 27, 191; shotgun, 76, 213

halibut, 165, 258
hawk, gray, 60
headquarters, 145
Heather Road, xxviii, 253, 280
herring, 271
Hilda, 232
Hitler and Nazis, xvii, 9, 39, 159
hoarding, 103, 126
Hogan, Giles (logging cousin), 108, 109, 110
Hogan, Kathy (Katharyn Lyle), v, xv, xvi, xxvi, xxvii, xxix, xxx, 98
Hoh River, 166, 280
Holland, 216, 245

Holmes, Mr. Hazen, 224, 260, 261, 262
honey, 181, 262
honeymoons, 264, 265
honeysuckle, 192
Honolulu, 123
Hood Canal, 6, 280
Hoquiam, xvi, xx, 44
Hostess House, 125, 278
hotel, old beach, xxix, 194, 195, 225, 265, 266
housework, 82, 83, 104, 105,106, 189
housing, xx, xxiv, 9, 97, 98
Hubbard squash, 129, 196, 197
huckleberry, 143
Humptulips, 108, 110, 151, 230, 280
Hyde Park, 153, 278

icing plant, 174
Ickes, Harold L., 166, 278
Indians, xxiv, 160, 162, 211
Iowa, 151, 153, 154
Ireland, 128
Italy, xvii, 3, 131, 144, 145, 241
Ivor, old, 50, 86, 93

jack pines, 77, 278
jam, 49
Japan, xviii, 3, 216; Archipelago, 13
Japanese, xv, xxvi, 10, 12, 13
Japanese Americans: evacuation of, xxv, 24, 48, 145, 151; induction of, 159; truck farmers, xxv
jellyfish, 233, 234
jetty, 130, 149, 170, 245, 246, 249, 267, 271
Joe, 197, 203, 204, 205, 215, 244, 252, 264, 265; wife Jenny, 264-265
Joe, wholesale grocer, 119,120, 121

Kaiser shipyards, xix, 122
Kalaloch, xxvii, 63, 64, 280
kelp, 130, 278
Ketchikan, 164
killdeer, 257
Kimberly Diamond Mines, 273
Kitchen Critic, v, xv, xvi, xxvii
Koreans, 10
Kress, 142, 222, 278

labor, 117, 118
Lake Ozette, xxii
land mines, 142
laurel, wild, 211
Lend-Lease, xvii, xviii, 99
Leningrad, 159, 163
Liberty ships, xix, xx
lieutenant's wife, 86, 90, 91
Life, 77, 186, 211
lighthouse, xiv, 60, 170, 222, 223, 255
ling cod, 52, 137
Little Hoquiam, 151
loaderman, loaders, 108, 109, 278
logger, 70; logging truck, 202
Lowery's Hotel, 225
lumber production, xvi, xx, xxi
luncheon, 27, 28, 29, 134, 135, 136, 218, 234
lupine, 41, 187

McArthur, Deputy Sheriff, 184, 185, 191, 210, 211, 212, 215, 270
MacArthur, General, xx, 9, 13, 23, 209, 273
McCleary, 44, 280
McDonald, Mayor, 174, 175
McNeil Island, 121, 278, 280
magazines, xxx, 34, 37, 77, 121, 155, 186, 211, 212, 216, 221, 243, 271, 274
Malay Peninsula, xix, 9
Marine Reserve, Washington, xviii
meat, 63, 84, 213
Melbourne, 44, 280
Midway Island, 48, 64
Milkmaid, 154
mole-hill break, 116, 127
Monterey cypress, 129
Morgenthau, Secretary of Treasury, 23
Motherwell, Robert, 257
Mt. Rainier, 197, 266, 280
Murrow, Edward R., xxvi
"My Day," xx, 19
myrtle, 40, 278

nasturtiums, 255, 276
National Guard: New Jersey, vii, 276; Washington, xviii; New York, 240, 241, 242, 276
National Geographic, 271
National Labor Relations board, xx, 139

Nazis, *see* Hitler
neighbors: from Blue Ridge Mountains, 207, 208, 209, 217, 244, 246, 250, 251, 258, 274; Jim, 153; mountaineer 207, 238, 239, 240, 274; Tennessee-born, 238; Tony Ceslev, 216, 221
Neilton, 167
nephew, 116; Robert Motherwell, 257
Neushkah River, 151, 280
New Deal, xx
New England, 116
New Guinea, 23, 72, 78, 93
New Jersey, 240, 241, 242, 276
newspapers, xxiv, 19, 95, 96, 150, 164, 202
newsreels, xxvi, 276
New York, 48, 59, 276; Yankees, xxx
New Yorker, xxx, 155, 243
North Africa, 146, 109
North Bay, 110, 280
North Beach, 210
North Cove, xiv, 71, 140, 219, 229, 248, 253, 262, 280
North Fork, 181
North Head, 166, 280
North jetty, 249
North River, 105, 151
North Spit, 97, 280
Norway, xvii, 220
Norwegian friend, Chris, 52, 53, 81

occupation, *see* army
Ocosta, xiv, xxviii, 280
octagonal summer house, *see* Blue house
Office of Civilian Defense (OCD), xx, xxii, 19
Office of Price Administration (OPA), xxiii, 99,100, 102, 119, 120, 137, 138, 151, 159, 165, 176, 187, 192, 217, 258, 259
Office of War Information (OWI), xxiii, 78, 83, 96, 131, 278
Olympia, 16, 18, 68, 97
Olympic Peninsula, xv, xxii, 36, 152, 180, 280
operator, 228, 247; *see also* telephone

parlors, 62, 174, 175
party line, 179, 180, 181; *see also* telephone
Patton, General, Jr., 154, 216, 261
Pearl Harbor, xix, xx, xxi, 2, 3, 12, 13, 41, 220
Pegler, Westbrook, 19, 279
permanent wave, 146, 147, 148

Philippines, xviii, xix, xx, 3, 23, 209, 267

plover, 77

plumber, plumbing, 55, 134, 136, 252

plywood, xx, 168, 175

poison gas, 9, 10, 114; gas masks, 42

Poland, xvii, 159, 161

Portland, xix, 68, 120

post office, 34, 42, 87

potatoes, 214, 273

price controls, xxiii, 9, 37, 192

PT boats, xx

Pure Food and Drugs Administartion, 217

Queets, 63, 65, 280

Quinault, 44, 86, 108, 151, 280

Quinault Indian Reservation, xxvii

radar, xxi

radio, 2, 46, 133, 159, 187, 184, 276

rationing: autos, 23; coffee, xxiii; dairy products, xxiii; fish, xxiii; gasoline, xxiii, 39, 81, 83, 137, 124, 217; meat, xxiii, 102, 149, 153; shoes, xxiii; sugar, xxiii, 49, 50; tinned foods, xxiii; ration books, 99, 158, 234, 272, 279; ration list, xv, xxiii, 99, 203, 273; ration points, 116; ration stamps, 110, 131, 158; blue stamps, 119; red points, 235; red stamps, 279

recipes: clams, baked, 41; salmon, 53; fresh baked tuna, 198; flank casserole, 236

Red Cross, 10, 188

Reykjavik, 84

Rhineland, xvii, 276

Rhine River, xx, 216, 245

riot, race: New York, 124; Detroit, 114; Zoot suit, 114

Robert, 114, 127, 169, 181, 187, 188, 190, 197, 204, 214, 220, 224, 228, 229, 243, 244, 260, 274; his family, 127, 167, 182, 204, 224; his father (Robert Rockwood), 114, 182, 183, 244, 245, 246, 266, 267; his grandfather, 127, 193, 228, 229; his mother, 190, 198, 245; his siblings, Gloriabelle, 167; Dorothy, 228, 229; Leonard, 193

Roger, 36, 46

Rome, 131, 145, 188

Rommel, Marshall, 155

Roosevelt, Eleanor, xv, xx, 19, 20, 21, 118, 174

Roosevelt, President Franklin, xv, xviii, xix, xx, xxv, 37, 39, 113, 117, 154, 161, 186, 216, 250, 251

rose, 265, 266

Rossitti, Tony, 44, 56, 192, 193

Ruby Beach, 166, 280

Russia, xvii, 15, 122, 161; Russian people, 11; steppes, 44; naval officers, 162; language, 163, 199

sailors, 67, 78, 275

salal, 171, 178, 179, 224, 279

salmon, 16, 36, 52, 53, 258, 268, 271

salmonberry, 30, 272

sand dollar, 263, 279

sand grass, 194

sandpiper, 161

sand verbena, 194, 279

Satsop, 151, 280

Saturday Evening Post, 37, 77

savings bonds, *see* bonds

scarcity: bacon 92; butter, 86; canned milk, 86; cheese, 86; cloth, xxiii; clothes, 159; food, 68; gasoline, 86; matches, 86; meat, 92, 113, 118; rubber, 86; sugar, 38

schoolhouse, 8, 29, 49, 79, 80, 225, 226

scrap drives, xxiv, 81

Sea Bride, 183

Seattle, xix, 18, 68, 101, 217, 224, 270

Senate Investigation Committee on OPA, 259

septic tank, 55, 197, 241, 252

shark boat, 164, 279; shark snapper, 52

sheriff, 184, 185, 191, 210, 211, 212, 215, 270

shipwreck, 61, 204, 267

shipyard, Aberdeen, xx, 112

shoemaker, 40, 41, 60, 201, 202, 251

shore patrol, 52, 75

Singapore, xix, 15, 135

skating rink, 123, 158

skunk cabbage, 249, 279

Smith boys, 97; Smiths, the, 162

Snake Hill, 237, 279

Solomon Island, 59, 74, 78

South Bay, xiv, 76, 143, 280; South Bay Bridge, 181, 237

Soviet Union or USSR, 51

Sparks, Ned , 42, 279

spindrift, 211, 279

Split Rock, 183, 223, 256, 280
Spokane, 98, 120
spruce, xvi
Stalin, 163, 258
starfish, 231
state park, 244, 270
storms, 246, 247, 252
Strait of Juan de Fuca, xviii, xxii, 281
strawberries, 192
strikes: coal mines, 99, 109, 114, 145, 203;
  transit workers, 199; airplane factory, 220;
  truck drivers, 199; maintenance workers,
  209
submarines, xxi, 6, 10, 11, 74
subsidies, 117
sugar xv, 33, 36, 39, 81, 270, 276
Sunset patrol, 38
surplus property, army, 168, 254, 255, 256
Swan Island, xix
sweet pea, 189

Tacoma, xviii, 120, 121,
tavern, new, 222, 223, 248
telephone, 179, 180, 181, 228, 229, 234,
  247, 248, 269
tide book, 66
tie house, 208
Tillamook Bay, 267, 281
Time, 216, 221, 274
Times, 19
Times Square, 113
Timoshenko, 45, 279
Tokeland, 44, 281
Tokyo, xxi, 10, 14, 33, 57, 220, 224, 238,
  245, 259
Tony, vegetable man, 44, 56, 192, 193
tower, water, 174, 175, 215
travel: bus, 16, 67, 106, 165, 236, 237, 252;
  train, 121, 155
Tripoli, 96
trollers, 170, 279
Truman, President Harry S., xx, xxi, 195,
  250, 273
tuna fish, 37, 137, 198, 268, 271
Twin Harbors State Park, xviii, xiv, 244
typewriter, 158, 172, 202, 203, 206, 243

Ukraine, 146
Umpty-Umpth, 241, 242, 276
USO (United Service Organization), xxiv

Vancouver, 68, 122
vegetable garden, 24, 44, 112, 130, 143, 179,
  186, 187, 189, 190, 196, 214, 238, 263,
  273; Victory Gardens, xv, xxv, 44, 61, 90,
  91, 129, 173, 214, 237, 238, 275
vegetable wagon, 56, 82, 192
venison, 142, 213
village store and post office, 14, 25, 34, 36,
  46, 87

wage controls, xxiii
Wake Island, 11
Walla Walla, 121, 281
want ads, 82, 104, 150
war correspondents, xxvi, 202
war game, xviii, 133, 154
War Production Board, xix, xx, xxiii
War Relocation Authority (WRA), 151, 153,
  163
war taxes, xxiii
washing machine, 32, 33, 34, 150
West Bridge, 112
Westport, vi, xiv, 52, 60, 131, 164, 168, 174,
  175, 215, 249, 254, 255, 256, 268, 281
Westwind, xxviii, xxix
whale, yellow-bellied, 205, 206
whale birds, 198, 279
Willamette River, xix
Willapa, xiv, 60, 187, 281
Willkie, Wendell, xviii, 176, 209
willow, 143, 149, 169
Wishkah, 99, 164, 281; Wishkah Street
  bridge, 19
women at work, 102, 122; manpower
  shortage, 236
Women's Ambulance Corps, 22, 23
wood, 76, 127; wood man, 260, 261, 262
work week, 15, 33, 96, 139
World War I, 209
writing, 243, 268
Wynooche River, 105, 151, 281